International Business Negotiations: Strategies, Tactics and Practices

Raymond C. Rody, Ph.D.
The University of Akron

© First Edition, 2002
Oceanprises Publications
ISBN 0-9676720-3-1

International Business Negotiations: Strategies, Tactics and Practices
Raymond C. Rody, Ph.D.

Published by:

ISBN 0-9676720-3-1

Printed in the United States of America

Acknowledgments

The author would like to thank the hundreds of people
around the world that have helped in the development,
production and completion of this text. A special thanks to
my numerous international business associates. Some of you
taught me the "hard way," but they were indeed valuable
lessons. I would also like to thank my international friends
from whom I have learned so much, both at home and
abroad. From you I have learned the "fun way."

Preface

A myriad of practices and strategies are used today in
international business negotiations. Business practices can be
defined as the business strategies, protocols, taboos, methods
of expressing ideas, ethics, and etiquette used in a country.
International negotiation strategies can be defined as the
persuasion strategies, systems of logic, methods of dispute
resolution, decision-making customs, contract law, and team
strategies commonly accepted in a country. This book sheds
light upon the salient business practices and highlights the
negotiation strategies and persuasion tactics that are likely to
be effective in the cultures studied within the text.

Table of Contents

INTRODUCTION

In the current global economy, over 5 trillion dollars in international trade takes place every year. Knowledge and understanding of international markets and of international negotiating strategies are essential ingredients in today's business world.

It is difficult, if not impossible, to adequately or easily categorize the international business negotiations methods used throughout the world. Countries have tremendously varied cultural traditions that influence the negotiation process and the eventual success or failure of cross-cultural business ventures, which is exactly why this book was written. Anyone considering negotiations across international boundaries must be knowledgeable about the history, values, proper behavior patterns, and traditional business procedures of the particular people they hope to interest. Success also demands that we be prepared to put aside the assumption that our own country's methods, procedures, and values are the only proper ones. A little flexibility, knowledge of where the other person is coming from, and the ability to build some mutual trust go a long way in the buying and selling of products on the international market.

There are, however, many negotiation procedures commonly and effectively used in business settings around the world. Chapter 1 highlights these negotiation strategies, such as persuasion techniques, prevalent negotiation styles, team strategies and maneuvers, and methods of dispute resolution. This chapter also examines the major factors one must consider when engaging in international negotiations, such as the basis of trust, concepts of time, and decision-making customs. The areas of protocol, taboos, ethics, and etiquette are addressed on a country-by-country basis in later chapters. Protocols and etiquette are so specific to each country that extensive comparison and contrast serve little purpose.

Chapter 2 deals with communications. Communication styles vary greatly across countries and cultures, and a basic understanding of differing styles is essential for success in international business. Otherwise, miscommunications or misunderstandings and even unconscious insults can become the focus of the negotiation rather than the intended topic. Thus, communication is important enough to merit its own chapter.

The remainder of the text (chapters 3 through 31) is designed to help formulate negotiating strategies for a particular country. The countries are listed in alphabetical order for ease of location by the reader. Each country-specific chapter provides a short history, current political information, economic data, demographics, and some cultural background for each nation. This information is provided in order to enhance understanding of why a particular country conducts business in a specific manner. Various aspects of a culture are integrated and interdependent; business life cannot be separated from the values, goals, beliefs, and behavior patterns ingrained in a culture by its past history and present social, economic and political conditions.

Last, keep in mind that the book generalizes about cultural practices and behaviors. Individual differences abound throughout the world. The text attempts to provide information and strategies that can be attributed to the general population for the countries presented. In addition, the text provides information to help you avoid a cultural faux pas. However, fine-tuning your international business negotiation strategies to fit the individuals you will meet is unfortunately a burden you alone must bear.

Chapter 1

International Business Negotiating Strategies

- *Negotiation Strategies*
- *Negotiating Concepts and Styles*
- *Preparation*
- *Strategies & Tactics*

The realm of international business negotiating is a vast catacomb of ideas, theories, and practices. Thus, negotiating strategies and styles are many and varied throughout the world. However, a select number of available negotiation strategies are acceptable and/or effective in most countries/cultures. The following negotiation strategies can be used around the globe with little or no modification.

Negotiation Strategies

The most critical part of negotiating is the negotiation strategy. A number of factors are involved when determining which tactics or practices one should use in an international negotiation. First, one must consider the opposition's concept of how negotiations should proceed—what is the style they are apt to use or approve of? Second, one must consider the level of interdependence. Third, what persuasion tactics and strategies can be used effectively, given the cultural backgrounds that will be present at the negotiation? Fourth, the opposition's view of conflict must be considered. Fifth, how should disputes, power issues, and the contract be handled? Sixth, what pre-planning, preparations, and information must be arranged or garnered? For example, what strategies and tactics are your opponents likely to implement and what type of initial presentation will have the most impact? Seventh, what additional concerns must be addressed that may effect the outcome of a negotiation? For example, value systems and cultural conditioning will effect the way one thinks, processes information, resolves disputes and makes decisions.

Negotiating Concepts and Styles

In the U.S. we view negotiations as a **joint problem-solving** process. Although we also engage in debate, bargaining and relationship building during negotiations, our primary view of a negotiation tends to be one of presenting the issues, discussing the issues and finding a resolution that is satisfactory to both parties.

The French on the other hand love to debate. A **debate** style of negotiating can be defined as making logical points, arguing, continuous conflict, etc. Therefore, a business negotiation void of debate would be a huge disappointment to the French. France is one of the few countries of the world to offer academic degrees in negotiating. Negotiating is viewed as an art form and debate should have a prominent role. The French view conflict as good. Their positive perception of conflict tends to enhance their desire to debate.

A common method of negotiating throughout the world is bargaining or more specifically distributive bargaining. **Distributive bargaining** is your basic transaction in which the buyer starts low and the seller start high and they meet somewhere in the middle. Another type of bargaining is **contingency bargaining** which involves the trading of products, items, services, personal favors, etc. for issues/concessions that have not yet been resolved in the negotiation. The Chinese love distributive bargaining. True, they spend a lot of time building relationships, discussing issues, and resolving conflicts. However, when you get to the end of the negotiation with a Chinese businessperson, be prepared to haggle. Haggling is an art form to the Chinese just as debate is an art form to the French. The Russians love distributive as well as contingency bargaining, but are best known for their skill in conducting contingency bargaining deliberations.

Another form of negotiating is **relationship building,** which is based on the creation of friendships, trust, and mutual understanding. The Japanese need to build a relationship when they do business. The Japanese tendency to view things from a long-term perspective also enhances their desire to build relationships. They expect to maintain relationships for a long time. Thus, the establishment of a relationship makes sense if one is to conduct business with someone for an extended period. In this way, the business relationship proves to be prosperous as well as enjoyable.

The last style of negotiating observed around the world is compromise. The British refer to it as shopkeeper diplomacy. This negotiating style requires both parties to make concessions willingly in order to promote harmony and to work towards a solution that is beneficial to both parties

Preparation

Pre-planning

Preparation in negotiations is crucial. When negotiating, knowledge is power. The organization of facts, supporting documents, and ideas in a presentation format are a critical step to achieving a successful transaction. Some of the most critical steps in preparation are as follows:

1) select an advantageous meeting site;
2) prepare an agenda that is strategically formatted;
3) have your questions ready;
4) bring proof sources (i.e., documents that support your claims);
5) formulate your goals;
6) list the people who will be involved in the negotiations from each side and identify their roles;
7) figure out who their decision maker is;
8) review the firms' past histories with each other and with other firms;
9) review your previous correspondence (i.e., faxes, letters, etc.); and
10) decide if you need an interpreter. If contemplating the purchase of goods, get competitive bids.

Meeting Place

The meeting place can play a critical role when negotiating. Always attempt to get the home-field advantage (i.e., your home office). If the home field advantage is not available or is impractical, go for a neutral site. The advantage of the home field is that you have all of your resources available (i.e., FAX, computers, assistants, etc.), the interruptions are your interruptions (i.e., you can decide if you want the negotiations to be interrupted) and time pressures will not be an issue. A hasty decision is often a bad decision.

What style of seating would you prefer during the negotiations (e.g., King Arthur's round table or a rectangular conference-table style)? Most international negotiators expect a conference table style with your team on one side and their team on the other side. It is advisable to give them what they expect, as long as it does not make you feel uncomfortable. You want them sitting happy with their guard down. Another seating issue is who is near the door and who will be facing the door. Most international negotiators want to be the farthest from the door and facing it. This perspective has historical roots and goes back to when people were slain during negotiations. If the King can see the door at all times and is a long distance from the door, the King will have more time to react. In addition, the knights were between the King and the door.

Once again, it is advisable to give them what they want, as long as it does not make you feel uncomfortable. After all, your weapon is a pen not a sword.

Agenda Setting

It is customary to have an agenda during most international negotiations. However, strict adherence to an agenda is rarely followed. Negotiation styles are so different around the world that it is very difficult to find an agenda that both parties will desire. However, you should still attempt to formulate an agenda that works in your favor, then accept deviations graciously and attempt to put the negotiation back on the agenda track when possible. Your agenda should include the following items:

1) topics in the order you wish to discuss them (i.e., leave their sensitive items until last and address the items critical to your firm up-front);
2) side meetings between key individuals;
3) style of the negotiations (i.e., point by point or big picture);
4) length of the negotiations;
5) start times, end times, breaks, etc.;
6) presentation times and the personnel who will make them (if all of the relevant personnel are not present, set a time when they will be); and
7) the decision and how it will be made. If you are able to address most of these issues before the negotiation begins, you will have fewer surprises and correspondingly a more successful negotiation.

Analysis of Competition and Potential Business Partners

Preparation would not be complete without a thorough analysis of one's counterparts. Collect as much information as possible regarding your competition and your prospective business partners in order to:

1) formulate your BATNA (Best Alternative To a Negotiated Agreement);
2) foresee possible issues; and
3) make adjustments for personal differences.

Health and Safety

When negotiating abroad, it is a good idea to check with your local health department regarding inoculations and medical precautions for your particular destination. Lost or stolen passports should be reported to the local police and the US Embassy or nearest consulate. Useful information on guarding one's valuables and protecting one's personal security while traveling abroad is provided in the State Department Pamphlet, "A Safe Trip Abroad." It is available from the Superintendent of Documents, US Government Printing Office, Washington DC, 20402.

Other safety issues and concerns about specific areas of the world are touched upon in each of the following chapters on particular countries.

International Negotiating Concerns

Cultural Influences

Cultural influences are powerful. Most of us have so internalized our culture's values, behaviors, attitudes, and goals that we are not even conscious of the impact our culture has on our thinking. Thus, we often judge other people negatively because they have learned different cultural patterns. How many times have you heard statements, said with contempt, that certain people do not know how to value time, or are lazy, or are inscrutable, or are too loud, too fat, or too this or that. The key to successful international negotiations is to understand that the global system includes many people with diverse ideas concerning what is good, what is right, and what should be done in any particular situation.

If we can understand where people are coming from, then we will better understand why they do the things they do. (Furthermore, they will have heard things about your culture and are also probably judging it in an ethnocentric way.) Especially in countries where relationship-building is essential for business agreements, knowing a culture's important values and attitudes can prevent statements or actions that cause misunderstandings, or even anger and the termination of negotiations. (The "we don't want to do business with someone who behaves so immorally, or strangely, or impolitely" syndrome.) Although many parts of the world have long been cosmopolitan and other parts are becoming more sophisticated regarding cultural influences, your own venture will be more successful if **you** are the one with the most knowledge and preparation. This enables you to accommodate and fit in (without compromising your own beliefs or values). Furthermore, you will be proud of your abilities and have a much more enjoyable time during your visit!

Understanding cultural influences is really the crux of this entire book. Each country's chapter will deal with their cultural attitudes toward values, time, proper attire, gift-giving, greetings, etiquette, and entertainment, as well as communication styles and negotiation strategies and philosophies. Within a complex nation like the United States, the appreciation and knowledge of subcultural variation has current popularity. How much more complex and crucial are international cultural influences on the business venture.

Basis of Trust and Friendship Development

In the U.S., short-term trust is based upon one's **intuition** and **"external sanctions."** If Americans meet someone and like him or her, they often trust that person to a certain degree (i.e., intuition). External sanctions are based on legal recourse. Because the U.S. has an excellent legal system, if improprieties arise legal action can be taken with a reasonable expectation of a fair resolution. Of course, a prerequisite for "external sanctions" is that the firm must be large enough to sue. External sanctions are rare in the field of international negotiations. Only the legal systems of the U.S., Canada, most of Western Europe, Australia and a few other areas are strong enough to enforce contracts in a fair and unbiased manner. In the USA, long-term trust is based upon dependability and credibility.

In Germany, trust is based on the "**past record**" of the firm or individual in question. In Spain, trust is based on one's intuition and **status** (i.e., a member of a prestigious family or a person endorsed by someone of importance). In Korea, trust is based on the **prior experiences one has had with the individual** in question. Koreans view the development of a relationship and mutually beneficial business transactions as the main method of establishing trust. In Japan, relationship development is the most critical element in the establishment of trust. If a relationship outside of the work environment cannot be established in Japan, then true trust will never be established.

Some basic trust building strategies are:

1) dependability (remember perceptions are the key);
2) be humble (especially in Asia);
3) honesty;
4) performance (show your stuff but stay humble);
5) favors (although each country has a different style);
6) information sharing (share a little, but not too much); and
7) set correct expectations. Having appropriate expectations is vital. If they are not disappointed, then the trust will not be broken.

Concept of Time

The concept of time can be broken into two components: punctuality and mono/poly chronic. Punctuality will be dealt with on a country-by-country basis in later chapters. "Monochronic" behavior is defined as "Doing one thing at a time." The concept of performing one task at a time in a "monochronic" culture is viewed as efficient, disciplined and using the best method of maintaining quality standards. "Polychronic" behavior is defined as "Performing many tasks at the same time." The concept of performing many tasks at the same time in a "polychronic" culture is viewed as efficient, skillful and stimulating. Germany, the U.S., Sweden, and Switzerland are "monochronic." Most of the rest of the world tends to be "polychronic."

Decision-Making Customs

Most countries practice either "**Top-down**" **decision-making** or "Consensus" decision-making. "Top-down" decision-making occurs when the senior official/manager of the firm makes the decision he/she views as the best decision. The "Top-down" manager may review the input of his/her subordinates, but the decision rests completely with the manager. The "Top-down" manager views the subordinates' feelings, ideas and satisfaction as irrelevant to the decision. The U.S uses the "Top-down" (also known as "Authoritative decision-making" or "Hierarchical") style of decision-making.

Japan uses the "**Consensus**" (also known as "Bottom-up decision-making") style. "Consensus" decisions occur when the employees analyze the situation, discuss the options and inform management of their decision. Management implements the unaltered decision of the employees. China uses a combined "Top-down/Consensus" style of management. In China the employees are asked for their opinions, ideas and position on decisions. Management reviews the employees' decisions, discusses everything with the employees and then a consensus between the employees and management is reached. Then management attempts to implement the mutually agreed-upon decision. The U.S. has its own version of "Top-down/Consensus" decision-making. In the U.S., the employees are consulted in order to make them feel they are part of the decision. Then management does whatever it wants without much regard to the employees' input.

Australia uses the "**Collaboration**" style of decision-making. Collaboration decision-making is most easily defined as a negations within a negotiation. Once the Australians leave the negotiation table they will debate/negotiate among themselves as to whether or not they all agree with the terms, prices etc. that were previously reached with opposing firm.

Selection of Personnel

Select personnel who are personable, adaptable, knowledgeable, and healthy travelers. Your opposites from the other country may look favorably upon position, family background and status, education, or age, and include persons with these characteristics on their team. In most instances you should mirror their team's composition. They may be insulted if low-level people are sent to talk to them. They may resent U.S. economic power and definitely do not want to be looked down upon. Remember they have probably learned and internalized the view that their culture is the best, just as you may favor yours. Some countries still favor male negotiators and will not take women seriously (a few may even refuse to negotiate). All want to make a beneficial deal for themselves, as do you.

Risk-taking Propensity

Some cultures admire and embrace risk and others avoid it like the plague. Australians and southern Nigerians are among the most enthusiastic risk-takers. In the U.S. risk is often appreciated as an opportunity, but information is avidly sought. The Japanese tend to be risk-averse.

Interdependence

Another issue to consider when attempting to persuade is the needs of the other party. Interdependence almost always exists within a negotiation. An interdependent relationship can be defined as a relationship in which both parties know that they can influence each other's outcomes as well as have their outcome influenced by the other party, and that both can benefit. Interdependence often impacts the negotiation's starting point, the style of negotiation and persuasion tactics used. The negotiator does not wish to offend an interdependent party. However, they also do not wish to concede too much. In international negotiations the complexity of interdependence can be greatly enhanced.

Power

Levels of power are intertwined with interdependence. However, desire for power is a one-sided arrangement (i.e., desiring the other party to be dependent on you without reciprocation). Negotiators seek power because they believe an advantage or leverage will help them obtain the agreement desired. Power in a business setting is **determined via** the following factors:

1) **asset specificity** (the size of non-transferable investments each side has made to specifically do business with each other);

2) **ease of replacement** (the ability to replace one's business partner with a comparable party and vice versa); and

3) **relative size** (the percentage of each other's bottom line each party represents). Influencing any of these factors changes the power relationship.

If one desires more power, then:

1) reduce your asset specificity while attempting to increase the other party's asset specificity;

2) research your BATNAs (Best Alternative To a Negotiated Agreement, i.e., other potential business partners); and

3) diversify (increase your other business pursuits or buy-out the competition). All of these alternatives are available to a firm in the long run. However, only number two is available in the short-run.

Strategies and Tactics

Discovery

Rule number one in negotiations is **knowledge is power**. A great negotiator always starts every negotiation by acquiring as much information as possible. Some of this falls into the area of pre-planning. However, once the negotiation team is at the table knowledge acquisition takes on the form of carefully crafted questions. Entire books have been written on how to ask questions. SPIN Selling. by Neil Rackham, is an excellent example.

There are two major forms of questions: closed-ended and open-ended. Closed-ended questions require a yes or no response. "Did you do any importing last year?" **Open-ended questions** require an elaborate response. "What problems did you experience with your international partners last year?" Open-ended questions are best for acquiring information.

Involvement questions are a good idea almost anywhere in the world. Involvement questions require your counterpart to elaborate on how business with you would benefit them in the future (How do you foresee our relationship adding to your growth in the future? or How would you solve this problem?). Involvement questions help you acquire information.

Rackham describes four types of questions in his text on SPIN selling. They are:

1) situational questions,
2) problem-solving questions,
3) implication questions, and
4) need pay-off questions.

Research has shown that the last three types of questions are the most effective in selling and negotiating.

Before going into the negotiation meeting your team should develop **questions that address problems with the status quo, questions that address possible solutions and questions that examine the benefits of this type of change**. Once you are at the table, start asking your questions, **but do not offer solutions immediately. Strategically formulate a response to the concerns raised, and use the acquired data during the presentation stage of the negotiation**.

It is best to **stay away from leading questions, which attempt to elicit particular answers or results**, unless you are very good at them and you really understand the culture. A leading question can easily lead to a cultural faux pas. For example, don't ask, "How would this transaction benefit you personally?"

Presentations

The presentation stage takes place at the beginning of the negotiation. It immediately follows the relationship-building and agenda-setting phases. However, in many cultures the relationship-building phase in quite lengthy and never really ends. The presentation stage sets-up the entire negotiation. Both sides usually make presentations. However, if one firm is offering a product their presentation will usually be longer. A presentation usually includes all of the data, information, etc. to help both parties make an informed decision.

Multinationals spend a great deal of time and effort preparing their personnel to make good presentations. Throughout the world the presentation is seen as a critical part of a business transaction. Although,

introductions and greetings are the first personal impression, the presentation is the first business impression.

The style of presentation varies greatly across cultures. In Germany, a presentation should be very detailed/technical and it is considered impolite to ask questions during the presentation. In Taiwan, it is considered imprudent to offer too much information during the presentation stage. In Japan, a presentation should utilize the latest technology, provide numerous visual stimuli, and be thoroughly rehearsed. In Brazil, the presentation should be conducted with flair and considerable oratorical powers. In Saudi Arabia, one should overstate the firm's capabilities. Although understatement is considered appropriate on a personal level in Asia, during a business presentation it is best to just be as accurate as possible.

Persuasion

Some of the persuasion tactics/strategies that are discussed in this text can be used in almost every culture. Unfortunately, many persuasion tactics/strategies are culturally specific; these are presented in their corresponding chapters.

A persuasion tactic is a statement or an act that is used to gain an advantage during a negotiation. For example, getting up to leave from the car dealership in order to reduce the price is a persuasion tactic. A persuasion strategy is an integrated system of tactics. For example, the good guy - bad guy scenario is a team persuasion strategy. Both members must execute several tactics in order to establish one as the bad guy and one as the good guy.

The first thing one should endeavor to accomplish, when attempting to persuade, is to get the other side to like you. Some of the universally-accepted methods of ingratiation (i.e., getting people to like you) are:

1) smiling,
2) listening,
3) enthusiasm,
4) gratefulness,
5) reciprocity,
6) helpfulness,
7) sincere flattery,

8) favors,
9) opinion conformity (agree with them)
10) mirroring (do what they do).

Although each culture varies somewhat on how they perform the aforementioned ingratiating strategies, try them. Even if you are a little bit off, it will probably be a big help to your business transaction.

Most of the world negotiates with misleading information (e.g., Asia, Latin America, parts of Europe and a good proportion of the U.S.). In addition, these cultures expect to be misled by others in order to save "face," etc. However, the subjects that each culture considers acceptable misleading territory can vary (such as real costs, past accomplishments, or even your personal life. So, you will need to do your research regarding which types of misleading information is permissible and you will need to develop strategies on how you choose to deal with it. You need to be able to recognize when the information may be misleading and you will need to decide whether or not you will mislead. In some cultures they will always assume that you are misleading, whether you are or not, because in their culture it is a way of life.

The persuasion tactics that can generally be used across cultures are as follows:

1) **The first person to quote a price loses.** The starting point may dictate the entire transaction. Your opponent may be willing to concede a great deal more than you anticipate.
2) **Ask for their list of technical requirements up-front.** If you allow your opponents to introduce technical specifications throughout the negotiation, the negotiations will be delayed and you will be forced to make concessions throughout the negotiation process.
3) **Get everything in writing.** Regardless of a culture's traditions or an individual's desire to avoid putting an agreement down on paper, it must be done. Throughout the world everyone likes to use the following situational manipulation methods:
   a) "It was just a misunderstanding,"or
   b) "Oh, I guess there was just a little miscommunication. That's all."

In some cultures it is best not to ask for a signature. However, it is almost always acceptable to ask the other party to write out their wishes, their concessions, your concessions and everyone's current understanding of the ongoing agreement. If you avoid this step, you will loose something at least 75% of the time.

4) **Be gracious and flexible while being tough as nails when it counts.** Being nice concedes nothing. A gracious negotiator earns the respect of everyone present. Then when it is time to make your move, everyone will at least listen earnestly. Getting their ear is half the battle.
5) **Don't take specific positions.** Certain facets of the negotiation may be very important to you and your firm. However, you must keep an open mind and not demand specifics. All of the items, in combination, that make up the agreement are what really counts. For example, if you insist on getting a specific price you may forgo excellent delivery terms, advantageous financing terms, etc. The worst case is that the position may cost you the entire deal.
6) **Insist on objective criteria whenever possible.** Don't spend countless hours negotiating "hear-say," "third party facts," and fabricated information. Get the other party to put forth supportive documentation. In other words, get the real facts.
7) **Yield to principle not pressure.** When the other party makes sense and supports it with documentation, it is time to yield on that point. However, never yield to threats, anger, emotional outbursts, or someone's unhappiness.
8) **Break if a member of your team is blundering.** If someone on your team is faltering, do not correct him or her at the negotiation table. Break and discuss it away from everyone else. If you make a member of your team look bad (i.e., "lose face"), then your whole team loses.
9) **Build trust through friendliness and limited information sharing.** Your ability to earn the trust of your opponent is critical to a successful long-term association. One can never be too friendly to the right people.

However, keep in mind that most of the world is very hierarchical. Therefore, being friends with a subordinate may preclude a friendship with his or her superiors. Sharing certain information is considered to be part of trust building. However, since most of the world places no value on intellectual property rights, don't share too much information. You may be viewed as foolish and receive nothing in return.

10) **Formulate your best alternative to the transaction.** What could you do if this transaction is terminated? Knowing your alternatives will keep you from conceding too much. This strategy is commonly referred to as BATNA (Best Alternative To a Negotiated Agreement).

11) **Use diffusion questions.** Diffusion questions are designed to reduce conflict. For example, when your opponent is very upset with an action or position your company has taken, you might say, "Then what would you suggest?"

12) **Show competence and commitment.** Have all your facts and support material readily available and make it obvious you are ready to negotiate forever.

13) **Use stalling and delaying tactics with vigor.** Stalling is a very effective negotiating strategy in most countries. Unfortunately most cultures are more adept at stalling than business people from the U.S. Don't be surprised to find out that your opponents know your exact airline departure date and time.

14) **Engage in relationship-building strategies** (Except for Northern Europe and North America, most countries believe this step to be critical.) Unfortunately, the topics that should be used to build relationships vary from country to country. An appropriate topic in one country is an insult in another. (For example, in Saudi Arabia, do not ask about the women in a man's family.) This whole area is a critical part of your preparations. Do not take it too lightly. Spend at least 15 hours specifically on this. Decide exactly what you will say, how you will say it, and what questions you will ask in order to build the relationship. You may need to learn about soccer in your opponent's country, or who their country's greatest artists were/are, or

who is in their family. You need to find out what is important, research it, study it, and formulate your potential conversations.

15) **Act disappointed.** Acting disappointed may allow you to get additional concessions and it always makes the other side feel like a winner. Most of the world is very good at this tactic. However, U.S. negotiators do a poor job of acting disappointed.

16) **Use confirmation techniques.** When making a statement it is often helpful to ask for agreement (e.g., …wouldn't you agree…?). Formulating your statement into a question promotes two-way communication. In many countries all you will get in response is a nod, but that is all that you need.

17) **Assume agreement.** If you act as if it is a bad deal, then they will probably say no.

18) **Never look too eager.** An opponent's perception that you will agree to anything is definitely counterproductive. Acting as if you might leave and thus terminate the negotiations might be too extreme, but a take-it–or–leave-it attitude on your part could be helpful.

The specific persuasion strategies that may be invoked or which are likely to be effective in a particular country will be covered in the persuasion section of the chapter on that country.

Team Strategies / Tactics

The use of teams for business negotiations has long been practiced by the rest of the world and is now gaining acceptance in the U.S. In the past, a lone U.S. negotiator frequently met with a Chinese team of fifteen. It is difficult for even the best negotiator to achieve excellent results when he is pitted against so many.

One common team strategy is the "good guy/bad guy" strategy commonly used by law enforcement officials. The "bad guy" scares you and the "good guy" supports you. The rationale is to force opponents to confide in the "good guy" so that he/she protects them from the "bad guy." In addition, the "bad guy" attempts to disrupt the opponents' train of thought and steer them away from their pre-planned strategies. This method of negotiating has proven to be effective in a number of situations, but should be used with care and modified to fit the culture.

Along with the personalities your negotiation team attempts to assume, the negotiation team must determine the role of each member. The roles of the team may include:

1) the facilitator (i.e., who will start the meeting, assume the leadership role, etc.),
2) the relationship builder (i.e., who will escort the opponents to the various meeting and functions, see to their needs, etc.),
3) the technical expert (i.e., who is going to address the tough technical questions),
4) the commercial expert (i.e., who will address the terms, conditions, factors that must be considered in international shipment, etc.) and
5) the closer (i.e., who will close on the major issues). The roles should be based on your team members' strengths and weaknesses.

It is important to share your weaknesses and strengths with your team members and vice versa before the negotiations begin. Also, discuss how each of you views the negotiation (i.e., win-win, problem solving, bargaining, etc.). Last, what will be your strategies and tactics as a team. For example, will you have planned breaks or interruptions?

Conflict

Views on conflict

If conflict must be avoided in a culture, the style of negotiation is extremely different from the techniques used in cultures that desire conflict. The French and Australians view conflict as good, and are among the very few cultures with such a perspective. The U.S., Germany, China, Russia, and the U.K. view conflict as a necessary evil. These countries expect conflict and are prepared to deal with disputes in an effective manner.

Japan, Mexico, Spain, and Saudi Arabia view conflict as an extremely bad problem. Heated conflict terminates business transactions, so harmony must be preserved in order for a transaction to be finalized. When faced with conflict-avoiding negotiators, one must be patient and use a great deal of tact. The time it takes to finalize a business transaction in a conflict-avoidance country

is three to four times longer than it takes to conclude a business transaction in a country that has no problems with conflict.

Methods of dispute resolution and systems of logic

Acceptable methods of dispute resolution and ideas of logical argument can vary a great deal from country to country. For example, the French like to practice "Cartesian" logic, which descends from the philosophy of Rene Descartes. Cartesian logic doubts everything until it is proven as a means of defining truth. In Saudi Arabia, emotions tend to be the most powerful means of resolving a dispute. The personal needs of an individual outweigh facts and fairness when making decisions in Saudi Arabia. In the U.S., we like to use empirical reasoning to resolve our differences. Other methods of dispute resolution found in international negotiations include dogma (i.e., authoritative proof or ideology), prior experiences, and intuition.

It is advisable to use the standard "Objection Handling System" when dealing with disagreements. The standard Objection Handling System requires you to:

1) feedback the objection (i.e., repeat the disagreement);
2) question the objection (i.e., ask for clarification as to their concerns);
3) answer the objection; and
4) confirm that their concern has been answered.

Steps one and two are identical in any culture. Just be polite, repeat the concern and ask for clarification. However, step three differs considerably across cultures because what is considered a reasonable style of argumentation or proof can be tremendously variable. You will need to study each culture in order to determine how step three should be executed. Step four is also inconsistent across cultures. You will want confirmation that everything is okay. However, how you ask for that confirmation will vary. Nevertheless, it is a good idea to employ the standard Objection Handling System in international negotiations, for the steps are the same. Only the execution style of step three and four varies.

Conflict reduction

There are numerous means of reducing conflict available to a negotiator. Intense conflict is often the reason a negotiation is terminated or forestalled. However once conflict has been reduced, progress may be made towards an agreement.

De-escalation is an excellent means of conflict reduction. De-escalation can be orchestrated via small concessions, active listening (acknowledging the other side's disagreement), or the separation of the parties via a break or reduced negotiating teams.

Conflict is often a by-product of miscommunication. First, the parties should restate the conflicting issues. Next, each party might agree to show empathy for, or at least attempt to understand, the other's concerns. With de-escalation and restored communication, a discussion of the issues may have a chance at resolution or conflict reduction. However, these simple techniques may be difficult to implement in international negotiation settings.

Contract Formation

All business people know that a well-drafted contract can avert later problems. International contracts must accommodate unique global differences, while offering the hope of legal enforceability. From its inception, the United Nations has devoted attention and resources to this enormously complex issue. Computer technology has made this daunting task easier. In this text only brief glimpses are offered into the legal international labyrinth. Brief descriptions of each nation's legal apparatus are offered. They are intended as academic introductions; if errors are noted it is my intent to correct them in future editions. The previous sentence is, of course, an informal contractual disclaimer. Contracts in their simplest form are agreements between people that offer the possibility of legal enforcement. Businesses use contracts to add the framework necessary for long-range planning.

Most nations have business laws and guidelines for the formation of contracts. They often include arbitration provisions for the resolution of contractual grievances. A rudimentary understanding of contract formation is desirable for business personnel since they often negotiate and draft contracts.

Contracts can take many forms. They do not even have to be written to have validity. A contract can be implied and created through conduct. When individuals organize and perform certain acts, even though no written contract exists, those actions can be construed as contractual. Under Brazilian law a contract can be claimed on the basis of notes, memos, correspondence, entries in books, and even on the basis of the oral testimony of witnesses. A contract can be formal or informal. Formal contracts are usually written and may use standardized forms. Informal contracts can have either an oral or a written format.

Contracts can be bilateral or unilateral. Bilateral contracts involve the exchange of promises binding both parties reciprocally. In unilateral contracts, one party seeks an outcome and once that outcome is realized the contract is fulfilled. Most contracts begin with an offer, which can be accepted or rejected. Rejection will usually terminate an offer; acceptance will usually implement it. When an offer is accepted, the offer and the acceptance create mutual assent between the contracting parties. It is during the offering stage of contract formation that the most intense negotiations usually occur. It is important in the offering stage to clarify the exact nature of the proposals being submitted. Some business cultures prefer open-ended contractual arrangements that allow negotiations to resume when necessary. In some instances time frame parameters do not allow for this, so schedules and agendas should be spelled out.

The United Nations commission on International Trade Law has developed model laws that cover a wide range of international transactions. In 1980 this commission produced an extensive document that has been ratified by most of the major trading nations. It offers guidelines for the formation of international contracts.

Promises that are negotiated become considerations that have monetary value, and services usually have measurable forms of accountability. These issues must be properly clarified. There are numerous factors that might mitigate against the enforceability of an international contract. The most obvious is the issue of the legality of the enterprise. Another factor is the capacity of the parties—do they have the competence to produce a legible and legally binding document? Enforceability can be jeopardized when relevant ordinances have not been properly followed, or the document not properly notarized. The formation of international contract enforceability issues will vary greatly from one country to another. It is generally true that the best evidence in a contractual dispute, when taken to court, is the written contract. Oral evidence seldom is allowed to alter a fully integrated written contract. When adversity strikes an international business venture, handshakes and good faith may have little value.

Once a contract has been fully performed it is discharged. However if a party fails to perform as stipulated in the contract, they may be charged with breach of contract. This can be quite complicated in international agreements and may involve numerous compensatory options if the contract is internationally enforceable. Under United Nations guidelines, a buyer must inspect the purchased goods, and give written notice within a two-year period of time if the merchandise was faulty, or forfeit all rights to compensation.

There are five major legal systems that impact the formation of international contracts. Each system has unique characteristics. In this context, we offer only superficial reference to them. The five major legal systems are:

1) The French Legal System,
2) British Common Law,
3) German Law,
4) The Scandinavian Legal System, and
5) The Law of Shari-a.

In addition to these five major legal systems there are numerous other minor systems. Later chapters will offer commentary on the legal constructs within a particular nation.

The French legal system has its roots in two thousand years of legal history. The coalescence of French law occurred between 1789 and 1803 when Napoleon commissioned French scholars to draft a civil code. Modern French law is a dynamic and still developing major legal system that continues to shape the global marketplace. The French legal system is often referred to as Napoleonic Law. Under Napoleonic Law all conversations, communications, memos, and previous contracts are considered to be binding agreements unless these agreements have been specifically addressed and altered in future conversations, communications, memos, and contracts. This legal system differs a great deal from British Common Law which views only the final agreement as binding (i.e., prior conversations, agreements, and communication are viewed as irrelevant).

British Common Law has a continuous history dating back to the customs of medieval England and the reign of Henry II (1154-1189). It is the product of four primary sources:

1) Legislation,
2) Judicial decisions,
3) Customs and
4) Legal writings.

Legislation, however, takes precedence over all other sources. British Common Law is the most extensive legal system because of the global influence of the British Empire. The U.S., the Philippines, Canada and the U.K. practice contract law that is derived from British Common Law.

German Law evolved out of territorial laws of the 11th century. Roman Law, refined and reshaped by the Italians of the middle ages, found its way into Germany through the canon laws of the church. The political transformation of Germany following the Napoleonic wars brought laws that favored absolutist rulers, yet provided advancement in the codification process. On January 1, 1900, the German Civil Code was adopted. This code, a product of its own historical period, eschewed comprehensibility, but those who understood it admired its precision. However, Austrian and Swiss codes that could be understood by the average citizen also emanated from this same tradition.

The Scandinavian system is a pragmatic one, which is only partially spelled out in written law and is subject to considerable judicial interpretation. It has had its own unique evolution among the Scandinavian nations of Denmark, Norway, Sweden, Finland, and Iceland. Scandinavian Law makes no distinction between private and commercial law and there are few formal requirements.

The Law of Shari-a is derived from the teachings of the Holy Koran. It has been supplemented by a steadily

PRIMARY NEGOTIATION STYLE

Relationship Building	Distributive Bargaining	Contingency Bargaining
Argentina[2]	Brazil[2]	Brazil[3]
Brazil[1]	China[1]	China[3]
China[2]	Hong Kong	Indonesia[3]
Greece[2]	India	Italy[3]
Indonesia[1]	Indonesia[2]	Mexico[3]
Italy[1]	Italy[2]	Philippines[3]
Japan	Mexico[2]	Russia[1]
Korea	Philippines[2]	Saudi Arabia[3]
Mexico	Russia[2]	Spain[3]
Philippines[1]	Saudi Arabia[2]	South Africa[N2]
Saudi Arabia[1]	Singapore[2]	Taiwan[2]
Singapore[1]	Spain[2]	Turkey[2]
Spain[1]	South Africa[N1]	United States
Thailand[1]	Taiwan[1]	
United States	Turkey[1]	
	United Kingdom[3]	
	United States[2]	

1 - Primary
2 - Secondary
3 - Tertiary

B- British Influence
D- Dutch Influence
F- French Influence
N- Native Influence

Debate	Compromise	Joint Problem Solving
Australia	Canada[B]	Argentina[1]
Canada[F]	Norway	Czech Republic
France	South Africa[B]	Denmark
Greece[1]	Sweden	Germany
United States[3]	United Kingdom[1]	Netherlands
		South Africa[D]
		Switzerland
		United Kingdom[2]
		United States[1]

growing body of statute law in each Muslim country to provide for the conditions of modern societies. Legislation is quite extensive in the commercial areas.

Last, one must keep in mind that the majority of contracts in the world tend to be implicit in nature. U.S. contracts tend to be very explicit and legalistic. Overdoing the legalistic side of the agreement will scare away potential international business partners in Japan, Brazil, and Saudi Arabia. Business people want to build relationships in these countries and the contract should reflect mutually prosperous long-term goals.

Follow-up

Although very helpful (and considered good manners), follow-up after a signed contract has never been seen as a critical part of business in the United States. In other parts of the world, the contract is merely a symbol of a desire to do business. Without follow-up, no business will exist. This is partly due to the inability to enforce contracts in other countries, but is primarily because of cultural expectations. Follow-up is probably most critical in Northern Asia. For example, thank you notes, pictures, phone calls, return visits, seasonal greetings, and continuous correspondence / relationship development are required in any major business transaction. The turnover of key personnel can terminate an international contract, for continuity is critical in international relationship development.

Chapter 2

Cross-cultural Communication

- *Context*
- *Non-Verbal Communication (i.e., kinesics)*
- *Communication Styles*

A crucial element that must be examined when one engages in international negotiations is cross-cultural communication. The various methods and styles of communication used across the globe can vary to the point of non-communication. In addition, communication reception methods can be radically different in contrasting cultures. Non-communication takes place in our own hometown and even within our own homes. When we span international borders, the percentage of encounters resulting in non-communication is often multiplied by a factor of 50. Obviously, the language barrier exists when borders are crossed. Yet, even when two individuals are both fluent in the others' languages, a massive amount of non-communication can take place if each is not cognizant of how communication is delivered, analyzed, and processed in the other party's country.

Context

A critical component of international communication is the "context" of the communication. Culture's impact upon language (i.e., "context") is traditionally classified on a scale from "low context" to "high context." "Low context" can be defined as a direct and explicit manner of communicating. In addition, less emphasis is placed upon personal relationships, risk taking is more common, and non-verbal communication is usually not a critical part of the communication process. The countries that typify "low context" are Switzerland, Germany, Sweden, the United States and the United Kingdom.

"High context" can be defined as an indirect and vague manner of communicating. In "high context" cultures a great deal of emphasis is placed upon personal relationships, usually a high level of uncertainty avoidance exists, and non-verbal communication is generally a critical part of the communication process. In addition, the concept of "saving face" is very important, conflict is avoided, and communicators usually share common experiences and understandings.

A sharing of common experiences and understandings is necessary for communication to take place in "high context" cultures. Vagueness is also inherent in this style of communication. Thus, communicators must have a mutual understanding of each other's gestures, slang, indirect statements, and methods of expressing ideas to

High Context Countries

Japan
Saudi Arabia
Indonesia
Philippines
China
Mexico
Brazil
Turkey
Spain
Thailand
India
Argentina
Korea
Italy

Low Context Countries

France
Russia
United Kingdom
United States
Sweden
Denmark
Australia
Germany
Switzerland (German)

communicate in a "high context" culture. The major factors enabling efficient communication to take place in a "high context" culture is the homogeneity of the culture's members and a high level of familiarity that often exists between communicators. When the members of the culture are homogeneous, the likelihood of understanding each other's style of communication is increased. The importance of personal relationships tends to be part of "high context" cultures and efficient communication depends upon this familiarity.

The concept of "saving face" will be referred to quite frequently throughout the text. "Saving face" refers to the avoidance of public humiliation. When an individual is embarrassed publicly he loses "face." Almost all countries that are "high context" cultures place an emphasis on "saving face." France is one of the few exceptions. In France "saving face" is not very critical. However, the French tend to be a "moderate to high context" culture. Countries that typify "high context" and put an emphasis on "saving face" are Japan, Saudi Arabia, China, Korea, Mexico, Brazil, and the Philippines.

The process of building a relationship during international negotiations is usually based on discussions that do not address business issues. These types of discussions will be referred to as "non-task sounding," "relationship-building," "non-substantive discussions," "non-directive discussion," "small talk," or "non-business discussions." Discussions related to business will be referred to as "substantive," "task-related," or "business-related" discussions.

Non-Verbal Communication (i.e., kinesics)

Non-verbal communication is a critical part of the communication message in the majority of today's cultures. Hand gestures or emblems convey a wide variety of messages. However, these messages may have an entirely different meaning in different countries. For example, the O.K. sign if turned downward is vulgar to a large portion of the world's population. Only Germans and U.S business people prefer the firm macho

View of Silence

Hate Silence	Uncomfortable with Silence	Like Silence	Love Silence
Brazilians	North Americans	Indonesians	Japanese
Australians	Germans	Chinese	
Italians	French	Koreans	
Spaniards	Swedes	Thai	
Mexicans	Russians	Taiwanese	
Saudi Arabians	British	Malay	
Argentineans	Indians		
Turkish	Swiss		
Filipinos	Polish		
	Canadians		

handshake. In the Philippines, handshakes are noticeably weaker, which has no bearing on a Filipino's character.

Hand gestures in Brazil are a critical part of communicating. Brazilians often speak simultaneously. Thus, non-verbal communication is an important communications medium because one is often fighting for the floor and others may not be able to hear the entire message. It is not unusual to see a Brazilian gesturing and talking in an aggressive and demonstrative manner. However, there is method to the madness. In fact, their style of communication is not madness at all. Brazilians can recognize over 100 gestures as having a specific meaning. Gesturing is a common and well-understood method of communicating in Brazil.

The Japanese also communicate via a great deal of non-verbal communication. However, their method of non-verbal communication is very subdued. The Japanese are taught to present a positive facade under all types of situations to hide conflict and embarrassment. However, their expression is subdued and rarely exposes their teeth. For example, Japanese women often cover their mouths when conversing or while sitting/standing in public to avoid exposing their teeth. The manner is which they cover their mouths determines whether or not they are hiding embarrassment, politely laughing, being flirtatious, or a myriad of other communication messages.

The Japanese are known to be masters of the art of detecting meaning from "facial expressions." Non-verbal communication is a critical part of the communication message in Japan because it is a very "high context" culture. Movements are to be slight and expression should be hidden or disguised to avoid losing face. Thus, the art of communication via minute facial expressions emerged in Japan. Other forms of non-verbal communication include body or hand movements (i.e., illustrators), eye contact, and posture, all of which may communicate a message, punctuate an important point, or display a particular emotion. For example, crossing one's legs or arms often indicates a defensive position, pointing a finger in the air may indicate significance, and looking at the floor often indicates subservience, depression, or discouragement.

Eye contact is a critical part of communication in the United States and most of Europe. We expect people to look us in the eye when conversing. Avoidance of eye contact in the United States and most of Europe implies that the communicator is lying. However, eye contact is seen as confrontational in most of Asia and the Middle East. It is appropriate to look at someone approximately 30% to 60% of the time in the United States. To a North American, eye contact levels that falls below the 30% mark indicate disinterest or deceit, while eye contact levels that exceed 60%, and/or pupil dilation indicates an interest in the person being viewed, not the conversation. The level of eye contact may reach only 10% in Japan, China, and Saudi Arabia, while in Brazil eye contact levels may exceed 90%. The term the "steady Brazilian gaze" is often used when describing the level of eye contact used in Brazil.

Body orientation, erectness, and posture also communicate messages. A slouched body posture usually indicates a lack of confidence. An expanded chest, a protruding jaw, clinched hands, and arched back and shoulders indicate aggression. Most of the world considers it vulgar to rest one's foot upon one's knee. To be on the safe side, one should always keep feet on the floor (i.e., whenever possible) during international business dealings. It is a good idea to "mirror" a counterpart's body posture and positioning during exchanges of information. U.S. companies teach their salespeople the strategy of "mirroring" and this strategy also applies to international encounters. It is also a good idea to sit straight in international settings. The rest of the world does not share our view of informality and comfort as a way of expressing positive feelings.

Communication Styles

How close should one stand (i.e., proxemics) in an international setting when conversing? In the United States we prefer an arm's length (i.e., 3 feet, or 1 meter – sometimes slightly less for women) when conversing. Most Asian countries prefers 1.5 meters for same-sex conversations and two meters for opposite-sex conversations. Latin Americans prefer a distance of two feet while conversing. Saudi Arabians prefer a distance of 6 to 12 inches while conversing. Thus, proxemic preferences vary a great deal across cultures.

To touch or not to touch (i.e., haptics) also varies. In the United States it is permissible for men to touch other men on their shoulders, arms and hands in a business

High Observance of Non-Verbal Communication

Japan
China
Korea
Thailand
Philippines
Brazil
Saudi Arabia
Mexico
Argentina
Indonesia
Spain
Italy
Russia

Low Observance of Non-Verbal Communication

United States
India
France
United Kingdom
Denmark
Sweden
Australia
Germany
Switzerland (German)

High Use of Non-Verbal Communication

Brazil
Saudi Arabia
Italy
Mexico
Turkey
Spain
Argentina
Russia
Philippines
Australia
United States
Thailand

Low Use of Non-Verbal Communication

France
Korea
Indonesia
United Kingdom
India
China
Japan
Sweden
Germany
Switzerland (German)

setting. It is also permissible for women to touch other women on their arms and hands. Likewise, it is permissible for men to shake women's hands in a business setting. In the United States, it is also permissible for women to touch men on their shoulders, back, arms, and hands in an informal business setting, although caressing is viewed as inappropriate. In a non-business setting different rules apply.

Styles of touch vary a great deal across the globe. Indian males often hug each other while simultaneously exerting a firm slap upon each other's backs. Handshakes are not practiced in every culture. Handshakes between women and men are the exception, not the rule, in international business settings. The French, Italians, and Brazilians kiss each other when greeting. It is best to keep one's distance in Asia. It is also best to keep one's distance from the opposite sex in international settings. It is acceptable to be very close, friendly and "touchy" in the Middle East when conversing with the same sex. The same is true for Brazil, Italy, Argentina and Mexico.

Vocalics (i.e., pitch, loudness, tones, rates and pauses) have different meanings in international circles. Loudness in Saudi Arabia means sincerity. Loudness in Malaysia means insincerity. Softly spoken statements indicate importance and sincerity in Malaysia. Almost everyone speaks too fast in an international setting. Due to language barriers, everyone needs to slow down their rate of speech when conversing with people from another country.

In the U.S. a pause is used to emphasize a point. Pauses just don't exist in Brazil. If you pause in Brazil you will lose the floor. Arabs love spirited and enthusiastic conversations. In most of Asia. long pauses are a way of life and silence is appreciated. Asians quickly tire of people who speak continuously.

Chapter 3

Argentina

- *Country Background*
- *The Argentine Culture*
- *Business Protocol*
- *Communication Style*
- *The Argentine Concept of Negotiations*

Argentina is the second largest country in South America, (after Brazil), and covers most of the Southeastern part of the continent. It is about three-tenths the size of the United States. One of the world's richest nations during the 1930s, Argentina fell into political and economic chaos during the 1970s, and then started a remarkable recovery in the 1980s and 90s.

Argentina, composed of 23 provinces, is bordered by the Atlantic Ocean and Uruguay to the east, Paraguay, Brazil and Bolivia to the north, and Chile to the west. Argentina has recently enjoyed friendly relations with most of its neighbors, although a few border tensions remain with Chile. Argentina's strategic position gives it excellent access to European, Caribbean and American markets.

Country Background

History

The Spanish settled in Argentina in 1516, and it quickly became an important colony due to its abundant silver and gold resources. The country's name comes from the Latin word *argentum*, which means silver. The Spaniards settled mainly in northern Argentina where they relied heavily on forced labor to mine the riches of the Andes Mountains. Indigenous Indians resisted the Spanish for a long time in the southern part of the country, which remained less developed in comparison to the northern part.

The inhabitants of the colony became disenchanted with Spanish rule at the end of the 18th Century and declared their independence in 1816. Argentina adopted its federal constitution in 1853 and became fully united in the 1880s. Argentina's Constitution is closely patterned after the U.S. Constitution. However, the Argentine Constitution has been suspended numerous times under various military dictatorships.

The Argentine economy benefited a great deal from the exportation of wheat and beef from the mid-1890s until World War I. However, the economy could not support the flood of European immigrants after the war and the onset of the Great Depression. The resultant economic and civil unrest led to military dictatorships that ended with the election of Juan Peron as President. Peron's presidency from the mid-forties to the mid-fifties promoted industrialization and self-sufficiency. The working class was able to increase wages, pensions and job security. Growing inflation eventually hurt Peron's presidency, and in 1955 he was ousted by a military coup that resulted in three decades of military rule.

Although Peron temporarily returned to power in the early 1970s, the military took over again in 1976. The ensuing dictatorship tried to eliminate all forms of opposition and resistance with methods that included torture, kidnapping and murder. This became known as the "dirty war," and thousands of people died or disappeared during that time. In 1982, perhaps to distract the Argentine public from internal problems, Argentina invaded the Falkland Islands, which it had claimed for more than 150 years. The ensuing defeat by Great Britain hastened the demise of the military, and the return of an elected president and the constitution.

Government

Argentina is a federal republic, with a government structure similar to that of the U.S. government in that it has executive, legislative and judicial branches. The elected president is the chief of state and serves a six-year term.

Presently Argentina enjoys a relatively stable political environment. Carlos Menem, elected president in 1989, introduced many democratic and free-market reforms. Despite high unemployment levels (currently around 15%), and opposition from other political groups, an elected government will probably survive.

Demographics

The terrain includes the famous and rich Pampas plains in the north, the plateau of Patagonia to the south, and the rugged Andes Mountains along the western border. The highest point at Cerro Aconcagua is 6,960 meters, while the lowest point at Salinas Chicas is below sea level.

Argentina has a population of 37 million inhabitants; over 85% are of European descent. The majority of Argentines are of Italian, Spanish and German stock, making Argentina the most European of all South American countries. Other ethnic groups include Yugoslavs, Japanese, Koreans, Russians and Arabs. Indigenous Indians, mestizos, and other nonwhites make up the remainder of the population.

Argentina's literacy rate exceeds 96%. Life expectancy is 71.9 years for men and 78.8 years for women.

Economy

European influence is apparent in Argentina's language, cuisine, architecture, fashion, education, and economy. Many Argentines have sophisticated taste and shop for the latest in European fashions. On the other hand, there is also a tendency to favor and support local products and ideas.

The 2000 per capita GNP was $12,900. Over one-third of the population lives below the poverty line. Considering the nation's vast natural and human resources, Argentina has yet to reach its economic potential. Obviously, the unstable governments of the past have inhibited Argentina's economic growth, but years of Menem reforms are starting to have positive effects on trade and private capital investment.

Argentina produces processed foods, motor vehicles, textiles, chemicals, steel, and many agricultural products. In 2000 it exported $26.5 billion worth of these goods to Brazil, the USA, Italy, Japan, the Netherlands, and other countries. During the same year, it imported $25 billion in goods from the USA (22% of all imports), Brazil (21%), Germany, Bolivia, Japan, Italy, and the Netherlands. Imports included machinery, fuels, chemicals, plastics, and consumer products.

Unfortunately, recent international economic turmoil have resulted in decreased investor confidence. High unemployment and a history of defaulting on foreign debts have also hindered economic growth, but the economy is improving and will probably continue to grow under the present political atmosphere. After decades of runaway inflation, the Argentine peso is currently pegged on a par with the U.S. dollar.

The Argentine Culture

Language

Castillan Spanish is the official language of Argentina. However, Argentine Spanish is unique due to an Italian influence, and many words are pronounced differently than in other Spanish-speaking countries. One of the most distinguishable variances is that the *ll* is pronounced

as *zh*. Thus, the word *Castellano*, pronounced /kahs-tay-yano/ in the rest of the Spanish-speaking world, becomes /kahs-tay-zhano/ in Argentina. Also, Argentine Spanish uses the *vostostros* form of the second person familiar, as opposed to the *tu* form, and requires a different set of verb endings.

While Argentines understand the Spanish spoken by people outside Argentina, and vice versa, there are different meanings for some words. It is not uncommon for an innocent word to mean something different or even vulgar in Argentine Spanish. Therefore, it may be necessary for negotiators to use translators familiar with the local dialect to communicate effectively.

There are several other languages spoken in Argentina by different immigrant communities. These include Italian, English and German.

Religion

The official religion in Argentina is Roman Catholicism. Although 92% of the population is nominally Catholic, less than 20% are practicing Catholics. Therefore, one can deduce that religion does not play a large role in current society or business culture. Other religions are present: Protestants are 2%, the Jewish are 2%, and other diverse, often indigenous, religions are found in the rest of the population.

Value system

Humanitarian values have traditionally been very strong in Argentine society. This, however, has recently given way to a wave of consumerism, especially in large cities. As in most of South America, the family plays a large role in defining individual identity and behavior. Although the older generation still looks to the church and traditional values, younger generations are endorsing other social structures that range from political allegiance to soccer organizations.

Argentines frequently make individual decisions, but these are influenced by the interests of the family or larger group. Kinship, loyalty and friendship play a large role in making decisions. Machismo is strong in Argentine society, although this is changing in upper levels of business and society. Women do not have the same business opportunities as men, and they still play a conservative role in society and business.

Class structure / Stratification

There is no rigid class structure in modern Argentine society, but great differences exist between the rich and the poor. The older generation tends to emphasize the traditional divisions between the upper and lower classes more than younger people do. Argentine social stratification tends to emphasize occupational or regional themes, rather than lineage.

Safety

Although crime has been increasing, Argentina's cities are still safer than most U.S. inner cities. Business people and tourists can normally travel quite safely in most parts of the country. The political situation is considered very stable at this time, although one might keep in mind the volatile nature of past Argentine politics and coups.

Business Protocol

Argentine business protocol is **very formal**. **Titles** are regularly used in business environments. These include *Doctor*, *Ingeniero* (engineer), *Abogado* (attorney), and *Licenciado* (most professionals who wear ties).

Unless close friends, co-workers regularly address each other by their titles. It's not a good idea to drop formalities when addressing Argentine business people unless they do so first. Women should pay particular attention to formalities in order to avoid any misinterpretations.

Greetings and etiquette

It is customary to **greet everyone when meeting a group** of people, unless this is not possible due to seating or room arrangements. Likewise, it is important to bid everyone good-bye so no one is offended.

A typical business greeting involves a **brief handshake with a nod**. "Air kissing" close friends or even strangers in social situations is very common. Although traditional machismo influences may prevent some men from making the first move to shake hands with a businesswoman, more men will now initiate handshakes with women.

Time

Like their South American neighbors, Argentines have a casual attitude toward time. They are **polychronic** and tend to be **15 to 30 minutes late for meetings.** Higher-ranking people will usually arrive later than lower-ranking individuals. However, some modern Argentine executives equate time with money and may be as punctual as their North American counterparts.

As a polychronic people, Argentines can tolerate constant interruptions and attend to many tasks simultaneously. While this may be frustrating to many visiting teams, discussion-focusing techniques can often keep the negotiations on track.

Typical business days in Argentina are from 9 AM to 5 PM with a one or two-hour lunch. Executives, however, may put in extremely long hours that may last till 9 or 10 PM. The siesta is alive and well in rural areas of Argentina, where it's not unusual to close from 1 to 5 PM, and reopen till late hours.

Like many Europeans, Argentines take four to five weeks of vacation each year, traditionally around January. It is therefore advisable to avoid business trips around Christmas or January.

Gifts

Business gifts are acceptable in Argentina, especially when there is a close relationship between individuals. **Gifts should usually be of high quality**, and popular items include imported liquors and electronics, which are relatively more expensive in Argentina. When a personal relationship exists, gifts for an associate's child are also acceptable.

Items to avoid include wine and leather goods since Argentina is known for these products. Also, gifts of knives are considered in bad taste since they symbolize the severing of friendship. Gifts that visibly advertise company logos are considered tacky.

Business entertainment

Business **lunches and dinners are common in Buenos Aires. However business lunches are less common in rural areas, since people may return home for lunch**. Most Argentines consider meals to be a social occasion and usually do not discuss business. Argentine cuisine mainly consists of Italian pasta dishes, German meat and potatoes, and asados or barbecues that follow gaucho traditions. Having wine with a meal is very common. Argentina has the third-largest per capita wine consumption in the world. Mexican cuisine is quite foreign to Argentina, and one should not assume that Argentines prefer or have ever eaten Mexican-style burritos, nachos and tacos.

Argentines are especially fond of social occasions and parties, and they often stay up late with family members and friends. It is therefore not unusual to receive and accept late invitations to bars and dinners. These occasions usually strengthen the relationship-building process and are well worth pursuing.

Dress

Business dress in Argentina is **conservative, but stylish**. They prefer subdued fashions and follow European trends. They tend to notice every aspect of a visitor's dress, from shoes to briefcase or suit. Therefore, it is essential to dress tastefully when visiting Argentina on business.

Ties are required for men, and white blouses are popular for businesswomen. Conservative attire is essential, and provocative dress by women is frowned upon.

Communication Style

Business language

Argentines use **a moderate to high-context language**. It is a homogenous culture, so the use of such language results in very few misinterpretations. Although most all Argentines speak Spanish in business situations, some will chose to use English, especially in the capital city of Buenos Aires. It is important, however, to employ an expert translator when negotiating in Spanish.

Generally, Argentines strongly dislike silence and employ small talk to fill in the gaps. Small talk is normal at the beginning and the end of the negotiations. It is wise to let the Argentine leader begin or end these topics. When engaging in social or small talk, it's essential not to offend the strong Argentine pride. Generally,

Argentines consider Buenos Aires as the Paris of South America and their country to be a sophisticated Europeanized nation.

Non-verbal communication

Argentines use many non-verbal cues as part of their communication process. Since most Argentines are of Italian or Spanish descent, they use many of the same hand gestures as their European cousins. An Argentine may place his hands on a colleague's shoulders or arms to emphasize a point or show friendliness. Hand gestures include placing the index finger under the eye and pulling on the skin, which usually means: "watch out for that person," and "no" is indicated by wagging the index finger back and forth and making a clicking noise with the tongue. Intense eye contact is normal. Lack of eye contact is believed to indicate insincerity or weakness.

Argentines are also very observant of non-verbal communication from others. It's important to be aware of one's own non-verbal behavior in order to avoid sending the wrong cues to the Argentine team.

The Argentine Concept of Negotiations

Selecting personnel

Selections for negotiation team members are based upon **status** and **rank. Education, experience** and **social position** also affect team selection. Therefore, visiting teams should attempt to equal the rank and social position of the Argentine team in order to avoid the appearance of inferiority or superiority. Additionally, since Argentines are socially oriented, it is recommended to bring individuals who are adept in social settings.

Negotiating style

Argentines look at negotiations as **joint problem-solving**. Therefore, they approach the negotiating process analytically, paying special attention to details. The Argentine style is similar to the Italian concept of **family interest and mutual dependency.** Argentines are capable of bending the rules to meet business objectives. Bribery and corruption have been somewhat commonplace in Argentine politics and business. Thus, **relationship building** is an important part of Argentine negotiations, and can help avoid being cheated.

Argentines can be tough negotiators and will concede slowly and begrudgingly. Negotiations take more time than they do in the USA or Europe. It is advisable to save some concessions until the very end, so that the Argentine team will perceive they are winning.

Issues discussed

Many important issues discussed are **relationship-based**. Argentines will spend a great deal of time on **non-substantive** issues, such as personal questions, unrelated business issues, sports, fine wines, arts, movies and world affairs. Soccer is probably the best ice-breaking topic in Argentina. Argentina has traditionally had some of the best soccer teams in the world and has won two world cups. Some consider Diego Maradona of Argentina to be the all-time best soccer player in the world.

Taboos include Argentina's political history and the Falkland war of 1982. It's important to remember Argentine pride when discussing political or social space issues concerning Argentina and its neighbors.

Establishing trust

Argentines tend to have long-term relationships that are based on trust and mutual respect. They usually gain trust by **intuition** and establishing **personal relationships**. These can be fostered through social activities, personal interaction and past experiences. Once trust is established, it is imperative to keep it through personal contact, business activities and social activities.

Persuasion

Argentines tend to rely on **intuition** and **emotional reasoning**. However, this does not preclude the use of **hard facts** in negotiations. Indisputable facts and figures will convince even the most ardent Argentine team, and accordingly prompt them to react without much emotion or personal feelings. In addition, stressing the mutual benefit of a deal increases an argument's validity.

Argentines may not haggle over price as much as other South American cultures. To them, growth opportunities and prestige are often more important than money.

The specific persuasion tactics that are likely to be effective in Argentina are:

1) **Get it in writing**. Write everything down throughout the negotiations. Use your copious notes as a proof source in the later stages of the negotiation.
2) The use of metaphors, emotional tactics, fear tactics, distraction tactics and diffusion questions can be very useful in Argentina.
3) **Avoid direct conflict**. It is acceptable to say what is on your mind. Thus, some indirect conflict and/or a little banter are okay. However, direct and serious conflict that causes someone to "lose face" will result in an emotional reprisal.
4) Take your time.
5) Certain requests that we might consider to be **corruption** are normal business practices in Argentina. Decide how you plan to initiate or respond to such requests.
6) Receiving the **technical specifications up-front** or in the beginning of the negotiation is a good idea.
7) **Build trust through information sharing**.
8) **Supported facts**. One needs to present logical/factual information that is accompanied by supportive documentation.
9) **Display your expertise**. A credible argument carries a lot of weight in Argentina. **Display/state your own, your team's, your firm's credentials and accomplishments when appropriate (i.e., on the business cards, when asked, for your team members, as supporting documentation, etc.).**

Resolving disputes

When negotiating, Argentines avoid confrontation and prefer to keep the discussions friendly and relaxed. If a dispute arises, it is best to employ **personal appeals** and emphasize the long-term benefits of the **relationship**. An attempt should be made to enhance the level of trust and goodwill that exists between the negotiating parties.

Group and individual dynamics

Argentines tend to be **individualistic,** but still respect their group affiliations. They work well as a team and they do not like internal conflict. They respect each other's social standards. Although they may display strong emotions, they will continue to work together as a team until the objective is reached.

Risk

Argentines are **moderate-to-low risk takers**, a stance due to their strong emphasis on family and personal relationships. This can cause longer decision times, an aversion to quick deals, and some frustration for foreign negotiating teams. Thus, extra meetings or trips may be necessary in order to obtain Argentine acceptance. Visiting teams are better off presenting low-risk long-term-oriented proposals, rather than lucrative but risky deals.

Decision-making

Argentine firms tend to use a **centralized top-down decision-making system**. Inter-level communications are rather weak. Upper management frequently sets the standards and will not solicit feedback from lower echelons. However, since Argentina is a rather paternalistic society, decision-makers will keep the well-being of their group in mind.

Since, Argentine decisions tend to take a long time, foreign negotiators should plan on an extended decision-time frame. The additional time is necessary in order to allow the Argentine team sufficient space and freedom to reach a decision, and should be used to maintain and enhance the mutual trust that has been fostered by the interaction to date.

Type of agreement

The Argentine legal system is based on the French and German civil law systems. The civil code covers most aspects of contracts and agreements. In addition, the Commercial Code supplements commercial and mercantile contracts. Agreements should be **written in detail with all terms and conditions specified**.

Argentina has traditionally welcomed foreign investment. Law no. 21382 enacted in 1976 sets guidelines for new and existing foreign investment. The Undersecretariat of Economic Policy must approve investments exceeding five million dollars.

NOTES:

Chapter 4

Australia

- *Country Background*
- *The Australian Culture*
- *Business Protocol*
- *Communication Style*
- *The Australian Concept of Negotiations*

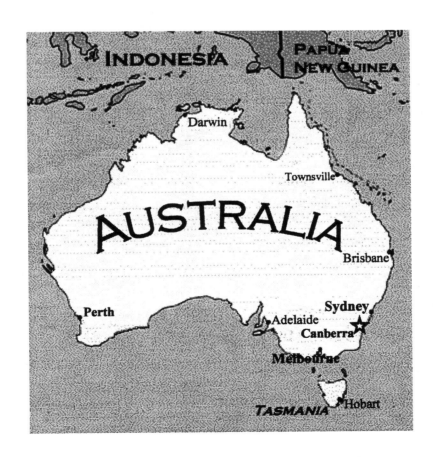

Australia is a continent of great diversity and contrast. It is approximately as large as the continental United States with a population of over 19 million people. Although a relatively young nation, modern Australia is an advanced country with many natural resources and a reputation as one of the world's favorite tourist attractions.

Country Background

History

After Britain lost America as a colony, the British government decided to settle its convicts in Australia, which had been explored earlier by William Dampier and Captain James Cook. On May 13, 1787, a fleet of 11 ships under the command of Captain Arthur Phillip sailed from England to start the new convict settlement. They sailed to Port Jackson, a few miles north of the present site of the modern city of Sydney. The settlement consisted of 1,030 people, 736 of them convicts. Other explorers gradually opened up the vast hinterland to new settlers, and convict transportation to the mainland ended in 1840.

The original inhabitants of Australia were hunters and gatherers who arrived on the continent about 60,000 years ago from Southeast Asia. This native population of about a half million people was decimated by European diseases and clashes with settlers. With the discovery of gold in 1851 in New South Wales, the immigration of free settlers greatly increased, and Australia today is a nation of immigrants much like the U.S.

Government

Although the English Queen is referred to as the Queen of Australia as well, Australia does not consider itself to be a constitutional monarchy, but rather a parliamentary democracy. The national governing body, the Australian Parliament, consists of an Upper and Lower House: the Senate, with 64 seats, is patterned after the American system, and the House of Representatives, with 127 members, is patterned after the British Westminster system. Australia is made up of the federal states of New South Wales, Victoria, South Australia, Western Australia, Tasmania, and Queensland as well as the Australian Capital Territory (Canberra) and the Northern Territory.

The Prime Minister heads the executive branch and is the head of government. An independent High Court heads the judicial branch. There are three major political parties: the Labor Party, the Liberal Party and the Australian Democratic Party. Australia is an active participant in the United Nations and is committed to international law and disarmament. It is particularly involved in assisting its developing neighbors in Asia and the Pacific. Currently 80 countries receive aid from Australia.

Demographics

Australia's 19,357,594 citizens (2001) are concentrated mainly on the southern and eastern coasts. It has one of the world's highest urbanization rates with 90 percent of its population living in 7 cities and the areas within 50 miles of the coast. Australian cities are modern and expansive. Most Australian citizens own their own homes and live in well-planned and serviced suburbs. Inner-city town houses of the Victorian and Edwardian eras have regained popularity. In some of the larger cities high-rise apartments are becoming a preferred way of life.

Ethnic groups are: 92% of European (mostly British) background, 7% of various Asian ancestries, and 1% from Aboriginal or other groups. Aboriginal population is rising, their traditions are being encouraged, and some of their land rights are being restored. Many of them still retain traditional life styles and choose to live apart from the rest of the population. The Australian government has become more responsive to their needs in recent decades and is currently encouraging Aboriginal self-determination.

Life expectancy is 77 years for men and 82.9 years for women. The literacy rate is an almost perfect 100%.

Economy

When Australian adventurers discovered gold, they transformed Victoria into the most important British colony in the world. Capital flowed in, the gold mining industry prospered, and agriculture flourished. The region became nearly self-sustaining by the end of the 19th century.

Australia continued to develop its western-style capitalist economy and in 2000 attained a per capita income of $23,200, which is higher than that of many European countries.

Natural resources include bauxite, coal, iron ore, copper, tin, silver, uranium, nickel, gold, tungsten, mineral sands, lead, zinc, diamonds, natural gas, and petroleum. The industrial revolution brought factories and jobs and added economic stability to this highly urbanized country. Australia pioneered industrial arbitration, adopting a minimum wage as well as an organized legal system for resolving industrial disputes. Australia is the world's largest exporter of iron ore, beef and wool, second largest for mutton and one of the top wheat exporters. Other significant agricultural products include barley, sugarcane, fruit , and poultry.

Australia's exports, worth $69 billion in 2000, included coal, gold, meat, wool, wheat and machinery. Major partners included Japan (19%), South Korea , the USA, New Zealand, the EU, Hong Kong, Taiwan and Singapore. Australian imports reached $77 billion in 2000 and included machinery, motor vehicles, computers, office machines and oil products. Major import partners included the EU (24%), USA (22%), Japan (14%), China and New Zealand.

The Australian Culture

Language

Although a few native languages are still used by Aborigines and some recent immigrants maintain their home languages, English is the official language and is spoken by almost all the population. Australian grammar and spelling are a mix of British, American, and unique Australian patterns. For example, the Australian majority party is spelled "Labor" (American spelling), not "Labour" (British spelling). Australian English contains a mixture of metaphors and swearing. The language is fairly uniform between regions.

Australians realize that others do not easily understand their language, particularly the dialect known as "strine". Strine is based on word condensation. For example, saying "Dijvagudweend" instead of saying "Did you have a good weekend?" Mastering this dialect is necessary to gain the acceptance of Australian workers.

It involves shortening words to one syllable and adding a long sound at the end. Therefore, a barbecue becomes a barbie, a mosquito a mozzi and the people are Auzzies.

Religion

Australians are predominately Christian, with Anglicans composing 26% of the population, Roman Catholics 26% and a variety of other Christian denominations making up 24.3%. Jews, Muslims, and Buddhists are also present. A significant proportion of Australians (almost 13%) claim no religious affiliation.

Value system

Although Australian ethics are based on Christian traditions, material progress is becoming more important than humanistic concerns. Individualism is very important and Australians find it easy to say "no." The prevailing attitude is that one's private life is not to be mixed with business. Friendships usually are confined to a few people and are generally specific to needs.

Most Australians have low levels of anxiety about life, since external structures (democracy, organizations, scientific method) have provided a great deal of stability to their daily lives. The nuclear family is the rule and is one of their strongest socializing forces. There are established traditions for almost every aspect of life. Areas of anxiety that do exist can center around meeting deadlines and performance objectives.

Class structure / Stratification

Australians are highly egalitarian and endorse a high standard of well-being for all. This value orientation greatly minimizes privileges normally associated with formal rank. Considerable emphasis is placed on one's ability. Traditional sex roles are changing rapidly, but women are still pursuing equality in pay and power.

The concept of "mateship" is unique to Australia. It involves deep trust, respect and the promise of long-lasting friendships. Mateship may also involve giving without expecting anything in return. It follows that the democratic and egalitarian treatment of all is important. Class differences do exist, based on ownership and control of property and resources. However, Australians don't like it when a person stands out, nor do they like being categorized. They are critical of those who would use wealth to exert power. They respect those who contribute their fair share and they tend to form judgments based on those actions.

Safety

Australia has a low crime rate. Petty street crime does occur, usually in the form of pick-pocketing and purse snatching. Violence is less apparent than in the United States, but it is on the increase, mainly in areas with youth unemployment or racial tension.

Business Protocol

Greetings and etiquette

Business etiquette is **quite informal. Australians value modesty and casualness.** They are usually quite friendly and easy to get to know, without the British reserve of their ancestors. It is acceptable for visitors to introduce themselves in social situations. They greet each other with hello or an informal "G'day." It is the custom to shake hands at the beginning and end of a meeting. Women don't usually shake hands with one another, but may give a kiss on the side of the cheek if they are acquainted. It is appropriate to present a business card at an introduction, but many Australians do not have them or give them out.

Time

The average work week in Australia is between 35 and 40 hours. Australians are **punctual for business appointments,** but **casual about time for social activities.** Australians go **point by point** when it comes to presentations and heavy discussions/negotiations. However, they still **like to throw in some casual conversation** during a meeting. Thus, Australia can be best characterized as **monochronic with an Australian flair.**

When travelling to Australia, one crosses the International Date Line. When flying westward from the United States to Australia, one "loses" a day. Going eastward from Australia to the United States causes one to "gain" a day. The normal Australian business day is from 9 AM to 5 PM Monday through Friday.

Gifts

Australians are not likely to give gifts in a business context. If invited to a home as a dinner guest, however, one may want to bring a small gift of flowers, wine, chocolates or folk crafts from home. An illustrated book from a foreign culture also makes a good gift.

Business entertainment

Australians do not usually like unannounced visits, so it is best to call ahead. In an Australian pub it is important to remember that **each person pays for a round of drinks.** Missing one's turn to "shout for a round" can make a bad impression.

Australians do not readily invite business acquaintances to their homes. With time and increased closeness, however, it is not uncommon to receive an invitation for a barbecue. It is important to distinguish between "afternoon tea" around 4 PM and tea which is the evening meal served between 6 & 8 PM. Supper is a late snack. Safe conversation topics include sports and sightseeing. Australians love sports, and are also proud of the unique qualities of their country. No other place in the world has the koala bear, the kangaroo, and other fascinating features. Politics and religion are taken seriously, so expect strong opinions if those subjects come up. Australians respect people with opinions even if contrary to their own.

Dress

Australians tend to **dress quite informally** and fashions follow North American trends. However, women wear pants far less than women do in the United States. Australia is in the southern hemisphere, so the seasons are the opposite of those in North America. Most of the country is tropical, but given Australia's great size, temperatures can vary considerably. Southern Australia has warm summers and mild winters, so light clothing is generally advisable. During the winter months, warmer clothes and rain gear are appropriate. **Business dress is generally conservative, with a dark suit and tie being customary.** Women may wear either a skirt and blouse or a dress.

Communication Style

Business language

Australians use **low-context communication** in their speech and expression. They love controversy, and disagreement is considered "lively conversation". They are assertive, independent, and seek to strengthen their individuality by acting against "others'" opinions. Australian humor often contains a certain amount of cynicism that could be construed as harsh or inconsiderate. Under stress, they tend to use humor to lighten things up.

Australians appreciate the art of understatement. Neither criticism nor praise is lavishly bestowed. They are often laconic and are noted for the brevity of their speech. Australians enjoy being candid and direct, which at times can be disconcerting for someone from another culture. This can even lead to breakdowns in effective communication.

Non-verbal communication

Australians tend to act casually and are friendly and cheerful, but resent authority or take-charge types. It is important in their presence to be up-beat and positive, and yet ready to mix it up with them because that is what they expect in a negotiation. They may lean forward and make good eye contact, and do not mind if others do the same.

They may also smile when facing controversy, and it's a good idea to do the same with them because that is the response they are culturally conditioned to expect. A negotiator's demeanor should be unassuming, but he/she should maintain eye contact, have friendly facial expressions, and generally act confidently.

The Australian Concept of Negotiations

Selecting personnel

Managers are generally chosen for their **efficiency in conducting meetings, and their ability to establish good relationships with subordinates**. In Australia, instructions are usually disguised as polite requests, and subordinates expect their bosses to give them instructions and let them perform their jobs without interference. Fairness in relationships is more important than closeness. Their concept of the boss consists of a coach who supports, encourages, and provides feedback to his subordinates.

Negotiating style

Australians **do not like high-pressure sales pitches,** and presentations that are filled with hype and excitement will not impress them. They value brevity, and find it difficult to be patient when a negotiation drags on.

Since Australians are inner-directed, they are not likely to modify themselves or their behavior to please others. **They view conflict in the negotiation process as good.** An Australian simply expects each party to present their viewpoint, everyone discusses the issues, and a resolution is worked out with neither side "taking it personally." The Australians view negotiations as an **informal debate.**

Issues discussed

Australians discuss **substantive issues at the negotiating table, but this usually occurs after establishing a relationship**. They often do this through finding common ground with their counterparts, and through inquisitive and friendly non-task sounding (i.e., non-business related discussions). A little non-task sounding is usually interjected throughout the negotiations.

Establishing trust

Australians tend to base their trust upon a **person's loyalty and commitment,** and on their own sense of that person's capacity for performance and consistent behavior. They will also note others' recognition, ranking and accreditation of that person.

Persuasion

In negotiating with Australians, it is important to present cases in a **forthright manner, outlining both the good and the bad.** Modesty is the better approach, casualness is the better demeanor, while hype and excitement will be counter-productive. Australians value profit over market share, so negotiators should stress the profitability of any proposed venture.

The specific persuasion tactics that are likely to be effective in Australia are:

1) Haggling over price is okay. The price will probably change around 25 to 30%. Both sides should start with reasonable prices.
2) Receiving the **technical specifications up-front** is a good strategy.
3) **Get it in writing**. Write everything down throughout the negotiations.
4) **Build trust through information sharing**. The Australians will expect a healthy exchange of information.
5) The use of metaphors, emotional tactics, threats, fear tactics, distraction tactics and diffusion questions can be very useful in Australia.
6) **Embrace conflict**. The Australians view it as positive, productive and fun.
7) It is **okay to be blunt** and to the point in Australia, even to the point of rudeness.
8) **Take your time**. Australians do not stall but often postpone unfinished items. Remember that Australians value brevity, yet they are definitely not in a hurry. In addition, Australians value their free time. Thus, if a negotiation drags on and little is accomplished, rather than simply agree on some of the items in order to finalize the transaction, Australians will most likely want to continue the negotiations the next day. So, do not start trading things so that you can wrap things up and go home, because you will be the only one making concessions.
9) **Speak with conviction and confidence.**
10) **Supported facts**. One should present logical/factual information that is accompanied by supportive documentation.
11) **Two-Sided Appeals**. Australians expect a fair assessment of the proposed transaction. Thus, a two-sided appeal, which provides both pros and cons of an argument/product, is likely to be an effective persuasion strategy.

Tactics to avoid include:

1) Do not use stalling, favoritism, or nepotism.
2) Never brag by saying I did this and I did that.

However, providing factual information with supportive documentation that shows the accomplishments of your firm or yourself, if it is related and presented in a humble manner, can be very helpful.

Resolving disputes

When an impasse is reached, it is not uncommon for an Australian team to confer with their supervisors and to use them as a sounding board for their personal and professional questions. To successfully resolve disputes, foreign negotiators must be **attentive to Australian concerns**, and be ready to modify their approach to accommodate the issues Australians feel are important.

Group and individual dynamics

Australians are **highly individualistic, but they also can work together in a team environment.** Since they view conflict as healthy and even constructive, they bounce ideas off of each other freely without much regard to personal feelings or rank.

Risk taking

Australians are **high-risk takers.** They are generally more willing to take risks than Americans, who may feel a little uneasy with Australians who without hesitation want to jump into action. Indeed, Australians are considered to be some of the highest risk takers in the world.

Decision-making

Australians are **collaborative** in their orientation toward decision-making. They believe quite definitely that decision-making procedures must be based upon management's willingness to allow subordinates to share in the establishment of organizational goals. Thus, all information is shared, subordinates consult with top management and then an agreement is reached. It seems the Australians view the decision-making process as a negotiation in and of itself.

Type of agreement

Australians prefer written agreements that discuss the contract in detail. Parties are usually free to choose between Australian and foreign law governing the contract language. Both the agent and the principal may stipulate specific courses for terminating the agreement. Australian agreements are based upon British Common Law.

The Australian government has imposed capitalization rules on Australian enterprises in which foreigners have a 15% or larger degree of control. Most Australian companies are formed by incorporation under the Companies Act. The only type of company in common use by overseas investors is a limited liability company.

NOTES:

Chapter 5

Brazil

- *Country Background*
- *The Brazilian Culture*
- *Business Protocol*
- *Communication Style*
- *The Brazilian Concept of Negotiations*

Brazil is the world's fifth largest country in area, and the sixth in population. It is slightly smaller than the USA, and it borders every South American country except Chili and Ecuador. Despite occasional setbacks, Brazil has transformed itself from a third world nation into an industrialized country with huge human and material resources. Economically, Brazil is second only to the United States in the Western Hemisphere, and is first in South America and the Southern Hemisphere. It is truly an economic giant garnering the world's eighth highest GDP.

Brazil has been a tourist attraction for many decades due to its beautiful natural resources, friendly people, and leisure/relaxed lifestyle. Despite heavy commercialism and urbanization, Brazil is still the land of samba, *Carneval,* and great beaches. This unique combination of natural beauty and resources has attracted many international businesses and ventures into Brazil in past decades.

Country Background

History

The history of Brazil differs from the rest of South America in that it was a colony of Portugal not Spain. The Portuguese discovered Brazil in 1500 and it quickly became their largest and most important colony. In 1808, the Portuguese Royal family fled from Lisbon to Brazil to escape Napoleon's armies. They ruled Brazil from 1808 until their return to Portugal in 1821. Dom Pedro I declared Brazilian independence in 1822 with very little resistance from the Portuguese. In 1888, the monarchy was overthrown and a federal republic was formed. During a four-decade span, the government was a constitutional democracy dominated by coffee growers and similar interests. Military and reform governments alternated control until military domination ended in 1989 with a popular presidential election.

Portugal's influence on Brazil during its 500-year history is evident through the language, customs, and political system. Portugal protected Brazil, its most important colony, from Dutch, Spanish, and French incursions for many centuries. Brazil is a Portuguese-speaking "island" in a sea of Spanish influence in South America.

Government

Brazil is a multiparty federal republic, which is similar in structure to the United States. The president, who is elected through universal suffrage, is both the chief of state and head of government. Brazil has had two free presidential elections in a row, which is a departure from the military rules and coups of the Sixties and Seventies. The legislative branch consists of a federal senate and a chamber of deputies, all of whom are elected by their constituents. The Brazilian judicial system is very similar to the Spanish and Portuguese legal systems. The highest federal courts are the 11-member Supreme Federal Court of Justice, and the 13-member Federal Court of Appeals.

Demographics

Brazil's population continues to expand and now amounts to over 175 million people. Almost 90% of the population live in 10% of the land, especially in metropolitan centers along the country's eastern coastline. Brazil has 11 cities with a population of one million or more inhabitants, including the capital, Brasilia. Sao Paulo is the country's most populous city with more than 16 million inhabitants, followed by Rio de Janeiro with 10 million. The Brazilian people are a mix of Europeans (55%), mulatto, which is a mixture of Caucasian and African (38%), Black (6%) and other minorities, such as Japanese and Amerindian. Although slaves were brought into Brazil during the height of the slave trade, they were generally treated better than North American slaves. Brazilian culture has traditionally been open-minded regarding racial integration. Great numbers of Brazilians are of mixed descent.

The Brazilian literacy rate is 83%, and education is supposedly compulsory until children reach the age of 15. However, only 17.4% of those ten years or older have ever attended a high school. The majority of the population does not regard education as seriously as people in the United States or Europe, although economic factors are usually the main reason for dropping out. It is hard to think of schooling when the family does not have enough to eat. There is even less emphasis on higher education, and only a small portion of the population, usually of wealthy background, obtains a university education. The per capita income is approximately $7,000. A large segment of the

Brazilian population is under 20 (approximately 40%). The Brazilian labor force has approximately 60 million workers.

Economy

Brazil is usually ranked in 8th or 9th place among the world's economy. Brazil is Latin America's biggest economy, and is host to many American-owned factories whose profits are essential to corporate America's comfortable bottom line. Brazil attained its economic growth despite bursts of runaway inflation (1000% in 1994), private and public corruption, and a lack of a unified economic policy. In its efforts to reduce inflation and stabilize its economy, the Brazilian government launched an ambitious reform program, known as the *plano real* in July of 1994. The plan called for a new currency and sweeping reforms that opened the market and deregulated industry. The plan apparently had a positive impact on the economy, and inflation dropped from 50% to 3% per month by late 1994. Recent turmoil in the global economic system has affected the Brazilian economy; but recent years have shown gradual improvement.

Brazil's vast natural resources remain as its major long-term economic strength. Mineral resources include bauxite, gold, iron, manganese, platinum, and timber. Brazil's giant agriculture provides the country with all its foods except wheat. It is the world's leading producer and exporter of coffee and orange juice, and second largest exporter of soybeans. Other agricultural products include rice, corn, cocoa, beef, and sugarcane.

Due to the disruption of imports in World War II, Brazilian industry grew considerably to meet local demand. This eventually led to a large industrial output, especially in the Sao Paulo area. Brazilian industry today produces anything from aircraft to footwear for local and export markets. Other industrial products include chemicals, motor vehicles, lumber, mining products, steel, and machinery.

Brazilian exports are about $55 billion per year. Major partners included Europe, Latin America, the USA, and Japan. Imports are usually around $60 billion per year. These included oil, capital goods, foodstuffs, and chemical products. Major partners included the USA, Europe, the Middle East, Argentina, and Japan.

The Brazilian Culture

Language

The official language is Portuguese. Brazilians do not appreciate people who assume that Brazil's language is Spanish, like the rest of South America. This may suggest that visitors do not know the culture, or that they do not appreciate the subtle differences between Spanish and Portuguese. Other languages spoken in Brazil include Italian and Native American languages. Brazilians, especially business people, are usually adept in more than one language, and many speak Spanish, French, and English fluently.

Religion

Between 70 to 80% of Brazilians are Roman Catholics, making Brazil the world's largest Catholic country. Other religions include spiritism, Protestantism, Judaism and Buddhism. Although religion does not play an important role in business and national affairs, it influences social behavior in Brazil. Religious Brazilians tend to be more personally conservative and family-oriented than those with less religious inclinations.

Value system

Family loyalty is probably the most important value in Brazilian society. Brazilians trust and help their family members tremendously as evident by widespread nepotism in the country. In fact, the family is more important in Brazil than in any other South American country. Brazilian families are extended, and they include relatives from both sides of a nuclear family, sometimes numbering hundreds of individuals.

Brazilians are passionate, but not hot tempered, and they have affectionate relationships. Another important value that Brazilian men share with Latin Americans is *machismo*. Since this includes a feeling of superiority and masculinity, Brazilian men frequently act "macho." They will open doors for women and always pay for meals with the opposite sex. Brazilian men also stare at women and may exhibit a general attitude of strength and dignity. Divorce in Catholic Brazil is both difficult and uncommon. Women emphasize their feminine attributes, and they have a very small share of business management in Brazil.

Hospitality is another common Brazilian value, and Brazilians entertain their visitors lavishly and openly. They also appreciate favors and reciprocate generously. It is rare for someone to say "no" when asked to do a favor, and most Brazilians will probably say "yes" even if they cannot follow through. Building relationships through hospitality and entertainment is a very important Brazilian practice. Finally, Brazilians are passionate about sports, and soccer in particular. Brazil has won four soccer World Cups, which is more than any other country in the world. Brazilians naturally consider their unique style and players as the best in the world, and they have strong rivalries with neighboring countries, especially Argentina. The majority of the male population enjoys playing and analyzing soccer, and Brazilians appreciate foreigners who share these qualities.

Class structure / Stratification

Although there is little outward racial bias in Brazil, the concept of class and status is very strong. Since class is based on economic and family status, the higher classes get most of the educational opportunities, and therefore, the best jobs in the country. Nepotism and the importance of family connections further enhance this.

Although the races seem to get along and intermingle freely in Brazil, the reality is that whites still control most of the wealth and power in the country. Only a small percentage of mulattos and blacks have transcended the vast economic and social barriers that exist in Brazilian society. Natives of the Amazon forest region face prejudice and economic barriers in their attempts to hold on to their land, resources, and way of life. Other old-fashioned ideas still exist today, such as 1) the upper class's refusal to do manual labor, 2) the use of servants for everyday needs, and 3) a heavy emphasis on business ownership and/or investments for income (vs. working for someone outside the family). One only needs to visit different parts of Rio and other Brazilian cities to see the vast differences that exist between the rich and the poor. Considering Brazil's tumultuous economy and family system, it is highly unlikely that this gap will narrow in the near future.

Safety

There is a fair amount of small crime in urban areas, especially in poor sections of Brazilian cities. This includes petty theft, burglaries, and fraud. The country has also had a history of death squads and other assassination groups that largely target poor city dwellers, street children, and political opponents. Visitors today are immune from most serious crimes, but should be wary of pickpockets and thieves in some areas. However, the hospitality of the Brazilian people toward visitors, particularly toward business people, is very evident.

Business Protocol

Greetings and etiquette

Brazilians use **warm and sometimes effusive greetings.** It is customary to shake hands with everyone at a meeting, starting with the ranking individual. As relationships progress, it is common to embrace, and women frequently kiss on the cheek. Although Brazilian etiquette is warm and friendly, it is better to err on the side of formality when in doubt, especially in the early stages of a relationship. Another important business practice in Brazil is exchanging business cards, printed in Portuguese and English, at the first meeting.

If a Brazilian associate business card or introduction has a title, such as *Doctor* or *Professor*, he should be addressed as such. Otherwise, visitors may address Brazilian associates using the term *Senhor*, or *Senhora*. Being an affable people, Brazilians will often drop titles from names, but it is best to wait for them to do so first.

Time

Brazilians are **very polychronic and relaxed about punctuality**. This is indicative of a culture that values human relationships more than hours and minutes. USA or European business people who are accustomed to punctuality should expect tardiness from their Brazilian counterparts. Although visitors should try to be punctual, they should plan on finishing some work or reading while waiting for meeting to begin. Business people should make appointments two weeks in advance, and should never drop by without an appointment or a phone call.

Business hours in Brazil are 8:30 AM to 5:30 PM, but top executives may start and finish the business day later. Business lunches may run longer than two hours, so plan accordingly. Although *Carneval* is one of the best times to visit Brazil and Rio, it is probably the worst time to do business. *Carneval* always proceeds Ash Wednesday, so visitors should avoid trying to conduct any business during that time.

Gifts

Gifts are not required at a first meeting, but they may be given afterwards, especially at social functions. These gifts can be neatly wrapped expensive pens, calculators, electronic calendars, popular foreign CDs or CD-ROMs. When visiting a Brazilian home, it is appropriate to bring chocolate, champagne, toys, or souvenirs for the children. Popular items include Disney or soccer apparel and equipment. When exchanging gifts, it is best to wait for the host to open his first, or to ask if it is appropriate to open them.

Business entertainment

Being friendly and gregarious people, Brazilians value business entertainment, and invite their counterparts to many dinners and social activities. **Business is seldom discussed at these dinners or activities**. Instead, the two parties usually converse about soccer, travel, and culture. It is best not to bring up controversial subjects during these dinners, such as the rain forest or relations with Argentina. Visiting business people should reciprocate by inviting their Brazilian associates to expensive restaurants, preferably at nice hotels. These dinners and activities are essential tools for building firm relationships with Brazilians.

Dress

Three-piece suits sometimes symbolize an executive position, while two-piece suits for men usually denote office workers in Brazil. Because the country is mostly tropical, light clothing made of natural fibers will be cooler and more comfortable. Since it lies in the southern hemisphere, Brazil's seasons are opposite those in the northern hemisphere. January is a summer month, and June is a winter one, so pack the right clothes for the season. Businesswomen in particular should dress professionally and conservatively to keep

the respect of their Brazilian counterparts. They should also avoid wearing green and yellow combinations that resemble the colors of the Brazilian flag.

Communication Style

Business language

Brazilians use a **very high context language,** often considered one of the highest in the world. Brazilians tend to say what others want to hear more than what they really mean. Therefore, it is essential for a negotiator not to take everything literally, and to try and clarify the context through patient and polite questioning. Brazilian conversation also tends to be emotional and sometimes loud. It is important for negotiators to recognize that emotionalism means sincerity, not anger. The main purpose of the Brazilian high context communication is their willingness to please, and not to disturb the harmony or "face" of the negotiations. Foreigners who must ask questions directly should consider prefacing their requests with an apology for being direct so as not to disturb the harmony of the group.

Non-verbal communication

Brazilians use **very expressive non-verbal communication**. It is common for Brazilian negotiators to touch frequently and to put their arms around their counterparts' shoulders. They also pat others on the arms, the back, or the stomach. Brazilians may look directly into others' eyes, almost to the point of staring. This, however, is considered a sign of sincerity. Generally, Brazilians have a much smaller space orientation than North Americans or Europeans. It is not unusual for them to get very close to someone when talking or listening.

It is very important not to use some North American or European gestures in Brazil. For example, the USA okay sign is an obscene gesture in Brazil, and Brazilians usually use the thumbs up sign to signal okay. Beckoning someone involves turning the palm downwards and waving toward the body.

The Brazilian Concept of Negotiations

Selecting personnel

Brazilian negotiators are usually educated and refined members of society. **Other than their inherited status, Brazilian negotiators also possess strong oratory and bargaining skills,** as well as friendly and affable characteristics that help them influence others. A new generation of Brazilian negotiators is being chosen because of their accomplishments and knowledge. It is not uncommon to see a negotiating team composed of a mix of people with status and others with knowledge. Women in Brazil do not have the same status as in the USA, and it is rare to have them in powerful negotiating positions. Since most companies in Brazil today are privately owned, it is more likely to have senior members of the family heading the negotiating team. Since whites own most businesses in the country, most Brazilian negotiators are Caucasian. Due to the sometimes complex Brazilian business structure, especially within government agencies, it is very wise to have a Brazilian contact or "expediter" to facilitate all meetings and transactions in the country. Additionally, although a large number of Brazilian business people speak English or another foreign language, it is a good idea to bring along a Portuguese-speaking negotiator or interpreter.

Negotiating style

Brazilians enjoy the art and process of bargaining more than North Americans or Japanese. To a Brazilian, getting to a solution is almost as important as the solution itself, and unlike some Europeans and North Americans, they do not appreciate direct and "bottom line" talk. Instead, they use **non-directive discussion, bargaining, and relationship building** in the negotiating process. Trying to rush the negotiations in Brazil is not a good idea, and may even be detrimental to the relationship. It is best to relax and try to deal with the affable Brazilians at their own pace. Coffee is served often, and sometimes one should take the time to drink and chat while conducting business. Brazilian negotiations can also be lively and even heated. Following their communication traditions, they may suggest solutions, rather than imposing their ideas.

Issues discussed

Getting to know their foreign associates is the Brazilians' first order of business. Therefore, the primary issues discussed are **relationship-based**, and rarely substantive. Brazilians may not feel comfortable in doing business with people they do not know or understand. As the negotiations progress, the ranking Brazilian negotiators will discuss the nature of the proposed business, but they may leave the details for subordinates to iron out after an agreement has been reached.

Establishing trust

Brazilians gain trust **based on past experience**. The various entertainment activities they share with foreign visitors help "break the ice" and enhance personal relationships. Casual conversations, nice dinners, family outings, and sporting events all add to the trust chest in Brazil. Brazilians will remember someone's past behavior, and may term it as "generous," "cheap," or "friendly." Once they establish a trusting relationship, Brazilians can be very supportive and easy to deal with. They will also continue their hospitable and warm behavior, and will do what they can to maintain the relationship.

Persuasion

Brazilians use **personal dogma and appeals as a means of persuasion**. Since human relationships are very important to Brazilians, they also use friendship as a persuasion tool. Using one's network of contacts in Brazil is very effective in certain situations. Emotionalism is much more profound than it is in Europe or the United States. Brazilians may mention emotional issues, such as past relationships and favors that the two parties have shared in the past. They will also refer to the notion that it is very important for industrialized nations to help the Brazilian economy, especially in lieu of some of these nations' claims of concern for deforestation and poverty among large sections of Brazilian society. One may even hear arguments such as: "If these nations are so concerned with Brazil and Brazilians, why don't they grant us favorable business deals or terms?" This Brazilian "logic" comes across as friendly and persuasive, despite its departure from "Western" logic and facts.

The specific persuasion tactics that are likely to be effective in Brazil are:

1) **Get it in writing**. Write everything down throughout the negotiations.
2) The use of metaphors, emotional tactics, fear tactics, distraction tactics and diffusion questions can be very useful in Brazil.
3) **Take your time**. Brazilians may stall and they are definitely not in a hurry.
4) Brazilians love to **haggle** and are quite lively while doing so. Expect both **distributive and contingency bargaining** tactics. The Brazilians almost always **"high-ball" or "low-ball"** a deal.
5) Certain requests that we might consider to be **corruption** are normal business practices in Brazil. Decide how you plan to initiate or respond to such requests.
6) Receiving the **technical specifications up-front** or in the beginning of the negotiation is a good idea in Brazil.
7) Brazilians tend to brag a little and use puffery. So, definitely build up your firm, your products/services, and yourself with slight **exaggerations, enthusiasm, and non-verbal demonstratives**. Brazilians will expect everything you present to be slightly exaggerated. If you use a conservative approach, the Brazilians may discount your offer (because they assume exaggeration), and your firm will quickly be eliminated from consideration.
8) **Speak with conviction and confidence.** Start out with a positive "Yes, our firm can meet your requirements." Brazilians tend to be great orators/story tellers and will expect the same from you and your firm.
9) Brazil is a very visual culture. Thus, **visual proof sources that are animated and nicely displayed** should prove to be effective props.
10) Brazil is hierarchical and individualistic at work and sport settings but collectivist in the home. General associational appeals are likely to be ineffective in business. However, referring to the approval of respected **higher authorities** in regards to your company, product, etc. may prove to be an effective method of persuasion.
11) Because Brazilians are an emotional as well as a socially-engaging group, the **presentation of possible future cooperative endeavors** and/or multi-firm interactive simulations should be very persuasive.
12) Use a **"big-picture"** strategy. Nothing is decided until everything is decided.

Tactics to avoid include:

1) **Avoid direct conflict**. It is acceptable to say what is on your mind. So, some indirect conflict and/or a little banter are okay. However, direct and serious conflict that causes someone to "lose face" will result in an emotional reprisal. Thus, avoid blunt and pointed statements.
2) Do not use fear tactics, ultimatums, threats, yelling, etc.
3) **Avoid Two-Sided Appeals**. Brazilians expect exaggeration, not factual analysis. A two-sided appeal, which provides both pros and cons of an argument/product, is likely to cause doubt and hesitation.
4) **Do not engage in extensive information sharing**. If you disclose too much, you will be viewed as foolish.

Resolving disputes

Problems may be resolved by **reintroducing friendship and trust into the relationship**. Brazilian negotiators also use their "hunch" and personal skills to resolve problems or misunderstandings. This may entail asking common friends and business partners to add their weight to the resolution process. Without using any empirical data or "Western" logic, Brazilians will remind their counterparts of the importance of resolving problems in order to continue successful negotiations.

Group and individual dynamics

Although they are a gregarious people who enjoy and cherish group situations, Brazilians **tend to be very individualistic**, and they may try to outdo each other during the negotiations. This Brazilian mentality is even manifested in soccer, where Brazilian players are known for their flair, and their ability to dribble skillfully through defenders. This individualism, however, is geared toward scoring goals and gaining glory, much as individual negotiators try to do great things on their own. Although not disruptive, Brazilian individualism contrasts greatly from East Asian teamwork. Despite this apparent lack of unity, Brazilians generally remain loyal to their team and company, especially when dealing with traditional adversaries from South or North America. In addition, group influences become more pronounced in family and home settings, which is similar to most of the Latin world.

Risk

Like their other South American neighbors, **Brazilians are risk-averse**. This is due to their desire to protect their families and businesses, their laid-back business attitude, and their unwillingness to put their careers on the line by taking additional responsibilities. Although they believe in financial gain, Brazilians would rather do this at a comfortable pace that guarantees reasonable returns and security. Therefore, presenting get-rich-quick ventures that carry risk does not appeal to Brazilians in general. They will more likely be interested in long-term relationships that guarantee reasonable returns. This may seem odd considering Brazil's roller-coaster economy during the 20th century.

Decision making

Reflecting their hierarchical society, Brazilians tend to make **top-down decisions.** This is especially true because of the large number of family-owned businesses in Brazil, where the male patriarch usually makes all the important decisions. These, however, may take place after consulting with middle managers and other influential members of the family or business. Once they arrive at decisions, Brazilian executives expect their subordinates to follow them strictly, but due to the Brazilian outlook on time, this may take a while to implement. Therefore, effective negotiators should endeavor to know the Brazilian decision-makers, and subsequently deliver their message.

Type of agreement

Brazilians consider a handshake and a word of honor as sufficient gestures to start a business relationship. They will, however, require **a written document that defines the implicit or explicit terms of the agreement**. Brazilian lawyers may get involved in such a document, and it is a good idea to hire a Brazilian law expert to review and/or help write the document.

Brazil's legal system had its roots in Portuguese Law. When it attained independence as a nation, it began to develop its own legal apparatus. Brazilians may say that a handshake and one's word of honor are sufficient gestures to begin a business venture, but their laws say something quite different. Under Brazilian Law a contract can be claimed on the basis of notes, correspondence, entries in books, and even in some cases based on the testimony of witnesses. Furthermore, there is no provision for the discharge of contractual obligations on the grounds of unforeseeable events. The prudent businessperson will seek legal counsel prior to the start of contractual negotiations in Brazil.

Chapter 6

Canada

- *Country Background*
- *The Canadian Culture*
- *Business Protocol*
- *Communication Style*
- *The Canadian Concept of Negotiations*

Canada is a young multicultural, multilingual nation, with a quality of life that is admired throughout the world. In size, Canada is the second-largest nation in the world, though much of its territory is too far north for current economic development. Strengthened by this vast land with rich natural resources and a diverse educated, energetic people, Canada showcases advanced technical and industrial development with the eighth or ninth-largest GDP in the global system.

Country Background

History

Immigration and resettlement is the dominant theme of Canadian history. Early Paleo-Indian migrations into Canada probably began over 30,000 years ago. Around 1000 AD, the Vikings sailed to Newfoundland, but their settlement was soon abandoned. The French established the first permanent European settlements in the early 1600s and developed a thriving fur trade with the aboriginals.

Early British colonies developed as the result of early interest in fishing and furs. John Cabot was sent to Canada in 1497 to claim land for England and to find a Northwest Passage to Asia, but Bristol merchants interested in establishing fisheries financed his voyage. As their settlements grew, trade in beaver furs became the most important British commercial activity.

Competition over control of the fur trade, the main basis of the economy for two hundred years, led to increased hostilities between France and England. In 1760 British colonial interests prevailed. However, the French inhabitants resisted assimilation and retained their language, culture and religion. In 1774 Britain passed the Quebec Act, granting official recognition to French Civil Law along with a guarantee of religious and linguistic freedom.

The formation of modern Canada, with ten provinces and three territories, took place in stages. Upper Canada (Ontario) and Lower Canada (Quebec) joined in 1838, forming the United Province of Canada, though this union went through various levels of conflict. In 1867, the Dominion of Canada was created under the terms of the British North American Act. This joined Canada East, Canada West, Nova Scotia and New Brunswick. From 1870 to 1949, the other provinces joined the

dominion. Not until 1999 did the Northwest Territories divide and the new territory of Nunavet become established. 80% of Nunavet's population is Inuit, making this the first territory to be governed by First Nations (aboriginal) people.

Government

Canada's government is a federation with parliamentary democracy. Considerable tension exists between the federal and provincial governments over the proper allocation of power. The titular head of state is the British monarch, represented by the governor general. The prime minister heads the government, leads the majority party in the House of Commons, and has extensive powers, but is answerable to Parliament.

The bicameral Parliament consists of the Senate and the House of Commons. The Senate is patterned after the British House of Lords. The usual number of 104 members are appointed from Canada's four main regions of Ontario, Quebec, the West and the Atlantic Provinces, with a few additional members from Newfoundland and the Territories. Senate appointees, largely individuals who have served their country well in one fashion or another, can serve until they are 75 years old. The 301 members of the House of Commons are elected by direct popular vote. The House is the major legislative body, for the Senate functions more as an influential deliberative and consulting group. The constitution requires elections at least every five years, with universal suffrage at 18 years of age. Almost three/fourths of all eligible voters participate in national elections.

Canada's legal system is primarily based on English common law, except for Quebec where French civil law prevails. The Supreme Court of Canada is the highest judicial body, followed by the Federal Court of Canada and the Provincial Courts

Geographics

Slightly larger than the United States, Canada is the second largest country in the world, with an area of 9,976,140 square kilometers. Extending from the Atlantic to the Pacific Ocean, Canada shares a border only with the United States to the south and west (Alaska). More than a million rivers, streams and lakes, constituting one quarter of the world's fresh water, are spread throughout the country.

In such a vast land, climatic conditions are variable. The four seasons vary according to latitude, ranging from the permanently frozen ice caps north of the 70th parallel to the temperate climate of southern Ontario and British Columbia. In the north, long summer days contrast with the almost constant hours of darkness in winter.

The terrain varies from the western mountains and temperate rain forest to the northern tundra. Prairie grasslands stretch from Manitoba through Saskatchewan into Alberta. Vast forests and woodland cover 54% of the land. Only 5% of Canada is well suited to agriculture, for much of the terrain is rocky, marshy, or mountainous, as well as too far north.

Demographics

Canada is a sparsely populated country with only 31 million people. Pre-1970 immigrants were primarily European; since 1970, most have come from Asia. Almost 90% of the population is concentrated along a narrow southern corridor bordering the United States. Approximately 62% of the people live in Quebec and Ontario. Nearly 17% of the population resides in the prairie provinces of Alberta, Manitoba and Saskatchewan. Another 12% are found in British Columbia, 9% in the Atlantic provinces and 3% in the Yukon and Northwest Territories. About 78% of the population reside in cities. The largest cities are sophisticated and multicultural Toronto in Ontario, French-influenced Montreal in Quebec, and western Vancouver in British Colombia. The capital is at Ottawa in Ontario.

Canadian life expectancy is 76 years for men and 83 years for women. The number of Canadians over 65 has greatly increased in the last 10 years. Ethnic origins are 28% British, 26% mixed backgrounds, 23% French, 15% other European, 5% Asian, and 2% Amerindian. Not all indigenous people are counted in the official census and some estimates put the numbers of Inuit, Aleut, and other First Nations people at 3 or 4%.

The literacy rate for the entire country is 97%. Nearly 16 million people are in the work force.

Economy

Before the 20th century, Canada was primarily an agricultural economy. Today Canada ranks eighth or ninth among industrialized market economies. Canada is self-sufficient in fossil fuels and the world's leading producer of hydroelectricity. In the Americas, only the United States surpasses Canada's per capita income.

Canada consistently has a trade surplus. The main exports are motor vehicles and parts, wood pulp and timber, petroleum and natural gas, aluminum and telecommunications equipment. The top agricultural exports are unprocessed grains, oilseeds, meat products and live animals. Over three-fourths of Canadian imports are with the United States, but other trading partners include Japan, the UK, Germany and South Korea.

Although the United States buys four-fifths of Canada's exports, much of this is a transfer between firms. Subsidiaries of Ford, General Motors, and Chrysler are Canada's largest manufacturers. Japanese auto plants also help to make transportation equipment Canada's leading manufacturing industry. Foreign investment reached a peak in 1970 when it composed 47% of all investments in Canada. Some Canadians have expressed concern over such large investment from abroad. In 1974, the government established the Foreign Investment Review Agency to examine foreign investment plans and ensure benefits to Canada.

The Canadian Culture

Language

Canada has two official languages with 59% using English and 23% using French. Another 18% speak other languages, such as Italian, German, Chinese, and Spanish. Many indigenous languages are still used, such as the Inuit and Aleut languages, Algonkian and Iroquois in the eastern sub-arctic, and Athabaskan in the west.

Although the number of Canadians speaking primarily French has increased, their proportion of the total population has declined from 29% in 1941 to 24% in 1991. The proportional change is because immigrants who settled in English-speaking areas have chosen English as their working language.

In linguistic and social terms, Canada is two nations. In Quebec, where French is the mother tongue for 80% of the population, the use of French is being promoted while English is being weakened under the impact of Quebec nationalism. Federally-funded efforts to promote bilingualism outside of Quebec have aroused hostility from English-speaking Canadians.

Religion

According to the 1991 census, four-fifths of the population categorize themselves as Christians, with 41% Protestant and 46% Catholic, half of whom live in Quebec. Of the Protestant denominations, the United Church of Canada is largest (12%), followed by the Anglican Church (8%). Other religions are Judaism, Islam, Buddhism, and small concentrations of Mormons in Alberta, Hindus in Toronto, Sikhs in Vancouver, and Hutterites, Mennonites and Ukrainian Orthodox in the prairie provinces.

Canadian society is highly secularized, with 13% claiming no religious affiliation. International business transactions are seldom influenced by religious factors.

Value System

Canadians share many cultural characteristics with the USA such as language, television, movies, books, magazines and music. But Canada has historically resisted absorption by the US, and has nurtured and developed its own writers, architects, artists, and filmmakers. To better promote Canadian arts, the government has imposed quotas on foreign content in the media. It has retained a close affiliation with Britain, first as a loyal colony and later as a member of the Commonwealth.

This contrasting heritage has made Canadian social values more conservative than those of the USA, with less concern for individualism and greater allegiance to authority. There is less violence and lawlessness even in the largest cities. Greater family stability is reflected in considerably lower divorce rates than in the USA.

Class structure / Stratification

The English-French division once reflected economic stratification. Canadians of French origin have earned less than the national average, while those of British ancestry have traditionally earned more. This disparity was even greater in Quebec where French-Canadians typically had lower-paying occupations and were underrepresented in the professional, technical and managerial positions. Modernization has tended to ameliorate some of these inequalities, but they fueled French-Canadian nationalism and a demand by some French-Canadians for an independent nation. However, most of the population acknowledges the economic advantages of continued linkage with the larger nation.

Although ownership of property and assets determine class, stratification is to some extent determined by occupation. Business owners, corporate executives, physicians and lawyers earn more and live in affluent neighborhoods. Teachers, civil servants, clerks and blue-collar workers comprise the middle-income groups. Few citizens are below the poverty index due to Canada's liberal social welfare programs. However, single-parent families headed by women, as well as many elderly women, are quite poor, while First Nations people have incomes that are half the national average. The bottom strata consists of marginal individuals involved with drugs, alcoholism, prostitution or crime.

Though class differences exist, there is no formal class structure in Canada. Within its cultural milieu individuals may transcend the limitations of their birth. Furthermore, the government has taken strides in the past two decades to eliminate social and economic inequalities based upon language or ethnicity. Health care is available to all citizens and immigrants who have permanent residence.

Safety

Crime rates in Canada are among the lowest in the world. If one takes simple precautions, keeps to well-lit streets, and remembers not to display valuables, one is unlikely to experience a problem.

Public drinking water is safe and food is usually prepared under hygienic conditions. Good medical care is readily available and of excellent quality in the cities. One should be aware that Canadian wilderness excursions can be dangerous. Some regions may require the use of insect netting and a variety of pesticides. Winter conditions can be unbelievable harsh. Visitors from tropical climates may require some physical preconditioning.

Business Protocol

Greetings and etiquette

Canadian business greetings begin with a smile and a firm handshake. Men usually wait for women to offer their hand. Direct eye contact is expected and is viewed as a sign of integrity.

The standard greeting "How are you?" is not an inquiry about one's health. The expected response is "Fine, thank you," and nothing more. In Quebec, French greetings are normally exchanged.

French-Canadians are very polite and concerned about propriety, ceremony and hierarchy. Their introductions will include the use of full names and titles. English-Canadians are less concerned with protocol and lengthy preliminaries.

Business cards are exchanged, with English the official business language. Impressions made at the initial meeting are crucial for success.

Time

Canada is a monochronic culture where punctuality is imperative. Tardiness is viewed in very negative terms. It is advisable to arrive a little early for all appointments. Early arrival will be noted and viewed in a favorable light. Any lengthy delays require a telephoned explanation. The working day generally includes scheduled meal and rest breaks. Business hours are usually from 9 AM to 5 PM, Monday through Friday. Industry specific information can be obtained through the local chamber of commerce or through trade associations.

Gifts

Gift giving in Canada is a complicated issue. It is better not to give a gift than to give an inappropriate gift that may be misinterpreted as an attempt to gain influence. Canadian laws prohibit government employees from receiving gifts associated with their employment. Businesses also keep a watchful eye, so do not give a gift that cannot be reciprocated.

It is advisable to let Canadians show you what gifts are acceptable. They will entertain you by offering a drink or invitation to dinner and a sporting event. When reciprocating, take care to go only slightly higher. Gift giving among business associates is traditional at Christmas, but tasteless extravagance is not.

Business entertainment

Canadians are friendly people eager to establish positive working relationships. Entertaining is an acceptable format for relationship building.

Business meetings are often conducted over lunch; whoever suggests lunch is expected to pay. Less common is the business dinner. Canadians tend to reserve their evenings for community and family activities. On rare occasions a business acquaintance may be invited to a Canadian home. Punctuality is expected and a modest gift of flowers or quality wine is appreciated.

Although it is advisable to wait for Canadians to bring up business issues at social functions, there is no set rule. Canada is a large complex heterogeneous country with varying regional customs. What may be acceptable in one area could be frowned on elsewhere. However, Canadians loathe any form of subterfuge or manipulation. Reciprocal forms of entertainment are recommended.

Dress

Canadian dress is stylishly conservative. Most men wear suits or sport jackets accented with a fashionable tie. Shoes are unadorned, dark and made of leather. Male business attire in Toronto and Montreal tends to reflect wealth and power while casual business attire is more common farther west. Women may wear suits or coordinated ensembles of blouses, skirts, jackets and pants but extremes in fashion are frowned upon. Hem lengths vary from just above the knee to slightly above the ankle. Makeup and hair styles tend toward understatement.

In choosing Canadian business attire, one must keep season and locale in mind; warm rain-resistant attire may be required.

Communication Style

Business language

Canadians of British descent are low-context communicators. The literal meaning of spoken words convey the actual message. In contrast, French-speaking Canadians are high-context communicators, with the spoken word only part of the total message.

Proper language usage is emphasized in the Canadian culture, but there are subtle communicative nuances. It is advisable to have someone fluent in French on the negotiating team. There are numerous regional and ethnic variations, for Canada's development as a country was based on immigration and resettlement. Its laws protect and encourage ethnicity and subcultural uniqueness. Local Canadian newspapers and magazines can offer helpful insights into regional characteristics. A growing amount of information about Canada is also available on the Internet.

Non-verbal communication

In resettling, immigrants tended to gather in regional clusters, maintaining their original cultural characteristics. Through assimilation, influences of the dominant culture were added. This has resulted in regional and ethnic variations in body language, gestures and other non-verbal patterns. Such non-verbal communication differences can be very subtle. Canadians stand about two feet apart when conversing. French Canadians may touch when conversing and are generally more animated.

Gestures are used in varying degrees, at times freely and expansively or at other times in a restrained manner. Nodding the head horizontally means "no", while shaking it vertically means "yes". Surprise is shown through raised eyebrows. Shoulder shrugging implies uncertainty. The palm held in front with the fingers together pointing up means stop. British Canadians tend to use fewer, less exaggerated gestures.

The Canadian Concept of Negotiations

Selecting Personnel

In Canada, ambition and academic accomplishments are valued attributes. Linguistic capabilities, honesty, tenacity, trustworthiness and a global vision are additional traits avidly sought. Previously successful negotiating experience is of course also desirable, as is technical expertise. Age, social class, race, gender and ethnicity are less crucial. Larger Canadian corporations will have personnel with most of these desired qualities. Smaller firms may have personnel with narrower, more provincial views.

Your team should mirror the Canadian team; negotiating experience and technical expertise are of special value.

Negotiating style

The Canadian negotiating style is generally open and direct. However, there are two official languages and two distinct negotiating styles.

The British-Canadian culture predominates in Ontario, British Columbia, Alberta, Manitoba, Saskatchewan, Nova Scotia, New Brunswick, Newfoundland and Prince Edward Island. British-Canadians tend to focus more on the theoretical issues. They will prepare thoroughly and be quite direct in their style, but not argumentative. The negotiating process may take longer than in the USA because these Canadians desire much information. They have a **compromise** approach to bargaining. Though concerned with time, they do not want to be rushed.

French-Canadians predominate in Quebec where the official language is French. There is also a strong French minority in New Brunswick and Ontario. French-Canadians have a more individualistic style which is more goal oriented. They can be aggressive and **like to debate** in negotiations. When not negotiating, they can be quite affable and will tend to focus on relationship building.

Both Canadian cultures value frankness and are willing to question. Both endorse lineal problem solving and the clarification of alternatives. Once a negotiating decision has been reached, both will readily explore timely implementation.

Issues discussed

Canadians will quite naturally favor their own self interests. However, they do value compromise. They will explore all issues forthrightly and expect others to do the same.

Canada consists of ten provinces and three territories, and each geographical division has its own unique characteristics. Some Canadians tend to feel greater loyalty to their home province than to the country as a whole. This provincialism can impede business expansions into other areas of the country. In Quebec there are strong separatist sentiments as well, with a passionate loyalty to the French culture. Regional differences may require discussion and clarification lest they impede long- term business objectives.

Establishing trust

In the negotiating courtship, establishing trust is an absolutely necessary ingredient. There are an infinite number of variables in the trust building paradigm.

British-Canadian business personnel tend to favor a cooperative negotiating posture. Trust to them ultimately means a legally-binding contract. The maneuvers between the first negotiating session and the final agreement are viewed as good-faith goal-oriented interaction. Their level of trust will increase as they progress toward the goal, providing the information they receive is accurate.

French-Canadians establish trust primarily through relationship building and past performance, will perhaps more readily assume a good-faith posture, and will rely more on intuition.

Persuasion

Canadians are committed to the concept of fair play. They like win-win business outcomes. It is advisable to initially focus on the more readily- apparent benefits. Well-planned, thoroughly- documented presentations appeal to them. All quantifiable facts should be shared openly and presented forthrightly. Oral presentations should be brief, clear and objective, with precise attention to detail.

The specific persuasion tactics that are likely to be effective in Canada are:

1) **Get it in writing**. Write everything down throughout the negotiations. Your thoroughness and astuteness will impress Canadians. Copious notes will diminish disagreements and facilitate contract formulations.
2) **Build trust through information sharing**. The Canadians will expect a planned exchange of information. The more information you provide up-front the more the Canadians will trust you.
3) It is **okay to be blunt** and to the point in Canada.
4) **Use Two-Sided Appeals**. Canadians base their decisions on extensive research. They have probably already completed extensive research regarding the negotiations' issues. By stating both the positive and negative aspects of the transaction, the Canadians will recognize and value your honesty.
5) Your initial presentation/offer is critical to a successful negotiation in Canada. The presentation/offer should de detailed, carefully-documented, and well-planned. This will create a favorable first impression with the Canadians.
6) **Demonstrate your knowledge and expertise in a tactful manner**. Do not brag about knowing-it-all. However, the incorporation of appropriate accomplishments by your firm, your staff, yourself, etc. into the presentation is an effective strategy.
7) **Supported Facts**. One needs to present logical/factual information that is accompanied by supportive documentation.
8) **Involvement questions and problem questions** should be effective in Canada. Ask your counterpart how they would envision (involvement question) the outcome of the transaction or ask them questions that expose a current problem (problem questions) they are having that a transaction with you could alleviate or solve.

9) **Tactics that are effective in the USA will normally be useful in Canada.** However, the Canadians are very averse to high-pressure, misleading, and/or scare tactics.

The persuasion tactics to avoid in Canada include:

1) **Avoid the use of metaphors**, emotional tactics, threats, fear tactics, distraction tactics and diffusion questions.
2) **Don't high-ball or low-ball.** Canadians expect a little haggling. However, prices rarely change more than 20%.
3) **Avoid stalling.** Canadians strictly follow schedules and deadlines.
4) Avoid extensive "small-talk." The Canadians will want to get down to business fairly quickly.
5) **Avoid misleading information**. It is likely to be detected and will result in the termination of the transaction.

Resolving disputes

One of the keys to resolving disputes is to do everything correctly in the first place, which can be a formidable task given the complexity of international business negotiations. Every step, even the time of day when an agreement was reached, can be important and should be recorded. All telephone and fax correspondence should be confirmed, noted and double-checked. Remember, verbal agreements might be binding in a Quebec courtroom but not in another province. Familiarity with provincial peculiarities is imperative.

Keep all language as simple as possible and include provisions for contractual amendments, such as foreign currency exchange fluctuations and shipping delays. Shipping products over a vast country can pose numerous problems.

Canadian courts have considerable expertise. International disputes are not so different from provincial ones and they have a lengthy history of fair play and impartiality.

Group and individual dynamics

The vast expanse of the country, the self-governing autonomy of the provinces and the lack of regimentation in the schools encourage individualism. With a minimum of stratification, success can be achieved through individual ability and effort. Individualism is, however, modified by strong familial, regional, and national loyalties. They are often willing to set aside personal self-interest in favor of larger regional or Canadian concerns. French-Canadian individualism is even more pronounced, but they will unite to favor their French-Canadian region and identity.

Risk

On a worldwide risk propensity scale, Canadians are near the median. They approach negotiations methodically, so all objective data is of interest to them. They will endeavor to minimize risk through logical exploration. They are process oriented and prefer to explore all issues sequentially. These propensities tend to make them moderately risk averse.

Decision making

Canadians are highly individualistic. Their decision making is decentralized. They tend to be methodical, sequential, and monochronic. Because they make incremental decisions, this form of processing tends to be time consuming.

Top level involvement is called in when logjams are encountered or when unusual decisions are required. Their decision-making flows out of the collective matrix of a highly egalitarian culture committed to rationalism.

Type of agreement

Canada's position in the global business community is unique. It is an independent economic entity, yet it co-mingles many of its economic policies with its southern neighbors. Canada participates in the Canada USA Free Trade agreement (CFTA 1989) and the North American

Free Trade Agreement (NAFTA 1994) between Canada, the USA and Mexico. Both the CFTA and NAFTA agreements have enabled Canada to expand its capital and management expertise. The net effect has been to open Canada more fully to international market forces.

Canada's financial and legal infrastructure generally offers highly developed, diversified services. These institutions provide excellent comprehensive contractual advice. Canadian business agreements are highly detailed, written documents. In Quebec, it is advisable to have the contract reviewed by a French-Canadian attorney, for the legal system differs.

NOTES:

Chapter 7

China

- *Country Background*
- *The Chinese Culture*
- *Business Protocol*
- *Communication Style*
- *The Chinese Concept of Negotiations*

With close to 1.3 billion people, China is the world's most populous country. If water rights are not included, it is also second largest in landmass, with a slightly larger land area than that of the United States. With its vast population and recent openness to the world, China is one of the globe's fastest growing economies and a most desired market for many industrialized nations.

China has a long coastline bordering the East China Sea, the Yellow Sea and the South China Sea. Many countries share its land borders, including India, Laos, Pakistan, Afghanistan, Nepal, Mongolia, Kazakstan, Kyrgyzstan, Tajikistan, Bhutan, Burma, North Korea, Vietnam and Russia.

Hong Kong is located just off the coast of China at the mouth of the Pearl River. It is comprised of Hong Kong Island, which is the administrative center, the Kowloon Peninsula, and the more rural New Territories, which include 236 islands. It consists of approximately 1,100 square kilometers.

The British returned Hong Kong to China when its 99-year lease expired in 1997. Hong Kong has long had a prosperous, bustling free-market economy, quite different from the economic system of China, the world's largest and most significant communist nation. Much mutually-beneficial trade has built up between the two areas, and China has agreed to a fifty-year transition period before the economic and legal system of Hong Kong will be changed.

Country Background

History

China is proud of being one of the world's oldest civilization and dates back to the Five Dynasties that existed from 2800 to 2000 BC. More than a dozen dynasties then ruled feudal China from 2000 BC to 1911 AD, when the empire broke into sectors and the first republic was established. As with Japan, European colonial powers forced China to open its ports during the 1800s. The Chinese were especially bitter when the British forcibly brought in opium, a substance the Chinese government had banned. China also went through a very difficult period between 1911 and 1949, when it was plagued by civil war and a foreign invasion by Japan. After Japan's defeat in World War II, the Chinese civil war ended with the defeat of Chiang-Kai-shek's Nationalist army by the communist forces led by Mao Zedong. The defeated Nationalists fled the country in 1949, and established the Republic of China on the island of Formosa (now Taiwan).

The People's Republic of China, which remains in control on the Chinese mainland, continued the country's tendency toward isolationism, though the Soviet Union gave support until ideological disputes split their unity in the 1960s. China remained closed to foreigners for the most part, and the country was largely self-sufficient. Over the years the Chinese also endured a number of purges and backlashes, best manifested by the Cultural Revolution of the 1970s. This student-led and government-supported movement attacked old values, the teachings of Confucius, and the perceived elitism of intellectuals.

China's modern trend of openness to the West, and the West's increased acceptance of China, took root in the late 1970s. Despite occasional setbacks, trade and cultural exchanges have increased every year. There is hardly a country today that does not have plans to enlarge its Chinese market, buy Chinese goods, or build a factory in China.

Hong Kong was once a quiet fishing village and a pirate haven in the South China Sea. It became an intermediate port used by Great Britain for delivering goods to China. Because of the island's ideal location in the center of Asia, Hong Kong was soon recognized as a link between the Central Kingdom of China and the Western World. The Opium War of 1839-1842 ended with the Treaty of Nanking, wherein China ceded Hong Kong to Britain and opened five Chinese ports to British traders. The Kowloon Peninsula, Stonecutters Island and the New Territories were ceded later in 1898, all under a ninety-nine year lease.

In 1984, a joint declaration between Britain and China stipulated that Hong Kong would revert to China at the end of the ninety-nine year lease. As of July 1, 1997, Hong Kong has been a Special Administrative Region of the People's Republic of China, under a one-country, two-systems principle. Under this agreement, Hong Kong retains a high degree of autonomy.

Government

China is a communist nation with universal suffrage for people 18 and older. There are no parties other than the Chinese Communist Party (CCP), but the people elect a few independent candidates to the National People's Congress (NPC), the legislative branch in China. The NPC appoints a cabinet, or a state council, which is headed by a premier and a vice-premier. The chief of state is the president, who is also elected by the NPC.

China has a judicial branch headed by the Supreme People's Court. The history of China's legal system is complex and confusing. The first Chinese Code, encompassing both criminal and administrative law, was drafted in 624 AD and was known as the Tang Code. Chinese law was heavily influenced by Confucian ideals. After China's legal system began to disintegrate in the nineteenth century, European laws were placed within this ancient legal system but were not particularly compatible.

In the twentieth century an anti-legalism period left China's legal system so fragmented it was difficult to tell what laws were in force. Many new laws were drafted from 1949 to 1965, when industrial and commercial enterprises were brought under state ownership. In 1966, the Proletarian Cultural Revolution irreparably damaged legal reconstitution for a decade. In 1977, the government moved in a centrist direction, further confusing the legal picture.

The new socio-economic system that emerged in the 1980's indicated the need for new laws in the economic sphere, but China was now bereft of a continuing legal tradition. The current constitution of December 4, 1982 is the fourth of the Communist era. An organized approach toward rudimentary codification was begun in 1986.

Law continues to be formulated in five-year plans, but the new laws frequently make no reference to earlier legislation that is amended or replaced. In 1993, several amendments to the 1982 constitution proclaimed a socialist market economy. Foreign investors need to be aware that China's current legal system is more a matter of politics and influence than a reliable, predictable process.

Demographics

China alone has 1.3 billion people who live in 644 cities and other areas with varying climates and geographic features. (Hong Kong's population would add only 6.8 million more to this total.) Since China consists mainly of uninhabitable mountains and deserts, only 11% of the land is fertile for agriculture. The majority of the population lives in approximately 20% of the country, making self-sufficiency even more challenging. The government has instituted a one-child program among ethnically-Chinese married couples. (Under the program, most minorities may have more than one child. Two children are also more common in rural areas.) This program, which fines parents for having more than one child and rewards them economically and socially for having only one, has helped curb population growth in China to 15.1 births per 1000 population, which is well beneath the world average.

The majority of Chinese are Han, or ethnic Chinese, who constitute 92% of the population. There are a number of minorities in the country, including Zhuang, Uygur, Hui, Tibetan, Manchu, Mongol and Korean. Having a slow growth rate of less than 1%, China's population is relatively mature, with the majority of the population (68%) in the 15-64 years-old group. Literacy varies between high rates in the cities and low rates in rural areas. The country's literacy average is 82%, with males at 90% and females at 73%.

Economy

With its doors open to trade and foreign investment and with increased reliance on market forces (called a socialist market economy), estimates place China in terms of GDP PPP as the world's second-largest economy or in sixth place in terms of real GDP. The most impressive figure in China's economy, however, is the estimated annual double-digit growth rate, which reached 12% in 1994, and 10% in 1995 (compared to the world average of 3 to 4%), and 8% in 2000. China has the world's largest labor force by far, totaling more than 700 million people. Much of the labor force, however, is unskilled by Western or Japanese standards, but the new market economy is changing this condition. Special Economic Zones and coastal cities have been favored places for foreign investors.

Hong Kong's economy has been nurtured by a government policy of maximum support and minimal intervention. Low tax rates created a fertile environment for an average GDP growth of 5.8% during the period from 1986 to 1996. Although Hong Kong's population is 1% of China's, its GDP is equal to 16% of China's GDP and it should have a significant influence on mainland China's economic future.

Some of the problems facing modern China include: 1) air and water pollution; 2) collecting revenues due from provinces, businesses and individuals; 3) keeping inflation in check; 4) reducing extortion, corruption and new economic crimes; 5) ensuring the survival (or phasing out the obsolete and unprofitable) of large government-owned enterprises; and 6) controlling the widening gap between various sections of the population due to the new economy.

Despite these problems, China's economy continues to grow, and more countries want to do business with it every year. China consistently maintains an excellent trade surplus. Chinese exports include textiles, footwear, weapons, machinery, toys, and other consumer goods. Its primary export partners include Japan, the USA, Germany, South Korea, and a large segment of the Third World. Chinese imports include steel, plastics, vehicles, machinery, oil and aircraft. The primary import partners are Japan, the USA, Germany, Russia and South Korea.

China's industries are quite diverse and include steel, machine building, weapons, apparel, cement, chemicals, food processing, vehicles and consumer electronics. Its southeastern seaboard, especially opposite Hong Kong and Taiwan, has seen a tremendous surge in production over the past few years. Agriculture has also benefited from the new system of private responsibility, and has seen a countrywide resurgence. China's agriculture accounts for more than 20% of their GDP and 50% or their labor force, making it self-sufficient in food. Agricultural products include rice, potatoes, peanuts, tea, barley, pork and livestock. China also produces cotton and other fibers in domestic and export quantities.

The Chinese currency is the yuan. Hong Kong still maintains its own currency, Hong Kong dollar (HK$).

The Chinese Culture

Language

The official language is Mandarin Chinese, which is spoken by the majority of the population. There are many other Chinese languages, including Cantonese, Shanghaiese, Fukienese, Hokkien, Hakka and Chin Chow. There are also many minority non-Chinese languages, especially in the western part of the country. Although the Chinese languages have different word meanings with different pronunciation, they all use the same writing system. Thus, all literate Chinese can read the same ideograms, which mean exactly the same in the different languages. In other words, the Chinese can read each other's languages fluently, without necessarily being able to speak them. This remarkable system, which was standardized in the third century BC, has held the Chinese culture and people together despite various separations that occurred through the centuries.

Another unique attribute of Chinese is that it does not have verb tenses, genders or moods, which hopefully makes it easier to learn. Chinese words are made of one, two, three or more syllables, each of which requires an ideogram, or character, to write. The majority of modern Chinese words have two syllables, which require two ideograms to write. Like most people, the Chinese are proud of their language and appreciate a visitor who can speak it. A popular Chinese greeting is *ni hao ma?* (nee how mah), which means "How are you?" The response is *hen hao, xie xie* (hern how, shay shay), which translates to "Fine, thank you." In the Hong Kong area there are two official languages: Cantonese and English. Documents and road signs are usually translated into both languages.

Religion

Chinese religions include Daoism and Buddhism. Moslems make up 2-3% of the population, and Christians another 1%. Confucianism has influence, but is more a philosophy than a religion. Though atheism is encouraged, many practice their religion, especially in rural areas. Religion does not play a large role in modern Chinese society, especially in the business arena. The religion of foreign business people or visitors is inconsequential to the Chinese unless they are there to support certain unapproved religious groups. Hong Kong also has no official religion.

Value system

When visiting enormous China, one has to keep in mind that there are differences between some areas of the country. Generally, northerners are extroverts who show their emotions much more than southerners. They are said to be warm-hearted, sincere and have a recognizable sense of humor. The southerners come across as more sophisticated, implicit, smooth and quite capable in business. There are also plenty of exceptions to these generalizations.

Being such an old society, the Chinese have values that go back thousands of years, and that have not only influenced China, but also much of Asia, including Japan and Korea. The teachings of Confucius (551-479 BC) still influence much of Asian and Chinese society. Confucian ethics and rituals of etiquette and ceremony remain a large part of business relationships. Confucius taught, among other things, propriety, which includes respect for human dignity, fairness and duty. This duty is to one's parents, elders, employers, customers and the state.

Other fundamental aspects of Chinese culture include friendship, face, favor and fate. Friendship, or *guanxi*, is probably the most important element in the Chinese value system. It is far more reaching than "friendship" in the Western sense, and it includes friendship, relationships, personal connections and more. If one has no *guanxi* in China, he has nothing.

Face is equally significant in Chinese culture, and it is very important for someone not to lose face, at least on the surface. It is even more important not to cause someone else to lose face by putting him on the spot, or forcing him to admit a mistake. "Favor" in Chinese society also carries a special meaning and significance. This includes reciprocity in relationships and transactions. A Chinese expects a return of favor, which, in many instances, is like a return on a social investment. The same applies to concessions and gestures of hospitality and friendship.

Fate is more than just destiny or luck. The Chinese approach may even include consulting the moon and the stars before making important decisions, as well as believing in lucky or unlucky numbers. Some businesses in China and Hong Kong will not accept certain telephone numbers since they may bring bad luck (or others may perceive them as bad luck), and will diligently try to change them into lucky numbers (such as 5, 8 and 9).

Chinese society also believes in *Yin* and *Yang*, an ancient belief that everything in the universe is held together by positives and negatives. This may mean wet and dry, light and dark, male and female, etc. The Chinese apply this philosophy to almost everything in life, including relationships, art, politics and business.

Another characteristic of Chinese society for many millenniums is conformity, without which it would have been very difficult for any government to rule vast China and all its inhabitants. The Chinese are accustomed to living with thousands or millions of others in the same city or area, just as they are accustomed to conforming to the laws and traditions that rule the land.

Although Hong Kong has been greatly influenced by Western values and traditions, it has always remained predominantly Chinese in its orientation. While Confucian values may have been diluted in Hong Kong, Confucian ethics are still prevalent in the people's behavior.

Class structure / Stratification

In olden times, Chinese society had a class system that placed scholars above farmers, laborers and merchants. In feudal China, only scholars could serve in government, and they enjoyed many privileges. In communist China, theoretically everyone is equal, but high government officials and their children generally enjoy more power and privilege than the rest of the population. During the Cultural Revolution of the seventies, intellectuals were considered public enemies and were often persecuted and/or sent to work in rural areas, but a university education is again an esteemed accomplishment. Today another important class is emerging: the entrepreneurs who are enjoying China's new openness to private enterprise.

Class structure in Hong Kong is essentially based upon economic status. Many businessmen have considerable wealth, prestige, and power. At the bottom of the social hierarchy are the *tanka* or "Boat People". In the past, these people were not allowed to move ashore or to marry into landed families. At the present time they continue to experience discrimination.

Safety

Most visitors to China observe the overwhelming friendliness and kindness of the Chinese people. Since the loosening of communism, however, crime and corruption have risen in many cities, especially in areas on the eastern seaboard that have seen tremendous growth. Chinese laws discourage crime by having some of the harshest sentencing on earth. Several crimes are punishable by death, including murder, rape, spying, arson, and pimping. Yet, despite the 3000 to 4000 executions per year, crime is growing in most of China's large trade cities such as Shanghai and Canton. The new wave of crime includes extortion, gambling, money laundering and theft. Many of these activities can be attributed to the widening gap between the haves and have-nots in these cities.

Foreign business people visiting China should try to avoid the seedy parts of any city, but should also feel quite safe and protected, especially at their hotels and at the homes of their Chinese hosts. The Chinese government is keen to keep foreign investment in the country and will do what it can to protect foreigners and their families from crime or other wrongdoing.

Business Protocol

Greetings and etiquette

Although most Chinese people shake hands when meeting someone, **it is best to wait for them to extend a hand before doing so**. A more traditional Chinese greeting involves nodding or bowing slightly. Another Chinese tradition that important visitors encounter at Chinese schools or factories is applauding the visitors as they enter. The polite response in this case is to applaud back and acknowledge the reception. The leader of a Chinese team usually enters first, followed by the second in charge and so forth. Therefore, it is important to recognize the leader and have someone of like status greets him at the head of the team.

Throughout their long history, the Chinese have become adept at greeting and treating their important visitors as dignitaries. This not only impresses the visitors, but some also think it softens them up for the upcoming negotiations and urges them to reciprocate. Chinese hospitality is apparent from the first moment one sets foot on their soil.

Titles are very important to the Chinese, and it is customary to call someone by his title, such as Bureau Chief, General, or Chairman. The best way to keep track of names and titles is to accept business cards (preferably with both hands) and to place the cards on the table in the same order of seating. Due to most people's unfamiliarity with Chinese names, this practice is quite acceptable in Chinese business circles.

Time

Unlike many Westerners who believe "time is money," the Chinese believe that *guanxi* comes first, and business follows. The Chinese business culture is **multi-focused and polychronic**, and it may take months or even years to reach and implement agreements. This is due to a strong cultural orientation that stresses long-term relationships, and therefore requires more time to know and understand a trading partner. Another reason for this is the Chinese relative inexperience in world trade, and their reaction to the speed at which Westerners usually conduct negotiations and sign contracts. As the Chinese economy continues to pick up steam, especially in the northern section of the country, the Chinese are beginning to do business at a faster pace. Much of the southern part of the country, near Hong Kong and in Shanghai, has already developed a rapid approach to concluding business.

The Chinese are generally **punctual** in business, and less punctual in social settings. Tardiness or cancellations of business meetings or social occasions are not appreciated, and may cause an affront. Business hours are from 8 or 9 AM till 5 or 7 PM in most areas. Almost everyone takes a siesta-style break between noon and 2 PM, including switchboard operators, which makes this a bad time to schedule any business. When some factories in China eliminated the siesta, productivity declined, and it only recovered when the siestas returned. Another bad time to schedule business is the Chinese New Year when businesses may close for as long as two weeks. Dates vary for the New Year since it follows the lunar calendar.

Gifts

During China's long feudal history, giving gifts was an important tool in making friends and gaining favors. This has not changed much in today's Chinese society, although the government prohibits its officials from accepting gifts. Most Chinese contacts and business people **expect gifts** from their foreign counterparts. Experienced business people suggest giving business-related gifts that will not cause any suspicion or impropriety.

Giving gifts in China is akin to saying "thank you" in the West. While Westerners are accustomed to thanking others for small favors, the Chinese expect more tangible things in return. They may even tell the potential gift giver what kind of gift they would like to receive. This is especially true of people who have established strong or long relationships, and very common among Chinese family members or relatives visiting from abroad. When giving or accepting gifts, use both hands, and do not open the gifts in front of others. It is common for the Chinese to decline a gift two or three times before accepting it, which is a matter of etiquette. Therefore, gift givers should offer a gift two or three times, as is the Chinese custom.

Business entertainment

China is the land of **lavish and frequent banquets**. Despite government regulations intended to curb excessive banquets for foreign guests, the Chinese still treat their visitors to large dinners and banquets. According to experts, there are many reasons for this custom. The first is that banquets are one of the few perks available to Chinese business people and government officials, who otherwise could not afford them. Second, banquets enable the Chinese to know the visitors and soften them up for the negotiations. Third, and foremost, banquets are one of the oldest customs in China.

Traditionally, the host sits in the middle of the table with his back to the door, while the chief guest sits to his left. While seating arrangements may vary slightly today, the tradition of seating the guest to the left of the host goes back to feudal China.

Vegetarians need not worry in China, where it is acceptable to decline any meat. It is a good idea to practice using chopsticks, and thus not attract too much attention when eating. Although the Chinese used spoons a thousand years before Europeans, today the preferred tool for eating is chopsticks. When using these utensils, guests must take care not to stick them upright in the rice, which, according to Chinese customary belief, could bring bad luck. It is also not proper to suck on chopsticks, and one should place them parallel to each other across the dish or bowl when finished. The Chinese will place bowls directly under the lower lips and push food with the chopsticks into their mouths. It is also acceptable to slurp long noodles into one's mouth.

It is important for Westerners in particular to treat their Chinese counterparts to equally lavish dinners and banquets in their respective homelands. Reciprocity is an important Chinese value, and they often complain about Westerners' lack of hospitality by Chinese standards.

Dress

There was a time in China when the "Mao suit" and other official dress dominated society. This has changed today, but Chinese dress is definitely conservative. Businessmen should wear **dark conservative suits, shirts and ties.** Loud colors should be avoided. **Women should wear conservative suits with neutral colors.** These should not have a revealing neckline, and should not reveal too much of the legs either. Women should also wear low-heeled shoes, even to dinners and banquets. Formal wear in China is much more relaxed than it is in Western countries, and it is rare for men to wear tuxedos (probably only to foreign embassy functions) or for women to wear evening gowns.

Casual wear is also conservative in China, and revealing clothes may be offensive for both sexes. Jeans are acceptable casual wear for men or women in most areas, as are conservative shorts when exercising.

Communication Style

Business Language

The Chinese use a **high-context** language when communicating. Their business language can contain many subtleties and hidden meanings in the interest of saving face or feelings. They will not, for example, use direct communications, such as "Let's get down to the bottom line," or, "Let's cut to the chase." The Chinese, who usually use tactful and self-controlled language, consider this type of communication ill-mannered.

Although many speak English, particularly in Hong Kong, Chinese negotiators will probably choose Chinese as the negotiating medium so they do not put themselves at a disadvantage. It is, therefore, necessary to bring a competent translator to the negotiating table. The Chinese business language is full of "polite escapes," which a clever negotiator will use to disguise his true feelings. For example, if someone says that something may be "impractical," the true meaning may very well be that it is a bad idea. Likewise, "perhaps" in a Chinese proposal may mean "should."

It is also important to have an experienced translator because the Chinese spice their language with many puns and connotations. Mandarin also has four different tones, and some other Chinese languages, such as Cantonese, have nine tones that can influence meaning. There are also hundreds of words that sound alike, but mean totally different things. The word *I*, for example, has 69 different meanings that range from "city" to "ant."

Non-verbal communication

The Chinese are **very conservative** when it comes to non-verbal communication and gestures. They do not like to be touched or patted on the back, especially by strangers. It is acceptable for people of the same sex to hold hands in public, since this is considered an act of friendship. People of the opposite sex, however, should not show public affection in China. The Chinese do not use hand gestures when speaking and may become distracted by a speaker who does. The same is true for facial expressions and highly charged conversations. Personal space is much smaller in China, so it is not unusual for Chinese to get too close to someone by western standards, and to keep this distance even if the Westerner withdraws.

It is best to keep a conservative posture and demeanor when dealing with the Chinese. When pointing, one should use an open hand, not just one finger. To beckon, one should turn the palm down and wave the fingers toward the body in a scratching motion.

Although the Chinese are not known for expressive non-verbal methods of communication, they are known for subtle non-verbal messages. The Chinese are very observant of another's non-verbal messages. So, one should do as their Chinese counterpart does and attempt to maintain a "poker face" during the negotiations.

The Chinese Concept of Negotiations

Selecting personnel

Change is taking place at a fast rate in China, and the Chinese today negotiate with people of all nationalities and beliefs. However, they have some preferences and reservations regarding a visiting negotiations team. One of the most common complaints they have regarding Westerners, especially Americans, is their lack of patience. To the Chinese, many Americans want to rush, take things too fast and try to make quick deals. All this contradicts Chinese cultural and business values, and although they are pragmatic business people, this undoubtedly leaves a negative impression on some Chinese.

The Japanese, who share many cultural values with China, have had tremendous success in that country because they understand Chinese customs. A negotiating team should show **inexhaustible patience and a high degree of etiquette** when dealing with the Chinese. This quickly develops into friendship and trust, which are followed by long-term relationships. This can be accomplished through good patience, manners, and personal traits that appeal to the conservative Chinese culture.

Negotiating style

Overall, the Chinese spend a good part of the negotiating process in **establishing trust and *guanxi***. Without friendship and trust, it will be hard to have very fruitful discussions. The Chinese are good bargainers and they will use **distributive bargaining** techniques to reach an agreement. They will not appreciate a negotiator who tries to force the issue by giving ultimatums or other strong means of persuasion. They do not like surprises when it comes to the substantive part of the negotiations, and they prefer everything laid out clearly. Another favorite Chinese negotiating technique involves stalling. While some may consider this a softening-up tactic, the Chinese say they may slow down things in the interest of future success. Other reasons for stalling may be the lack of a decision-maker at the table and/or the gridlock of Chinese government red tape.

The purpose of negotiations to most Chinese is establishing good long-term business relationships. Their belief in the *yin* and the *yang* plays a role in allowing them to sacrifice a little so they may gain in the long run, a belief also shared by the Japanese. These beliefs are the products of thousands of years of civilization, and they should be taken seriously by a visiting team.

Issues discussed

The issues discussed by Chinese negotiators are usually **relationship-based and substantive**. As stated before, the Chinese are more interested in long-term relationships than fast profit, and they will probably want to know what kind of relationship the other side is willing to offer, and whether this will be a lasting one that has long-term advantages. Other discussions center around the type of products or services offered. The Chinese are always interested in new technology, and they will listen intently to presentations that showcase new technologies and services. Other discussions may take place to establish friendships and to satisfy professional curiosities. This may include asking someone about his work place, what kind of office he has, how many people work under him, how large is the company, etc.

Establishing trust

The Chinese have mixed emotions about foreign people and things. Some are fascinated by everything foreign. Others do not trust foreigners, especially Westerners and the Japanese, due to China's experience of occupation and exploitation by some of these powers. Yet, even with the bitterness that many Chinese harbor against Japan, that country is supremely successful in conducting business in China. Most Chinese consider Americans benevolent and friendly people. Unlike the Japanese, however, Americans do not share many cultural traits with the Chinese, and they may have to work harder to earn their trust. The keys to earning Chinese trust are establishing **guanxi and good experiences** with them. The Chinese are cautious at first, but they find comfort in friendship and positive experiences. Therefore, foreign business people should ensure that they always leave their Chinese counterparts with a good impression.

Persuasion

The Chinese method of thinking may be frustrating to some Westerners. While most Europeans and Americans would rather concentrate on one subject or task at a time and think in linear and inductive terms, the Chinese **tend to look at the whole picture in a holistic way**. The concept of the *yin* and *yang* plays a large part in Chinese logic. If something sounds too good, then there must be a down side to it. If it sounds bad, then there might be some good out of it. While Western negotiators may discuss price, quality and service, the Chinese look at the broader picture of a company's previous attitude toward China and the common future of both sides.

The Chinese generally prefer harmony and little conflict. To them, it is possible to achieve a win-win situation that considers the interests of both sides. However, they are not naive in business. In fact, they believe that "the marketplace is a battlefield." One of the most powerful influences on the Chinese negotiations style is Sun Tzu's ancient volume, *The Art of War*. This book, which is full of philosophical anecdotes, has certainly influenced Chinese society at large. For example, regarding compromise, Sun Tzu advised, "allow someone more latitude at first, and then keep a tighter rein on him later." For the Chinese, concessions are acceptable as long as they bring future gain.

Based on their experience, the Chinese use many problem-solving tactics, including using friendship and emotion to sway people, using competition and multiple bidders to apply pressure, going back to anything that the other side has said or wrote that may help the Chinese position, and finally, changing the negotiation team to change the terms of the discussion.

The persuasion tactics that can be generally used with the Chinese or will be used by the Chinese are:

1) Chinese love to **haggle** and are quite lively while doing so. Distributive bargaining is a favorite pastime. However, given the chance, they will also engage in contingency bargaining. The Chinese will almost always **"high-ball" or "low-ball"** a deal. Embrace haggling and go at it as a way of life and you will do okay. Side Note: People negotiate the fee to use a restroom. Haggling *is* a way of life.

2) Chinese love to use the ploy "We are only a poor third-world country" (i.e., **shaming**) in order to seek compromises in their favor. Even though your particular Chinese counterpart may have more money than you have ever dreamed of having, they may still use the "poor-mouth" strategy and "undeveloped nation" argument. Sidestep this issue by stating that you desire a relationship that is beneficial to both parties and don't concede anything.

3) **Get everything in writing**. The Chinese will attempt to put all of your requirements in writing while omitting theirs. The agreement will still change after it is in writing, but at least it will be a little closer to the original agreement if it was previously written down and agreed upon by both parties. Remember, as previously mentioned, the Chinese view business as they do warfare or sports, and the rulebook may be different.

4) Like most of Asia, the Chinese will imply that they have influence with government officials or with important individuals. You may wish to **imply that you have influence** with certain people that are relevant to the transaction.

5) **Stalling** is a way of life in China. It is a favorite technique of Chinese businessmen. Remember the cost of labor in China. It costs the Chinese practically nothing to have several of their employee's delay you for months. Get used to it. Plan on it. Use it to your advantage.

6) **Diffusion questions** are often used.

7) **Metaphors, stories and analogies** are a good idea in China.

8) **Distraction tactics** are useful in times of conflict and will definitely be used by your Chinese counterparts.

9) Certain requests that we might consider to be **corruption** are normal business practices in China. Decide how you plan to initiate or respond to such requests.

10) Receiving the **technical specifications up-front** or in the beginning of the negotiation is a good idea in China.

11) **Start small and build. If your Chinese counterparts are required to infuse cash** into the agreement they are likely to prefer a small initial transaction. It is advisable to accept the smaller transaction. Thus, business may start slower than you prefer. However, this lays the foundation for future business. However, **if only your party is infusing cash** into the transaction the Chinese are likely to wish to proceed at **full-speed-ahead.** In this scenario, it is your side that might wish to move cautiously.

12) Expect the Chinese to use the **"big-picture"** negotiation style. That is, nothing is decided until everything is decided. You should probably plan on a similar strategy.

13) China is a hierarchical as well as collectivist society. Referring to the **approval of others** and especially the approval of **respected higher authorities** in regards to your company, product, etc. should prove to be an effective method of persuasion.

14) Discussion of harmonious future beneficial business relationships is an integral part of Chinese as well as other Asian business cultures. It is the basis for most introductory business toasts. Although this style of influence is very indirect, it can serve to alleviate tensions, provide minor support for argumentation, etc. Your **presentation of possible futuristic cooperative endeavors, the use of positive imagery,** etc. should be beneficial during business presentations and negotiations.

15) Based upon the collectivist nature and desire for harmony in China (as well as much of Asia), the **"Feel-Felt-Found"** objection-handling tactic should prove to be effective when delivered in a harmonious and non-

confrontational manner. Unfortunately, objections are often not clearly stated in China.

Tactics to avoid include:

1) **Do not self-promote**. Humility is considered a virtue.
2) **Do not engage in extensive information sharing**. Profuse information sharing is seen as foolish.
3) **Avoid Two-Sided Appeals.** Even though the Chinese believe in yin and yang (which is similar to the pros and cons), a two-sided appeal, which provides the other side with some negative information, would appear amateurish.
4) **Avoid direct conflict**.
5) Avoid extensive direct eye contact, elaborate demonstratives (although reserved non-verbal behavior is okay), and touching.
6) Do not use fear tactics, ultimatums, threats, loud voices, etc.

Resolving disputes

In the Tang Codification system, which formed the roots of ancient Chinese Law and the apparatus for the settlement of disputes, was not included among the written legal codifications. The Chinese followed Confucian ideals that believed that law was a reflection of morality and justice rather than a legal system of control. Today the apparatus for the resolution of disputes is so fragmented, localized and ephemeral as to defy understanding of what laws or regulations are currently in force. Therefore it will take *guanxi, creativity and patience* to solve problems with the Chinese.

Group and individual dynamics

The Chinese are **very group oriented**. One of the strongest entities in Chinese society is the *danwei,* or "work unit." To Westerners, workers in *danweis* are almost like indentured servants, and until recently, it was difficult to impossible to move from one unit to the next. This system required conformity and obedience, and anyone who deviated from the rules faced disciplinary action and a bad record. Even after relaxing *danwei* transfer rules in the late '80s, it is still

difficult to transfer or exit the system. Therefore, it is difficult to find many Chinese who are individually-oriented. They would be surprised by any of their negotiations counterparts who do not show loyalty to the group. The Chinese may replace individual negotiators or the whole team in case of a breach of group loyalty and discipline.

Risk

In accordance with their group mentality and need for security, the Chinese take **very little risk** when conducting business. Risk usually carries with it potential for loss or quick profit, and most Chinese are not interested in either. They are, in accordance with their culture, more interested in establishing long-term relationships that will benefit them over an extensive period.

Decision making

China's long history is distinguished by dynasties and rulers that ruled with an iron fist. The Chinese suffered under strict and cruel rulers, and prospered under benevolent and caring ones. Unless that ruler or dynasty fell to a new dynasty, one man usually set and changed the rules as he and his closest advisors saw fit, with little regard for public opinion and dissension. This trend began to change during China's communist rule from 1949 until the mid-1980s. In the 1950s an organization's (*danwei's*) top managers began sharing some of their decision making power with their subordinates. Subordinates began to obtain a greater voice and were truly empowered by their superiors and the new Chinese communist culture. However, managers still maintained some of their control. Today, China is considered to use a combination of "Top-down" decision-making along with "Consensus" decision-making. The term used to describe China's decision-making style is "Top-down Consensus." Management always consults with employees regarding decisions that will affect the employee. Thus, decisions are made together.

China's new young and educated professionals may still find themselves implementing rules that they feel are wrong or outdated. China is a country that has hierarchical traditions and is therefore, at times, slow to change. For example, an engineering group may still implement old techniques since top management is familiar with them. This situation is common in China since older managers rarely update their education, and rely more on their status and authority. Young engineers who attend technical updates seldom get the chance to voice their opinions, and therefore have to follow old procedures that are behind the times. Thus, some businesses and governmental organizations may resemble a top-down approach to decision making. However, this is a worst- case scenario. Chinese businesses do have their share of competent managers and dynamic companies who embrace change. In summation, decision making in China is best characterized as **"Top-down Consensus."**

It is interesting to note that in Taiwan the traditional Chinese decision-making style is still used. Top management makes all of the decisions and middle managers simply implement the rules and ensure that the workers obey them faithfully. Subordinates are rarely involved in decisions and are never empowered. Taiwan definitely uses a "Top-down" style of decision-making.

The frustrating aspect of Chinese management and decision making to foreign negotiators is the mind-boggling layering system that is characteristic of a "Top-down Consensus" style of decision-making. There are few systems in the world that are more layered and complicated. A simple decision may have to go through a number of committees and agencies for final approval. Chinese bureaucrats are also masters at "passing the buck," which limits their responsibility and increases their chance of political survival. New, unproven companies with very few connections can experience a staggering amount of red tape. Once a company establishes itself in China and has the *guanxi* and connections, business becomes much easier.

Type of agreement

For many Westerners, an agreement is a binding process or document that both parties must fully adhere to. The Chinese concept of agreement is fundamentally different from the Western one. To the Chinese, an agreement may simply be an accord to *start* a relationship, and not necessarily to end negotiations. This is why the Chinese **prefer a loosely-worded commitment to do business, not a detailed and carefully-worded document outlining all aspects of the relationship.**

One should also keep in mind that public notaries in China handle many of the affairs that are left for lawyers in the USA. During the Cultural Revolution; lawyers were often attacked and fell out of favor with most of the population. Recognizing the necessity for business laws, and the need to respect international copyrights and patents, the Chinese are developing their business laws at a fast pace. However, most public transactions and business contracts still involve Chinese notaries, not lawyers.

Chapter 8

Czech Republic

- *Country Background*
- *The Czech Culture*
- *Business Protocol*
- *Communication Style*
- *The Czech Concept of Negotiations*

The Czech Republic, established on January 1, 1993, is one of the newest nations in Europe. Its present status has evolved out of a tumultuous and lengthy political history.

Country Background

History

More than 2500 years ago, the Czech people lived on the plains of central Asia. A peaceful agrarian people, they were driven westward by Mongolian raiders known as the Avars, who enslaved them. Under the leadership of a tribal chief called Somo, they defeated the Avars in 620 AD. Determined to keep their freedom they built permanent defensive settlements of wood and stone.

A century or two later, two Greek Christian missionaries brought the Christian faith and taught them a new alphabet. In the 9th Century they united to form the Maravian Empire, but were soon defeated by the Magyars, invaders from neighboring Hungary. Around 900 AD Queen Libussa and her consort, the peasant Premysl, founded the first dynasty. The Romans who had invaded the area centuries earlier had named it Boiohaemia after a Celtic tribe. So it was that the Premsyl kings came to rule over a kingdom that was called Bohemia.

In the 13th Century they expanded their borders to the shores of the Baltic Sea in the north and to the Adriatic Sea in the south. During the reign of King Charles IV (1316-78) the kingdom achieved its greatest cultural and political development when he became the Holy Roman Emperor and established Prague as the capital of the Empire. He undertook ambitious building projects and in 1348 founded Charles University, the oldest university in Central Europe.

In 1526 Czech lands became part of the Austrian Empire whose rule lasted for several centuries. The mid-18th century saw the rebirth of Czech nationalism, but it wasn't until 1918 that Tomas Masaryk conceived the idea of re-uniting the Czech and Slovak lands into the nation of Czechoslovakia. President Woodrow Wilson endorsed the move and for the first time in centuries Czechs ruled their own land.

Masaryk's first Republic became a significant economic force and at one point ranked 8th in the world in GDP per capita, though much of this success was due to a considerable infusion of German capital. As Hitler rose to power in Germany, his attention focused on the Sudetenland, an area bordering Germany with a significant German population. A meeting in Munich between Hitler, Mussolini, Chamberlain of the UK, and Daladier of France produced the Munich Pact, which ceded part of Czechoslovakia to Germany. Within a year Germany occupied the entire country.

At this time the Soviet Union offered to help Czechoslovakia if the Western allies followed suit. This gesture along with later Soviet resistance to Hitler helped pave the way for the Czechs to nominally embrace communism.

For several years after the World War II, Czechoslovakia was an independent state again. In the elections of 1946, the communists won 38% of the vote. They were then able to take control of the government and elected Klement Gothwald president in 1948.

Many Czech communists were inclined to be independent, and in 1968, many forces combined to rebel, unsuccessfully, against Soviet domination. In 1989 Gorbachev agreed to complete independence. On January 1, 1993 in a series of complex economic and political compromises, a peaceful division of Czechoslovakia into the present countries of the Czech Republic and Slovakia was negotiated.

Government

Democracy is a popular concept in the Czech Republic. The nearly two-decade administration of Tomas Masaryk was a shining example of democracy in Central Europe between World Wars I and II. The liberal communist experiment of the Dubcek government in 1968 challenged 20 years of hard-line communist rule. The intellectual-led human rights movement of the 1980's was driven by democratic ideals.

The current government is a multiparty parliamentary democracy. All citizens over 18 can vote. The president is the chief of state but his/her duties are primarily ceremonial. The prime minister is the head of the government. The parliament is divided into two houses, an upper Senate and a lower Chamber of Deputies. The

Supreme Court heads the judiciary. The legal system is a civil law system based on Austro-Hungarian precedents. The present constitution was brought into existence in 1992.

Geographics

The regions of Bohemia, Maravia, and Silesia have all played a role in the development of the current republic. They share a common language, culture, and ethnic background.

Bohemia is the largest and most western region of the country. It is basically a flat plateau surrounded by mountains and forests. The Bohemian Mountains, bordering on Germany, are rich in coal and uranium ore. The forested area produces lumber and wood products and the fertile soil makes it ideal for raising crops and livestock. To the northeast lie the Sudetic Mountains, which border Poland. The region is home to a number of important industrial cities. The Bohemian basin, the heart of the region, has farmland that is irrigated by the country's two largest rivers, the Vltava (Moldau) flowing northward and the Elbe flowing westward.

To the East of Bohemia is Maravia, a region of lowlands that is home to industry and mining. Brno, in the southwest, is the country's second largest city and one of Europe's largest textile centers. The Maravia River in the east forms a fertile valley where many crops are grown. To the northeast is Ostrava, an industrial center where coal is mined and iron and steel are produced.

The third historical region, Silesia, contains the Karvina basin, a rich source of coal. The northern section of Silesia has fertile lowlands used for farming and raising vegetables.

The landmass covers 78,864-sq. km. and borders Germany, Poland, Slovakia, and Austria. The capital city of Prague has been a leading cultural center since the 14th Century.

Demographics

The population of 10.3 million people has remained stable for several years. The average size of a household is 2.5 individuals. Prague, the largest city, has a population of over one million people. Other large cities include Brno 385,000, Ostrava 327,000 and Plzen 175,000. The ethnic divisions are: 81% Czech, 13% Moravian, 3% Slovak, and less than 1% each of Gypsies, Poles, Germans, and Hungarians. Literacy is 99%, reflecting the fact that the country has long had an excellent educational system, which tends to emphasize scientific research. Life expectancy is 72 years for males and 79 years for women.

Economy

Historically, the Czech economy has been one of the more prosperous in Europe. However, the Nazi invasion and World War II caused tremendous destruction. Immediately after the communists took office in 1948, most privately-owned property and businesses were nationalized. Market economy procedures were abandoned, and central-planning strategies caused the growth of bureaucracy and inefficiency. The focus was on basic necessities; prices and salaries were controlled and did not change for decades. Jobs were secure, and some said this led employees at stores, hotels, etc. to become surly and inattentive toward their customers.

Extraordinary changes have taken place since 1989, and the Czech economy is now the healthiest of the former Eastern Bloc countries. Much of this has been due to the fiscally conservative government of Vaclav Klaus. Inflation was initially almost 100% in 1990, but it was gradually brought under control and in 2000 stood at 4%. Retaining government control of essential enterprises such as transportation, housing, and health care eased some of the pain of transition to a market economy.

One of the more important economic developments since 1989 was the return to privatization of property owned by the government. A system of restitution with privatization vouchers was established. The Prague stock exchange opened in 1993 and by the end of 1996 over 90% of the formerly state-owned firms were back in private hands. Enormous amounts of foreign capital have poured in and greatly aided the transformation. The Czech work force is highly skilled and labor costs are lower then in Western Europe.

Unemployment remains high in the Czech republic ranging from 7 to 9% in recent years. The work force of 5.3 million is employed primarily in industry (40%), and services (55%).

Industrial strength is based in heavy industry, transportation equipment, chemicals and food production. Tourism is now a considerable source of income. Chief agricultural products include potatoes, wheat, barley, hops and sugar beets. The Czech Republic maintains a slight trade deficit. The GDP PPP has grown steadily from $30 billion in 1993 to $132 billion in 2000. However, in recent years, the real GDP has remained flat. The currency, the Czech koruna, remains strong.

The Czech Culture

Language

The Czech language is part of the Slavic family and is rather similar to Russian, Polish, and Slovak. It uses an alphabet similar to English except that it has 40 letters rather than 26. Strict phonic rules apply so that each letter has a specific sound.

The biggest obstacle to learning Czech is the way verbs, nouns, and adjectives change their endings according to their function in sentences. Despite its complexity, the Czech language is beautifully descriptive. It would be well worth one's time to learn a few polite phrases.

Religion

Though there are numerous churches, the Czechs overall are not a very religious people. Catholicism reigned throughout Europe during the Middle Ages, but by the beginning of the 15th century, voices in Bohemia cried out for reforms. Jan Hus was instrumental in the development of Protestantism. After the reformation, Catholicism was never strongly re-embraced. Under communism religion was discouraged. Judaism was firmly established as early as the 10th century, but by the end of World War II only a handful of Jewish people survived.

Those Czechs who do worship are predominantly Catholic but the number of active members is relatively low. It seems Czechs are somewhat agnostic, preferring independent thought and their own folk traditions to that of organized religion; 40% consider themselves atheists, 39% are Catholics, 13% miscellaneous, 5% Protestant, and 3% Orthodox.

Value system

Czechs occupy a geographical central position in Europe, and tend to feel that they occupy a special place in the world, a sort of bridge between east and west. This has helped produce a value orientation of non-conformity, which is not to say they are rebellious or temperamental. It is a quietly defensive trait that has probably evolved out of centuries of having to contend with foreign occupations. It can best be described as an independent ability to make light of adversity and find a way around it.

The husband is considered to be the head of the household but they are expected to share in the raising of children because most women work outside the home. Communism supported basic equality for women, and for the most part women have legal, political, educational, social, and economic equality with men.

Literature, art, and music have always played a central role in Czech value systems.

Class structure / Stratification

In 1989 when the Czech Republic initiated a program of privatization, a two-stage voucher system was developed. The first stage included the establishment of joint stock companies. The management of each of these companies was required to prepare a privatization proposal. The proposals then were submitted to and evaluated by the minister of privatization, against competing proposals that could be submitted by anyone domestic or foreign. This stage was completed in June 1993.

The second stage has consisted of the auctioning of the vouchers for each joint stock company. The "coupon privatization" process enabled citizens to purchase privatization points that they could exchange for shares in state-owned companies. This was completed in March 1995. By then, nearly 80% of the economy was wholly or partially in private hands. It is estimated that the private sector now accounts for 70-80% of the Czech Gross Domestic Product.

It is the intent of these policies to support the development of a large middle class, which will increase political and economic stability. These policies are also designed to provide support for the new Czech entrepreneur and a new class of owners.

Currently the average Czech has a higher standard of living than any other eastern European country. Nevertheless, it is far below what wage earners earn in even the poorer countries of Western Europe. While the majority waits for things to improve, the rich continue to get richer causing increasing economic stratification. This may create some political turmoil for the Czech government as it evolves its own form of free enterprise.

Safety

The Czech Republic does not appear to be a dangerous place, but statistics indicate that the rate of theft and violent crime are dramatically rising. However, many people feel it is still safe to take a late metro or to walk through town alone at night.

The most common crimes are pick pocketing and car theft, especially in the tourist areas of Prague. It is a good idea to keep your bags close at hand and your cash in a money belt or hidden on your person and to be particularly wary in crowds.

Traffic safety is another commonly expressed concern. By western standards, there are inadequate traffic controls and it is not uncommon to be caught up in high-speed tailgating types of driving situations on the local roads. Fortunately, the public transportation system is well-developed and safe. Buses are preferable to trains. Taxis are not cheap and are often operated by entrepreneurs who believe it is fair game to separate foreign passengers from their money. Therefore, use taxis with caution, especially in Prague. It is sensible to ask the fare before agreeing to use one, as exorbitant fees are a common occurrence.

Members of the public safety system (police, fire, etc.) are well-trained and motivated but often lack sufficient manpower and resources to do their job well.

Business Protocol

Greetings and etiquette

When it comes to doing business in the Czech Republic, the rules are essentially the same as in the West. The Czech greeting protocol is formal and involves a **firm and brief handshake**. It is important **to shake hands with everyone present when arriving and when departing**. However, it is best to wait for a woman or older person to extend their hand first. It is considered impolite to keep the left hand in one's pocket while shaking hands with the right. It is also considered impolite to chew gum or to talk with your hands in your pockets.

In formal situations it is preferable to be introduced by a third person, while in informal situations it is not unusual to introduce oneself. The appropriate way to **introduce** two parties is to give the name of **the younger or lower ranking person first.** The use of titles is strictly adhered to on business cards and Czechs have great respect for education and professional status. First names are not used in business situations. **Mr., Mrs., etc**. followed by the persons last name is the accepted practice.

Time

Czech business negotiators are **monochronic** and **punctual** and expect the same from their guests. However, they are usually not in a hurry and take things at a more leisurely pace then most Western Europeans, Northern Asians or North Americans. The workday usually begins at 8 AM. Meetings are usually scheduled between 9 AM and noon or between 1 and 3 PM.

Vacations are generally 4 weeks a year, and the period from mid-July to mid-August is the most popular. It is advisable to make appointments by phone or telex at least 2 weeks in advance. A full month should be allowed for appointments made by mail.

The Czech Republic is one hour ahead of Greenwich Mean Time (GMT + 1) or six hours ahead of U.S. Eastern Standard Time.

Gifts

Businessmen do not normally expect to give or receive expensive gifts. If one were inclined to bring a gift, a moderately-priced imported wine or liquor, a pen, or a pocket calculator would be well received. When invited to a Czech's home it is appropriate to bring flowers or a houseplant. The floral bouquet should have an uneven number of flowers but not 13. Roses are reserved for romantic occasions and lilies for funerals, so the bouquet should be consistent with the nature of the occasion.

Business entertainment

Historically, business meetings have been confined to offices. Business lunches were rare; the only meal one shared with a business associate was a celebratory dinner. They did not regard relationship building as an essential part of the negotiating process. However this practice was due in part to restrictive government regulations. The Czechs are not very gregarious and some prefer to be with their family rather than at a business dinner. Thus, business entertainment in the Czech Republic remains an optional activity.

Business lunches have become more popular, but breakfast meetings are very rare. Business topics may be discussed before and after the meal but not while food is being consumed. Whoever makes the reservations will be expected to pay the bill. Invitations for dinner to a Czech's home are rare and should be considered a great honor. Toasting is a common practice and is initiated by the host.

Dress

Business dress tends to be **very conservative**. Generally, businessmen wear dark suits, ties, and white shirts, while businesswomen wear dark dresses or suits with white blouses. Formal executives tend to wear their jackets throughout business meetings even in warm weather. Business attire is also appropriate for most formal evening events. For outings in the country, casual attire is suitable as in the US, and jeans are universally accepted as long as they are neat and clean.

Communication Style

Business language

The Czech language is **low to medium in context**. Czech, English and German are all considered acceptable languages for conducting business meetings. The native Czech language is preferred, however, and therefore arrangements to use a translator should be considered.

Because Czechs often base their business relationships on personal sentiment, cordial relationships should be established with your potential business colleagues, partners, or clients. However, Czechs have disdain for superficiality and small talk, and will expect to get quickly down to business.

Non-verbal communication

For a people **not given to emotional displays, body language** is not a particularly noteworthy aspect in their communication. It is more helpful to be aware of what Czech's don't do, so that one may avoid giving offense. Handshakes are the extent of most physical contact. However, eye contact is very important. When shaking someone's hand, always look them straight in the eye. To get someone's attention, one may raise one's hand, palm facing out with the index finger extended. When entering a room, the highest-ranking person goes first and men enter before women if they are of the same age and status. When a man and woman walk down the street, the man walks closest to the curb. When sitting, keep your feet on the floor or cross one knee over the other, never rest your ankle on your knee, and never prop your feet on anything other than a footstool.

The Czech Concept of Negotiations

Selecting personnel

A key factor to consider in selecting personnel for negotiating with the Czechs is flexibility. In dealing with the Czechs, one should expect the unexpected. Goals can usually be achieved but not in a necessarily prescribed manner. Czechs are relatively new to international negotiating and are still working out their own strategies, but **negotiators are usually chosen on the basis of their knowledge and experience.**

Women can be successful members of the negotiating team. The Czechs regard women as a novel addition to the process. Optimally, women should be rather feminine and non-aggressive.

Negotiating style

Negotiating with the Czechs is **rigorous problem-solving**. They do not necessarily have a built-in desire for compromise. When a Czech businessman presents an offer, he may consider it to be exactly what he expects to get. This is not to say there is no room for negotiating; it's just that you cannot expect him to be willing to give in much. Whereas a Westerner might be accustomed to making an offer where he has left room for negotiation, the Czech may simply lay all his cards on the table with a take-it or leave-it approach.

Czechs are exceedingly polite in most business situations and this can get in the way of productive haggling. If you find yourself at a particularly crucial and sticky point in the negotiations, you may find your Czech counterpart avoiding eye contact, or speaking to a third party instead of directly to you. He may change the topic of conversation or engage in a weighty silence. You may find yourself trying to ease the discussion along while covering all the salient points. At this juncture one must keep one's cool. Be patient. If you feel like expressing disapproval, do so gently without being condescending or unfriendly. Give your counterpart time, but don't acquiesce too much or give away any of your own leverage.

It may even be desirable as a negotiating strategy to call a halt and take a break. If you've established a good business-negotiating environment, chances are you'll be able to work out a reasonable accord. Not all business negotiations with the Czechs are arduous. **Many Czech businessmen are perfectly comfortable with straightforward negotiations and good problem-solving approaches.**

Issues discussed

Initially, a few minutes of conversation will probably focus on trivialities, your flight, your accommodations, where you are from, or your impression of their country. Other safe topics include sports and beer and the beauty of the countryside or the historical significance of the city, etc. Political issues are best avoided. These conversations help lay the groundwork for the more extensive **substantive conversations that follow**

Basis of trust

It is important to establish a level playing field where both sides have equal say and neither is superior to the other. Do not give advice unless it is sought. Czechs do not take kindly to unsought council. Your best chance for success is to mingle fully in the culture and learn to appreciate it and to then express this appreciation as genuinely as possible. Any haughtiness or acts of superiority will completely undermine the establishment of trust.

Czechs value individual achievement and they like to test the boundaries of the relationship. They may want to enhance the business climate by offering an invitation for dinner and cocktails. To the Czechs, it is these unannounced events that often help make things work. They feel that trust is essential before a business deal can be finalized. Thus, trust is gained through **past performance, intuition and relationship building.**

Persuasion

Czechs are very conscious of feelings, in fact many business transactions succeed or fail based on the opinions formed about one another. This is not to say that Czechs are emotional in business dealings. The average Czech is not outwardly emotional, rather he is inwardly conscious of feelings. This can be difficult to recognize. Non-response from the other party may well be an avoidance of the issue. Remember also that Czechs tend to be non-confrontational, and snags or stumbling blocks in the course of a negotiation may become insurmountable. It is important to recognize the danger signs: lowered eyes and silence could be a signal that there is a problem.

Some people like to equate the Czech style of doing business with the Germans, and in many ways they are similar. Both view **empirical reasoning** as the best method of persuasion. However, they are very different when dealing with conflict. German's tend to be blunt and to the point even if it causes conflict. Conflict is merely a necessary evil to German negotiators. Severe conflict may mean the end of negotiations with your Czech counterpart.

Western business negotiations often infuse a sense of urgency into the process while the Czech counterpart may choose to sit and wait. The Westerner then gets nervous and often gives in. It is important to remember that the Czech businessman probably wants the deal more than you do. So it is important to stay calm, be patient and friendly, and wait. Sometimes a good strategy, if the negotiations have dragged on for an interminable period of time, is to withdraw or reschedule. This gives the Czech time to reflect and lets him know that you have your own time constraints.

The specific persuasion tactics that are likely to be effective in the Czech republic are:

1) **Supported Facts**. One needs to present logical/factual information that is accompanied by supportive documentation.
2) **Get it in writing**. Write everything down throughout the negotiations. Take copious notes. Writing it down is expected and will not be considered rude or aggressive.
3) **Build trust through information sharing**. The Czechs will expect a healthy exchange of information.
4) **Demonstrate your knowledge and expertise in a tactful manner**. Do not brag about knowing-it-all. However, the incorporation of appropriate accomplishments by your firm, your staff, yourself, etc. into the presentation is an effective strategy.
5) The Czech Republic is a hierarchical but individualistic society. Referring to the approval of others will not be effective. However mentioning the approval of **respected higher authorities** in regards to your company, product, etc. should be effective.

6) Czech businesspeople tend to be fairly analytical. **Summarizing previously-agreed-upon technical benefits** should be well received.

Tactics to avoid include:

1) Avoid the use of metaphors, emotional tactics, and fear tactics.
2) **Avoid direct conflict**.
3) Do not use ultimatums, threats, loud voices, etc.

Resolving disputes

Many disputes can be avoided by a careful exploration of the proposal at hand. A **thorough analysis** may often pinpoint the areas of concern and can then be the focus for resolving the dispute. Too often Westerners fail to keep their cool, to listen calmly and patiently. Czech negotiators give in very slowly. If your Czech counterpart turns non-communicative, he may be merely contemplating and after some reflection may come back with a more reasonable response. So don't acquiesce too quickly or you may lose some of your leverage.

Group and Individual Dynamics

While Czechs are **highly individualistic**, they also can make strong team players. The culture values privacy and individual accomplishment, but also encourages discipline and discourages deviation. This combination of strong individualism and group cohesiveness creates excellent teamwork.

Risk

The Czechs are basically a **risk-averse** culture. This can be seen in their cautious behavior during business negotiations. It is not uncommon for them to explore, with great thoroughness, verification of compliance to their country's laws. Their tendency to do methodical and logical systems analysis is another facet of the need for certitude before progressing. Individual entrepreneurs can occasionally act quickly, particularly if it's not their money on the line

Decision making

Most decisions in Czech companies are made from the **top-down**. Negotiations might typically start with the lower-echelon people. This of course, reduces the pace of negotiations, which for the Czechs is familiar and comfortable. The final decision-making process will eventually be made by the top executives.

Type of agreement

The Czech legal system is in a state of disarray. It will take a number of years for legislation to catch up with the political and economic changes that have taken place. In the present situation one should never feel at ease until one has the contract signed and the cash in hand. **Czechs prefer verbal** rather than written agreements, but written contracts will clarify issues and offer a better chance of enforceability. **Contracts written** in English or other languages are valid but if there is a version **in the Czech language, it prevails in any dispute**. Retaining a lawyer who is familiar with both Czech law and western practices is essential.

NOTES:

Chapter 9

Denmark

- *Country Background*
- *The Danish Culture*
- *Business Protocol*
- *Communication Style*
- *The Danish Concept of Negotiations*

The Danish nation is an old civilization with a long and complicated history, numerous wars, and many changes in rulers. Its monarchy, one of the oldest in Europe, originated in 950 AD. Today it is a sophisticated society noted for its progressive policies, wide spread tolerance of diversity, economic prosperity and liberal social welfare system.

Country Background

History

Some stone tools have been found in Jutland (i.e., the Danish Peninsula) that are estimated to be 200,000 years old but the first solid signs of habitation follow the last ice age around 11,000 BC. By 4000 BC, agriculture and permanent settlements had been established. By the eighth century, the Vikings had become strong enough in terms of their numbers, tools, and boats to engage in trading and resettlement ventures from the Baltic sea to France and England.

Viking shipbuilders perfected reliable sailing ships that had no need for deep water. They could be sailed or rowed and could go up rivers and land on coastlines. It was this ship that permitted the Vikings to explore, to trade, and to establish domination over a considerable portion of northern Europe.

In the late 9th century, a Norwegian Chieftain, Hardegon, conquered the Jutland peninsula. Gorm, the oldest of Hardegon's sons, established the first monarchy in Denmark. Gorm's son, Harald Blatond, completed the conquest of Denmark and took the throne in 950 AD. He introduced Christianity to the Danes. Denmark expanded and ruled England from 1013 until 1042. As time progressed, there were numerous wars with Sweden and Norway as well as civil wars within Denmark. When Copenhagen was founded in 1167, Denmark ruled most of Sweden, Denmark and Northern Germany.

The 19th century was the golden age for Denmark as it became a center for the arts, philosophy, and literature. This enlightened age challenged the monarchy to adopt more democratic principles. In 1849, a new democratic constitution established a parliament with two chambers, the Folketing and the Landsting, whose members were elected by popular vote.

During World War I, Denmark remained neutral. As a result of Germany's defeat, Denmark was able to recover part of Schleswig under the Treaty of Versailles. During World War II, Denmark again sought neutrality, but Germany invaded. During the Nazi occupation, Denmark was able to rescue 7000 Jewish Danes by sending them to Sweden. In 1945 allied forces liberated Denmark.

Government

Politics in Denmark is more than a decision-making process. It is a source of entertainment and discussion for the Danish people. Its system is a constitutional monarchy with Copenhagen as the capital city. The crown holds great executive power and appoints the Prime Minister (who is the head of government) and the cabinet ministers.

The current legislative structure is quite simple. It consists of a single chamber parliament called the Falketing, which is responsible for enacting legislation. Elections can be held at any time but must be held at least once every 4 years. All citizens who have reached the age of 18 can vote. At present, 9 political parties are represented in the parliament. It is rare for a single political party to hold a majority. Therefore, Danish politics is a never-ending series of discussions and compromises with the more serious problems permanently under review.

In addition to the national political structure, a new supranational structure is emerging since Denmark joined the European Union. Roughly one-third of all recent legislation in the Danish national parliament is a direct result of laws pushed through by the European Union movement.

Denmark has a civil law system, judicial review of all legislative acts, and a Supreme Court whose judges are appointed for life by the queen.

Demographics

Denmark covers an area of 43,000 square kilometers (16,630 square miles) not including Greenland and the Faroe islands. It has a population of approximately 5.4 million people. Denmark is ethnically homogenous and consists primarily of Nordic Scandinavians. A large

German minority lives in the south, primarily in Jutland. Greenland is also part of the Danish realm and is predominately Inuit.

The population is 85% urban with 38% residing in the 4 largest cities: Copenhagen with 1,340,000 is the largest; Arthus has 275,000; Odense has 182,000; and Aalborg has 160,000 people. Nine years of primary education is compulsory. All education is free but continuation beyond the secondary levels is based upon grades and test scores. Denmark has a literacy rate of 99%.

Economy

Denmark's world economic rank is around 25th depending on the year and the type of measure used. Danish per capita income is among the highest in the world. With high-tech agriculture, modern corporate industry, and extensive government welfare measures, its citizens enjoy a very high standard of living. It has a total work force of 2,900,000 with 54 to 46 the ratio of men to women. The Danish economy is quite strong, despite the fact that the government commits almost half of the GDP for social services and transfer payments to the disadvantaged.

Unlike its Scandinavian neighbors to the north, Denmark has maintained a low inflation rate of 2 to 3% with fiscal stability over the past decade. This is good for the economy, but unemployment is around 5 to 6%. The new center-left coalition government is trying to reduce the high unemployment rate and budget deficit, while maintaining low inflation and the current trade surplus.

The government does not have any ownership of capital. Privately-owned companies provide all basic services such as ambulance and fire-fighting services, but they are state-funded.

Nearly two-thirds of the land is under cultivation. Of 77,000 farms, the majority are still owned and operated by families. The average farm size is 36 hectares. Although small and family-operated, they do use high-tech agricultural methods to produce efficiently. Farm products include wheat, potatoes, sugar beets, and barley, and 75% of Denmark's food production is exported.

The raising of livestock is another important industry. Denmark leads the world in the exporting of canned ham. Danish dairy farms also supply the milk used to make the country's famous cheese and butter cookies. Denmark has Europe's largest fishing industry. About 20% of the catch is used to produce fish oil and fishmeal.

A key factor in Denmark's economy is its industrial base, which provides about 17% of the nation's employment. Important industrial exports include home electronics, furniture, silverware and porcelain. Other significant industries are food processing and manufacturing machinery.

Denmark maintains an enviable trade surplus. Its exports includ meat, fish products, beer, and machine tools. Most of these products go to Germany, Sweden, the UK, Norway, and the USA. Imports included petroleum, machinery, chemicals, grain and foodstuffs, textiles, and paper. These imports to Denmark also came from the same partners.

The Danish currency is the kroner.

The Danish Culture

Language

Danish is a language within the Germanic group of languages, with special affinities to the Latin-based languages of southern Europe and the German and Nordic vocabulary and grammar of the north. Danish is the only official language and is spoken by all Danes. There are a lot of regional dialects and some groups of Danes have difficulty understanding one another.

Most Danes are taught English and German in school and some are fluent in these languages. There is a small minority in Jutland who speak German. The study of the Danish language is mandatory for all immigrants, so most of them can speak it to some degree. It is quite common for Danes to have some degree of fluency in two or more languages.

Religion

The Evangelical Lutheran Church, established in 1536, is an integral part of Denmark and is supported by the state. Around 95% of the population are members and all newborns automatically become members. However, the Danes are not a very religious people. Only about 3% of the population attends church twice a month or more. Most Danes claim that they believe in God and about 50% attend church a few times a year, primarily at Christmas and Easter. There is complete religious tolerance. The Roman Catholic Church has around 28,000 members nationwide, and there are a small number of Muslims..

Value system

Denmark is a rather homogeneous culture so they tend to view themselves as a united people. There are slight regional differences; people from Zealand tend to view people from Jutland as lackadaisical, while those from Jutland perceive Zealanders as snobbish.

Danes are often described as individualistic and reserved. Their family ties tend to be close-knit and newcomers usually find it difficult to establish friendships. They are an industrious people who take considerable pride in their work and strive to produce quality products. They also speak out, question authority, and few truths are accepted as universal.

One of the best ways to become part of Danish social life is by joining one of the numerous organizations that espouse a variety of causes. Most Danes are avid protectors of the environment. They are humanistic and have numerous organizations and a social welfare system to help those less fortunate. There is a general commitment to the Law of Jante, which implies basically that no one is better than anyone else. A deep-rooted sympathy for the labor movement exists in Denmark, and working conditions and wages are among the best in the world. The Danes also have a strong commitment to international humanitarianism. Denmark spends about 1.5 billion annually on foreign aid to about 21 selected countries with low GNPs. Much of this is tied to the recipient country's commitment to democracy.

Class structure / Stratification

In business, as well as in social life, connections are not as important as they are in many other countries. There is little corruption, so one cannot buy favors. There is a consensus in Danish society that everyone is either equal or should strive to be equal. There is even intolerance toward those who do not want to be equal, especially those who want to be better, or worse yet, richer. A wealthy ship owner reported that he decided to sell his Rolls Royce and buy a more ordinary car because he got tired of getting the finger in traffic from other drivers.

Another aspect of this equality complex is the reluctance to serve. If there are no masters, there should be no servants, so it is not uncommon for the lowest employees to act like bosses.

The middle class comprises the vast majority of the population, and there is a small upper class. The generous Danish social welfare system prevents any citizen from falling into the depths of despair.

Denmark is also a forerunner in equalizing income disparities between genders. Before most other Europeans, the Danes passed legislation mandating that women must be compensated at the same level as their male counterparts. The current work force of 2.9 million has approximately 1.3 million working women.

Qualities that command respect and determine status in Denmark are age, experience, and knowledge. These are the trademarks of the successful business people.

Safety

For a number of years, humanitarian Denmark has had a permissive attitude toward crime. The question of the rights of the criminal overshadowing those of the victim is commonly debated. As crime rates have soared, the consensus seems to be moving toward increased restrictions on criminal behavior.

The number of reported crimes has more than tripled over the past 30 years. One-fifth of all Danish families are affected by crime every year. Most of it is petty crime but there is also an increase of break-ins and violent crimes.

For most Danes, the answer to increased crime has been insurance. Since the perpetrators cannot be effectively dealt with, you simply insure yourself and your belongings. Danes also lock their doors, install burglar alarms, and lock steering mechanisms on their cars.

Business Protocol

Greetings and Etiquette

The Danes are a somewhat reserved people and they are not particularly gregarious. Introductions are, however, somewhat similar to the American way in that a **firm handshake** is appropriate. **Women greet the same way as men,** and one should always **greet in the order of hierarchy and status. The highest-ranking** person, regardless of gender, will be addressed first. It is appropriate to stand during introductions in all settings. It is also appropriate to shake hands when saying goodbye.

Business cards are exchanged in the same fashion as in the United States. A courteous gesture would be to have a Danish translation on the back of one's card. It is also **customary to state one's title or position** in the company when first introducing oneself.

Courteous and respectful behavior is highly regarded by the Danes. They tend to view Americans as culturally ignorant, overly friendly, and at times too aggressive. For these reasons it is probably best for Americans to be **polite but reserved** in their greetings and introductions with Danes.

When it comes to addressing others, Danes prefer to be informal, but it would be advisable to follow their lead in determining the appropriate time for informality. When dining with Danes, one might consider using one's utensils in the European fashion with the fork in the left hand and the knife in the right hand. When toasting (Skol), it is proper to lift one's glass and acknowledge all the other diners at the table. This is accomplished by smiling and looking each diner in the eye, beginning with the person seated to one's right. One could add to this favorable impression by learning a few Danish words or phrases for such occasions.

Time

Denmark is a **monochronic** culture. In addition, **punctuality is important.** If one is delayed and cannot make an appointment on time, it is advisable to call and apologize for the delay, else they might assume you don't value their time.

In Denmark about 96% of all workers are in unions, which means employers have to pay overtime rates. Consequently, Danes rarely work more than 39 hours per week. Normal working hours are from 9 AM to 4 PM, Monday through Friday. Offices are almost always closed on Saturdays and Sundays as weekends are considered family time. Danish law mandates vacations in Denmark and most workers are entitled to five weeks per year. July is the most popular month for vacations along with Christmas and Easter.

Denmark time is GMT +1 or six hours ahead of U.S. Eastern Standard Time (EST +6).

Gifts

Gifts are optional. Danes will act appreciative and express their gratitude directly even if the gift is not something they desire. It would be in **poor taste to bring a promotional gift.** The gift should be wrapped, as this is customary in Denmark and they will open it immediately. If one chooses to bring a gift, fine quality liquor or something unique from one's own country would probably be appreciated. If you are invited to dinner, bring flowers and a bottle of wine.

Business entertainment

The Danes are a highly-motivated people and are not averse to talking business over lunch. While business lunches are usually dedicated to business conversation, dinners are normally a more relaxed social event. Reservations are often made at upscale restaurants where wine will be served. Since conversations at dinner will not involve business issues, topics such as soccer or current affairs might be chosen. Personal topics should be avoided. Entertaining at home is a common practice. Clients are expected to bring their significant other to these functions.

Dress

Danes are not particularly known as good dressers. For most occasions **an ordinary business suit is quite adequate for a man.** A **ready-to-wear dress is fine for a woman.** One seldom sees women wearing suits in Denmark. Danes often wear casual attire to business meetings or even formal parties. Jeans with a shirt and tie are very common attire.

Communication Style

Business Language

Despite the small size of the country there are considerable regional differences in how Danes communicate. Traditionally, Danes from the rural districts of western and northern Jutland are calm and careful in choosing their words and their dialect is somewhat different. It also takes a little longer to establish rapport with them.

City dwellers in Copenhagen are typically fast talking, quite open, and can be very frank in expressing themselves. It is not uncommon for them to express a criticism directly and they seem to welcome a good argument. Danes like to be direct and forthright, with emotions playing a secondary role to logic and common sense.

Danes utilize a **low-context language.** They do not like to be interrupted. It is customary, therefore, for topics to be dealt with sequentially, and it is inappropriate to interrupt or change the topic until one is certain everyone has had their say.

Most Danes speak two or more languages with English being the most common second language. In the fourth grade, English becomes a required subject for the remainder of the student's education.

Non-verbal communication

Body language among the Danes is quite subtle. Danes exhibit **very little non-verbal behavior** or touching. They like to poke fun at southern Europeans who use their hands and arms to do a lot of gesturing. Danes like to let their mouths do the talking. They normally only touch their closest family members, so anything more than the introductory handshake would be considered inappropriate.

Danes also do not show much emotion with their facial expressions. They appreciate eye contact and their spatial needs are about the same as Americans, at least two feet apart.

The Danish Concept of Negotiations

Selecting personnel

As previously noted, Denmark is a non-authoritarian culture. The boss is considered to be a coach or team leader. Status is determined by age, experience, and above all, professional competence. Business hierarchies are purely functional and there is a lot of sideways communication across hierarchical lines.

Negotiators are chosen on the basis of their **knowledge and expertise.** Past job performance and professional competence are qualities that will favorably impress the Danes. You would probably not want someone on your team who is authoritarian or someone who is superficial and unable to handle criticism. Overall, it would seem that a **predominantly male and mature team** would have the best chance for success.

Negotiating style

Danish business people are tough time managers. It is best to write them well in advance to schedule a meeting. Danes regard work as a very serious matter. They like to have a tightly structured agenda for all meetings. They prefer to meet only when it is absolutely essential and then they want to get right to the point. They take little time for any pleasantries, small talk, or deviations from the agenda. They will come to a negotiation prepared, organized, and ready to discuss business.

Bargaining is unlikely since the Danes will want most terms and prices predetermined, allowing little room for negotiations. Logic and brevity are key values to Danes and a company's reputation and past performance are the best indices of future success. Danes are quite result-oriented and will explore every angle for the best solution. Thus, the **problem-solving** approach to negotiating best characterizes the Danes.

Issues discussed

In 1994 a Swiss-based management institute published a survey in which they concluded that Denmark came out on top when the quality of the work force was considered. The Danes are very hard workers and are highly efficient. It follows that they will want to discuss only those issues that are absolutely relevant. Usually lower-echelon employees work out the underlying issues while the top-ranking Dane will focus on the big picture. Relationships are of little importance. Small talk is frowned on, and only the **substantive** and business-related issues crucial to a negotiated settlement would be of interest to most Danes.

Establishing trust

Initially, with little or no data to guide them, Danes will attempt to establish trust on the basis of their **intuition. Within a short while,** however, they will be testing those initial assumptions against the indices of one's **performance.** They invariably will persist in their faith that if **past performances** have been exemplary, then it is likely that future performance will also be satisfactory. It is important to not exaggerate, but simply state the facts in any presentation. Reneging on a promise will usually terminate a business arrangement.

Once trust is established, Danes like to do business with those who are familiar to them. If a company or an individual performance is satisfactory to them, the likelihood of a long-term business relationship is very good.

Persuasion

A good way to impress the Danes is through **empirical data and logic.** Danes appreciate active people who take the initiative and get things done. Emotional outbursts are anathema to them; they prefer the intellect. Any presentation should be thoroughly researched and carefully prepared **with charts, graphs, pictures, product samples and other visual aids** that illustrate the advantages of the product or service under consideration.

Danes want to get to the bottom line as quickly as possible. Arguing is an acceptable negotiating strategy with them. They have little fear of losing face since they view business transactions as something apart from themselves and not reflective of their personal self-worth. Do not take offense if they become caustic, because that is part of their argumentative style. Try to remain upbeat and positive, and to conclude the meeting in that way.

The specific persuasion tactics that are likely to be used and or likely to be effective in Denmark are:

1) **Get it in writing.** Write everything throughout the negotiations. Take copious notes.

2) **Build trust through information sharing.** The Danes will expect a healthy exchange of information.

3) Receiving the **technical specifications up front** or in the beginning of the negotiation is a good idea.

4) **Supported Facts.** One needs to present logical/factual information that is accompanied by supportive documentation.

5) Your initial presentation/offer is critical to a successful negotiation In Denmark. The presentation/offer must include the benefits the Danish firm will derive from the transaction along with the corresponding supportive documents. During the presentation, all options should be weighed, thus providing a logical path to your conclusions.

6) **Two-Sided Appeals.** The Danes will likely have completed or will complete extensive research regarding the negotiations. Thus, a two-sided appeal is likely to be an effective persuasion strategy. Two-sided appeals provide both the pros and cons of an argument/product. Of course, when making a two-sided appeal, make sure the pros outweigh the cons.

7) It is okay to be blunt and to the point in Denmark. Remember the Danes view conflict as a necessary evil. So, make your points and support them. The Danes will view this as an appropriate persuasion strategy.

8) **Summarizing previously-agreed-upon technical benefits** just before asking for a major consesion should be helpful .

9) Use a **point-by-point** presentation as well as negotiation style. They will use it and expect the same in return.

Tactics to avoid include:

1) Avoid the use of metaphors, emotional tactics, fear tactics and distraction tactics.
2) Do not use ultimatums, threats, loud voices, etc.
3) **Avoid stalling.** The Danes want to get down to business.
4) Do not use favoritism or nepotism.
5) Avoid extensive "small-talk."
6) Do not brag about personal achievements.
7) Haggling over price is okay but the price will probably not change more than 15 to 20%. So **do not "high-ball" or "low-ball."**

Resolving disputes

Public-limited companies in Denmark have a supervisory board. In companies with more than 35 employees, this supervisory board is made up of equal numbers of management and employee representatives. In a dispute, all participants are encouraged to voice a considered opinion, but consensus is less important than everyone being fully informed. Over the years, the Danes have developed considerable expertise in the resolution of disputes. The tactics they usually adhere to involve **presenting the facts** or data to substantiate one's position, which hopefully will convince those who are opposed to change their mind.

Groups and individual dynamics

The Danes are a complex and contentious group of people. They tend to take sides in a variety of chronic antagonisms toward one another: pedestrians despise motorists, dog owners detest cat owners, the rich reject the poor, and the poor abhor the rich. On the other hand they love their country and are very proud of it and almost universally believe it is the best place on earth to live. **They are highly individualistic and opinionated and yet work well together in teams.** Individually they are highly motivated and energetic, collectively they are well educated, and are considered to be the most effective and efficient national work force in the world.

Risk

Fiscal conservatism on a collective level is typical of business practices in Denmark. Danes would rather a company grew slowly on retained earnings than take on debt in order to increase the growth rate. They believe in hard work and planning, and producing valuable products that will sell because of their superior quality. These factors, the Danes believe, will lead to success **with a minimum amount of risk.**

Decision making

Most Danish firms practice **top-down** decision-making. They are similar in many ways to American management structures in that they are multi-tiered and hierarchical. Much of the responsibility and decision making is placed on the shoulders of the CEO. However, Danes are good communicators and welcome input from every facet of their corporate structures. Consulting all levels of the corporate structure serves as an empowerment strategy that ensures cooperation and fosters a sense of teamwork throughout the organizational structure.

Type of agreement

Denmark is second only to Sweden as the country with the most laws and regulations. Danish law has evolved out of French law and there are various mandates that indicate a **verbal agreement is as binding as a written one.** Danes, however, **prefer written contracts** to oral ones, and they will want to have it **spelled out quite clearly with all terms and agreements specified.** Since English is the international language of choice in most instances, they would probably find it acceptable to have the contract written in that language.

Chapter 10

France

- *Country Background*
- *The French Culture*
- *Business Protocol*
- *Communication Style*
- *The French Concept of Negotiations*

France is one of the oldest nations in Europe. It is also the largest West European country with the world's fourth or fifth largest economy. France was an important colonial power and many countries today, especially in Africa, look to France as a "mother country" and share French ideals and systems of government. France has kept up a strong cultural and economic network with many of its former colonies, plus a number of overseas departments (French Guiana, Guadalupe, Reunion, and Martinique), overseas territories (Mayotte, St. Pierre and Miquelon), and dependent areas like French Polynesia, New Caledonia, etc.

France borders three bodies of water (the Atlantic, the English Channel and the Mediterranean) and seven countries (Belgium, Germany, Luxembourg, Switzerland, Italy, Monaco and Spain). It is a permanent member of the U.N. Security Council and an important member of the European Union.

Country Background

History

The French are descendants of Celtic Gauls, who were conquered by Julius Caesar in 51 BC. King Clovis united France in 486 and extended Frankish rule over much of Europe. France became the strongest unified kingdom in Europe by the time of Charlemagne's death in 814.

The French monarchy remained the strongest in Europe until 1789 when the French Revolution overthrew the monarchy and established the First Republic. Then Napoleon established and ruled the First Empire from 1804 to 1815. Napoleon started a series of French conquests into Spain, Germany, Russia, and even Egypt. It took a number of alliances, a Russian winter, and many great battles to finally check French expansion at Waterloo in 1815. Most historians today consider Napoleon a military genius and an able administrator. The French naturally honor him as a great hero and leader, and "Napoleonic law" still governs French business and legal matters.

However, the Napoleonic wars weakened the French government and economy. It took France the remainder of the 19th Century to fully recover. Meanwhile, a unified Germany invaded France during the Franco-

Prussian war. The rivalry between Germany and France also manifested itself in two world wars in the 20th Century. The Second World War was particularly difficult for France, which endured German occupation and political division. Following the war, France became involved in two unpopular conflicts in their former colonies, Vietnam and Algeria, both of which gained their independence at a high cost to themselves and to France. The country started to stabilize when the Fifth Republic began in 1958, and this recovery is manifested in today's high standard of living.

Government

France is a multiparty republic with executive, legislative and judicial branches. The people elect a president every seven years. The president, who is the chief of state, appoints the prime minister to form and head the government. The choice of prime minister and government usually reflects election results. According to the Fifth Republic's constitution, the government decides on national policy, but the president has the power to dissolve the lower house of parliament and to call for new elections.

The bicameral Parliament has a Senate with 321 members serving nine-year terms who represent not only the 22 regions of France, but also overseas departments, territories and French nationals abroad, and the National Assembly with 577 members elected to serve five-year terms. France is a democratic country whose citizens can vote when they reach the age of 18.

The president appoints judges of the Supreme Court of Appeals after nomination by the High Council of the Judiciary.

Demographics

France has a total area of 547,030 sq. km., about twice the size of Colorado. The terrain consists of large flat plateaus and rolling hills, with the Pyrenees Mountains to the south and the Alps to the east.

With almost 60 million inhabitants, France has one of the lowest population densities in Europe. A low fertility rate has existed for many decades. The literacy rate for people 15 and over is almost perfect at 99%. These figures add up to an economically stable society with relatively small families and a mature labor force. Life expectancy is extremely high: 75 years for males and 83 years for females.

Ethnically, the French are Celtic and Latin, with Teutonic, Slavic, North African, Indochinese and Basque minorities. Strong urbanization occurred after World War II, and more than 70% of the population now lives in cities. Paris alone has more than 8.5 million people, with other cities, such as Lyon, Marseilles and Lille each surpassing more than a million inhabitants.

Economy

France's economy is powered by a highly-skilled labor force of over 25 million people, consistently maintains a low inflation rate, and is always ranked among the top five nations in the world. In addition, their standard of living and per capita income are continually rated among the top ten countries.

France is one of the world's leading technological and industrialized nations. Their industry produces everything from satellites to advanced weapons and cars. Other industries include tourism and services. France also has some of the most fertile land in Europe, and has possessed one of Europe's most productive agricultures for many centuries. More than 85% of French soil is arable. Rich agricultural resources make it largely self-sufficient, as well as a major exporter of wheat, dairy products, and wine.

Although France is a major exporter of goods to many of its former colonies, its major trade partners today are its European Market neighbors. France maintains an excellent trade surplus every year. Exports include machinery, transportation equipment, aircraft, chemicals, foodstuffs, agricultural products, iron, steel and clothing. More than 16% of exports go to Germany. Other major trade partners include the UK, Spain, Italy, Belgium, and the USA.

Most of France's imports come from the same partners. Imports include crude oil, chemicals, iron, steel and agricultural products such as tropical fruits and non-temperate foods.

The French franc (F) was formerly the French currency. In 1999, France joined several other European countries in usage of the euro or European Currency Unit (ECU or XEU).

The French Culture

Language

French is the official language. Local dialects, such as Breton, Flemish and Catalan, are declining rapidly due to a recent resurgence of French nationalism. French is a delicate language that was used in international diplomacy for many centuries. It is also the official language of the European Union (along with English) and many international sports governing bodies, such as the Olympic Games, the International Football (soccer) Federation and many car and motorcycle racing organizations. French also remains as the first or second business language in many of the former French colonies.

To the French, their language represents their highly cultivated culture and ideals that make up French society. It is the language of Voltaire, Moliere, Hugo, Zola, Descartes, and other great writers and philosophers. The French are extremely sensitive to people who demean their language. Likewise, they respect and open up to those who show a good appreciation and understanding of the French language and culture.

Religion

Although there is no official religion, over 90% of the French people are Roman Catholic. Protestants represent less than 2% of the population, Jewish people 1%, and recent North African Moslem immigrants about 1%.

Unlike other dominantly Catholic countries, such as Mexico, Catholic teachings do not play a large role in everyday life. The population growth rate, for example, shows that most French people practice birth control. Historically, however, France has been a leader of the Catholic world, with the Papacy looking to French monarchs as important political allies and supporters. France also influenced its colonies through Catholic missions and schools that are still in existence in most of their former colonies in Africa and elsewhere.

Value system

The French are very aware of their contributions to the arts, literature and etiquette. Parisians are especially cultured, and may appear snobbish even to other Frenchmen. Parisians know that their French capital was not only home to French artists and intellectuals, but also the cultural center and refuge for some of the greatest non-French artists of western civilization. Picasso, Dali, Miro and Modigliani are a few of the foreign artists who lived and worked in France. Some of this nationalistic French pride, however, is giving way to a more European sense of identity, especially among young people who value European unity and strength.

The French appreciate a person with great talents and culture, but they deeply value an individual's privacy and seldom delve into personal lives. It's not unusual to have a deep discussion with a complete stranger in Paris, then part ways without exchanging names or dropping formalities. Informality is sometimes looked on as intrusive and disrespectful, as is prying into personal issues upon first meeting someone. After establishing trust, however, one can drop formalities, but should keep up with French etiquette.

The French are also strong individualists who do not mind disagreements and nonconformity. It is acceptable to publicly express one's satisfaction or dissatisfaction.

Class structure / Stratification

Influenced by their political and social history, there are class divisions in France. Although a country with strong socialist leanings and a middle-class majority, the upper bourgeoisie still retains much of the true influence and power in French society, especially in large industry and business ventures. Generally, the culture recognizes lineage and connections, as well as the educational and social privileges of the elite.

Much of the working class in France believes in socialism, and a small number believe that communism is the only road to equality. The range of classes produces occasional mistrust and alienation between various segments of the population. This has been manifested in the severe labor strikes that have occasionally paralyzed France. One byproduct of these strikes was a quiet loosening of stringent hierarchical control over subordinates.

There is some hidden racism in French society, especially toward French citizens of African or Arab descent. This has increased with the resurgence of nationalism in some sections of society and recent concerns about terrorism..

Safety

Millions of tourists and business people visit France, especially Paris, every year. The French population is very law-abiding, but as in all industrialized nations, there are high crime areas in almost every major city. Some port cities, such as Marseilles, have more criminal activity than the rest of the country. France has also experienced political violence in the past few years, ranging from riots to bombings in Paris and other cities. Visitors should use caution and avoid seedy areas of the cities. The French countryside, on the other hand, is legendary for its beauty and peacefulness.

Business Protocol

Greetings and etiquette

When dealing with the French, one must sometimes remember that etiquette is a French word. **The French shake hands during introductions or meetings.** French handshakes are not as firm as they are in the USA or Germany, and men wait for women to offer their hands first. Business people should always present their business cards, which are printed in French and English. In social situations between friends, men and women kiss on the cheeks or touch cheeks and kiss the air (*les bises*).

Titles in France are much more important than in areas such as North America or Australia. It is customary to address a retired army officer or business executive by his last title for the rest of his life. To address such an individual by his first name is a major breach of etiquette in French society, so it is important to find out or listen to the titles of all French contacts. Likewise, if the visiting team members have high or important credentials, they should mention them or have them printed on their business cards. Women should be addressed as *Madame*, whether speaking English or French. Some women will point out that they prefer to be addressed as *Mademoiselle* (Miss), but generally, *Madame* is acceptable at first. Visitors should expect the common use of last names in France, and should use first names only after the French initiate the practice. To the French, this adherence to etiquette shows good manners and respect. Once they establish trust and friendship, however, they drop formalities and start building a lasting relationship.

Time

The French are **polychronic** and can tolerate constant interruptions and do many things at the same time. However, unlike many polychoronic cultures the French are **very punctual**, always **keep appointments,** and **maintain schedules.** Although they maintain schedules, the French are also known for their flexibility, and they may change appointments, schedules, and delivery dates if conditions so dictate. One should also keep in mind that the lifestyle in southern France is more leisurely than the rest of the country, and so punctuality is not as important as it is in the north.

Most French get four or five weeks of vacation per year, which they take in July or August. Therefore, do not plan any important business during the late summer months, when the business sector virtually shuts down for vacation. A typical business day in France is from 8:30 AM to 6:30 PM. Lunches may last for two or even three hours, and they often include fine food and conversation. The French proclaim that they work hard, but they work to live and not vice versa. They appreciate their time away from work.

Gifts

Although **gifts are not expected or necessary in business,** it is wise to ensure that gifts do not offend French taste. For example, one should not leave his business card with a gift, or give gifts that show a company logo or have little value, such as key chains and cheap pens. When attending social functions, one may bring fine chocolate or liqueur, which should be presented before the party. It's not a good idea to bring wine since the hosts probably have carefully selected the wine for the occasion.

Business entertainment

The French **appreciate good conversationalists,** and, although they normally appear business-like and private, they will open up to those who gain their trust and admiration. Long power lunches usually start with

conversation about the food and the ambiance, rather than business. If the French host initiates business talk, one can respond in turn. Table manners originated in France, so it is important to keep the hands on the table at all times, and to use and place the fork and knife properly. (It is uncouth to switch the fork and knife when eating in most French homes. The knife stays in the right hand, and the fork in the left.) Foreign visitors who are not familiar with French table manners can observe and follow, or they can consult an etiquette manual for such information. Whoever initiates the business luncheon usually pays for it. Hotel and fine restaurants are better for such meals since they are quieter than cafes.

Paris is a legendary city for fine art museums and other cultural attractions. It also offers a great variety of night life, fine dining, and entertainment for millions of visitors each year. The rest of France is equally inviting and beautiful, with excellent skiing in the French Alps and scenic resorts and beaches in the south. The French people value visitors who appreciate France's vast cultural and natural resources.

Dress

There are probably only a handful of countries in the world that are as fashion conscious as France. Whenever visiting France, business people **should invest in the best clothes they can buy for business.** Conservative dark suits are suitable for men working in the north. The south has its own style and colors, but a conservative cut also works in business situations. Women should wear business clothes and not try to compete with their French counterparts. Most western business suits will work fine for women in France. The French may be fashion conscious, but they are practical people who will ultimately judge a person on his or her merits, not on the price of their suit. However, visitors should only dress down when the hosts start doing so.

Communication Style

Business language

The French use a **low to medium-context** language when communicating. Since it is acceptable in their culture to express negative and positive feelings, the French will often say what they feel about a proposal or idea, even if not complimentary. Following their rules of logic, they do not expect this to negatively alter the negotiations, but view it as a reason to work for solutions.

What pushes French communication into the medium-context range is the use of long-winded stories and explanations that allow for the use of Cartesian logic. So, although the French are trying to be direct, and often even think they are being direct, their delivery may be far from direct. However, at other moments they can be blunt, rude, etc. and thus extremely direct.

As stated earlier, the French are proud of their language, so if a negotiator cannot speak French, it is a good idea to apologize for not knowing the language, and to hire a translator. This not only satisfies French pride, but it may also smooth the translation process and cause the French team to ensure that the guests understand the whole context of the negotiations. If the negotiations take part in French, or some of the French negotiators speak English, foreign negotiators should expect different connotations for some words. For example, the French verb for "ask" is *demander*. So if someone "demands" something in French, he is merely asking, and not demanding as in the English connotation of the word. Another important linguistic consideration is to use the more formal form of *vous* (which means "you" in the plural form) rather than *tu* ("you" in singular form), since the latter may seem too personal and even disrespectful.

Non-verbal communication

The French use **direct eye contact** when communicating, which some cultures may find intimidating. They may also use facial expressions signifying surprise, acceptance or displeasure, but they tend to be conservative in using body language. They have a keen visual sense, which is used to observe colors, patterns and designs.

The thumbs up sign means "O.K." in France. The USA sign for "O.K." (forming a circle with the thumb and forefinger) means "zero" in France and should not be used to signal "O.K." Generally, it is best to keep non-verbal communication to a minimum and to communicate clearly and pleasantly whenever possible.

The French Concept of Negotiations

Selecting personnel

Your ideal negotiating team for France should have at least one French-speaking member who understands French culture, can argue logically, and can gain the respect of the French as a worthy adversary. Individuals negotiating in France should be **intellectually gifted, cultured, well-dressed, dignified and tactful,** since these will be the talents exhibited on the French team.. The French will expect a decision maker to be present on your team and will usually respond in kind.

Status in their own country may help negotiators, but the French, who often think of themselves as culturally superior, will respect those whose cultures have also contributed to civilization. This is perhaps why the French have a grudging respect for the British, Germans and Americans. All three nations have had differences with France at some point in history, but they also respect France's leadership in many areas and vice versa. The French also have a special relationship with their former colonies, and they frequently view those educated under a French system as intellectual equals or protégés.

If a negotiating team does not have the "ideal" personnel for France, it is a good idea to hire a good translator and to study French mentality and culture to prevent losing ground at the negotiating table.

Negotiating style

The French frequently **use Cartesian logic, which does not take anything for granted until it is demonstrated.** (Cartesian thinking is based on the philosophy of Frenchman Rene Descartes who coined the phrase, "I think, therefore I am."). The French are usually very thorough and well-prepared, and negotiations may take the form of a logical debate. To argue effectively, one must use profound knowledge, expertise and logic. The French tend to be deductive. They like to establish principles first, then analyze the situation by breaking it up into intricate parts in order to come up with a logical solution.

The French also view conflict as constructive, and will not shy away from confrontation to attain their goals.

Thus, do not be surprised by attacks directed towards one's company or products. However, personal attacks/ confrontations are not acceptable nor appropriate.

The French expect their adversary to be fully prepared, and they enjoy discussing the minute details that lead to an agreement. Win-win situations, often advocated in North American cultures, are considered compromises in France, and are not always desirable. The object is to have honest and direct negotiations to reach a logical resolution.

In France, negotiating is a **formal debate**. The French have a long history of teaching negotiations, being the language of preference for diplomatic negotiations, and being viewed as great negotiators. In fact, France has offered university degrees in negotiations for years. So, expect a variety of tactics, strategies, and maneuvers from your French counterparts. It is very likely that they will be very adept at negotiating.

Issues Discussed

The issues discussed in French negotiations **are substantive** and directly related to the purpose of the discussion. The French do not dwell on small talk or personal issues, and avoid both whenever possible. Some, especially those from Middle Eastern or Latin American cultures, may find the French attitude of neglecting personal relationships cold or rude, which is not intended. Following their own logic, the French spend the majority of the negotiating time on direct negotiations.

Bases of trust

The French build trust based on **status, education and past performance.** The French may appear mistrustful, and they are not easily impressed, especially by people who boast or make big promises. Instead, they prefer individuals with educational credibility and good social and business status. They prefer anonymity in social and business life, without addressing personal questions. They also don't like "chumminess," and consider it a screen to hide true emotions. Once the French establish trust, however, their relationships can be deep, loyal and enduring.

It is important for foreign bidders not to make outrageous or risky bids, but instead, to make reasonable offers that show good planning and realistic outcomes.

The French appreciate business relationships that will last, rather than one-time deals that won't, no matter how extravagant or profitable.

Persuasion type

To influence the French, one must play by their rules and **present arguments in a logical, analytical manner**. They are not put off by confrontation and view it as necessary at times to achieve the desired results. Also, unlike many other cultures, such as in Asia, the French do not necessarily respect conformist thinking and attitudes. Being the "devil's advocate" in France is considered clever and acceptable, especially when this leads to finding alternative solutions that best suit the situation.

The French also appreciate elaborate presentations with visual support and materials that show all the facts. Clarity is important to the French, who will interrupt and stop the process to clarify small items during a presentation.

The specific persuasion tactics that are likely to be effective in France are:

1) Haggling over price is okay. The price will probably change around 25 to 30%. Both sides should start with reasonable prices.
2) Receiving the **technical specifications up-front** is a good strategy.
3) **Get it in writing**. Write everything down throughout the negotiations. All conversations, memos, previous contracts are binding in France until they are superseded. You may wish to review your notes with your French counterpart.
4) **Never brag** by saying I did this and I did that. Instead, provide factual information with supportive documentation that shows the accomplishments of your firm or yourself.
5) **Build trust through information sharing**. The French will expect a useful exchange of information.
6) The use of metaphors, threats, and even fear tactics can be very useful in France.
7) **Embrace conflict**. The French view it as positive, productive and fun.
8) It is okay to be blunt and to the point in France.

9) Take your time. The French do not stall but they are definitely not in a hurry.

10) Your initial presentation/offer is critical to a successful negotiation in France. The presentation/offer must include the benefits the French firm will derive from the transaction along with corresponding **supportive documents.** During the presentation, all options should be weighed, thus providing a logical path to your conclusions. In addition, an **historical overview is advisable. This is part of the Cartesian system of logic.** The historical overview provides a track record of success and displays thoroughness. **Active participation** from others or questioning during presentations should be encouraged.

11) **Speak with conviction and confidence.** The French are a very proud people and tend to speak with eloquence as well as bravado. You will need to do the same.

12) **Surprise tactics** are acceptable strategies as long at they are artfully and tastefully executed.

13) **Summarizing previously-agreed-upon technical benefits** should be well received.

14) **Metaphors, stories and analogies** can be used if they are delivered in the context of a Cartesian argument.

15) **Distraction tactics and diffusion questions** are useful in times of conflict and will be used by your French counterparts.

16) Like the Chinese and the Americans, the French view an effective tactic as an acceptable tactic, provided it is professional, related to the business at hand, tastefully executed, and complies with their system of logic.

Tactics to avoid include:

1) Avoid supplification and emotional demonstratives. Crying will get you nowhere.
2) Avoid extensive "small-talk."
3) Do not brag about personal achievements.

Resolving disputes

The best way to resolve disputes in France is to follow a logical path to fix the problem. The French are easiest to please **with logic and facts, rather than charisma and emotion,** provided the relationship between the parties remains congenial and productive. Although they may appreciate those who disagree with them, the French may not take too kindly to some types of criticism, especially if it is directed against national or personal pride. Face saving is important, so always leave room for personal pride in the negotiations. The French may appear stubborn and difficult to budge on some issues. This occurs when they think that their adversaries do not offer enough evidence to continue the negotiations, or when they seem too arrogant and disrespectful. A good negotiator should ensure that French pride remains intact at all times, and that the level of negotiations remains professional and informative.

Commercial courts resolve French commercial disputes. The judges of these courts are merchants, not professional judges. Articles 1442 to 1507 of the French Civil Procedure Code deal specifically with arbitration proceedings. French Law distinguishes between domestic and international arbitration, and both are recognized and accepted. However, this legal apparatus has a lengthy history of failing to provide adequate injunctive relief for grievances.

Group and individual dynamics

The French culture places a **high value on individualism.** Unlike individualism in the USA, however, the French version does not necessarily mean self-reliance, but has more to do with nonconformity and independent thinking. The French, unlike most business cultures, do not necessarily have strong loyalties to their companies, and they certainly do not possess blind loyalty. It is their tendency to question everything, and to explore the truth whenever possible. The French may be more interested in people who exhibit similar tendencies and who disagree with them than in those who agree. Likewise, they can be hard to please and may disregard a person's achievements. Instead, they may look more at the makeup of the person: his individuality and eccentricity.

By other cultural standards, especially the Japanese and Chinese, the French are not good team players. More precisely, **they may not be interested in being good team players**. This is perhaps due to a traditional, and often despised, top-down management system. The various labor strikes and tense labor relations demonstrate the uneasy relationships between different classes in France. They are also vivid reminders of the individualistic and independent nature of French people in all walks of life.

Outsiders, however, can rarely exploit this Achilles heel in French business. Despite their disdain for other classes, the French are excellent judges of what's good for them, regardless of their feelings toward their superiors or companies. They will remain tough negotiators who know what's best for themselves, their companies, and for France, regardless of their individualistic tendencies.

Risk

The French are **risk averse.** They prefer to make their decisions based on rational, well-analyzed decisions, not on luck or trust. In accordance with this, the French will scrutinize high-risk ventures or proposals, and they will probably refuse or alter them drastically. The French may do business with high-risk partners, such as Australians, as long as their end of the bargain holds very little risk. Their rational business approach dictates that they always weigh the positives against the negatives, and that they plan in a manner that guarantees or promises a high level of success.

Decision making

The French bureaucracy has traditionally been known for its rigid **top-down control and decision-making**. The 1968 nationwide labor strike and ensuing disruptions have somewhat changed the thinking of many companies, especially in the private sector. However, the government sector remains largely autocratic, with little delegation of power to subordinates. This is perhaps a reason and a result of the mistrust between the classes in France.

Large companies and their top executives greatly influence the private sector in France. Traditionalists still retain most of the power and delegate very little to subordinates, while younger companies and executives

share more of the power and treat their subordinates as equals in the work place. From a negotiations standpoint, it is astute to find out who makes the decisions on the French team, and how much influence others may have in making that decision. Since the French government is involved in many business ventures, one can expect the decisions to adhere to governmental policies, including those that affect the European Union. It is wise to study these policies and to hire a local expert when necessary.

Type of agreement

One must remember that **under Napoleonic law, all written agreements are binding, including memos and letters**. Verbal agreements on the other hand can change without notification. It is advisable to have contracts brokered through an agency. In a highly structured culture such as France, expertise is very important. An agency with well-trained personnel can guide a venture through the rather daunting legal obstacle course. Following their risk-averse attitude, the **French prefer well-structured and detailed contractual agreements**. Since agreements are usually **written in French**, it is advisable to have a translator or French lawyer review the written agreement before signing it.

French Law has its roots in two thousand years of well-documented history. The coalescence of French Law and the advent of political centralization basically occurred between 1789 and 1803. In 1799 Napoleon commissioned French scholars to draft a civil code. This code became effective in 1804 and was followed by a commercial code in 1807 and a criminal code in 1810. This body of law evolved into contemporary French Law, which is now being influenced by France's leading position in the European Union movement. The legal methods to conduct business in France are principally governed by the commercial and civil codes. These codes are currently being reviewed in order to achieve compliance with European Union directives. The French are also attempting to provide a complete computerized official data base in an online information library concerning legal matters.

Chapter 11

Germany

- *Country Background*
- *The German Culture*
- *Business Protocol*
- *Communication Style*
- *The German Concept of Negotiations*

Germany is the leading European economic power, and historically one of the most influential and important countries in Europe and the world. The reasons for Germany's longtime prominence include its industrious people, its technological edge, and its central European location. Germany is bordered by the Baltic and North Seas to the north, and by nine European countries.

Compared to France and other European countries, Germany is a relatively young nation. In its 125-year history, it has at times equaled or overshadowed its rivals economically, technologically and militarily. Germany emerged from two crushing World War defeats to accomplish economic and rebuilding miracles. Today the German standard of living is the best among Europe's large countries. Although its GDP is lower than Japan's, Germany conducts much more trade than that country, and only the United States exports and imports more goods than the Federal Republic of Germany.

Country Background

History

Although Germany technically became one nation in 1871, the history of the Germanic peoples is much older. Beginning in the eighth century AD, Charlemagne ruled over an empire of German-speaking peoples. After Charlemagne's death, his empire fell apart, but the word "Deutsche," which means "German," became synonymous with the people who spoke that language east of the Frankish lands in Western Europe. The nation is usually dated from 911 when Conrad became King, but German lands were dotted with unstable kingdoms and loose alliances throughout their feudal history. Germany also became the European battleground for the schism between Catholics and Protestants, and during the Thirty-Year War (1618-1648), much of Germany became a wasteland.

Prussia emerged as the dominant German power in the 19th Century. Prussian industry and the military took full advantage of the Industrial Revolution and became the most efficient in Europe. Prussia defeated Austria in its quest to unite the German Empire, and under Bismarck's leadership, subdued France as well. Riding on this wave of success, Prussia convinced the southern German principalities to join the northern Prussian confederation. Thus, the German unified nation traces its independence to 1871, when King Wilhelm I of Prussia was proclaimed German emperor.

This highly successful empire, however, was on a collision course with England and France. This culminated in 1914 with the outbreak of the First World War. Although initially successful, German advances halted in costly and protracted trench warfare. This, coupled with labor and civil dissension at home, led to a sudden capitulation by Germany. The end of the war led to hard financial times and the market crash of the late 1920s. The Nazis ascended to power in 1933, and although they brought some stability and jobs to a tired country, they also steered it toward extreme repression at home and another destructive war with its neighbors.

As a result of military defeat in WW II, Germany lost several of its eastern territories, was divided into four sections and occupied by the USSR, the US, the UK and France. After the unification of the latter three parts into West Germany, East Germany remained under a communist government until 1990, when both parts of the country were again unified.

Government

Following World War II, a transitional constitution and basic set of laws were established as part of the military occupation. The Federal Republic of Germany became a sovereign and independent nation in 1955 when the USSR officially terminated its state of war with Germany. A final peace treaty was signed in 1990, which served as an enabling document for actual reunification with the eastern German Democratic Republic on October 3, 1990. Germany is now a federal republic with 16 *Lander* (states), five of which are from the former German Democratic Republic. The *Lander* share national decisions, but enjoy considerable legislative, judicial, and administrative independence. A democratic system, which includes universal suffrage for people 18 years of age and older, provides these states with proportionate representation at the federal level. The executive branch includes a president, a chancellor who heads the government, and a cabinet elected by the Bundestag. Considerable effective legislation emanates from the cabinet or ministry level. The legislative branch consists of two chambers: the Federal Assembly (Bundestag) and the Federal Council

(Bundesrat). The Assembly has 669 multi-party representatives elected through direct and proportional representation.

The German Republic is a unified state in terms of its civil, commercial, and procedural law, as well as virtually all its tax and revenue legislation. The legal system is based on German civil law with indigenous concepts. Germany's constitution, known as Basic Law, was enacted in 1949 and became the constitution of reunified Germany in 1990. The Bundestag and Bundesrat each elect half of the judges for the highest court, the Federal Constitutional Court.

Demographics

Reunited Germany has a population of 83 million people. Although 92 percent of the population is composed of ethnic Germans, the country has also integrated a number of ethnic groups into its workforce since the 1960s. These include Turks, who make up the majority of "guest workers," Italians, Greeks, Russians, and Poles. The population growth rate of ethnic Germans is very low at 0.01 %. Minority growth rates, especially among the Turkish population, are much higher. The German population is well educated through an excellent school system, with a literacy rate of 99 percent.

Economy

Germany rose from the ashes of World War II to become the leading European economic power and third-ranking world economic power. The vast majority of its GDP comes from the country's western sector. Reunification came with a high cost for both sides. Among them are a 9.9% unemployment rate and the annual transfer of large sums to modernize and integrate the east German economy.

A highly skilled labor force of nearly 40 million workers fuels Germany's market-driven economy. Germany has traditionally been one of the strongest manufacturing countries in the world. In addition, Germany has always had a strong service-oriented economy and has one of the world's best trade-surplus figures.

Except for coal, Germany is relatively poor in natural resources. Like Japan, it imports oil and natural resources to fuel its powerful industry, which produces some of the world's highest quality machines, vehicles,

tools, chemicals and steel products. Agriculture constitutes a small section of the economy and the country depends on imports to fulfill its food needs. Germany's main trading partners are its European neighbors, especially France, which has enjoyed a special trade and cultural relationship with its old nemesis since World War II.

German exports are approximately $600 billion, 88% of which were manufactured products. Main trading partners were France, the U.K., the USA, the Netherland, Italy, Belgium-Luxembourg, Eastern Europe, Austria, and OPEC. Imported are approximately $450 billion worth of goods and raw materials, 74 % of which are manufactured products, 12 % in fuels and raw materials, and 10 % in agricultural products. France again is the primary trading partner, accounting for 11 percent of Germany's imports. Others included the Netherlands, Italy, the USA, Japan, the UK, and Belgium.

The German Culture

Language

Except for some foreign workers in Germany, 99 percent of the population speaks German. Although only one official language is taught in the schools, there are many dialects spoken in various parts of the country. Bavarian and Swabian, for example, are southern dialects that differ from the northern dialects spoken around Hamburg and the Rhineland. Most Germans can also speak a foreign language, such as English or French.

Religion

Germany is the birthplace of Martin Luther and the Protestant religion. The country today is about evenly split between Protestants and Catholics. Most of the northern part of the country is Protestant, while the majority of Catholics live in southern Germany. There are also small Jewish and Moslem minorities in the country (most Moslems are Turkish guest workers). Just as in most European countries, religion does not play a large part in German society or business, and Germans in general are very tolerant of others' religions.

Value system

Although there are many values shared by all Germans, the country's long *lander* (state) traditions have produced differences among Germans. It is a common perception that Bavarians and southern Germans are much more gregarious and laid back than their northern countrymen. Northerners are known for their hard-working ethic, eastern Saxons for their stoic behavior, and western Rhinelanders for their cosmopolitan nature, though such generalizations do not always apply.

Most Germans, however, believe and act in accordance with their "German" values. These include discipline, respect for authority, formality, propriety and neatness. While some younger Germans may not always adhere to these codes of behavior, German society in general was founded upon these values. Germans value common sense and good analytical judgment over emotionalism. They will rarely show public emotion or act contrary to established codes, and they respect privacy and confidentiality. Opera spectators, for example, will rarely shift in their seats or say a word for the duration of the performance. Likewise, public greetings and farewells are rarely emotional or loud. Their history during World War II, which has alienated many Germans from their past, has caused them to become more tolerant toward their minorities than their forefathers.

Class structure / Stratification

The German peasants did not revolt against the aristocracy as their French counterparts did during the French Revolution. Some historians claim that the German peasantry never revolted because the gap between the classes was not as wide as in other countries, and the relations between the different strata in society have been more harmonious. This is still true in modern Germany with a large, relatively well-off working class/middle class. There are still some titled individuals in Germany, many of whom are distinguished by the "von" in their last names. The German aristocracy, however, unlike the British or French nobility, has always been closer to the people and less ostentatious. There are also very powerful business families with both inherited and newly acquired wealth and prestige.

There are biases against foreign workers, especially Turks. The majority of these "guest workers" were invited during the sixties and seventies to offset manpower shortages in German industry. Many have since settled and started families in Germany, but have not fully integrated into the German way of life. Since the manpower shortage in Germany has ended, many Germans feel that these foreigners take away jobs and are a burden on the economy. However, many of the foreign workers take menial jobs that highly skilled Germans do not want. Unfortunately, neo-Nazi youth groups have targeted these minorities in sporadic attacks. The German government, as well as the majority of the population, welcomes these workers and there are many efforts to help them integrate into German society. Most Germans are very wary, as well as weary, of their past, and do not want a repeat of Nazi policies.

Safety

Being a law-abiding and well-organized society, there is much less crime in Germany than in the USA. Apart from the rare violence and counter-violence against poor foreign workers, Germany has also had some political violence from internal terrorist groups attacking the German "establishment." Most of the leaders of these groups have been captured and the organizations are no longer a cause for concern. Visitors and tourists to Germany can feel quite safe, especially since they are rarely targeted by terrorists.

Business Protocol

Greetings and etiquette

German protocol and **greetings are usually formal.** All meetings usually start with a firm handshake between men and possibly between men and women if the woman offers her hand first. Handshakes are also the norm at departures. When shaking hands, it is considered good form not to reach over others' extended arms. An erect posture is also important to Germans, and it signifies inner discipline and dignity. Conversely, a laid back attitude, or putting hands in pockets during introductions, is impolite and even disrespectful. In most regions, men stand when women enter a room, but not vice versa. Also, when introducing others, it is customary to introduce the older or senior ranking member first.

Unless they are very close friends, it is rare to address business associates by their first names in Germany. Formality in address is widely used, and it is traditional to address all men as "*Herr*," and ladies as "*Frau*." "*Fraulein*," which is the equivalent of "Miss," is rarely used in business circles, and is usually reserved for young girls. When addressing titled individuals, it is common to use "*Herr*, or "*Frau*" and the title. So a male doctor may be addressed as *Herr Doctor*, and a female professor as *Frau Professor*. As in most nations, it is a good idea to ask a secretary or another associate for advice regarding name pronunciations and titles. Most German business people, however, can read English business cards, and there may not be a need to print those in German.

Common German greetings are: "*tag*" for hello (pronounced tak), "*guten morgen*" for good morning, and "*auf wiedersehen*," or "*biss spater*" for good-bye.

Time

Germans are known for their punctuality, and Germany is considered a mono-chronic society. Whether in business or society, Germans are rarely late, and they have little tolerance for tardiness from other people. Visiting business people should schedule appointments well in advance (two to three weeks), and should always try to be on time to prevent loss of respect from their German counterparts.

Many German businesses do not open at all on weekends, and there are government regulations that largely prohibit doing business on Sundays. Germans usually take more vacation time than Americans, thus making it difficult to meet with decision-makers during the summer months.

Gifts

Exchanging gifts is not a part of German business culture, but there are exceptions. Gifts should be of good quality, but not too expensive. They may be given to long-time associates when visiting their homes or during Christmas and other holidays. Christmas gifts can be similar to those exchanged in the USA and other countries. Flower bouquets and foreign liquors are both appropriate gifts when visiting German homes. Since there are some regional traditions concerning the variety and color of flowers, it is best to ask a florist to help pick the right ones for the occasion. Scotch and brandy make good gifts to less conservative Germans, but

presenting beer is a bad idea throughout the country, especially since German beers are considered superior to any imports.

Business entertainment

Business entertainment is not as important in Germany as in other countries. Compared to the Japanese and other East Asian cultures, German business entertainment is insignificant, and may be limited to simple lunches. This is indicative of a very serious business culture where personal relationships are neither encouraged nor fostered. Factory tours are probably more important in most of Germany than elaborate dinners or entertainment. This, however, may not be true of all Germans. Bavarians, being more gregarious than their northern countrymen, may invite clients to some of the many activities that distinguish their state, such as *Oktoberfest*.

Lunches are the most common business meals in Germany, and although one may discuss business before or after eating, this rarely happens during the meal. Germans rarely invite business associates to their homes, and it is considered an honor to receive an invitation to a German associate's residence. Since business is rarely discussed, the conversation may revolve around art and culture. Guests should not bring up sensitive subjects such as the Second World War or lost lands to the east. Local and international soccer teams are good topics of conversation for those who know the sport. Almost every major German city has a premier soccer team that competes with the best of Europe.

Dress

Germans **traditionally** dress conservatively in business, with **dark suits, white shirts/blouses and sedate ties**. However, **recent trends include more color,** power ties, etc. Social events, such as the opera or business parties may require tuxedos for men and evening gowns for women. Germans tend to dress casually on weekends, when jeans, shorts, sandals and sport shirts are common.

Communication Style

Business language

Germans use a **low-context language** when communicating. They tend to communicate directly and unemotionally. Logic is foremost, and it is rare to bestow or receive compliments, or to try to influence others through prose and emotion. Such traits are especially true of northern Germans, but may not necessarily describe the Bavarians to the south. Bavarians may seem friendlier and more understanding than their other countrymen, but they too prefer to communicate factual information.

This apparent German "coldness" should not be construed as unfriendliness. It is merely the result of a very disciplined and well-rooted business culture that does not mix business and personal feelings, or facts and emotion. Therefore, Germans may be turned off or impatient when they encounter emotionalism or very high-context communication. Traditionally, many high context cultures, such as those in South America or the Middle East, have had difficulty dealing with German negotiators, but have eventually learned to respect and appreciate German honesty and quality. Since German is not as popular as English internationally, most German negotiators use English when negotiating with others, including Asian, African and South American nationals.

Non-verbal communication

Germans **exhibit very little non-verbal communication and touching.** They also require more space between people than North Americans do, and are uncomfortable with touch and most facial and body gestures. Germans in general value dignified and reserved behavior. Correct posture, clear speech and good grooming are much more important than friendly and communicative gestures. Most Germans are very polite and reserved in public, and will not shout across a street or show affection outdoors. Many, however, are gregarious and may smile and try to put their counterparts at ease.

Germans are very private at home or at work, and it is common to work behind closed doors. Visitors should always knock before entering an office or room. "Chumminess" and personal intrusions are not appreciated, especially in the north, and **it is impolite to rearrange office or home furniture to sit closer to a German colleague.**

The German Concept of Negotiations

Negotiating style

German negotiators come **prepared and well organized** for the negotiating process. To the Germans, a negotiation is a means of achieving a satisfactory business arrangement through a **problem-solving** process. In that context, personal conflict is viewed as being unconstructive, as is lack of preparation, stalling, and other techniques that do not employ empirical reasoning. Following the German credo for producing high quality products, Germans tend to sell their products and services on their merits and value. Their traditional lack of "hype" is sometimes mixed with what may be construed as arrogance and a possible disdain for competitive products of lesser value. This attitude, however, can be supported by the excellent reputation of German products, despite their high prices. As evident from Germany's export figures, German negotiators are doing an excellent job of selling their products and services worldwide.

Issues discussed

The issues discussed by German negotiators are **substantive and business related**. They rarely discuss non-substantive issues at the negotiating table, such as family, recreation and politics. Being a monochronic society, Germans concentrate on the task at hand. It is uncomfortable for Germans to engage in non-task sounding and "small talk." After all, their meticulous preparation and organization are geared toward logical discussions of the issues at hand. This is not to say that they do not exchange pleasantries with their counterparts at the beginning of meetings, such as asking about their trip, hotel accommodations and so forth. Finally, the German reputation for punctuality is enhanced by their ability to stay on track and within their agenda. Therefore, they have a tendency to remind others to stay within the working agenda in order to accomplish the tasks at hand. German negotiations are more expedient than in countries (e.g. Spain, Italy, Japan, Korea, China,

Mexico, Brazil, etc.) where agendas tend to be ignored and relationships must be established before the negotiations can proceed.

Selecting personnel

German negotiators are chosen on the basis of their knowledge and experience. The majority of German managers, especially in industry, have engineering backgrounds. Others have economic and business knowledge. German negotiators bring to the table a vast amount of technical expertise and competence in their fields. Since they also value experience, the majority of negotiators and top managers are men in their fifties. Although women have made great inroads in German society, men still dominate top management.

Even though many large German companies were started and run by families since the Industrial Revolution, few of these families still own or directly control many of today's top industries. Unless members of these families are highly qualified to be top managers, they seldom interfere with managing or try to influence their former interests.

Other German managerial traits include strong character, discipline and linguistic skills. The majority of German managers can speak English fluently, and may be fully prepared to negotiate in that language.

Group and individual dynamics

Germans **may be highly individualistic; however, they make excellent team players**. This is not unusual in a culture that values privacy and individual accomplishment, but also encourages discipline and discourages deviation. Some German negotiators may "act important" and try to impress others with their knowledge or status. This combination of strong individualism and cohesive teamwork makes German negotiating teams among the most formidable in the world. This is especially true when they have the upper hand, or when the negotiations follow the German dictum of thorough preparation and empirical discussion.

Although Germans are not as homogenous as the Japanese, or as nationalistic as the British, they have a strong "German" sense that keeps them united. Despite strong regional identities, being "German" is the main thing that these regions or individuals have in common, and this pride is apparent.

Establishing trust

Being a society that encourages empirical thinking and logic, Germans **do not rely upon intuition or building friendships to establish trust, but rather base trust on past experience**. Germans prefer a clear understanding of intentions, as well as clearly defined contracts to honor these intentions. If trust is broken, it may be very difficult to reestablish it with Germans since they value facts and past history.

Risk

Considering their recent history and cultural orientation, **Germans are low risk takers**. For the most part, German society believes in hard work and just reward. There is also an industrial philosophy that believes in producing valuable products that sell because of merit and quality, not because of luck or chance. This, added to the country's painful memories of the great depression during the Weimar years plus the political and military gambles and horrors of World War II, have produced a culture that values planning and contingencies, not risk. The German government, however, has traditionally helped business at home and abroad. By belonging to several trade organizations and being the leading EU member, Germany helps ensure that the majority of its business is with trustworthy partners who are bound by the same rules of business. German firms have shown a tendency for creativity and success with the least amount of risk.

The Germans use in-depth analysis in order to avoid risk. Their appreciation of analysis complements their desire for technical degrees, low risk, and facts. Since in-depth analysis takes time, German negotiations take longer than negotiations in the USA, Australia, Canada or the U.K.

Persuasion

Following their dictum, **Germans both listen to and render logical arguments as a means of persuasion**. Emotional pleas, favoritism and threats are not effective means of influencing German negotiators, especially in the private sector. Instead, **negotiators should use**

empirical data, charts, and well-prepared presentations that show the benefits of a plan or a proposal. An effective presentation should contain all the necessary technical and mathematical data and figures and an explanation of the methods for implementing the plan. They also value the "bottom line," as it is known in American business. In many ways, the German business culture is similar to the USA system. (This is probably due to the massive numbers of USA citizens who possess German ancestry. Thus, German, as well as British culture, has had great impact upon USA business customs.)

Germany's large import figures demonstrate that they are excellent clients/buyers. Despite viewing German products as superior, they import almost every known product. By exporting expensive goods and importing less expensive ones, the country can continue its outstanding surplus balance, which has contributed to their high standard of living. Since their economy is now one of the largest and most successful around the world, they also perceive a long-range advantage in assisting and doing business with certain developing countries.

The specific persuasion tactics that are likely to be effective in Germany are:

1) Your **initial presentation/offer is critical** to a successful negotiation in Germany. The presentation/offer must include the benefits the German firm will derive from the transaction along with the corresponding supportive documents. During the presentation, all options should be weighed, thus providing a logical path to your conclusions. In addition, a historical overview is advisable to provide supporting documentation, show a track record of success, and display thoroughness to the Germans. However, active participation or questioning from others during presentations should be avoided.

2) Receiving their **technical specifications up-front** is an excellent strategy. The Germans are very technically oriented. You will need to be able to meet technical specifications as dictated.

3) **Get it in writing**. Write everything down throughout the negotiations. Take copious notes. Your German counterparts will be taking notes. Writing it down is expected and will not be considered rude or aggressive. Do not rely upon the final contract (even though the final contract will be very detailed and in writing). Having items agreed upon throughout the negotiations in writing will be a great help in Germany. Once it is in writing it becomes a logical argument with a concrete basis.

4) **Build trust through information sharing**. The Germans respect intellectual property rights and will not push for information that is proprietary. However, they expect a healthy exchange of other information, because they believe it is the best way to execute the problem-solving style of negotiation.

6) **Reply to correspondence immediately**. Silence is considered to mean acquiescence in Germany (both culturally and legally).

7) **Speak with conviction and confidence.** Germans are a very proud people and tend to **overstate** their **ability** to accomplish a requested task. You need to do the same. Start out with a positive "Yes, our firm can meet your requirements."

8) **Expertise** goes a long way in Germany. To render a credible argument, one must possess expertise (i.e., yourself, your team and your firm). However, do not brag. **Display/state your credentials and accomplishments when appropriate (i.e., on business cards, when asked, for your team members, as supporting documentation, etc.).**

9) It is okay to be rather **blunt and to the point** in Germany. Germans usually view conflict in business as a necessary evil. Make your points and support them. The Germans will view this as an appropriate persuasion strategy.

10) **Supported Facts**. One needs to present logical/factual information that is accompanied by supportive documentation.

11) **Two-Sided Appeals**. The Germans will probably have completed extensive research regarding the negotiations. Thus, a two-sided appeal, which provides both pros and cons of an argument/product, is likely to be

an effective persuasion strategy. Of course, when making a two-sided appeal make sure the pros outweigh the cons.

Tactics to avoid include:

1) Avoid the use of metaphors, emotional tactics, threats, fear tactics, diffusion questions and distraction tactics.
2) Do not use stalling, favoritism, or nepotism.
3) Avoid "small-talk"
4) Do not brag about personal achievements.
5) Haggling over price is okay but the price will probably not change more than 15 to 20% in Germany. So **never "high-ball" or "low-ball."** In addition, it is probably best to wait to the end to discuss price. Both sides should start with reasonable prices, attempt to meet each other's specifications and other requirements, and then the minor price issues can be resolved.

Resolving disputes

If problems arise while negotiating with Germans, refrain from emotional fixes and instead opt for well-prepared solutions. This may require counter or **follow-up presentations, more data, and a desire to return to the objectives of the negotiations.** Other remedies include writing formal letters of explanation or apology as a means to reestablish the relationship. This may be especially effective in case a team member caused the problem. Although German negotiators are usually unemotional and impersonal, censuring an offending individual may restart the process, especially since it is hard to reestablish trust with Germans.

Should serious legal conflicts occur one could take consolation in the fact that the German courts offer pragmatic and reasonable options. Germany has ratified United Nations and European Union treaties that compel courts to resolve international contract disputes by truly international means.

The outcomes regarding breach of contract in German Law are similar to those of Anglo-American Law. Problems usually arise when there are irregularities in performance. The statutory regulations regarding irregularities in performance are very complex. However, a tenet of German Law is that "agreements shall be interpreted according to the requirements of good faith." A contract can therefore be voided if one party can demonstrate a disadvantage has occurred that is incompatible with the requirements of good faith.

Decision making

German **decision-making starts from the top down**, with plenty of data, fact-checking and studying by top management. German executives are some of the most hands-on managers in the world. Since they have strong technical backgrounds, they are able to evaluate all the data and make decisions based on facts. Although Germans are known for their punctuality, the decision-making process is slower than in the USA, and Germans will take their time to arrive at a satisfactory decision. When a decision is made, it flows through the organization as scheduled, and the German system of paternalistic management and organizational discipline ensures its timely implementation.

Type of agreement

After reaching a verbal agreement, Germans like to draft a **carefully written document** that spells out the overall and detailed aspects of the agreement. This reflects the German low-risk propensity, as well as their tendency not to trust quickly. Preferring careful planning to unknown quantities, they plan for contingencies and do not leave much room for future interpretation or deviation. This may seem excessive to other cultures that base their agreements on relationships. In this case, the German team may alter the contract to accommodate the other team, but without increasing its own risk.

Contract law

In both Anglo-American and German Law, contracts can be established orally. Written contracts are preferable because of their presumed verity. Some legal transactions also require public authentication. German embassies can provide that service.

German contract law is straightforward in nature. When one party makes an offer it is considered a proposed contract. When another party accepts the offer it is considered binding. The main tenant of German contract law is merely that the offers and acceptances must be clear and obvious in all of their component parts. Thus, under German Law a contract can be produced through the correspondence of and acceptance of an offer. Contract formation under German Law revolves around issues related to declarations of intent. A contract can be nullified if there is a perceptible defect of intent. Therefore all correspondence should be prudently drafted, since the words and the conduct of the participants form a causal linkage toward the legal outcomes.

German Law can bind the offering party. To avoid this complication, the use of clauses such as " subject to change" permits the exploration of options without legal obligations. If a contract is formed by telephone, a letter of confirmation must forthrightly follow. If the letter deviates from the oral agreement, but is accepted, the letter modifies the agreement. The letter is said to have constitutive effect. If not acceptable, the recipient of a letter of confirmation must refute it immediately, since silence is viewed as acquiescence. Under the German Contract Terms Act, issues of price for goods and services must be determined within four months of the date of contract. German law views an agreement as a blueprint routing the participants toward a mutually agreed-upon goal.

German law is consensualist. It looks for the common intent, the legal capacity, and the good faith of the contracting parties. Anglo-American law differs in that it interprets a contract literally according to its terms and has no general requirements of good faith.

Germany's membership in the United Nations and the European Union influences German domestic law. The Uniform Law for International Sales (United Nations Convention 1980) defines proposal and acceptance. Briefly, this law says a proposal for concluding a contract will constitute a binding offer if it is sufficiently definite and indicates the intent of the offeror to be bound in the case of acceptance. An acceptance must indicate the offeree's assent and becomes effective when it reaches the offeror. The Maastricht Treaty on European Union was ratified by the German Budestag and entered into force on November 1, 1993. Currently, this treaty is a political statement of intent, not a legally binding commitment. Thus, this treaty influences but does not replace German domestic law.

Chapter 12

Greece

- *Country Background*
- *The Greek Culture*
- *Business Protocol*
- *Communication Style*
- *The Greek Concept of Negotiations*

Greece is the land of Athens and Sparta, of Aristotle and Plato, Hercules and Apollo. It is an ancient land of myth and celebrated history.

The Olympic Games began in Greece. The earliest concepts of democracy are credited to their early philosophers. Athens became a city of unparalleled political and cultural accomplishments which influenced the Roman Empire, later the Byzantine Empire, and ultimately the entire world. Some say that the culture, art, and other traditions of ancient Greece laid the basis for Western civilization.

A peninsular country with almost 2000 islands, Greece has long been a sea-faring nation. Early population growth and lack of enough fertile land forced many Greeks to migrate and found overseas communities. The Greeks possess an adventurous and entrepreneurial spirit. Aptitude, attitude, and necessity have given the Greeks an international outlook. Their worldwide shipping industry, trading centers on every continent, and prosperous emigrant communities bear witness to the fact that they are an immensely enterprising and adaptable people.

Country Background

History

Between 10,000 and 3,000 BC, the development of agriculture and other early stages of settlement and social evolution took place in the peninsular land known as *Hellas*. Larger villages built between 3500 and 3000 BC indicate a growing complexity in social organization. Ultimately, this culminated in the growth of powerful city-states. Greek influence was centered in Athens, whose art, drama, architecture and philosophy are still admired today. Ancient Greek city-states had a variety of political systems from monarchy/oligarchy to democracy. The people in the city-state of Athens developed the first state-level democratic system in the world during this period. The early city-states had many conflicts with each other. The modern Greek state still deals with regionalism.

Greece has a lengthy history of occupation and domination by outsiders. Conquest by the Romans, the Turks, and Germany with its Italian and Bulgarian allies,

has made the Greek people fiercely nationalistic. Yet when there are no external threats, their ferocity is at times turned inwards in civil strife.

During the Second World War, resistance to the occupying forces was pursued by a variety of guerrilla bands, which fought among themselves almost as much as they fought the Nazis. When World War II came to an end, the presence of these competing guerrilla organizations led to a civil war from 1946 to 1949. Royalists wanted a return of the monarchy, while communists wanted a government like those in Eastern Europe. The civil strife ended when neighboring Yugoslavia left the Soviet orbit and closed its borders to the Soviet-backed Greek communists. The Agreement of Yalta placed Greece in the Western Alliance. The United States took on the responsibility for Greek reconstruction from an impoverished Great Britain.

Greece was a constitutional monarchy at this time. Governments came and went in rapid succession. Distressed by the inability of parliament to maintain stability, King Constantine often operated outside the guidelines of representative government. In 1967 a military coup caused the exile of the king to Italy. The junta, led by Col. George Papadopoulos, brought Greece some stability and a small degree of economic prosperity, but at the cost of lost human rights. Thousands of political opponents, mostly leftists, were imprisoned and many organizations outlawed. Papadopoulos staged his coup based on the propaganda that the communists were going to take over Greece. It is rumored throughout Greece that the CIA aided Papadopoulos. This in turn caused some anti-American sentiments, both during and following the fall of the junta.

By 1973, opposition to his authoritarian regime forced Papadopoulos to institute reforms. He proposed abolishing the monarchy, restoring civil liberties, and promised free elections. General Ioannides, the head of the Greek military police, decided that the reforms were too liberal and staged a coup in late 1973, before the elections and changes could be implemented.

Within a year this new coup had yielded to the demand for free elections. Former Prime Minister Konstandinos Karamanlis returned from his self-imposed exile in France to help form the new Greek Republic in 1974. A new constitution was adopted and the current presidential parliamentary system created. Karamanlis also prepared and completed Greece's entrance into the European Union. Greece has had peaceful democratic transitions from one government to the next since that time.

Modern Greece is currently dealing with several international controversies. A series of territorial disputes involving the six-mile offshore limit with Turkey have been complicated by the discovery of oil in the region, and Greece and Turkey have nearly gone to war over these issues. Conflicts also exist with neighboring Albania involving the treatment of ethnic minorities in each country and feared threats of territorial annexation. Most complicated has been the conflict with the Former Yugoslav Republic of Macedonia (FYROP) over the latter's name, flag, and territorial aspirations. FYROP chose the name Macedonia for the country and put Alexander the Great's 16-pointed star on its flag. The Greeks responded that this new Slavic nation had no right to the name, the star, or any more land, that the name Macedonia and the star were Greek, and such stealing of a culture should not be given international support. (The region always known as Macedonia has an ancient Greek history). As a result of a Greek embargo and other pressures, FYROP gave up the star and renounced all land claims, but still wants the name. The UN admitted the new nation under the rather awkward name, The Former Yugoslav Republic of Macedonia. The situation is calmer now, and negotiations continue between FYROM and Greece.

Government

Greece is now a presidential parliamentary republic. The President is elected by the parliament for a five-year term and assumes the position of chief of state. The president is served by an advisory body, the Council of the Republic. However, the Prime Minister is the official head of the Greek government. The Prime Minister leads the majority party of the unicameral parliament. There are currently 300 seats in the Parliament, which is called the Greek Chamber of Deputies. Currently the primary political parties in Greece are the Panhellenic Socialist Movement (PASOK), New Democracy Party, the Communist Party, the Coalition of the Left and Progress, the Democratic Social Movement, and the Political Spring Party.

Suffrage at 18 years is both universal and compulsory.

The legal system is headed by the Supreme Judicial Court. The President appoints judges on the Supreme Court after conferring with a Judicial Council. The Judiciary is divided into Civil, Criminal and Administrative Courts.

The Greek Civil Code is largely a successful synthesis of Roman and modern legal concepts. It has taken into consideration previous civil laws and adopted new elements from European codes. In the case of commercial law, the French code has been applied. Greek law treats citizens and foreigners, men and women, equally. The rights of property and possessions are enumerated and protected by statute. The economic domain is basically not government controlled.

Geographics

The land area of Greece is 131,940 square kilometers, a little smaller than the state of Alabama. It has 13,676 km. of coastline and land borders with the following countries: Albania, Bulgaria, Turkey, and the Former Yugoslav Republic of Macedonia. The peninsula is practically surrounded on the east, south and west by the Ionian Sea, the Mediterranean Sea, and the Aegean Sea. Its location on the Aegean Sea and southern approach to the Turkish Straits have favored their shipping industry. The climate is temperate with mild wet winters and hot dry summers. The terrain is mostly mountainous, some ranges extend into the sea as peninsulas or chains of islands. The elevation extremes are 0 at sea level to the highest point, Mount Olympus, at 2,917 meters.

Natural resources include bauxite, lignite, magnesium, nickel, chrome, marble, bentonite and perlite. In land usage, 19% is arable, 8% is in permanent crops, 41% is in permanent pasture, 20% is forests and woodlands, and 12% is unclassified. Severe earthquakes are the most serious natural hazard. Environmental problems include air and water pollution. However, Greece has been very proactive in its attempts to curb environmental contamination. For example, the Aegean Sea is very clean. Most of the pollution is located near major population centers and major shipping ports.

Demographics

The Greek population of almost 11 million is quite stable with near zero growth. The majority considers themselves to be ethnically Greek. There are small provinces in the north that identify themselves as Greek Muslims.

Since World War II, the population of Greece has shifted noticeably toward the area around Athens in the south and Thessaloniki in the north. At the present time approximately four million people reside in and around Athens, the capital of Greece. Thessaloniki, the second largest city has over 400,000 residents, but only four other cities have populations of over 100,000: Patras, Herakilon, Volos and Larisa.

The long tradition of emigration from the Greek mainland began in the eighth century BC when Greeks began to colonize the Mediterranean and Black Sea areas. Overpopulation, foreign trade, and self-improvement remain the primary incentives for emigration, though specific political and economic factors have varied. After 1974, emigration stabilized to a rate of a few thousand persons annually.

Nearly 5% of the total population and 7.5% of the work force is foreign. Substantial portions of some national groups are in the country illegally. An estimated 500,000 Greeks resided in the former Soviet Union and returned to their homeland at a rate of 3,000 annually in the 1990's.

Current government policy is designed to aid Greek citizens to return from abroad and to accept Greek immigrants from the former Soviet Union. In general, Greece does not encourage naturalization of immigrants. It is cooperating with other EU countries to develop common migration policies and a reduction of illegal immigration.

Greece has a literacy rate of 95%. Life expectancy is 76 years for males and 81 years for females.

Economy

After World War II, the Greek economy underwent a significant transformation. The natural environment favored agriculture, herding, and fishing, but manufacturing and services emerged as major areas of economic activity. In 1940, over 50% of the population lived and worked in agricultural areas, but in the 90s less than 25% remained in rural areas. Tourism continues to be a major source of income. Shipping is another major industry.

Domestic economic growth in Greece was impressive for several decades. The period from the late 1950s to the late 1960s has been characterized as the era of the "Greek economic miracle," during which the gross domestic product (GDP) grew at the fastest rate in Western Europe, averaging 7.6% annually. Industrial production grew at an average rate of 10% over the same period, and manufacturing exports surpassed agricultural exports for the first time in Greece's history. Per capita income (PPP) in Greece grew substantially from about $500 in 1960 to $17,200 in 2000.

The present economy has dynamic and profitable investment opportunities as evidenced by significant rises in the Greek stock market. However, the public sector of the Greek economy has generated large deficits that have led to an accumulating public debt. These conditions created macroeconomic imbalances that forced successive governments to implement stabilization policies with restrictive monetary practices, income restraints, and increased tax burdens, which tended to stifle economic growth. The rate of inflation in the late 1990's remained above levels considered acceptable by the European Union. The government's hard drachmae (the Greek currency) policy and public-sector wage restraints are largely responsible for the downward trend in inflation, which is at the lowest level in 26 years.

Certain areas of Greece's industry and service sector are currently making impressive progress. Especially encouraging is the growth in food products, textiles, telecommunications equipment, banking, and business services. Some Greek exports have shown significant growth and some Greek financial markets have gained strength in neighboring Balkan countries undergoing transition to market economies.

Greece tried to enter the new European Monetary System, the "euro," during 1998, but a few required economic indicators did not meet the EU's specifications. However, Greece has now reduced its inflation to less than 4% per year, their currency is stabilizing, and their stock market is doing very well.

The Greek Culture

Language

Greece is linguistically homogenous; only an estimated 2 or 3% of the population are unable to speak the Greek language. Greek is a direct descendant of an Indo-European language that was spoken by civilizations in the northeastern Mediterranean for centuries before Christ. The Greek language, in it's several variations, has been used to record an unbroken literary history stretching almost 3000 years. No other European language can make such claims. Modern Greek retains many of the linguistic qualities of its earlier antecedents. Nevertheless the chief linguistic problem for Greeks has been a dichotomy between the spoken language and the traditional literary language. This divergence has produced three forms in varying degrees of use.

Koine, was developed from an Athenian dialect and became the spoken language of Alexander the Great's empire. The New Testament and all of Greek literature for 10 centuries was written in this language. As Koine was influenced and modified by other languages in the Byzantine period, scholars also preserved the Greek (now known as Attic Greek) that had been used by the classical writers.

In the late 18th century, language became a political issue as people debated which form of Greek would be most appropriate for an independent state. Some thought Attic Greek best represented their national language while others favored Koine, the language extant in Constantinople. A third group favored a modified form of Demotic Greek, the modern spoken language. Demotic Greek finally prevailed as the official language.

Religion

An estimated 97% of the country's population belongs to the Greek branch of the Eastern Orthodox Church, commonly known as the Orthodox Church of Greece. The Greek Church became independent of the patriarchate in Constantinople in 1833, shortly after Greek independence. In many respects, church and state are not separated in the western sense. In spite of reforms in the 1980's and the loss of some influence since World War II, the Orthodox Church remains the official religious institution. Principles of the faith are taught

in school, and the state financially supports the church. However, freedom of religion is guaranteed by law, and there are small minorities of Muslims, Roman Catholics, Protestants, and Jews.

Value system

Greece is considered to be the historical home of democracy and although other forms of governance have at times been espoused, it has always returned to a democratic form of government. Since 1974, Greece has compiled a generally positive human rights record. However, international human rights organizations have noted incidents of discrimination and some other violations of basic rights. Before 1974, Greek citizens were imprisoned for publicly expressing communist beliefs. Reports of torture and ill treatment have emerged from Greek prisons in the past, but Greece now follows the policies of the European Union.

One finds great respect for education because of Greece's venerable classic heritage and because education is seen as the key to social advancement. In the 1970's the centralized education system underwent major reforms. However, a shortage of university and research facilities created a brain drain as many students were forced to attend universities abroad and did not return home after their education.

At the individual level, life is influenced heavily by family, friends, and organizational ties. Friendships are deep and carry significant obligations. It is the extended family and deep friendships that give structure and security to the individual.

There are a number of contradictions in Greek culture. On the one hand they profess a strong work ethic, but casual approach to life. They profess value for group consensus, but a resist its consistent accomplishment. While the individual is held responsible for decisions, failures are frequently attributed to external circumstance rather than one's own behavior. Greeks have an inherent trust in people because of the social interrelationships between extended families and friends, but there is also a social hierarchy with some bias against certain ethnic groups, religions, and political opponents.

Although many of the superficial aspects of traditional social behavior have changed, especially in the cities, modern Greek society still retains elements of a much more traditional set of values, such as the protection of a family's reputation. However, divorce rates have increased in recent years.

Class structure / Stratification

Except for the differences between rich and poor, Greece is a relatively homogenous country. The main factors that bind a culture together, such as race, language and religion, are uniform. The main consideration for preferment in the Greek culture is whether a person can be trusted, rather than his/her qualifications, expertise or performance. A predisposition toward nepotism, political affiliation, regional affiliation, and personal influence known in Greece as *messon*, permeates the fabric of every Greek organization. The technocratic ideal of rising to the top on merit and performance is secondary to this more ancient value. Intertwined with this cultural imperative is the family structure, which is the basic social unit for all strata of Greek society.

Since the nineteenth century, upward mobility through education has become quite common in Greece. Greece's class system became more flexible than that of many other European countries.

Historically, women have been viewed as inferior. They were expected to care for the family and remain in a domestic context while being submissive to the opinions and demands of men. At the present time, Greek women have emerged from these constrictions. Through pressure brought by economic needs and the women's movement, social legislation in the form of the Family Law Act of 1983 made equality of the sexes the law of the land. Women are gradually moving into government circles. Several Greek administrations have had women in leadership roles and a number of women have been elected to the national legislature.

Safety

One should remember to get all the immunizations that are recommended for that area of the world. Be careful in the selection of food and drink. In Greece, bottled water is advisable. However, in Athens the water is safe to drink.

Minor crimes such as pick pocketing, purse snatching, and taxicab con games can occur in popular tourist areas throughout the country. Unfortunately, crime has recently increased, perhaps due to an influx of indigent illegal immigrants. Lost or stolen passports should be reported to the local police and the USA embassy or nearest consulate.

Business Protocol

Greetings and etiquette

Upon meeting others, Greeks will use a handshake or an embrace or kiss. Close friends of the same sex may kiss and embrace when they meet. For most **business introductions a firm handshake is expected**. The order of Greek names is the same as in the United States: given name first, followed by the person's surname. Greeks seldom use first names when doing business and then only among colleagues of similar age and status. **Older people are highly respected and are always addressed formally**. Any attempt to address them in their native tongue will be regarded as a compliment.

Greek **etiquette** tends be fairly **formal**. When handing out business cards, it is advisable to have one side printed in Greek. One should present the card with the Greek side up and positioned so the print is facing the recipient.

Time

Greece is basically a **polychronic** culture. They are people who like to do many things at once and **do not greatly concern themselves with punctuality**. This orientation has evolved out of their belief that people and relationships are a higher priority than hours or minutes. However, Greeks **will expect their foreign business counterparts to be punctual**.

Greek office hours are 8 AM to 5 PM. Lunches take between 15 to 75 minutes. Late lunches between 1 PM and 2 PM are very common. Appointments should be made in advance out of courtesy; a week in advance is usually sufficient.

Governmental offices are open from 8 AM to 3 PM. Bank hours are from 9 AM to 3 PM. Store hours vary, however. They tend to follow: 1) a 9 AM to 7 PM pattern, or 2) a 8 AM to 1:30 PM opening, with a break, followed up by a 4 PM to 7:30 PM opening.

Greece is two hours ahead of Greenwich Mean Time (G.M.T.+2), or seven hours ahead of USA Eastern Standard Time (E.S.T.+7).

Gifts

The Greeks are a **very generous people**. If one compliments an object too enthusiastically, it may be given to you. It is not necessary to give gifts at an initial meeting. Giving a gift too soon could be interpreted as trying to move things along too quickly. However, **after a relationship has been established, it is appropriate to give pens, pocket calculators or leather desk accessories**. While these gifts can be small, the giving is more important than the gift itself. One should avoid too lavish or too inexpensive a gift or one that has the company logo on it. If you are invited to a businessman's home, one can bring small gifts for the children of the host/hostess. Flowers or a cake will be appropriate for the hostess.

Business entertainment

Greeks are **natural hosts** and they are known for their enjoyment of life, which is one of the reasons Greece is so popular with tourists. Greeks want to make money but they like to have fun while they are doing it. **Frequently business is done over a cup of coffee in a coffeehouse or tavern.**

Lunch is usually served between 12-2 PM. In restaurants it is not uncommon for customers to be invited into the kitchen to look into the various pots to make one's selections. Often many dishes are ordered and then shared by everyone at the table. In Greece, as in many other cultures, the elderly are served first.

Dinner is eaten late in the evening. A festive atmosphere of drinking, dancing, and entertainment that can last late into the night often accompanies dinner.

If one is invited to a Greek home, one will probably be offered seconds and thirds of food in an insistent way. The acceptance of more food is a way to compliment your host.

Dress

When doing business in Greece, **men** should wear **suits and ties** in the winter. In the summer, Greek businessmen may dress more casually, but usually still wear a suit and tie. In Greece a nice sport jacket and dress pants are considered to be the equivalent of a suit, so this is permissible attire. Greek ties tend to be solid colors, so tone down your tie.

Women should also dress conservatively and wear a **dress or suit with heels**. If one is invited to someone's home, women should wear dresses or dressy pants.

In Greece, dress is not a clear guide to status, and there are wide variations in taste and style. Greeks do not always dress up to go to work, nor do they necessarily dress down when they want to enjoy themselves. However, we suggest you dress formally and conservatively just to make sure you do not commit a fashion faux pas.

Communication Styles

Business language

Greeks tend to be **medium to high-context** in their business language usage. They place considerable emphasis on building strong relationships. In order to protect or enhance these relationships, Greeks may use subterfuge or they may tell their counterparts what they think they want to hear. Greek is a very rich and colorful language and it is culturally acceptable to exaggerate and dramatize in order to build friendship and trust. They are, however, shrewd and tough negotiators and enjoy the art of bargaining. One should withhold judgment and be patient, particularly if one is from a low context culture with expectations of getting right to the point. It is also possible to work out a fair deal for all parties because the Greeks are by nature generous and pragmatic in business matters.

Cell phones are even more popular in Greece (and for that matter most of the world) than in the United States and are often used for business conversations. Incoming cell phone calls are free.

Non-verbal communication

The Greek are a warm and friendly people; when introduced they shake hands firmly and make good eye contact. In business communications, **personal contact is very important,** even in the smallest matters. They prefer to meet face-to-face rather than over the phone, and there is a general mistrust of written communication.

One of the **non-verbal mannerisms** commonly utilized in Greek culture includes a slight upward nod of the head, which means "no." However, Greeks also use the same side-to-side movement as Americans to mean "no." Another non-verbal way of saying no is to lift the eyebrows upward. An affirmative response is indicated by a nod downward. Greeks typically use facial expressions to accentuate a positive or negative response.

Historically, females will issue a puff of breath through pursed lips in order to ward off the "evil eye". To call someone to you, the Greeks extend the arm, with the **palm up or down,** and make a scratching motion with the fingers.

When dining, male guests of honor are usually placed to the right of the hostess and female guests to the right of the host. One should keep the wrists on the table when dining, rather than in one's lap. Some foods are eaten with the hands and one should imitate the host in this regard. To signify when one has finished eating, cross the utensils in an "X" shape, knife under the fork.

The Greek Concept of Negotiations

Selecting personnel

When assembling a negotiating team, one has to consider many variables as well as a whole host of cultural nuances. An intermediary is desirable but not necessarily essential. In Greece the negotiating process will be seriously compromised if the relationship factor is not properly attended to. A **Greek intermediary** could offer advice and council to teammates prior to and in the midst of negotiations. This person could, in advance, make all the logistical and tactical arrangements that are necessary for a team to function smoothly. In addition, the intermediary will obviously be Greek, and thus understand the language, non-verbal nuances, and the Greek culture.

Greek negotiating teams will be selected on the basis of **status and or filial** considerations. Since most companies are family-owned, it is quite common for a family member to be a member of the Greek team. **High-ranking** senior team members will almost always be present and those with the highest status will make the final decisions.

Negotiating style

One can expect the Greeks to come **well prepared** to the negotiating process. They are shrewd and tough negotiators, and **they enjoy the negotiating and bargaining** process. For centuries this area has produced outstanding entrepreneurs and the principle of 'go getting' is one of the intrinsic values of Greek culture. Although Greeks truly value friendship and family, modern Greeks are materialistic and the standard for the good life is based on possessions and status. This does not mean one cannot get a fair deal in Greece. Modern Greeks are pragmatists who will search for practical and expedient means to make a deal work.

Although Greeks will come well prepared, they will react more favorably to proposals put to them by people who have cultivated a **relationship** with them. They will spend time in small talk while evaluating their business counterparts. They may begin talks by discussing the previous day's economic news. Lunch may be suggested at a restaurant, and one should reciprocate by inviting them out to dinner. If one is invited to a Greek home for dinner this is a further level of acceptance.

As previously noted, Greek is a rich and colorful language and the Greeks love to use it fully. **Exaggeration** is an integral part of their cultural conditioning. They **love drama and debate, to haggle and bargain**, and the more fully one can enter into this process, the better. Keep in mind that drama demands that one emote, use expressive gestures, loud voices, etc. Remember that when the Greeks are expressing themselves in this manner, they are not arguing or fighting, but merely communicating in the Greek style.

Greeks do not expect you to accept their first offer. If you do, they may feel short-changed and suspicious; they may even not trust you. So, leave some room to negotiate and maneuver.

Issues discussed

As with any relationship-based high-context culture, business negotiations are best approached as though it were a meeting among friends. Initially, generalized topics that may or may not be related to the more substantive issues will be the main fare. **Once a relationship has been established and a degree of comfort achieved**, the Greeks may be ready to get into the issues of pricing, time horizons, production schedules, and other **substantive issues**.

Modern businessmen are usually open-minded, efficient and up-to-date on modern business practices. Most will have business degrees and/or international experience. Most Greeks speak conversational English, and a few speak French, German or Italian. Patience is important when dealing with the government, due to the red tape and bureaucracy.

Establishing trust

Trust is a major consideration for upward- mobility opportunities within a Greek company, as well as for successful negotiations. Nepotism and personal influence are more important than a person's qualifications, expertise or past performance. It is only **out of mutual understanding and personal relationships that trust can be established**, which necessitates a lot of business entertaining. Business partnerships will be based upon genuine accord, and written contracts tend to play a less significant role. The time is well spent if both sides thoroughly understand the nature of the agreement and the necessary commitment of personnel and resources.

Persuasion

The Greeks use a blend of **logic, emotion and dogma** in their persuasion efforts. They tend to be quite charismatic and are in turn highly impressed by the **charisma** of others. They tend to be open-minded, quite gregarious and enjoy discussions, debates, and the

bargaining process, but it is difficult to change their perspective once it is firmly established and they have formed a strong opinion.

The specific persuasion tactics that are likely to be effective in Greece are:

1) **Get it in writing**. Write everything down throughout the negotiations. Take copious notes. Use your notes as a proof source throughout the negotiations.
2) **Build trust through information sharing**. The Greeks will expect a healthy exchange of information.
3) Greeks love to bargain and **haggle** and can be quite lively while doing so. Greeks will probably **"high-ball" or "low-ball"** a deal.
4) **Metaphors, stories and analogies should be** structured so that they appeal to the Greek sense of **personal ideology** and their **situational-specific** concept of fairness.
5) **Diffusion questions and distraction tactics** are useful in times of conflict.
6) You may want to try the "multiple yes close" that is based on the Socratic method of persuasion. The "multiple yes close" attempts to obtain multiple agreements to minor issues before asking for a major concession.
7) Personal appeals can be effective in Greece.
8) Authoritative proof that is based upon the ideology held by your Greek counterpart (i.e., dogma) would be very effective.
9) **Summarizing previously-agreed-upon technical benefits** should be well received.
10) You may wish to **imply that you have influence** with certain people that are relevant to the transaction.
11) **Supported Facts**. One should try to present logical/factual information that is accompanied by supportive documentation.
12) Greeks tend to use a little puffery. So, definitely build up your firm and your products/services with **entertaining but professional exaggerations, enthusiasm, and non-verbal demonstratives**.
13) **Speak with conviction and confidence.** Greeks tend to be excellent orators and will expect the same from you and your firm.

14) **Visual proof sources that are animated and nicely displayed** should prove to be effective props.

Tactics to avoid include:

1) Avoid direct personal conflict.
2) **Avoid non-professional behavior**. Greeks can be playful, friendly, etc. but they remain professional at all times during work or leisure.

Resolving disputes

Greeks tend to process information from a fairly **subjective** orientation. This often leads them to be more impressed with **situational** specifics than with universal or generally held rules and laws. Their **personal ideologies** will frequently win out over objective facts if there are any contradictions between them.

There are numerous contradictions and divisions within the Greek culture. Having evolved from competing city-states to a national entity has resolved little of the internal factionalism that divides Greece. This factionalism can complicate business undertakings and lead to disputes. Foreign investors need to be aware that if Greeks cannot get along with one another, relationships with those from outside the culture may be even more complicated.

The cornerstone of the Greek legal system is the constitution of 1975. The Code of Civil Procedure, Articles 867- 903, has provisions for arbitration. The code establishes, encourages, and extensively regulates the proceedings of the arbitration process.

If the dispute is a contractual one, the obligations arising out of the contract are determined by the appropriate law on contracts (Article 25). Foreign judgments are recognized and executed if they are legally enforceable in the country in which the judgment was rendered.

Group and individual dynamics

The Greeks are a relatively homogenous people in terms of ethnicity and language, and yet their country has a history fraught with factionalism. They are **highly individualistic**, yet they have very strong family ties. They are loyal to their friends and their respective companies, yet individual achievements are very important to them. Greeks thrive on opposites. This mindset is all-inclusive and all-embracing, and they love contradictions, contrasts, inversions, and antitheses. Opposing is as natural to a Greek as conformity is to a German. The Greek mind is never happier than when it is involved in a convolution of thought and logic. Socrates lives.

Risk

Greeks are **low in their propensity for taking risks**. Their strong family ties tend to make them risk averse. They also like to build relationships before making a business commitment so they move more slowly in their business ventures. However, Greeks are also individualistic, pragmatic, and contradictory, so while they may be generally risk averse, they are also daring enough at times to go with a risky venture.

Decision making

Since most Greek companies are family-owned, families and friends are taken into consideration when decisions are made. Decision making, however, is a **top-down** process made by either the owner or a manager who has the owner's trust.

Type of agreement

Agreements with the Greeks can take many forms. The business environment is generally unregulated and relatively free, so a wide range of contract styles are permissible. The **French Commercial Code was the primary source out of which the Greek Commercial Code evolved** and the principle of contractual freedom prevailed within it. In the portion of the civil code dealing with contract obligations, the most frequently encountered types are covered. It is assumed that **contracts will be drafted (i.e., written) to the legal specifications of the respective parties.** Greek Law defines companies as partnerships, limited partnerships, limited partnerships by shares, limited liability companies, silent partnerships, and cooperatives.

The Greeks have the largest lawyer to population ratio of any country in Europe and their contractual law is quite sophisticated.

Chapter 13

India

- *Country Background*
- *The Indian Culture*
- *Business Protocol*
- *Communication Style*
- *The Indian Concept of Negotiations*

The Republic of India, committed to modernization, is a country with vast potential and enormous challenges. Visitors from other cultures can be overwhelmed by its diversity. Enormous untapped potential beckons the international businessperson in this second largest human marketplace of the world.

Country Background

History

There is archaeological evidence of an extensive civilization that thrived from 3000 to 1700 BC along the Indus River valley. Excavations have revealed planned cities in geometrical patterns, multi-storied buildings, underground sewage systems, organized garbage collection, large granaries and public and private baths. A prosperous merchant community that possibly traded with similarly-advanced cultures in the Persian Gulf, Mesopotamia, and Egypt peopled these Harrapan city-states.

Around 1500 BC the Aryans began arriving from central Asia. They gave India its Brahmanical culture, its caste system, and Sanskrit, the language that is the basis for most modern languages of India. The Vedic period (1500 to 600 BC) is regarded as a golden age when gods walked the earth and communicated with men.

Around 1000 BC, the center of Indian culture and politics shifted from the Indus to the Ganges Valley. Alexander the Great's arrival in 327 BC had little impact. His departure after only two years left a political vacuum that was quickly exploited by Chandragupta Mourya and his advisor, the Brahmin Kautilya. They were able to establish an empire that covered the Indus and Ganges plains and extended as far north as Afghanistan.

Chandragupta's son extended their control and when his grandson, Asoka, conquered Kalinga in a terrible slaughter, he renounced warfare and converted to Buddhism. Asoka governed for thirty-seven years and established the largest area under one rule until the British arrived. Asoka's legacy is one of moral and social responsibility to all living things. His decrees created sanctuaries for wild animals and he identified certain species of trees for protection. This is one of the earliest examples of environmental action by a government. The lion pillar of Asoka survives as an official emblem, and is found on every Indian coin and currency note.

After Asoka's death in 232 BC, the empire was divided and conquered by the Indo-Greek kings, descendants of the followers of Alexander. Menander, the best known of them, extended his power into the Punjab from 155 to 130 BC, leaving a Hellenistic stamp on the culture. Later conquerors were the Scythians and Huns from central Asia, the Arabs, the Turks, the Mongols from the north and west, and the Ahoms from Burma; all of these remained to become a part of India's complex human mosaic. These invasions also resulted in greater contact between India and its neighbors to the north and south, east and west, and advanced trade and commerce throughout the subcontinent and the Mediterranean world. Literature and the arts flourished, while institutions of higher learning taught mathematics and science.

By the sixteenth century power was being traded back and forth among Mogul Muslim invaders and Hindu rulers. By the seventeenth century, the Moguls were firmly in control, but were unable to unite the country and subdue the Hindus. By the end of the seventeenth century, their empire collapsed. The effects of their two hundred years of rule in northern India are still evident today in the language, literature, architecture, and religion.

The British utilized India's diversity to divide and conquer. They first intruded as a commercial enterprise (the East India Company), for their initial aim was trade, not territory. Eventually the British created their own bureaucracy, promoted western civilization, dismantled the indigenous legal, social, and educational systems and replaced them with their own administrative structures.

A mutiny in 1857 made the British realize that their policies of westernization could not be pursued with complete insensitivity to Indian opinion. In 1858, the British government bought out the East India Company. The purchase price was added to the public debt of India; thus India itself paid for the cost of becoming a British crown colony. The British developed the infrastructure and by 1900 India's railway system was the best in Asia. A rising middle class embraced certain western concepts with enthusiasm. Western democratic ideals awakened this new and influential class to ideas of freedom and equality and enhanced the possibility of questioning religious assumptions. It was out of this climate that Gandhi began his re-thinking of the Hindu religion and political process.

Mahatma (meaning "great soul") Gandhi re-shaped the philosophy of nonviolence (*ahimsa*) into a force for political and economic change. During the first decade of the twentieth century, Indians were demanding a larger role in the governing of their country. After World War I, the independence movement gained momentum. In 1930 Gandhi led the salt march and a boycott of British products was declared.

World War II depleted the British Empire's resources, but the Indian independence movement gained strength. On August 14, 1947 the British granted India independence. Later that same year, religious conflict between Hindus and Muslims lead to the division of India's territory into India (as we know it today), western Pakistan and eastern Pakistan (the eastern part later became Bangladesh). This partitioning led to the uprooting of 12 million people in three areas and 200,000 were killed in religious rioting. Religious differences and resultant hostilities still disrupt India's harmony today.

Government

India is a federal republic. Their constitution was adopted in 1949 and inaugurated on January 26, 1950. Legislative power is vested in a parliament consisting of the president and two houses. The Council of States (Rajya Sabha) has no more than 250 members, most of whom are indirectly elected by state and territorial assemblies, and the remainder are appointed by the president. The House of the People (Lok Sabha) has 543 elected members and two appointed by the president. Members are elected by universal suffrage, granted to all citizens who have attained the age of 21 years.

The president is the head of the government and is elected to a five-year term by an Electoral College consisting of selected members of both houses of parliament and the legislatures of the states.

The judicial system is headed by a Supreme Court, which has a chief justice and not more than twenty-five judges appointed by the president. This court has

exclusive jurisdiction in any dispute between the union and the states or in any question of law that involves an interpretation of the constitution.

The High Courts are the courts of appeal, and their decisions are final except in cases where the appeal lies within the jurisdiction of the Supreme Court. Provision is also made in the constitution for lower criminal courts called Courts of Session and Courts of Magistrates.

India has a complex array of political parties. Some are national parties and some are state parties. The National Congress Party, established in 1885, is the best-known political organization, but others have won recent elections. There are political parties that appeal to the Hindus or other religious or regionally defined groups, as well as several Marxist and socialist groups.

Demographics

The Republic of India is geographically the seventh largest country in the world with over one billion people, the world's second largest population. There are 24 different languages that are spoken by a million or more people, and numerous other languages and dialects. India has 25 states and 7 union territories, each with its own language, style of dress, religious rituals, and local customs.

India's current population growth rate is 1.55% per year. If this birth rate continues, India will become the world's most populated country in 20 years. One-third of the population is under the age of 15, which re-affirms the projected continuance of growth. Eighty percent of India's population resides in villages and rural areas, and the majority of them are involved in agriculture. In terms of ethnicity, 72% of the population is Indo-Aryan, 25% is Dravidian, and 3% are of Asian or other descent. Literacy rates as of 1995 were 38% for women and 65% for men. Life expectancy in 2001 was 63.5 years for women and 62.2 years for men.

Geographics

The Indian landscape is split into three sections. The Himalayas, the world's greatest mountain range, are in the north. Below them lie the northern plains, which are home to almost half of the Indian population, making it one of the most densely populated regions of the world. The third section is the peninsula, which consists chiefly of the Deccan plateau. Hills, escarpments and rocky valleys separate this plateau from the northern plains. The Great Indian or Thar Desert covers the westernmost parts of the northern plains. China, Tibet, Nepal, and Bhutan border the country on the north. To the northwest lie Pakistan and Afghanistan. To the east is Bangladesh and Myanmar. To the east and south lie the Bay of Bengal and the Indian Ocean. To the west is the Arabian Sea.

The Indian climate varies from year-round tropical heat in the south to sub-freezing cold in the northern mountains. Between these extremes, it is possible to discern four seasons. In the unrelenting heat of the summer, March to May temperatures on the plains can climb to 113 degrees Fahrenheit, and hot winds can raise dust storms. The monsoon rains advance across India sometime between June and September. The rain-laden clouds of the monsoons are turned back by the Himalayas, and forced to drop their moisture over the plains. This brings humid sticky weather from mid September to November. December to February is a relatively cool and dry period when most of India enjoys its best weather. The nights are cold in Delhi and the other northern cities, but days are sunny and pleasant.

Economy

After gaining its independence, India pursued a semi-socialist economic path in which the government assumed an important role as planner, investor, manager, and producer. This high level of government regulation acted as a deterrent to foreign investment. At the same time, India also pursued a path of self-reliance, which was fairly successful in feeding its multitudes. Concurrently, it also pursued more efficient and sophisticated agricultural methods. At present, it is the world's second largest producer of rice, with yields that make up 21% of the world's entire volume. It also produces 10% of the world's output of wheat. It is a leading producer of peanuts, milk, cheese, tobacco, cotton, sugarcane, and rubber. Large-scale agribusiness is forcing out many small traditional farmers, and has accelerated movement to the cities in a search for work.

India is blessed with a rich supply of mineral reserves: iron, manganese, and chromite are particularly abundant. Other natural resources include copper, bauxite, zinc, lead, gold, silver, diamonds, and limestone. India has only moderate amounts of oil and natural gas, which meet about half of its needs, but it has plentiful coal reserves. India not only possesses an enormous pool of human labor, it also has a well-established, well-educated, and talented array of engineers, scientists, doctors, lawyers, and technicians. It is India's dream to become a world leader in science.

Only 20% of the total population are well-educated, and these elites operate and control the industrial and governmental apparatus. Each segment of the skilled labor pool is either unionized or organized; work stoppages and strikes are frequent and lengthy. India's professional and trade organizations have established cross alliances and affiliations with national political parties. These factors tend to complicate an already complex political and economic environment.

The finance industry in India is highly regulated and largely government-owned. The Bank of India regulates the circulation of bank notes, operates the credit system, and manages the country's foreign exchange reserves. Other banks have been established which help promote specific industries and foreign trade.

India's government-owned railway system, the 6th largest in the world, carries the bulk of India's products and public traffic, but there has been a steady increase in motorized transport. A grid of highways links all the major urban areas. About 50% of the highway network is unpaved, and many rural areas are inaccessible by bus or auto. There are international airports at Bombay, Calcutta, Delhi, Thiruvananthapuram, and Madras. Three modern seaports, at Bombay, Calcutta, and Madras, are capable of handling an impressive amount of tonnage in foreign trade.

Shortly after gaining its independence, India embarked on an impressive program of industrialization, leading toward a diversified industrial base. A number of basic industries are publicly-owned and operated by either the states or the central government. There are also numerous private producers, including some large industrial conglomerates. The Tata Iron and Steel Company in Jamshedpur is privately owned and is one of the largest and most successful companies. Indian corporations have also developed satellite operations in Southeast Asia, Africa, and the Middle East, which are managed by indigenous personnel.

The largest proportion of manufacturing employment is in the textile industry, which was initially developed during the British occupation to meet the demands of its empire. Cotton is the most widely utilized fabric. However, jute, wool, silk, and artificial fibers are also produced.

The distributive consumer-goods industries have been largely concentrated in urban areas. In order to foster greater economic benefits to rural areas, and in an attempt to alleviate metropolitan congestion, the state governments have sponsored numerous industrial parks that offer cheap land, reduced taxes, and other concessions in order to entice private-sector investment. This program has helped increase employment and consumerism among India's rural poor.

For a number of years after gaining independence, India was considered a difficult nation in which to do business. Foreign investments were only allowed when they could contribute technology unavailable in India. Nearly every aspect of production and management was monitored and controlled, and many foreign firms abandoned their projects. Five-year plans have featured mixed economic policies with both capitalist and socialist elements, and have usually involved large government expenditures.

The collapse of communism in Russia in 1991 thrust India into a complex ideological and economic dilemma. The Indian government's response was to initiate exploratory discussions with the United States, purportedly involving military cooperation and joint-defense projects. The Indian government also introduced a new industrial policy, which essentially removed most licensing requirements, reduced the sectors reserved for government enterprises, and increased the ceiling on foreign investments.

In 1998 the Indian government made it clear when it released its annual budget that it will proceed with ambitious plans for infrastructure development and self-reliance. As of 2000, India had a GDP PPP of $2.2 trillion, reflecting its status as the largest market in south Asia. While this is an impressive figure, the per capita GDP PPP was only $2,200. The majority of the population lives in poverty, is poorly educated, and is essentially unemployable in any field other than agriculture.

Exports totaled $43 billion in 2000 and consisted of textiles, jewelry and gems, chemicals and leather goods. Primary export trading partners were the USA, Hong Kong, Japan, the UK, and Germany. Imports amounted to $61 billion and consisted of oil and petroleum products, machinery, fertilizers and chemicals, which came primarily from the USA, Belgium, the UK, Germany, Saudi Arabia, and Japan.

The Indian Culture

Language

The official language is Hindi, spoken by about 30% of the population. English, a legacy of the British Empire, is used for many official purposes. The Indian constitution also recognizes many regional languages; the most widely spoken are Telugu, Bengali, Marathi, Tamil, Urdu, and Gujarati. There are a number of other languages that are spoken only in regional areas.

Religion

While Indians are a very spiritual people, India itself is a secular state. All forms of worship are permitted and the state does not recognize any one religion. The principal religions are 82% Hindu, 12% Muslim, 2.3% Christian, 2% Sikhs, and some Buddhists, Jains, and the Parsis, who practice the Zoroastrian religion.

Value system

India's value system, as complicated as its religious belief system, evolved out of India's rich and varied religious traditions. Furthermore, India has numerous subcultures, which may be at odds with the more pervasively-held beliefs of the larger culture.

In terms of family values, one could say that they are a moderately-collectivist culture in which it is highly desirable that one's individual actions be in harmony with one's family and peer group. Family lines of loyalty are extended, and distant cousins are treated like brothers. Marriages are arranged, and dowries are given from the bride's family to that of the groom's.

For centuries India had been a largely agrarian-oriented culture. The twentieth century brought urbanization, industrialization, education, technology, and mobility.

When a young couple moves from a rural area to a big city, they weaken the traditional influences of their extended family. Women are also getting more education, which opens new employment options.

Western values have begun to influence India, particularly in the urban areas. The Indian government is generally supportive of this process because they want their citizenry to be able to compete in the world marketplace.

Many traditional values are being retained. There is still great respect for the elderly; the oldest person is always introduced first. The caste system, outlawed by the Indian government, still exists to an impressive degree with great power over individual lives.

Class Structure / Stratification

Under the caste system, stratification was based on one's birth into a particular caste. Castes were thought to be determined as a result of Karma, a concept in which what one presumably did in a previous lifetime determines one's current station in life. This belief is tied to the concept of reincarnation, a belief that all forms of life are in a continuous cycle of birth, death, and rebirth.

Though officially outlawed by the government, discrimination on the basis of caste remains prevalent in Indian politics and business. There are four traditional or main castes that are further subdivided into numerous subcastes. Foremost are the *Brahmans* or priests, who had to maintain a high level of purity in order to remain in contact with the gods, and tend to be members of the current economic upper class. The *Ksatriyas* were initially the warriors and the rulers; their descendants have made the transition into politics and the military. The *Vaisyas* were the merchants and farmers who had businesses and owned land. Then come the more numerous *Sudras*, the peasants and laborers, who are usually uneducated and lacking in skills. At the bottom are the Untouchables (the unofficial fifth caste or the *outcasts*), those who worked with what were considered unclean objects in such occupations as trash collection, sweeping and even barbering. Skin color (*Vama*) is also a part of India's caste system and class structure; lighter complexions tend to be of higher caste.

Safety

In today's business climate, the issue of one's personal safety has become complex and requires careful consideration. Once a relatively safe place, India has had dramatic increases in the crime rate in recent years. The tourist or businessperson should watch out for pickpockets and purse-snatchers.

As in many other countries, crime has become a sophisticated enterprise. Criminals tend now to work in teams. Tourists or visiting business people are quite vulnerable, but India does its best to protect visitors. Uniformed and officially-designated personnel are at the airports, bus stations, and train stations in part for the protection and convenience of foreign travelers. Try to remember to utilize them, and be certain that the next leg of your transportation from departure to destination is properly arranged.

Another factor to consider is possible harm to one's physical health. Drink only bottled water. Avoid fresh salads or any food that has been washed with tap water and not cooked before consumption. Eat in the best restaurants that you can afford and try to eat food that has been thoroughly cooked. In most countries it takes at least six months before your body is capable of developing a degree of immunity to the local microorganisms. Be certain to get all recommended immunizations and vaccinations.

Business Protocol

Greetings and etiquette

Shaking hands has become an almost universally-accepted greeting among international businesspersons, and shaking hands with male Indian business representatives is an acceptable practice. However, Indians utilize another common greeting, the namaste gesture. This involves placing the hands together with fingers pointed up, bowing slightly, and saying "*namaste*," which in Sanskrit means, "I bow to the divine in you."

When introductions occur between men and women in India, be cautious and wait—usually there is no physical contact. Hindus and Muslims both have prohibitions against physical contact with the opposite sex. If a Muslim touches or is touched by the opposite sex, he must go through a ritual purification before his next prayer. These prohibitions are often taken very seriously. If an Indian woman does not offer her hand, a polite half bow or a simple hello is appropriate.

Titles and professional designations are very important, and should always be used. The person who is oldest or has the most status should be introduced first. First names are only used among close friends. Business cards are exchanged in the usual fashion and there is no need to have them translated. Personal questions should not be asked unless the individual is a close friend or associate.

Indians do not normally use good morning, good night, and goodbye types of greetings, and thank you is not a part of their etiquette. They might instead say *"namaste"* in an especially humble way, the tone suggesting the appreciation they are trying to convey. Traditional greetings are important and are appreciated. Muslims often greet each other with an Arabic phrase (*assalaom aleikum*), with a bow, and with hands held palms together under the chin. A Muslim may also use a secular greeting, *aadab arz* (I offer you my greeting). This is done while raising one's right hand, with the palm facing inward and to the forehead as in a salute.

Time

India is a polychronic culture. The business or private sector tends to be more punctual and time oriented than the public governmental sector. Punctuality has never been a high priority. The Indian concept of time has emerged from centuries of a less measured and almost fatalistic approach to life. They do not believe that hurrying or promptness will change anything.

Normal business hours are from 9:30 AM to 5 PM, but it is not uncommon for junior and mid-level Indian businessman to work as late as 10 PM, and then go out for dinner. The next morning they may not start work until 10 AM. Senior employees tend to work from 11 AM to 6 PM.

Indian businessmen do expect foreign businessmen to be on time, which can be attributed to the still-prevailing British influence. There are also numerous holidays and one needs to be cognizant of that factor when scheduling appointments.

Gifts

Gift giving in every culture walks a fine line between bribery and thoughtful, sincere, good business practices. *Baksheesh*, or bribery, is a tricky dance in the complicated maze of Indian bureaucracies. Bribery is illegal and is publicly condemned; therefore anyone who engages in it might be arrested and there are periodic crackdowns and arrests. Nevertheless, *Baksheesh* remains a factor in the way business is often done in India. The gift of money is sometimes used to finalize a transaction. In reality, if one seems too concerned about propriety, one may miss out on investment opportunities. Quite often the monetary values may be insignificant, but gifts are often necessary to keep people motivated and the wheels of business turning. It is acceptable to give a business associate a gift. Nevertheless one must be aware that codes of conduct in this regard vary by region of the country and the sector of the economy being dealt with. Also, tact should always be used when presenting a gift.

A good rule of thumb is that a gift given to someone in government should be rather small and inexpensive. More elaborate gifts can be given to facilitate private-sector transactions. When presenting a gift, remember the colors black and white are considered unlucky, green, and red are associated with positive imagery, and that yellow and orange are associated with spiritual beliefs. So, it is safest to wrap your gifts in red and green. Flowers, Indian sweets, and food make good gifts. The gift is usually not opened in the giver's presence.

Business entertainment

Business entertainment is a more generally accepted persuasion tactic than gift giving. It has fewer negative connotations, and is more widely appreciated as a normal part of business relations.

The main factors to consider with business entertaining is to be cognizant of religious and regional prohibitions. It is not just remembering that Muslims will not eat pork and Hindus won't eat beef. There are other subtle cultural nuances that vary within each region of India. An ounce of research into these regional sensitivities will be worth pounds of goodwill over the long haul.

In general, lunches are preferable for business. Indian breakfasts and dinners tend to be private and family-oriented affairs. Tea and small talk normally precede the introduction of the business agenda.

It is permissible to drink alcohol (although not with Muslims), but it is not advisable to do so with anyone. Most Indians will be comfortable with a vegetarian menu. Private clubs or restaurants that provide an air of exclusivity and elegance will be the most appreciated. It is customary to be slightly tardy for business meals.

During the meal it is customary for the host to repeatedly inquire as to whether or not the guests are being accommodated in terms of food and drink. The traditional Indian response is the *namaste*. This gesture is used to indicate when one is sated.

When the meal is complete, do not be overly profuse in expressing gratitude. It can be misinterpreted; it is best to error on the side of understatement. Reciprocity is always appreciated, and is the safest form of gratitude. Your Indian counterpart will almost always offer to pay, and may be quite insistent, but this is an expected and ritualized gesture on his part.

Evening entertainment is also quite common in India. Membership only nightclubs are prestigious and popular for men. Normally, a driver will be provided. Appropriate eveningwear for men is casual long pants and a short-sleeve shirt.

Some American businesspersons have found that it is preferable to minimize both gift giving and business entertaining in India. Faced with the Foreign Corrupt Practices Act back home, they are obliged in many instances to say no to officials who expect under-the-table forms of remuneration.

Dress

Western attire, with the exception of leather products, is proper for all business meetings. Western women should wear conservative clothing; business suits are fine. Western women should avoid clothing that is flashy or shows too much skin and stay away from yellow and orange colors. Many Indians will themselves wear western-style business suits and ties. Light suits in light colors are preferable, particularly in the hotter regions.

Some Indians will wear traditional garb, which may include a turban, or a *dhoti*, a single length of cloth wrapped around the body. More prominent Indians may wear the sherwoni, a long coat traditionally worn by rajahs or government officials. In many larger cities, traditional robes that conceal the face and body of Indian women have been replaced with more western-style garments. Indian women currently wear a mix of ethnic, regional, and traditional Indian garments, as well as Western styles of attire. Traditional Indian garments can reveal the region a person comes from, the traditions that region represents, the language, and what caste she is a member of. The manner in which a woman's garment is wrapped and colored also reveals elements of status and class. The dot on Indian women's foreheads is not a caste mark, but is simply an adornment.

Communication Style

Business language

Anyone who spends time in India begins to discover that the elements of dress, language, food, and customs change as you move from one region to another. The Constitution of India recognizes 15 official languages. Hindi has been, and still is, promoted as the national language, but it is useless in Southern India, where there is almost violent opposition to its usage. English functions as a neutral language link between the different regions of the country, and is the most common business language. While only 10% of the population speak it fluently, it is very common for Indian businessmen to speak English. Translators are therefore rarely needed.

India is a **high-context culture** with a rather passive aggressive style. They prefer to communicate in a climate conducive to harmony and congeniality. Their communication patterns involve numerous subtleties. Like many other Asian cultures, they seldom say no, and will endeavor to avoid a negative response since they view it as brusque and impolite.

Non-verbal communication

India is a diverse multicultural nation. However, there are some cultural taboos in the non-verbal domain that the majority of the Indian population observes. Indians point with their chins, never with their fingers. When they wish to beckon someone, they put their hand out palm-down, and make a scooping motion with their fingers. They use their left hand for personal hygiene tasks, and therefore do not touch food or other people with their left hand. Indians do not touch each other on the head or the ears; the head is the seat of the soul, and the ears are sacred appendages. The feet are considered unclean. When sitting, keep them flat on the floor and try not to let them come in contact with another person. When an Indian attempts to walk through a room full of seated people, he/she will try very hard not to step over anyone. If Indians stands with their hands on their hips, everyone assume they are angry and sending an aggressive message. Indians normally stand 3 feet apart when conversing. They frown on any displays of public affection. Whistling is considered impolite, and winking is considered not only impolite, but also sexually suggestive and insulting. They tend to have a high level of eye contact. Southern Indians move their head from left-to-right several times while their face always remains forward to non-verbally indicate "yes." This style of indicating "yes" is very similar to the USA method of indicating "no." Although not exactly the same, it is often mistakenly interpreted as a "no" by Americans.

The Indian Concept of Negotiations

Selecting personnel

The Indians will select individuals who display coolness under fire. They look for resilient people who are flexible and capable of compromise. Indian negotiators usually are very realistic in their definition of the bottom line, and they are masters of understatement. They try not to show emotion, seeing it as a weakness, and generally try to turn the emotional element to their advantage.

However, they are relationship builders and will strive to establish rapport, so if possible everyone can enjoy a win-win situation. Indians tend to view the negotiating process as a mutually beneficial problem-solving event. The Gandhian principle of "firmness for a good cause" is deeply ingrained.

As in many cultures, it is a common practice for foreign corporations to hire an intermediary. The connections this person has may determine the success or failure of the entire venture. It is through this intermediary that introductions will be made, doors will be opened, and the pervasive nepotism dealt with.

Status is a critical factor in the Indian organizational pyramid. Many companies are family-owned, and status is determined by lineage. Leadership in most Indian companies is selected from within a controlling family's extended membership. Indians value technology, and they will always try to include technical expertise on their negotiating team.

Your team should include a technical expert, a high-ranking company executive, an Indian cultural expert, and a great negotiator. Other members of your team should be associated with the tasks necessary to complete the negotiations.

Negotiating style

The Indian negotiating style has been honed for thousands of years. It comes out of a lengthy history of sharp bartering in the marketplace. Their style is non-confrontational and relaxed. They are patient, amiable, low key, and are usually formal and procedurally sound. They exude an aura of humility and shun high-pressure tactics.

In keeping with this negotiating posture, it follows that Indians correlate loudness with dishonesty. Throughout their culture, loud and aggressive people are viewed as dishonest and untrustworthy hucksters.

Technical expertise is greatly admired by Indians. Therefore any presentation that features technical expertise will automatically appeal to them. If you are prepared to offer competitive technology, and technical follow-up assistance, they will find it very appealing.

Issues discussed

Initially, relationship-based issues will be paramount. Indian negotiations will evolve out of the establishment of rapport and camaraderie. Once friendships are established, the substantive issues will follow. However, often several meetings are necessary before substantial issues are discussed. Infrastructure services, governmental regulations, and the availability of credit are other issues that might be discussed.

Establishing trust

Trust is a by-product of relationship building. With Indians trust is earned through the development of both a business and a personal relationship. During relationship building they will be watching and evaluating you. The two parties can talk about business as well as family, children, culture, art, cricket, soccer and other subjects that reveal personalities and character in order to establish a working relationship. Ask your colleagues what is *pukka* or the proper thing to do.

Indians may wish to start with a minor transaction. Once trust is established, they may expand the business dealings.

Persuasion

You will have a chance to be persuasive if you come thoroughly prepared, if you can maintain a patient low-key demeanor, and if you can offer a technically-sound product. If you are capable of accomplishing these, you will be mirroring back to the Indians the very attributes they are cultivating in themselves. Your presentation should be understated; Indians despise arrogance.

The specific persuasion tactics that are likely to be effective in India are:

1) Indians will be impressed with logical and factual presentations that are accompanied by supportive documentation.
2) **Build trust through information sharing**. Indians will expect a healthy exchange of information.
3) Receiving the **technical specifications up-front** or in the beginning of the negotiation is a good idea in India.
4) Indians will use **stalling** tactics, so plan on it, and use a few of your own.
5) **Take copious notes**, and try to get even preliminary arguments **in writing**. Concrete steps like this will almost always provide the structure you will later need in formulating the final contract.
6) Your team should decide in advance where you are going to draw the line on dealing with *Baksheesh*. Sometimes it is better to let them know that you would rather have no deal, than a bad deal, but don't get self-righteous.
7) Indians are masters at influence peddling, and indeed you will undoubtedly need some of it. Play the same game; let them know you have influence too, and that you are willing to use it propitiously.
8) Indians like to **haggle** a little bit and at times can be quite lively while doing so. Distributive bargaining is a big part of their daily lives. Indians will usually **"high-ball" or "low-ball"** a deal.
9) **Diffusion questions** are often used since direct conflict should be avoided.
10) **Metaphors, stories and analogies** are a good idea in India.
11) **Fatalistic reasoning** can be used effectively to build rapport and give minor support to one's arguments. It is also effective when technical details are not available or are circumspect. For example, "We were destined to do business."
12) India is a hierarchical as well as collectivist society. Referring to the approval of others and especially the approval of respected higher authorities in regards to your company, product, etc. should prove to be an effective method of persuasion.
13) Indian businesspeople tend to be fairly analytical. Summarizing previously agreed upon benefits or listing the pros and cons of the agreement can be an effective persuasion method in India.

Tactics to avoid include:

1) Indians dislike the words "no" and "I." Avoid their use while interacting and attempting to persuade. For example, never say "No, that is a bad idea. I think you should do this."
2) Do not hurry, speak quickly or raise your voice. These tactics are viewed as low-class and are usually reserved for bargaining at flee markets, etc.
3) Do not brag. Humility is viewed as a positive trait in India.

Resolving disputes

Indians have a different orientation toward time than most westerners, and this can be an area of potential conflict. Time lines will have to be gone over again and again. Indians desire harmonious relationships and favor an unhurried pace, while westerners are more motivated by the time-is-money mantra. Indians are realists, and they are willing to compromise. They will be open to any approach that offers equal benefits for all. Indians are competitive, and they tend to have high individual aspirations. This would seem to indicate that they might place their own success ahead of the team. However, most Indian companies are family-owned and defections from family commitments are rare.

Risk

India is a culture that is steeped in the belief that life is an unending cycle of birth, death, and rebirth. Most Indians believe in reincarnation and Karma, which gives them a fatalistic orientation toward life. This belief system allows them some latitude in taking risks, for it gives them a degree of emotional freedom—they are not going to take it so personally if they fail. They are not so worried about saving face that they are unwilling to take some risks in an effort to succeed.

Decision making

India's current organizational and business framework evolved out of a patriarchal and extended-family network. Decision-making patterns are always top down. In the top-down decision making model, subordinates do not question those in authority.

Types of agreement

Corruption is prevalent in India and its presence can be an obstacle to reaching an agreement. The government bureaucracy is cumbersome and can impede the swift transactions that are possible in today's computerized global marketplace. However, India wants to change and is changing.

The Indian legal system is well developed and is based upon British jurisprudence. Oral agreements are considered binding, so be circumspect and careful when making oral commitments.

India is one of the world's most heterogeneous cultures, and all retail markets are locally owned. Its telecommunication system is still being developed. The majority of their population is basically illiterate. All of these factors militate against successful networking agreements. Immense market potential beckons, but remember distribution channels are limited, particularly in the rural extremities.

Indian businessmen prefer written agreements that are working documents, rather than binding contracts. Written agreements that broadly outline the nature of the undertaking appeal to them more than legalese jargon. They are practical businessmen, and they believe that once operations are underway, the finer points of the agreement can be spelled out. This of course ties in with their need for relationship-based organizational networking.

NOTES:

Chapter 14

Indonesia

- *Country Background*
- *The Indonesian Culture*
- *Business Protocol*
- *Communication Style*
- *The Indonesian Concept of Negotiations*

The Republic of Indonesia, the largest archipelago nation in the world, consists of 13,667 islands, 6000 of which are inhabited. It has a land area of 1.9 million square kilometers (733,590 square miles). The islands stretch over more than one-tenth of the Equator between Southeast Asia and Australia. The archipelago, also known as *tonah air*, which literally means 'land and water' but is understood as 'fatherland,' stretches across an area longer than the United States.

Since Indonesia straddles the equator, the climate is hot and humid and runs from wet to relatively dry, varying with location and season. Five islands make up 90% of the Indonesian land area. They are Kalimantan (the southern two thirds of Borneo), Sumatra, Irian Jaya (the western half of New Guinea), Sulawesi, and Java. Although Java makes up only 7% of the country, it is inhabited by 40% of the Indonesian population. Java is the most densely populated island in the world. The largest city, capital, and center of trade is Jakarta, with over 10 million people.

Country Background

History

The Indonesian archipelago has been populated for thousands of years. The earliest settlers were probably people from Malaysia. Fragmentary stone and metal inscriptions dating to the beginning of the fifth century AD indicate influence from India. The Hindu kingdoms had a flourishing trade and commercial relations with the Chinese. As these commercial contacts developed, the Indonesian culture absorbed various foreign influences and converted them into an indigenous mosaic
.

The introduction of Islam into the archipelago was closely tied to the rise of the city of Malacca, which was founded on the Malay Peninsula about 1400. From its founding to its capitulation to the Portuguese, Malacca was a major center of Southeast Asian commercial activity, and it also became a focal point of the Islamic faith. Islam spread from Malacca to Java and then to eastern Indonesia.

In the late sixteenth century other European powers, such as the Spanish, English and Dutch began to encroach. Within a century, the Dutch had won commercial predominance over their European rivals, and in increasing measure affected Indonesian historical development for the next several hundred years.

The Dutch came to Indonesia, like the Portuguese, to develop a monopoly over the spices of the Malaccas (i.e., Malaysia and Indonesia). The Netherlands' government blended Dutch merchant interests into the United East India Company, which was chartered in 1602 and became increasingly involved in the politics of the archipelago. Nationalist sentiments grew during the nineteenth and early twentieth century, but the Dutch maintained control until World War II. Under Japanese rule, Indonesian nationalism grew more rapidly to maturity. With the Japanese surrender to the allies in 1945, the nationalist leaders declared Indonesia to be an independent republic. A government was set up under Sukarno's presidency. Shortly afterward, Dutch troops arrived to reclaim their colony and the stage was set for the revolutionary struggle that fluctuated between negotiation and open conflict for the next four years.

On Dec. 27, 1949, the Netherlands transferred sovereignty to the new nation. President Sukarno led Indonesia from 1945 to 1965. During these years, the economy declined and Indonesia's close ties with the communist bloc discouraged assistance from western nations. In 1965, an anti-communist coupe was accomplished by the military under General Suharto, who executed hundreds of thousands, many of whom were ethnic Chinese.

Suharto looked to the west for economic aid and encouraged foreign investment. Elections held in 1968 gave Suharto the presidency. His Golkar party and total elimination of all opposition gave him victories in all ensuing elections for the next 30 years. Suharto was pressured into resigning in 1998 due to the Asian financial crisis, which caused widespread poverty and amplified dissatisfaction with the corruption and oppression that marked his rule.

Government

The government of Indonesia was structured as a unitary republic. The 1945 constitution vested highest authority in the People's Consultative Assembly (MPR-*Majelis Permusyaworaton Rakyat*), but the governmental system went through a gradual evolution. What emerged out of the internal strife and power struggle was a highly centralized system of presidential government.

The Indonesian Constitution divides the powers of the state into the executive, legislative, and judicial categories, but without expressly providing for checks and balances. The president is the chief executive and the supreme commander of the armed forces. He is elected indirectly every five years by the MPR and is eligible for re-election. The president is answerable only to the MPR that meets once every five years. In times of emergency he may declare martial law and issue emergency ordinance. The president may also exercise the power to declare war, make peace and conclude treaties with foreign states and change or abolish administrative agencies by decree.

The Indonesian constitution assigns judicial authority to the Supreme Court and other courts established by statute. There are four types of courts: general, religious, military, and administrative. Indonesia has a very complicated legal system involving 3 kinds of law; adat (customary law), Islamic law, and the Dutch-imported European law.

The Indonesian General Elections Act was adopted in 1969; a person must be 17 years of age to vote and 21 years of age to hold any public office. They must be able to speak the Indonesian language and read and write. By law certain categories of individuals are not permitted to vote or to stand for election. Principally among these are former members of the Indonesian Communist Party or members of any other organization outlawed by the government. The responsibility for determining who is eligible to vote is under the command of the *KOPKAMTIB* (the powerful military agency for domestic security and intelligence). All candidates for office also had to be approved by the military. Much pressure from students and others may end some of the military's powerful prerogatives.

Demographics

Population exceeds 228 million, the fourth largest in the world. The population growth rate is high—1.6%. Life expectancy is 66 years for males and 71 years for females. Literacy rates are 90% for males and 78% for females.

As a geographically divided archipelago with many diverse ethnic and religious groups, Indonesia struggles to maintain unity. People of Malaysian ancestry, who migrated to Indonesia in several different waves over the past 3000 years, make up the majority of Indonesia's population, and are considered to be indigenous. Indigenous Indonesians can be subdivided into Javanese (45%), Sundanese (14%), Madurese, Buginese, Batak, Doyak, Balinese, Minangkabau as well as a number of others. The Chinese constitute the largest number of nonindigenous-Indonesians (appox. 5%). Some nonindigenous-Chinese-Indonesian families have lived in Indonesia for 300 years.

Economy

Industrial output has been based on diverse natural resources, including crude oil, natural gas, timber, metals, and coal. Petroleum production and the mining of hard metals are highly developed industries in Indonesia. These areas evolved as self-contained operations that had little impact on the other sectors of the economy and the benefits of these resources were not directly accessible to the general population. Wealth has been channeled to those at the top.

Plantation crops, rubber, palm oil, textiles and plywood are also critical to the Indonesian economy. Agricultural products include rice, cassava (tapioca), peanuts, rubber, cocoa, coffee, palm oil, copra, poultry, beef, pork, eggs and a variety of tropical products, but agriculture constitutes only 17% of the nation's GDP.

In 1997 a severe economic recession crippled a number of Asian rim national economies including Indonesia's. Within a period of months the Indonesian stock market and the value of the rupiah went into a free fall. At its low point, the rupiah had lost 80% of its value. The rupiah has recovered a bit, but the economy is still weak.

Exports consist of oil, gas, wood, textiles, furniture, and rubber. Imports are likely to be machinery, chemicals, fuel, and foodstuffs. Indonesia's total work force is approximately 99 million. According to official figures, unemployment is about 15-20%, but others have even higher estimates. Japan is Indonesia's most important trade partner (21% of exports and 12% of imports) and supplier of aid, the USA is second, and Singapore is third, followed by the EU and Korea.

The Indonesian Culture

Language

The Republic of Indonesia has designated Bahasa Indonesian as the official language. Written in the Roman alphabet, Bahasa Indonesian evolved out of the "market Malay" trade language used throughout the region during the colonial era. The selection of Bahasa Indonesian as the official tongue was a conscious effort to unify all Indonesians; as a trade language, it did not have the literary history or prestige of other Indonesian tongues (notably Javanese). All advertising, media, and official communications are required to be in Bahasa Indonesian, and it is taught in all elementary schools. Bahasa Indonesian is similar to the national language of neighboring Malaysia, which is called Bahasa Malaysian. However, Malaysia was a British colony so English influenced Bahasa Malaysian. Indonesia was a Dutch colony so the Dutch language influenced Bahasa Indonesian.

Religion

Early traders and settlers brought Hinduism and Buddhism to Indonesia and the Majapahit Empire merged the two into a single state religion. Islam arrived in the sixteenth century, and eventually became Indonesia's major religion (88% of populaion). As with earlier religions, the Indonesians adapted Islam to suit their needs, especially on the island of Java. Indonesia is the world's most populous Islamic nation. However, Islam in Indonesia is fragmented into numerous sects, many of which are antagonistic toward other Islamic sects, both inside and outside of Indonesia. Most of the Muslim population lives on the island of Java. Hinduism is practiced by only 2 percent of the population, mostly on the island of Bali. The Chinese population tends to follow Buddhist-Taoist or Christian teachings. Some tribes in remote areas still practice their traditional religions. About 8% of the population are Christians.

Value system

For centuries Indonesia was a society heavily influenced by life in small villages, where members were jointly responsible for the common welfare and the public order. In Indonesian thinking, the primary community is the village.

In the villages of Indonesia today, certain features of the original social organization remain. Members of the community are still responsible for the common welfare. This includes the obligation to help one another in times of distress. The village headman has the role of being the guardian of tradition. His stature as headman is determined by two factors: length of residence in the village and amount and type of land held. The highest status is gained from the control of food-producing lands, notably paddy fields.

As Indonesia became urbanized, new forms of status developed. The village man with the most contacts in the large urban centers was accorded prestige and patronage for his influence and social control. When Indonesia formed a constitution and elected representatives, this was the sort of man each village elected as a representative.

Indonesians also have brought with them from their lives in the village a strong belief in the supernatural for protection and security. This faith goes beyond any one religion, although most Indonesians are at least nominally Muslims. This faith in the supernatural retains elements that pre-date Hinduism, Buddhism, Islam and Christianity. Many government officials and entrepreneurs adhere to a mystical form of spirituality called Kerbatinan, a metaphysical search for inner harmony and guidance in decision making.

The majority of Indonesian business people are Chinese. They place considerable value upon work, family, education and the accumulation of wealth. Modernization has also affected the values of urban Indonesians. Television and movies, as well as magazines and newspapers, have had impact.

Class structure / Stratification

Indonesia is a hierarchical and socially complex society. Internal divisions within groups further complicate the multiplicity of ethnic groups, each with a different basis for social organization and kinship structure. A growing number of landless peasants combined with limited urban resources mean that dispossessed migrating peasants simply join the marginally-subsistent urban poor. Social divisions and pervasive poverty have lead to violence and riots, which is out of character for most Indonesians.

Among the Chinese Indonesians, external cohesiveness is balanced by a clear internal differentiation between the Totok, those who retain a strong affinity for China, speak a Chinese regional dialect, follow Chinese religious practices, and are generally of pure Chinese ancestry, and the Peranakan, a larger group who have been in Indonesia for generations, speak Bahasa Indonesian or a local language by preference, and have a mixed Sino-Indonesian ancestry. Social stratification among the Chinese is based on education and wealth, primarily the latter. A very wealthy man is respected in the Chinese community whether he is educated or not. Social mobility in the Chinese community is linked to the fortunes of retail trade where relatively great wealth can be quickly amassed or lost.

Among urban Indonesians, lifestyles range from the elites to the homeless. The elites often participate in a westernized regional lifestyle with private country clubs, gated and guarded homes, gardeners, maids, etc. Among the elites, knowledge of one western language, preferably English, is considered desirable, and a degree from a western university carries with it a considerable amount of prestige. The upper echelons of the military and the bureaucracy, along with top businessmen (who are often the same people), make up the largest number of the elite. The latest additions to the well off are the technocrats, whose education and expertise have provided impetus to the industrialization of the country.

Over the past 30 years there has been a rapid growth in the number of educated people. Students are often educated at considerable sacrifice on the part of their parents and sometimes extended family. The sacrifice provides the young person with access to the government bureaucracy, the officer corps of the military, or a profession.

The great mass of the urban unskilled workers live in substandard housing even by third world standards. The neighborhoods are usually composed of individuals from the same ethnic or religious group, or of migrants from a single rural locality. The urban *Kampung* begins as a squatter settlement in an area behind the houses of a city block. Within this enclosure amenities are either inadequate or totally absent. The larger metropolitan areas also have significant populations of homeless beggars, vagrants, and thieves.

In most Indonesian organizations there is a strong authoritarian hierarchy structure that demands the obedience of subordinates. Although there are ethnic identities, there is also a strong national identity that is taught to all children in the primary school years. The husband is considered the head of the household but the wife is not considered to be of inferior status, and both are expected to cooperate in maintaining their household and family.

Safety

Remember to get all of the vaccinations and immunizations that are recommended for travel in this part of the world. Don't eat raw foods that haven't been cooked or that have been washed in local tap water. Carry or purchase bottled water or use purification pills. You will need to drink plenty of water because the hot humid climate can easily cause dehydration.

Minor crimes such as pick pocketing, con games and minor thefts occur in popular tourist sites throughout the country. Carjacking and breaking-and-entering can also occur.

Business Protocol

Greetings and etiquette

Indonesian greetings and business etiquette is **highly formal**. One should take time when exchanging greetings with Indonesians. A hurried introduction may be interpreted as showing a lack of respect. Most Indonesian **handshakes are more like handclasps; they are rather limp and usually last around 10 seconds**. For special emphasis, the handshake can be intensified by placing one's hand over the heart.

Most ethnic Indonesians are Muslim or Hindu. Traditionally there is no physical contact between men and women in these traditions. However, if a westernized Indonesian man or woman offers to shake hands, it is advisable to do so. Among Indonesian Chinese, a handshake and/or a bow is appropriate. The traditional Muslim Indonesian salutation is to use the world *selamat* or *Salom* and place one's hands together in front of one's body and bow from the waist. Among all ethnic groups, public displays of affection, even kissing on the cheek, is considered unacceptable.

After introductions have been made, the visiting businessperson can **offer his or her card to each person present**. The preferred method is to present your card using your right hand, or by using both hands. When you give your card to a recipient be sure the print is facing them so they can read it. The recipient will receive the card using both hands. He will look at it very carefully before putting it away. You should do the same when a card is given to you. Never put a business card in the back pocket or write upon a business card; either action might be misconstrued as a defilement of a card. Your business card should be printed in Bahasa Indonesian, English and possibly Chinese since ethnic Chinese constitute the majority of Indonesian business people. Your card should contain as much information as possible, including your business title and qualifications.

When being introduced use their **title and their last name** or **Mr., Madam, Mrs., or Miss**, plus their name. Names are considered sacred by most Indonesians, so it is important to pronounce it correctly. Many Indonesians have only one name.

Time

Indonesians are **polychronic**, but they are generally **punctual for business** appointments. Indonesians expect foreign business people to be on time for business appointments, especially when meeting someone of higher rank or social standing. The Indonesian term *Jom haret* (rubber time) refers to their cultural attitude toward time. For any event other than a business meeting, one can expect Indonesians to be late. The **casual attitude toward time** allows for appointments on short notice. However, large corporations may require the scheduling of appointments more than one week in advance. The typical workweek runs Monday through Thursday 8 AM to 4 PM, then half days on Friday and Saturday mornings. Muslims will take at least one hour off on Friday to pray. Observant Muslims will fast from dawn to sundown during the month of Ramahdan. One should be careful not to eat or drink in front of a fasting Indonesian Muslim.

Gifts

Gifts are a traditional part of Indonesian culture. The giving of gifts is more important than the gift itself. Gifts are given to celebrate a variety of occasions: when one returns from a trip, when one is invited to an Indonesian home, when a visitor comes to tour your office or workplace, and often for services rendered. Within the Chinese culture one can expect the recipient to decline the gift several times as a matter of etiquette before finally accepting it. If they accept your gift they will put it aside until you have left. Once they have accepted your gift, it is important to tell them you are pleased that they have done so. If they were to open your gift immediately this would imply that they are impatient or greedy. Food makes a good gift for many occasions. However, avoid bringing food to a dinner party; to do so would imply that the host couldn't provide enough. Cassette tapes of songbirds make good gifts for Indonesian bird enthusiasts.

Beware of certain cultural prohibitions in the giving of gifts. For instance, do not give pork or alcohol to a practicing Muslim. Also do not give a toy dog or pictures of a dog since Indonesian Muslims think a dog is unclean. For the Chinese, do not give gifts of straw sandals, clocks, a stork, handkerchiefs, or gifts (or wrapping paper) where the predominant color is white, black, or blue. All of these are associated with funerals by the Indonesian Chinese. Also, gifts that suggest the severing of a relationship such as knives, scissors, or other cutting tools should be avoided. If giving flowers, give an equal number since odd numbers are considered to be unlucky. For the Hindu, all leather products are inappropriate since they do not eat beef or use cattle products.

Business Entertainment

In Asian cultures, business entertainment is a cultivated art. **Business lunches and dinners** are usually arranged personally and over the phone and later confirmed by one's secretary. Whoever made the invitation and reservation usually pays. Do not order the most expensive item on the menu, unless your host insists. It is **customary to have a drink** before sitting down to eat. Food is usually served buffet style.

Once a pleasant atmosphere is established and soup has been served, business might be discussed. At more formal occasions, seating will be arranged and prominent guests will be introduced. A guest speaker is often the highlight. Light entertainment might be provided. Business events of this nature are the basis for relationship building, which sets the stage for business opportunities.

Jakarta nightlife has a lot to offer. For protracted business dealings, it is quite common to engage in an evening of **social activities that include dinner, drink, dancing** etc. Hostess bars, *karaoke*, and disco clubs seem to be favorites. Toasting is expected. Please keep in mind that traditional Islamic followers will refrain from drinking alcohol.

Avoid discussing politics, religion, and local problems in Indonesia. Some good subjects to discuss include third party business transactions, family, local attractions and sports.

Dress

Because Indonesia is hot and humid all year long, business dress tends to be **casual**. Standard formal office wear for **men is dark trousers and a light colored long-sleeved shirt and tie, without a jacket**. Many businessmen wear a short-sleeved shirt with no tie. **Businesswomen wear long- sleeved blouses and skirts**. Stockings and business suits are reserved for more formal occasions. One should dress conservatively until the degree of formality can be determined. Foreign businesswomen should wear a standard western business suit if an invitation specifies a "lounge suit". Jeans and open-necked batik shirts are appropriate casual wear. Shorts should be avoided. Women can wear sandals to most occasions. On entering homes, shoes are removed. Clothing colors should be dark since bright and vivid colors are considered inappropriate. Muslim and Hindu sensibilities require women to wear blouses that cover at least their upper arms and skirts should be knee length or longer.

Communication Style

Business language

Indonesian is a **high-context language**. They are **comfortable with silence** and frequently are **indirect or vague**. It is considered impolite to disagree, so they rarely say "no". A foreign businessperson is expected to be perceptive and understand the difference between a polite and hesitant "yes (which really means no)" from

an actual yes. If an Indonesian qualifies a statement such as "it might be difficult," this means "no". Chinese Indonesians may indicate a "no" by sucking air through their teeth; this sound always indicates a problem. Another way of indicating "no" is to pretend the question was never asked. Bahasa Indonesian has at least twelve ways to say "no" and many ways to say, "I'm saying yes, but I mean no". These subtleties are lost in English and westerners might interpret this as being deceitful, but Indonesians are simply being polite by their own cultural standards. It is considered polite among Indonesian Chinese to offer both positive and negative options to all decisions. For example, they ask, "You want dinner or not?" This can sound somewhat aggressive to foreigners.

Indonesia has been an oppressed country for most of its entire history. Corruption and deceit have been the norm. Therefore, trust is almost never given nor expected in return. People are often afraid to say their true feelings. The educational system is very weak and training programs within firms are often nonexistent. Thus, they have a non-trusting poorly-educated work force that is afraid to say what they really mean. This effects communication. Individuals often tell long stories and end up communicating nothing at all. Later it is explained, "it was just a misunderstanding." Misunderstandings are an everyday occurrence in Indonesia. Last, most workers are accustomed to a management style that is dictatorial in nature and that uses verbal punishment as a major management tool.

Non-verbal communication

Indonesians are **very observant of non-verbal behavior**. Saving face is a very important aspect of their lives. If an Indonesian expresses anger in public then he/she has shamefully lost face and will not be trusted or respected. Losing face or being embarrassed publicly is known as *malu*. One result of *malu* mentality is that Indonesians may allow a person to make a mistake rather than risk embarrassing them by correcting them publicly. Indonesians may smile or laugh in situations that might be considered inappropriate by westerners. A smile may hide embarrassment, shyness, bitterness, discord, and/ or loss of face. Indonesians may laugh when conflict arises and are expressing anxiety, not frivolity. Some nuances in body language are considered inappropriate or even obscene, such as pounding the fist into the palm of the hand. Standing tall and erect with one's hands on one's hips is interpreted as an angry and aggressive posture. Showing the soles of the feet or shoes is considered impolite. One should never touch someone's head, including a child, because many Indonesians consider the head to be the seat of the soul. Both Muslim and Hindu Indonesians consider the left hand as unclean so one must use only the right hand to eat or accept gifts. For Indonesians it is impolite to point with the fingers. One should point with one's right thumb and a closed fist, (like a hitchhiker). This gesture is also used to mean, "You go first". To beckon someone hold out the hand palm-downward and make a scooping motion with the fingers. Beckoning to someone in the western way with the palm upward and wagging a finger can be taken as an insult.

Indonesian Concept of Negotiations

Negotiating style

Indonesians prefer to do business only with people they know and like. The establishment of a **business relationship** takes time but it is vital for the success of the enterprise. The pace of business negotiations in Indonesia is slow. To complete a business deal, one should expect to make several trips over a period of months. Indonesians expect to take their guest out to dinner and get acquainted in a social setting. Thereby they are able to judge what type of people they are dealing with.

They tend to prefer a **"big-picture" negotiating posture rather than a point-by-point approach**. The "big-picture" approach allows them to be more subjective, flexible, change their minds, and to rely on their feelings and their desire for harmony. Those with higher education or who have been educated abroad will be more objective when negotiating and will be more comfortable with a point-by-point approach, although they will still prefer a big-picture system of logic.

Government intervention can impact negotiations. The Indonesian constitution gives governmental agencies dictatorial control over all natural resources and the right to intervene in any and all business arrangements. A legitimate licensing fee versus a bribe to a government bureaucrat to avoid governmental intervention is a very "gray" area.

Issues discussed

Indonesians prefer to discuss **relationship-based issues first**. For them, business negotiations are best approached as a meeting among friends. They prefer to discuss generalized topics that are only **indirectly related to organizational success**.

After a relationship is established, they will **start** to discuss **substantive** issues in an indirect manner. Then issues such as pricing, time lines, production schedule, etc. will be discussed in a friendly but aggressive manner. Be prepared for **haggling, long-winded stories, distraction and more**. The Indonesians are good negotiators, they enjoy the process, and they are great at stalling/taking their time. Thus, you will need to discuss many relationship-based issues at the beginning and throughout the negotiations. Then you can participate in a long and tough, **although very friendly**, negotiation.

Selecting personnel

Indonesians show considerable deference to a superior; they are impressed by **experience, rank, age, and wealth**. The sex of the personnel is an important consideration. As in most Asian cultures, males are considered more proficient and superior to females, particularly when it comes to business matters. Therefore, the negotiating team that an Indonesian firm will select, and your firm should attempt to mirror, will tend to be **male, older, educated, able to listen, work harmoniously with colleagues, and always defer to superiors**.

Groups and individual dynamics

The well-being of the **group** outweighs the importance of the individual in the Indonesia value system. Indonesians tend to socialize in large groups (i.e., 6 to 20 individuals) rather than smaller groups (i.e., 3 to 5 Individuals). Individuals will not speak up against each other in public. To do so would cause both parties to lose face.

When dealing with Indonesians **individually they tend to loose their allegiance to their group** (e.g., the Indonesian government). This type of behavior occurs in almost all cultures. However, the swing in allegiance is often more pronounced in Indonesia. If you need someone to give you a decision that is contradictory to the group's benefit, but is in the best interest of the individual, then attempt to negotiate with this individual separately. If you have the major decision-maker opposing you, then attempt to get a group decision (in a group setting). It is likely that the decision-maker will defer to the group's wishes in order to maintain harmony.

Indonesians are very team oriented. Indonesians tend to process information associatively. Independent thinking is discouraged in their educational system. Therefore, consensus, hierarchy and long-term harmonious relationships are highly desirable.

Establishing trust

Initially, Indonesians rely heavily upon their intuition in the establishment of trust. Because establishing trust is important, they engage in business entertaining, socializing, and take a long time to complete transactions. It is out of a **lasting relationship** that long-term trust is established. Because Indonesians place so much importance on personal relationships and mutual understanding, business partnerships tend to be based primarily on genuine accord, with the written contract playing a less significant role. It is therefore important that any agreement be well understood by both sides.

Risk

Indonesians are very **low** risk-takers. They have had a turbulent past with a lot of insecurities. Thus, they prefer to move slowly and cautiously. Many will consult oracles and psychics. They believe luck and good fortune are possible so they seek it out spiritually and subjectively.

Persuasion

A pushy hard-sell approach is not well received by Indonesians. **Harmonious** negotiations, the establishment of rapport, the building of a relationship, patience, and a review of the benefits to all parties will lead to desirable results. Indonesians are not swayed by step-by-step logical approaches and **subjective factors** will carry more weight.

The persuasion tactics that can be generally used with an Indonesian or will be used by Indonesians are:

1) Indonesians love to bargain and **haggle** and can be quite lively while doing so. Indonesians will almost always **"high-ball" or "low-ball"** a deal.

2) As a negotiation progresses, Indonesians may use the ploy "We are only a developing third world country" (i.e., **shaming**) and will seek compromises in their favor.

3) Indonesians like to imply that they have governmental influence or influence with important individuals. You may wish to **imply that you have influence** with certain people that are relevant to the transaction.

4) **Stalling** is a way of life in Indonesia. Although it is not always intentional, it almost always happens. Plan on it and use it to your advantage.

5) Always **get everything in writing** in Indonesia. If you do not, it will surely change.

6) Short visual presentations are best. Elaborate on-key items only. Indonesians want to enjoy the process. Aesthetic support documentation is helpful (colorful charts, etc.).

7) **Metaphors, stories and analogies** are often used in Indonesia.

8) **Personal appeals** can be useful if used in moderation.

9) Emotional tactics occur at lower-management levels.

10) **Diffusion questions and distraction tactics** are useful in times of conflict. They will be used very frequently in Indonesia.

11) Deny conflict exists.

12) Certain requests that we might consider to be **corruption** are normal business practices in Indonesia. Payment for help/favors is interwoven into the society's fabric. On a daily basis, people pay or give gifts for proprietary information, governmental assistance, etc. Decide how you plan to initiate or respond to such requests.

13) Use a **"big-picture"** strategy. Nothing is decided until everything is decided.

Tactics to avoid include:

1) Avoid direct conflict.

2) Do not use fear tactics, ultimatums, threats, yelling, etc.

3) Avoid surprises at the table. Up-front surprises promote conflict and reduce harmony. However, surprises behind the scenes are to be expected.

4) Do not self promote. Humility is considered a virtue.

5) Do not engage in extensive information sharing. Information is protected in Indonesia. Profuse information sharing is seen as foolish.

Resolving disputes

Western negotiators have to be patient and careful with their words when dealing with Indonesians. Indonesians can take an extremely long time to broker a deal. They emphasize mutual trust in their negotiations. The Indonesian approach is to **deny or avoid a problem** because it can effect harmony and jeopardize the relationship. Therefore, disputes can be difficult to resolve and one may have to take the position that no deal is better than a poor deal.

Decision making

Decision making in Indonesia is not a simple process. In most instances, decisions are made from the **top-down**. Authority and hierarchy are a way of life in Indonesia. However, consensus-seeking has deep historical roots within the Indonesian society. This model was first developed in the villages where all interested parties were welcome to participate. They strived for balance and conciliation without resentments or grudges. Based on these historical values, a **consensus is often sought** with input from all segments of the organization's personnel and then the **person with the highest rank will make the decision**. On the surface, this is identical to **top-down-consensus** decision-making in Mainland China. However, unlike China, the group is never given any power in Indonesia. Rather the belief exists that the headman will do what is best for the society or firm. In many ways, although for different reasons, the Indonesian decision-making style is much like that of USA. However, only verifiable facts from a USA employee are considered. Listening to anything beyond the facts is merely seen as a means of making the employee feel empowered. In contrast, an Indonesian's goal is to produce harmony within the firm via a top-down decision-making style. In addition, intuitive and spiritual guidance is often sought.

Type of agreement

A deal is never complete until all paperwork is signed. The **written contract** or oral agreement is not as important to Indonesians as the quality of the relationship and whether or not it is harmonious. A written contract is difficult to legally enforce in Indonesia. If over the course of the negotiations a **strong harmonious friendship** has developed, **then any contract inequities can be readily ironed out** so that harmony prevails.

Since Indonesians (especially the Chinese) often consult astrologers, the signing may be delayed until a "lucky" day arrives.

Contract law

Although Indonesians are receptive to international investment, there are enormous risks, for disputes will be resolved within a reputedly corrupt judicial structure. From the days when it was a Dutch colony, Indonesian Law was pluralistic. A number of heterogeneous systems of law existed side by side: European law, Oriental law and Adat (native common law). There is an unwritten rule that if parties enter into a transaction for which there is no Adat Law provision, then European Law is assumed to prevail. However, as previously mentioned, legally enforceable contracts are currently out of the question. Indonesia is not a member of the WTO (World Trade Organization) and does not accept compulsory ICJ jurisdiction.

Indonesia's multi-tiered, antiquated, legal apparatus seems to present an obstacle to international trade. Its reputedly corrupt government has resisted reform from the IMF and US Agency for International Development. A risk-averse investor would not consider Indonesia, while others may believe fortunes can be made under exactly these circumstances.

Currently, the constitution is under revision, and the legal community is reforming its body of law. A trend toward open market guidelines began in 1967 with commercial law revisions, and continued with the 1992 insurance law and the limited liability company law of 1995. The latter replaced some 400 obsolete ordinances. This trend could improve Indonesian business stability and the enforceability of contracts.

Chapter 15

Italy

- *Country Background*
- *The Italian Culture*
- *Business Protocol*
- *Communication Style*
- *The Italian Concept of Negotiations*

Italy has been a leading nation in artistic and scientific innovation, as well as the homeland of the old Roman Empire and of the Holy See (Vatican City) for many centuries. Possessing Europe's fourth largest economy (behind Germany, France, and the United Kingdom), Italy is today a leading economic power with a strong industrial base and one of the world's best tourist destinations.

Italy's central location in the Mediterranean Sea has long been a strategic advantage. Though on a peninsula with 7600 km. of coastline, Italy shares a land border with Austria, Switzerland, France, Slovenia, and San Marino in its northern areas.

Country Background

History

The early history of the Italian peninsula precedes the mighty Roman Empire, which at its height controlled much of Europe and the Mediterranean. Anthropologists have found evidence of Italic tribes that inhabited the area as early as 2000 BC. The Roman Republic (and later Empire) flourished from around 300 BC until 326 AD when Constantine moved the imperial capital from Rome to Constantinople. Following this shift of central power, Italy experienced a period of political division and instability that lasted until Italian unification in 1861.

Italy endured its dark ages between 400 and 1000 AD as rival cities and states fought each other when they did not face foreign invaders. The Renaissance, which lasted from 1300 to 1494, produced some of the world's best art and science, but Italy remained sharply divided into many city/states and a papal domain supported by France and other European nations. Foreign dominance in Italian affairs came from Germany, France, Spain, and especially Austria, Italy's strong neighbor to the north.

Considering Italian disunity and regionalism, unification took a very sudden and unlikely course. In 1860, a small force of Italian irregulars led by Giuseppe Garibaldi sailed from Genoa to liberate Sicily, and consequently, the rest of Italy. This force succeeded against all odds, and King Victor Emmanuel II became the ruler of a united Italy in 1861. Since the king and the "liberators" came from the north, northerners had a much higher

representation in Italian government than southerners for many years to come. This rift between North and South remains even today as the industrialized North and the laid-back South vie for influence and power.

Italy fought World War I alongside the Allies, and against its historical nemesis, Austria. As a result of the allied victory, Italy won back some Austrian-annexed lands. With the development of Benito Mussolini's Fascist regime, the country entered World War II unprepared, on the German side, and rather half-heartedly. This may be why the Italian military did not fare well, and why Italy was the first of the Axis powers to surrender and switch sides. Early capitulation spared Italian cities the destruction that afflicted the Japanese and German homelands. Thus, Italy emerged from World War II with less destruction than Germany, but with a weak and disheartened economy. Mass urbanization followed, with strong industrial and agricultural development, especially in the north. With some of the world's most beautiful and historic cities, Italy encouraged tourism to help the country recover economically and to regain its prestige and place in the world.

Government

Italy today is a republic with 20 administrative regions. A president and a prime minister head the executive branch. A bicameral parliament consisting of the Senate and the Chamber of Deputies makes up the legislative branch. Approximately three-fourths of each chamber is directly elected and one-fourth is elected according to regional proportional representation. Italian government has been less steady than other European governments, and many successive administrations have been plagued by corruption. Recently, however, Italian justice has taken strong measures to ensure democracy and minimize corruption.

The Constitutional Court represents the country's highest judicial branch. Italian law, originally grounded in classical Roman law, was transformed by renaissance scholarship. German and French codifications were later influential. Further changes came in the 1980s when Italy adopted an adversarial approach to its code of criminal procedure. It also then established ITALGUIR, the largest and most comprehensive legal electronic database in Europe. Italian law is currently undergoing further change brought about by European Union directives that prevail over Italian national laws.

Demographics

With an area of 301,230-sq. km., Italy is slightly larger than Arizona. The climate is primarily Mediterranean, but is Alpine in the far north while being hot and dry in the south.

Italy has a zero population growth rate with the population hovering around 56-57 million for many years. The majority of Italy's population is composed of ethnic Italians, with small German-, French-, and Slovene-Italian groups in the north, as well as small Greek and Albanian-Italian groups in the south. Life expectancy is 76 years for males and 83 years for females. The literacy rate is 98%.

Economy

The Italian economy is ranked either sixth or seventh in the world. Their per capita figure is usually in the top five. The economy has been characterized by a dramatic shift from agriculture to industry after World War II. Although heavily dependent on oil and raw material imports, Italian industry rivals even the might of German and British industry in some areas. Italian industrial products have benefited from the country's strong artistic and engineering traditions. Exotic Italian cars, for example, are some of the world's most coveted and expensive automobiles. Likewise, while the rest of European industry (excluding Germany's BMW) has completely given way to the Japanese motorcycle industry, many Italian firms still produce quality motorcycles that compete with Japanese products worldwide. The fashion industry has also benefited from Italian artistry and tradition, with Milan and other Italian cities rivaling Paris and New York as world fashion centers. Thus, the "Latin flare" reputation that accompanies Italian products has given them a distinct marketplace in Europe and across much of the world.

Italy's has consistently maintained a healthy trade surplus. Exports include textiles, clothing, motor vehicles, metals and chemicals. European Union countries lead the way with a combined 54% share of all Italian exports. The USA follows at 8% and OPEC nations at 4%. Import commodities include machinery, petroleum, chemicals, metals, food, and agricultural products. Import partners include the European Union at 56%, the USA at 5% and OPEC countries at 5% (mostly oil imports).

The national currency is the lira. However, Italy also switched to the Euro or European Currency Unit (ECU or XEU) in 1999.

The Italian Culture

Language

Italian is spoken by almost all of the population. Exceptions are some German, French, or Slovene speakers in a few northern regions. Although there are many regional dialects in Italy, all Italians can communicate with one another using the common language. Italian is the language of the Renaissance, which gives the people a sense of pride and unity, even in a strongly regionalized country. English is widely spoken by most Italian executives.

Religion

The population is predominantly Catholic. Although there is no official religion in Italy, the church has traditionally had a strong grip on the Italian social fiber. This has gradually decreased, as evident by the consistently low birth rate among Italians (9 births per 1000), which is much less than that of other Catholics worldwide. This decline in church influence is especially true in urban areas, where socialist and communist traditions date back to the 19th Century.

Value system

Family, often a large and extended one, governs the lives of most Italians. This is supported by Italy's history, which fostered a great mistrust of authority, and a feeling of "family first" among most Italians. Family loyalty transcends the great differences between the country's north and south. The industrialized north is full of private enterprises that are owned and managed by old families, while the south is heavily dependent on the public sector. Yet, family unity is strong in both parts of the country, and it transcends business and political affiliations.

Northerners are industrious, cosmopolitan and sophisticated. The business pace in Milan and Turin rivals that of London and Munich. The pace south of Rome and in Sicily is more laid-back and people are more passionate in their outward behavior. Therefore, one could say that northerners are serious, while southerners are relaxed. Likewise, northerners may prefer privacy to the southerners' openness. Most of all, the two are different in how they see each other. Northerners see southerners as being lazy, while the south accuses the north of being too serious and stuck-up for its own good. These differences have polarized social behavior and are the subject of many debates in the country today (even fostering a northern idea to secede from the overly-dependent south).

Class structure / Stratification

In addition to north/south differences, primary class differences are between the rich and the poor. Since race, language and religion are largely uniform in the country, there are few manifestations of stratification other than economic class and the power and status which accompany wealth. Like the German aristocracy, the Italian aristocracy remained fairly close to the people and historically encouraged sharecropping and more equality. Inherited titles today do not mean much more than that, and aristocrats are equal to the poor under Italian law.

Many women historically worked in Italy, and they have recently made great strides in terms of economic position and independence. The low birth rate suggests that many women today are choosing careers over raising a family. When Italy led the world in silk production a few centuries ago, women were primarily responsible for the cultivation of the silk farms. Today, women designers and fashion magnates take part in Italy's gigantic fashion industry.

Safety

Italy is one of the world's most visited countries, with millions of tourists flocking into its historical cities every year. This is heightened by an excellent visitor support system and good hotels in most of the country. Crime is relatively low except in certain enclaves that are still fighting central control. These include Sicily, which for generations has been the springboard for the Mafia and its operatives. Italian justice is waging a war to rid the country of crime and corruption, and although the cost is high at times, indications are that justice is winning the battle. Visitors should use common sense, avoid stays in areas known for crime or lawlessness, and take the usual precautions with money and valuables.

Business Protocol

Greetings and etiquette

Italians are generally warm and friendly. They treat most visitors as friends, and it is easy for them to put others at ease. **It is customary to shake hands with both men and women. Acquainted women may kiss each other on the cheek, and close male friends may hug and slap each other on the back.** It is very important, however, to always address Italians by their earned title, such as *Dottore* (doctor, or professor), or *Avvocato* (attorney). This is essential because of Italy's historical reverence for men of letters and arts.

Guests are usually introduced before the hosts, and special attention is given to the highest-ranking member of the group. It is also acceptable for someone to introduce himself, and to exchange business cards printed in English or Italian.

Time

There are two variations when it comes to the value of time in Italy: a monochronic north, and a polychronic south. **Most Italians may be considered polychronic. They prefer the finer things in life to deadlines and agendas, and they can do many things at the same time.** Northern Italian business people, especially in the industrial towns of Milan, Bologna and Turin, are very business-minded, and they usually conduct business efficiently and punctually. Pressure and deadlines do not faze the Milanese who are known worldwide for their business and industry.

Gifts

Inexpensive, but elegant gifts are appropriate in Italian business circles. These could be flowers or chocolates to secretaries, or quality illustrated books for associates. Crafts or folk items from the negotiators' country of origin always make good gifts. Promotional gifts that have a company's logo are not well appreciated in Italy. It is also a little risky to present Italians with wine or clothes, since most Italians rightfully consider themselves experts on wine and fashion, and it may be hard to satisfy their excellent taste.

As in many countries, it is inappropriate to give certain items that connote death or sadness. These include handkerchiefs, knives and certain flowers. It is best to check with local flower shops concerning the best kind of flowers to buy for each occasion.

Business entertainment

The country that contains Venice, Florence, Rome and Turin is considered by many as one of the best for business entertainment. Visitors can enjoy Rome's historical sites, view Florence's countless art treasures, or go for a gondola ride on the waterways of Venice after doing business. In addition, Italy is known for its restaurants and other entertainment venues that make it an ideal place for business entertainment.

Italians will frequently extend dinner invitations to their clients, who should oblige, even if they feel tired or full. While dining at a restaurant, the atmosphere may be very jovial in the south or subdued and delicate in northern cities. It is best to follow the lead of the host, and to keep one's hands on the table at all times. Italian wine is for sipping, not for drinking large quantities, which can be considered quite vulgar. While Italian family dinners can be large affairs, business dinners typically include only a select group. If a visitor extends the invitation, he should consult with a local expert (or ask his host's secretary) about an appropriate restaurant. The host should also try to secure good seats by slipping the waiter a generous tip *before* the meal.

Business is rarely discussed at the meal. The best topics of conversation include Italy's fascinating history and the local soccer teams. Italy has arguably the best soccer league in the world, which in turn attracts top players to play on famous Italian teams. Some of the better-known teams are AC Milan, Juventus (Turin), Lazio and Roma. The Italian National team is internationally successful, having won a total of three World Cups, second only to Brazil. When conversing about soccer, it is important to realize that most Italian males take the sport very seriously, and one should not antagonize them or side with a rival club. Conversational taboos include fascism, World War II, North-South economic and social issues, and organized crime.

Dress

Although good clothes are a measure of someone's success and status, one should keep in mind that Italy is one of the most fashion-conscious countries in the world, and it is hard to compete with Italians in this regard. Business people should always try to dress elegantly and tastefully. **Dressing conservatively in expensive suits and ties (preferably Italian-made and cut) may be the safest bet for men. Women should dress in elegant business suits** (also preferably Italian), and they should not try to "outshine" Italian women nor wear very "modern" outfits, lest they choose the wrong ones for the local fashion. Casual clothes in Italy are equally elegant and chic, so one should watch what one wears even on "off days."

Communication Style

Business language

Italians use a high-context language when communicating. They may "beat around the bush" before reaching a point as part of their tendency to save face. They may also tell their counterparts what they want to hear, rather than the truth, which may impede the relationship. Italians do not like aggressive language or threats. Instead, they value friendly prose that appeals to the parties' feelings of friendship and trust. Italians have historically enjoyed poetry, good prose and rhetoric as a means of communicating.

The majority of Italian executives speak English, but with varying degrees of proficiency. It may be necessary to hire a seasoned interpreter to help translate the contents of the meeting.

Non-verbal communication

Italians have a reputation for using **many gestures, facial expressions and other forms of non-verbal communication**. While this is true in most of the country, some northerners use very few exaggerated gestures, especially when compared to their southern countrymen. One of the most prominent features of Italian non-verbal communication is using the hands almost simultaneously with conversation. The hands sometimes seem to mirror the tone and emotion of the conversation. The more emotional an Italian, the more hand and face gestures are used. Other socially acceptable gestures include sounds such as whistling and clicking the tongue. Many of these gestures will vary regionally, so they should be taken in the context of the conversation and the individual exhibiting them. One should keep in mind, however, that high-ranking executives and business officials are less likely to exhibit many gestures when negotiating or representing their country.

The Italian Concept of Negotiations

Selecting personnel

Italian negotiators are **selected on the basis of their status and rank**. Many large and successful enterprises are still owned by closely-knit families. These extended families have executive representation and like to negotiate on behalf of their interests. This does not mean that a Mr. Ferrari will be present at Ferrari negotiations, but a member of the extended Ferrari family will probably attend or lead the negotiations. Family status alone, however, does not earn someone a place at the negotiations table. Most Italian industrial families have invested heavily in educating their heirs in running these profitable businesses, and therefore, many "family" executives have earned their rank. Considering that many on the negotiating team may not be family members, it is fair to say that knowledge and education are the other elements that make up an Italian negotiator. It is interesting to note that a certain "industrial aristocracy" has existed in northern Italy for some time. It is not unusual for members of industrial families to intermarry or work for each other.

Based on these facts, Italians may prefer to negotiate with people of rank and status. Since relationships are important, Italians may also prefer personable counterparts who show interest in Italian traditions and history. Being of Italian descent may help break the ice, especially if the person demonstrates Italian "feelings," or is related to influential people.

Negotiating style

Italian business relationships are based on **mutual dependency.** Italians believe in mutual obligation where both parties must deliver to satisfy the honor and needs of their families. These characteristics are not surprising considering the Italian city/state and family-dominated

history. The object of negotiations during these times was to enhance the position of one's family or city. When the city/states needed each other to combat outside aggressors, they formed alliances that benefited all of them. However, they have never lost their strong sense of individual identity.

Italians are also masters of skirting or bending the rules if these interfere with business or profit. One must remember that Machiavelli and his *Prince* are Italians, and this book has greatly influenced Italian thinking, especially during hard political and economic times. Machiavellianism professes that all politics are naturally corrupt, and therefore, using any means possible to achieve a solution is justifiable. Thus, opportunism and cunning may be justified means to achieve the desired result.

Realistically, Italians know that they are not the world's only shrewd negotiators and that trust is necessary for long-term benefits. That is perhaps why **relationship-building** is so important to them. The modern Italian businessperson knows that the world is a big place with an abundance of competitive services and products. Italian industry has known this for many decades, and has cultivated a niche as makers of stylish and coveted products that can sell themselves to the right market. Italians also have to negotiate for sorely-needed natural resources, as well as a variety of services and products. Building relationships helps them gain the trust of their associates, and helps guarantee fair conditions for everyone.

Issues discussed

When negotiating, most Italians will engage **in non-directive discussion and relationship-building issues**. This, however, may not be true of some younger executives from the northern part of the country, who prefer to discuss substantive issues. Since mutual dependency is important, most Italians feel it is essential to establish strong relationships with their business counterparts. This may involve "small talk," as well as inquiries about one's family, job and country.

Establishing trust

Italians largely **use intuition to establish trust with foreign negotiators**. They also measure trust based on the current status of the relationship. If a person comes across to the affable Italians as trustworthy and dependable, he will probably earn their trust. If a relationship exists already, Italians will generally want to keep it and expand it.

Persuasion

A foreign negotiator should endeavor to persuade Italians of the mutual benefits of the deal. They strongly believe in mutual dependency and obligation. Italians can also be influenced **through emotion and intuition**, so it is worthwhile to pursue an emotionally-charged path when trying to impress them.

Facts and figures will not necessarily be as effective in Italy as they are in the USA or Germany. Instead, negotiators should appeal to the personable nature of Italians and their desire to work with those who are equally friendly.

Italians are proud of their contributions to the Western Renaissance and to other fields of arts and science, so it helps to appeal to their sense of superiority. It is useful to remind them of how much a foreign company wants to do business with an Italian firm, and of how it would benefit that firm to build a long-lasting relationship with their company. Italians do not appreciate threats or ultimatums, which may mean the end of the negotiations.

The specific persuasion tactics that are likely to be effective in Italy are:

1) **Get it in writing**. Write everything down throughout the negotiations.
2) **Build trust through information sharing**.
3) **Two-Sided Appeals**. A two-sided appeal, which provides both pros and cons for both parties, highlights interdependence and a sharing of risk, and presents a cooperative upfront disclosure, is likely to be an effective persuasion strategy.
4) The use of metaphors, positive emotional tactics, distraction tactics and diffusion questions can be very useful in Italy.
5) Take your time with your presentations, rate of speech and length of time spent at the negotiations table. Italians do not stall but they are definitely not in a hurry.
6) Italians love to **haggle** and are quite lively while doing so. Expect both **distributive and contingency bargaining** tactics

(contingency seems to be the favorite). The Italians will almost always **"high-ball" or "low-ball"** a deal.

7) Certain requests that we might consider to be **corruption** are normal business practices in Italy. Decide how you plan to initiate or respond to such requests.
8) Receiving the **technical specifications up-front** or in the beginning of the negotiation is a good idea in Italy.
9) Personal appeals can be effective in Italy.
10) Associational appeals should be effective in Italy. For example, "Our product is #1 in Germany and England."
11) Authoritative proof that is based upon the ideology held by your Italian counterpart (i.e., dogma) would be very effective.
12) **Summarizing previously-agreed-upon technical benefits** should be well received.
13) You may wish to **imply that you have influence** with certain people that are relevant to the transaction.
14) **Supported Facts**. One should try to present logical/factual information that is accompanied by supportive documentation.
15) Italians tend to use a little puffery. So, definitely build up your firm, your products/ services, and yourself with **entertaining, enthusiastic, and non-verbal demonstratives**.
16) **Speak with conviction and confidence.** Italians tend to be excellent orators/story tellers and will expect the same from you and your firm.
17) **Surprise tactics** are acceptable strategies as long at they are artfully and tastefully executed.
18) A discussion of harmonious future interdependent business relationships relates ideally to Italian business logic. Thus, a **presentation of possible futuristic interdependent endeavors** should be beneficial during business presentations and negotiations.
19) Based upon the generally collectivist nature of Italy and their acceptance of personal as well as emotional appeals, the **"Feel-Felt-Found"** objection-handling tactic should be effective.

20) **Visual proof sources that are animated and nicely displayed** should prove to be effective props.

Tactics to avoid include:

1) **Avoid direct conflict.** However, a little indirect conflict usually occurs, is acceptable, and often advantageous. It is important to know the correct amount of "spice" in Italy. However, especially avoid personal conflict.
2) **Avoid overly analytical or dry presentations.** Try to have a little fun during all aspects of the negotiations.
3) **Do not speak in a monotone voice.** Use variations in rate, tonality, and pitch.
4) **Do not hurry to complete the transaction.** Allow for breaks, side conversations, etc. A level of enjoyment must be maintained.
5) It is best to **avoid fear tactics.**

Resolving disputes

Once again, subjective feelings are equal to, if not more important than, objective ones when dealing with Italians. One may resolve a dispute by simply **regaining the Italians' trust and obligation. This may involve personal pleas** as friends, as well as reminding the Italian side of the importance of the business relationship between both parties.

Group and individual dynamics

Reflecting Italy's history of clannish families and cities, Italians find comfort within their family or group. When it comes to protecting and increasing family or company interests, Italians are very **motivated and group-oriented negotiators.** As demonstrated by the many accomplished Italian artists, athletes and scholars, however, Italians can be formidable individuals with obvious talents and abilities.

Risk

Like most family and relationship-oriented people, **Italians are natural low-risk takers.** This usually means not doing business with unknown quantities or people, as well as avoiding risky investments or trade. Italy's healthy post-war economy was built largely on meeting existing demands, not on risky investments.

Even to this day, many small Italian industries produce only enough products to fill existing orders. This is especially true of Italy's exotic car manufacturers, which are largely based in northern Italy and are owned by wealthy founding families. Forecasters predicted that many of these makers would go out of business by the 1980s or become absorbed by larger companies such as Fiat. Although some companies were partially sold out, the majority are still around 20 years after they were supposed to "disappear." This is largely due to cutting down risk and excess spending, and concentrating on what they do best, which is building exotic cars. Building fewer cars than the forecasted demand avoided the risk of surplus inventories.

Decision making

Once again, family hierarchy dictates an important factor of Italian decision making. Most Italian firms today, even those that are not run by families, **adhere to the top-down decision-making system.** This system, however, is very paternal and caring, always taking into consideration the group's needs. One of the most significant aspects of this system is the ensuing delegation of responsibilities. Unlike Germany, where this flows through the company structure, Italian delegation usually involves certain individuals that are entrusted to see the project through. This is usually based upon company politics, the individual's level of competence and other factors that remain unknown to foreign negotiators. A good example is that the head of a department may not necessarily take charge of a project affecting his area. The project may be delegated instead to a handpicked individual who has the means and connections to accomplish the job.

Type of agreement

Italians believe in binding **written agreements,** but these are considered open to future interpretation and flexibility. As mentioned earlier, Italians like to bend the rules if they find them too inflexible or unrealistic. Machiavellianism is still alive in some Italians who will try to get the best possible terms initially, or if not successful, at a later date. In general, however, Italians honor and respect their contracts, especially if they have a hand in making or amending them. Italian Commercial Law is highly detailed. It offers rules, regulations, and legal provisions on every conceivable business structure.

Chapter 16

Japan

- *Country Background*
- *The Japanese Culture*
- *Business Protocol*
- *Communication Style*
- *The Japanese Concept of Negotiations*

Japan rose from a crushing defeat in World War II to become the world's second most-powerful economy. Only the USA and Germany export more goods than Japan, and Japanese products have earned a worldwide reputation for quality and value.

Japan is composed of four major islands: Hokkaido, Honshu, Kyushu and Shikoku. The capital, Tokyo, is on the eastern coast of Honshu. The country's total area is slightly smaller than that of California, and it is strategically located east of the Asian continent between the Sea of Japan and the North Pacific Ocean. Coupled with the country's long history of isolation, this location contributed to a strongly-knit society and a culture with unique social values and beliefs.

Country Background

History

Anthropologists trace the Japanese to Asian peoples who crossed over from the Korean peninsula and some Pacific islands. According to Japanese tradition, Japan was founded in the year 660 BC by Jimmu Tenno. Emperors ruled Japan, but feudal families and shoguns overshadowed their rule until 1868. Much of Japan's social and political structure developed during the country's long feudal history, and except for a few isolated influences, Japan remained closed to the outside world for most of its existence. Some foreign influences included the introduction of Buddhism from Korea in 552 AD, as well as the various arts and values of Confucianism from the Chinese culture. Kublai Khan's Mongols tried to invade Japan in 1274 and 1281, but were thwarted both times by fierce samurai warriors and a typhoon wind (called *kamikaze*) that destroyed the Mongol ships.

It was not until 1542 that the islands had Western visitors, a few Portuguese sailors who landed on the shore. The Japanese were duly impressed with the sailors' firearms, and trade with the West quickly followed. Jesuit missionaries who later accompanied traders introduced Christianity and shipbuilding knowledge. While Christians were tolerated at first, they were subsequently persecuted because they showed more loyalty to the church than to the shoguns. The Dutch and the British had some success since they brought trade without any

religion. In 1624, all Spaniards and some Portuguese were expelled due to religious and cultural hostilities. In 1636, all Japanese were forbidden from leaving or returning to Japan as the country completely closed its doors for approximately the next 220 years.

In 1853, Commodore Perry of the US Navy entered Tokyo Bay and demanded that Japan open its doors to Americans. Having been secluded for hundreds of years, Japan was behind the times in technology and weapons and could not militarily stand up to the West. Consequently, in 1854 the USA and Japan signed a peace and friendship treaty, which allowed the USA to trade with Japan and use its ports for that purpose. By 1856, the USA, Russia and Great Britain all had rights to use Japanese ports and facilities. Many Japanese were bitter about the extraterritorial policies that these powers exercised against their homeland.

Japan's *meiji* era, or "enlightened rule," started in 1868 when the emperor was restored to absolute power for the first time in seven centuries. This era was characterized by strong industrial and military modernization, largely influenced by Western models. The Japanese, who had always adopted the best from Eastern cultures, now upgraded their navy using the British Royal Navy as a model, and their army using German army principles. As Japan modernized and prospered, it also grew in population, and the need for more land and resources resulted in a strong desire to expand into Korea and other parts of Asia.

World War II was preceded in the Far East by rapid and successful Japanese expansion into Korea, Manchuria and China. When the Chinese and Russians tried to check Japan's advances, Japan's modern army and navy defeated them both. The whole world took note of Japan's victories, which were accomplished in part because of Japanese success in negotiating alliances and playing large powers against each other. Although some government officials opposed further conquests, the military-industrial machine could not be stopped. Japanese interests in Asia collided with European and USA interests in the region, and Japan attacked Pearl Harbor in 1941. After Japan's painful defeat of World War II, the USA occupied the country until 1950. A new era began, with a democratic government and an industrial resurgence only equaled by post-war Germany and South Korea.

Government

Japan's government is a constitutional monarchy with a parliamentary government. The emperor is a figurehead who does not rule, but provides an important symbol and connection to the past. Japan has an executive branch headed by a prime minister who leads the government, a legislative branch consisting of an upper House of Councilors as well as a House of Representatives, and a judicial branch with a Supreme Court. Japan's government closely resembles a combination of characteristics from the USA and parliamentary European nations. Citizens 20 and older elect representatives for their respective areas.

Japanese politics are dominated by a few political parties, mainly the Liberal Democratic Party, which has had the largest share of power for many years, the Social Democratic Party, and other smaller parties. The government, through demilitarization, subsidies and other policies, has played a crucial role in transforming Japan into an economic superpower.

Demographics

Japan's population has surpassed 126 million people. Most Japanese live in the narrow coastal plains that comprise a small part of this mostly mountainous country. Japanese cities are among the most densely populated in the world. The Japanese are a homogenous people; 99.4% of the population is ethnically Japanese. The remaining .6% are primarily of Korean descent. More than 99% of the population is literate, and the Japanese educational system is one of the best and most demanding in the world. Life expectancy is extremely high: almost 78 years for males and 84 years for females.

Economy

Japan has the world's second-ranking economy after the USA. Considering Japan's government and industry cooperation, strong work ethic, educational system, mastery of high technology, and low defense spending (roughly 1% of GDP), it's no wonder that it is one of the world's great economies. More impressive is Japan's fast ascent to a global superpower after its World War II defeat.

Japan accomplished all this despite its heavy dependence on imported raw materials and fuels. Japanese products, which at one point had the reputation of being inexpensive copies of Western models, are now considered of the highest quality. Japanese industry produces excellent automobiles, electronics, machinery, telecommunication equipment and many more items for export or domestic use. Government-supported agriculture produces enough rice for local consumption, but the country imports more than 50% of its other required grains and fodder. The Japanese have a great appetite for fish, and their fishing fleets bring in 15% of the global catch.

Although Japan's economy slowed in the 90s, unemployment was 4.7% in 2000. Business confidence is rather low as Japan remains mired in its worst recession since World War II. In its 1998 year-end report Japan's Economic Planning Agency said, "Japanese business and government leaders avoided the painful steps needed to recover from the bursting of Japan's speculative bubble economy of the 1980s." That collapse sent real estate and stock prices plummeting and left banks with billions in bad loans. Japan continues to be strong in its exports which consist primarily of machinery (50%), motor vehicles (19%), and consumer electronics (3%). Major export and import partners include Southeast Asia, the USA, Western Europe and China. Japan imports manufactures (54%), fossil fuels (16%), foodstuffs and raw materials.

The Japanese Culture

Language

The Japanese have a few dialects, but standard Japanese, which was originally spoken by the educated people of Tokyo, is the language of the country. Japanese have distinct styles to express degrees of politeness, honor, respect and familiarity. Unlike English, Japanese verbs fall at the end of a sentence and there is no future tense. The language adapted *kanji*, which is a set of Chinese characters, more than 1500 years ago. Additional sets called *kana* were developed since *kanji* was not enough for the language. Japanese literature reads from top to bottom in columns running from right to left.

O genki desu ka means "how are you" in Japanese. "Hello" is *konnichawa* in the day and *konbonwa* in the evening. "Good bye" is *sayonara*, and "thank you" is *arigato gozaimasu*.

Religion

The Japanese are a very tolerant people when it comes to religious differences. The majority of the people practice Shintoism, which is a religion unique to Japan, or they may practice Buddhism and Shintoism concurrently. Christians make up 1% of the population, and there are many other religious and social influences, such as Taoism and Confucianism. Although the Shinto religion supported the emperor through the years, Japan does not have an official religion.

Value system

Living in one of the world's most densely populated areas has given the Japanese a strong sense of group loyalty and association. This, coupled with strong Confucian influences, has produced a harmonious society that avoids confrontation and supports the group at the expense of individualism. Japanese society in general shuns those who break away from the group and set individual or selfish goals. This is why saving face in Japan is as important as it is in China and most of the East. The Japanese are very careful to save face and try not to put others in a situation that may cause conflict. In line with Confucian thinking is the importance of status in Japanese society. Unlike Western thinking, where everyone is to be treated equally, the Japanese are very aware and respectful of status. This includes someone's age, education, title, company affiliation, occupation, family ties, relationships and gender. Although some of these traditions have relaxed a bit with the younger generation, it is customary for many to bow to their elders, their bosses, and other people with higher status.

This Confucian discipline is evident in every aspect of Japanese life and business, where it is unusual to find insubordinate employees or any disrespectful citizens who succeed in society. The Japanese, whether at home or abroad, usually behave politely and reservedly. Some claim that the Japanese have a sense of cultural superiority and strong ethnocentrism, which was developed through centuries of isolation and independence. Their values, coupled with a strong work ethic, have contributed to a highly stable and productive culture that avoids conflicts while stressing teamwork and cooperation. Anxiety does exist, however, since the Japanese must work very hard to succeed and save face. Recent surveys show that Americans are happier with their lives than the Japanese, who work longer hours and have less time for social interaction and leisure.

Class structure / Stratification

Modern Japan does not have the divisions that existed in its feudal history when ruling families dominated the social structure. Other than the imperial family, there are no rigidly-inherited divisions in present Japanese society. There are, however, differences in wealth, power, and control over resources, which constitute the usual class structure of a modern capitalist society. Differences in status, which can be based on factors other than class, also determine widely-accepted roles governing everyday life.

One of the most important differences between Japanese and Western societies involves the accepted roles of women. In highly-industrialized and technologically-advanced Japan, women have not attained anything resembling equality in the workplace. For the most part, they assume only traditional family roles in society. There are very few women in high management positions. This may be changing, however, especially among those who prefer a western lifestyle. As stated earlier, other social factors influence status: Japanese society reveres its elders, as well as the highly-educated and well-connected.

Safety

Japan has an extremely low crime rate, which is not surprising considering its cultural values, group conformity, and education levels. The large Japanese police force is just as educated and disciplined as the rest of the population. In 1980, for example, only one shot was fired in the line of duty! As traditional values erode in some sections of society and economic insecurities increase, crime has gone up in some areas. Many neighborhoods today have watch groups that carefully monitor their areas for protection from outsiders. Today's problems include increased drug use among the nation's youth, small crimes associated with homelessness and poverty, and organized crime. Overall, however, the population's good manners and strict values impress visitors to Japan.

Business Protocol

Greetings and etiquette

Japanese protocol is generally **very formal, conservative and polite**. The first meeting between high executives is known as *Aisatsu*. This meeting may very well be the most important, as it is essential to make a good impression on the Japanese. Since they are very familiar with Western habits, the Japanese **may shake hands when greeting someone.** A more traditional greeting involves a bow with the hands placed against the thighs. The depth of the bow indicates the level of respect or status, so one should be careful to learn what is considered proper for certain individuals. When exchanging greetings, the Japanese use direct eye contact, so it is best to do the same. Often, the meeting is strictly social with just an exchange of formalities and no business is discussed. Companies already doing business together may also arrange *aisatsus* to welcome new executives.

Exchanging business cards that are printed in Japanese and English is a very important procedure during the first meeting. A business person should present his card after the greeting in such a manner that the Japanese person can read it. When receiving business cards, it is polite to receive them with both hands, and to take a few moments to read them carefully in front of the presenter, which indicates respect for the person's rank and status.

The proper way to address a Japanese business person is by the last name, plus *san* (i.e. Suzuki san), which means "Mr." or "Ms. Suzuki." It is not a good idea for foreigners to suggest that the Japanese call them by their first names. In cases of informality, it is best to suggest using a foreigner's last name without necessarily adding *san*. Also, when foreigners introduce themselves to the Japanese, it is not proper to use *san* after their last names, which may appear pretentious.

Time

The Japanese are **generally polychronic; however, they are very punctual**, as well as efficient time users. In keeping with their long-term outlook on business, they avoid hasty situations and like to take their time before deciding. However, once deadlines are established, the Japanese are very efficient and dedicated to meeting goals. Western negotiators should show patience and respect when dealing with the Japanese, who use time differently, and rarely seem rushed.

By working long hours, the Japanese can be punctual, take their time, and meet deadlines. The average workweek in the country is 48 hours over five and a half days. Some companies have recently switched to a five-day workweek, but the Japanese dedication to work remains very strong compared to the rest of the world. It is not unusual to see many managers go to dinner and then return to work until 9 P.M. or longer.

Gifts

Gift-giving is common at Japanese companies, especially during midyear and at the end of the year. Giving gifts is more important than the gifts themselves, so the value of the gift is not important. The best gifts are foreign items that are hard to obtain in Japan, such as scotch, coffee-table books, Swiss chocolate, or toys for the children of associates. The Japanese do not usually open gifts immediately, but if they do, they act restrained and do not exude exuberant thanks. This should not be misconstrued as judgment on the value of the gift.

Private company executives may discreetly give much more expensive gifts to other executives or associates.

When visiting a Japanese home, it is considerate to bring flowers (not white, which signifies death), candy or Japanese cake. When giving flowers or other assorted objects, one should not give four items, since the number four is an ominous one in Japan, much like the number 13 in the USA If you must refuse a gift, be sure to explain that it is due to your firm's policies and return the gift in private.

Business entertainment

Business entertainment in Japan is more frequent and significant than in most countries. In fact, the Japanese business entertainment budget is larger than the country's defense budget, which may seem incomprehensible in some parts of the world. To many Japanese businessmen, the process of building relationships with associates begins after business hours at local restaurants and bars. Perhaps one of the reasons why Japanese women have not made strong inroads in business is that these activities normally do not include women, and some take place at "hostess bars," where it may not be a good idea for women of any culture to be seen. Bars and restaurants are not the only venues for business entertainment in Japan, and there are a number of other alternatives that are suited for mixed company. These include *sumo* wrestling, *karaoke*, and for those with a taste for local culture, traditional Japanese theater and entertainment. Foreigners should act enthusiastically at any of these events, and show appreciation to their hosts. If foreigners are involved in a protracted negotiation, they will probably be invited to a *karaoke* establishment and should definitely attend. Thus, foreigners should practice a few traditional songs before their plane leaves for Tokyo.

The Japanese enjoy hosting these events, and they normally pay for them. They usually order food for their guests, which is convenient, considering most menus are in Japanese. Building trust, friendship, and enjoying the evening are the main objectives of these social activities. Business is rarely discussed, although this is acceptable provided your Japanese counterpart is the one who moves the conversation to business topics. Once the two sides establish trust and friendship, it will be much easier to communicate and discuss business. The Japanese may invite some guests to their homes after a few formal meetings, and this is considered an honor. When visiting a Japanese home, guests should remove their shoes at the door, and they will most probably sit around a low table with their legs crossed or to the side. Since this may be uncomfortable for many Westerners, the family may offer them a backrest. Guests who show good form will probably impress their Japanese hosts more than those who seem uncomfortable and bothered. When eating, it is important not to point chopsticks at anyone, and to place them on their special rests when done. Visitors should try to reciprocate by inviting their Japanese associates to dinner and entertainment. They should also insist on paying, especially if the Japanese paid for the last outing.

Dress

Dress codes for business people in Japan are straightforward. **Dress conservatively for the season**. Men should wear a tie and a conservative suit, and women should wear a conservative business suit with neutral colors, and should never wear pants or showy clothes for business. **Tall Western women should especially try not to wear heels**, since they may otherwise tower over their Japanese counterparts. They should also refrain from wearing too much makeup, jewelry, perfume or other attention-getting items that the Japanese may consider flamboyant and gaudy. A woman who tries hard to look different or attract attention may be ignored or looked down upon.

Men and women should wear good business shoes, but when they visit Japanese homes, they may consider wearing slip-on shoes since they may have to remove them. They should also remember to bring many changes of clothes for various occasions, especially since the Japanese are a very clean people.

Communication Style

Business Language

The Japanese use **a very high-context and complex language**. In keeping with their manners and self-control, they frequently make ambiguous statements that are not intended to deceive, but are rather part of their intricate language and communication style. For example, a Japanese negotiator may say, "We will consider it," when in fact he means "no." The total and true meaning of statements is not literal since the Japanese language expresses feelings more than other languages. Therefore, it is up to the foreign negotiator to ask key questions to distinguish the true meaning of certain statements.

When negotiating in Japanese, one cannot underestimate the value of competent and knowledgeable interpreters. Japanese interpreters need to understand the complex subtleties of Japanese, especially in the business arena.

Possible Seating Arrangements at the Aisatsu or Negotiations

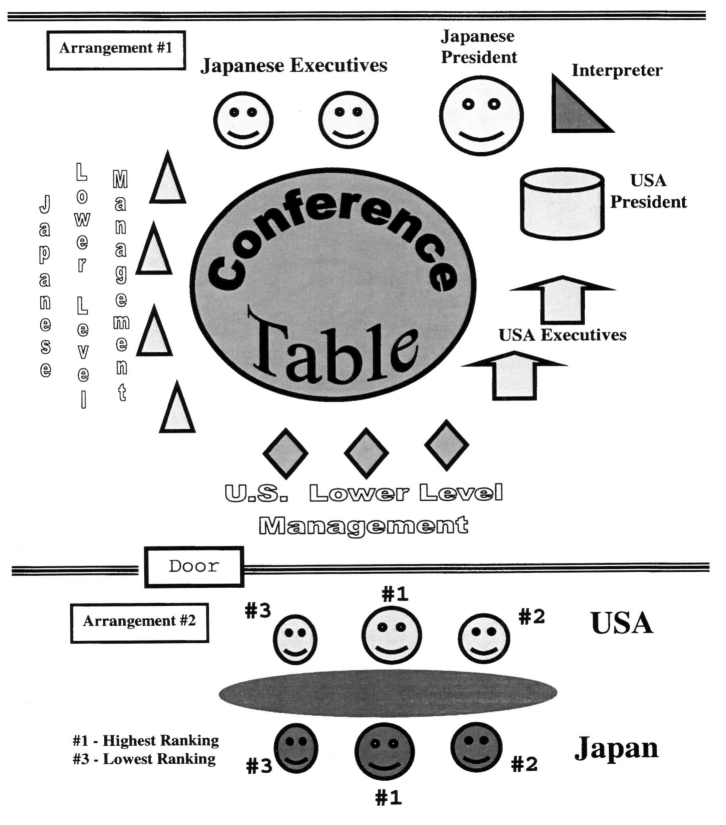

Arrangement #1

Japanese Executives

Japanese President

Interpreter

USA President

Japanese Lower Level Management

Conference Table

USA Executives

U.S. Lower Level Management

Door

Arrangement #2

#3 #1 #2 USA

#1 - Highest Ranking
#3 - Lowest Ranking

#3 #1 #2 Japan

Companies that hire interpreters should test them and prepare them thoroughly to prevent major misunderstandings. Negotiation chronicles between Japan and the USA are full of stories of misunderstood statements, even at the highest levels of government. It is, therefore, important to allow interpreters sufficient time to formulate their translations and to interpret accurately. It is also tactful to look at the person who is being addressed, rather than at the interpreter when communicating.

Tone, volume and pace are very important parts of Japanese communications. Good listeners and interpreters may be able to decipher much of the hidden meaning in Japanese narratives by paying attention to how it is delivered.

When the negotiations take place in a language other than Japanese, it is important to speak slowly to ensure that the Japanese comprehend what is said. Although many may speak and read English, it is difficult for most Japanese to understand American English or other languages when they are spoken rapidly.

Non-verbal communication

The Japanese are **careful observers of all non-verbal behavior**. They are very conservative when it comes to gestures or hand movements. **It is best to keep dramatic gestures and other movements to a minimum when dealing with the Japanese.** It is impolite to point at someone, so instead wave the hand with the palm up toward the indicated object. Beckoning someone is similar to the Chinese method of moving the fingers with the palm down. The American "OK" sign means "money" to the Japanese, and some Western gestures do not mean anything, such as shrugging the shoulders, or winking between friends. The Japanese are encouraged to maintain a pleasant demeanor from childhood. A pleasant façade usually means pleasure but it is also a means of self-control and patience.

After greetings, the Japanese generally do not engage in much direct eye contact. Instead they may look at a document or a prop while talking. Also, they are more comfortable with silence than most other people and use silence to think and formulate responses. Although

Terminology

Gaijin:	Foreigner
Hai:	Yes, I hear you
Honne:	True Self (real personality)
Ie:	Insider (as in the inner group)
Sayonara:	Good bye
Soto:	Outsider (outside the group)
Tatemae:	Façade (face one puts on)
Wa:	Harmony
Wakarimashita:	Understood

Japan is much more crowded than many Western countries, the **Japanese, unlike the Chinese, prefer to remain farther apart than do North Americans**. Backslapping and other types of male touching are extremely rare and uncomfortable. Male-female public displays of affection are equally rare and inappropriate.

The Japanese Concept of Negotiations

Selecting personnel

Before assembling a negotiating team for Japan, most companies have to secure a reliable *shokai-sha*, or introducer. Companies may secure introducers from other companies doing business in Japan, banks, Japanese trading companies, or international law firms. The *shokai-sha* may also act as an intermediary during the negotiations, so choose one who is knowledgeable and experienced. The other obvious person needed for conducting Japanese negotiations is a competent and experienced interpreter. Since introducers are normally high-level personnel, it may be best to hire another person to act as the interpreter.

When selecting the rest of the negotiating team, a company should consider the following qualities in individuals: **listening ability, respect for Japanese values, status, team orientation, loyalty, sociability and an attractive personality.**

People with these qualities make excellent counterparts for the Japanese, who are more interested initially in building long-term relationships than bargaining over details. A good listener, for example, will understand the subtleties of Japanese verbal and non-verbal communications, and will negotiate patiently and quietly. A person with high connections or status will receive reverent treatment from the Japanese, who will often do their best to entertain and impress him. Being a collective society, the Japanese value team effort and loyalty, and they will respect those who demonstrate equal qualities. In fact, they will look down upon adversaries who exhibit disloyal or insubordinate behavior toward their company. Finally, since much of the courting relationship involves business entertainment and after-hours meetings, it is helpful to have energetic individuals with good people skills and attractive personalities.

Another important consideration when assembling a negotiating team is having enough people. Large Japanese companies traditionally use large teams composed of individuals who perform different tasks. Some foreign executives think they can do the job with a small staff, and therefore find themselves outnumbered and outgunned by the Japanese, who are formidable team players. A typical Japanese team consists of an introducer, operational staff, middle managers, a team leader (often a CEO), an interpreter, and possibly a mediator. Foreign companies conducting important negotiations should try to match the number of Japanese negotiators, and not send only top managers who think they can do it alone.

Negotiating style

Observers will quickly note the **subtle and low-key approach of Japanese negotiators, which differs greatly from that of Chinese and Korean negotiators**, Japan's closest neighbors. As in their highly structured society, the Japanese employ and follow a number of traditional principles in business negotiations.

Japanese Team Members

Shokai-sha:	**Introducer**
Staffu:	**Initial Negotiators**
Kacho/Bucho:	**Middle Managers**
Schacho:	**CEO**
Chukai-sha:	**Mediator**

Wa, **or maintaining harmony, is probably the most pervasive and important** of these. The desire to maintain harmony is perhaps the reason why Japanese communication is sometimes vague and subtle. By masking rejection, for example, the Japanese can effectively maintain cooperation and continue the negotiation process. *Wa* also dictates mutual respect and cooperation throughout the negotiation process.

Japanese business also revolves around the concept of *amae*, which may be translated into "mutual dependency." In other words, the Japanese believe that buyers and sellers need each other, and therefore must take care of each other's needs. The Japanese believe in providing buyers with all their needs, and similarly expect not to be taken advantage of. In reality, since some buyers will undoubtedly try to take advantage of sellers, the Japanese usually leave room for maneuvering when it comes to pricing and other conditions. The Japanese will usually listen intently to the proposals, then ask questions and continue the discussions. To them, **negotiations are friendly meetings to work out the details of an already-accepted outcome.**

Finally, it is very important for foreign negotiators to maintain their patience and composure. By doing so, they will not rush into making deals due to time constraints, or worse, cancel them altogether. The Japanese may use stall tactics knowing Western preoccupation with time and deadlines, and a foreigner who becomes frustrated may lose a potential deal as well as any future business.

Issues discussed

Since the Japanese believe firmly in long-term relationships, the most important issues discussed in Japanese negotiations are **relationship-based**. By Western standards, the Japanese spend a disproportionate amount of time on non-substantive issues. These include gaining familiarity with their counterparts, as well as asking them about their company structure, objectives and policies.

Bases of trust

Traditionally, the Japanese foster lifelong relationships based on trust and mutual respect. This is perhaps why business entertainment is so important. The Japanese learn about the character and trustworthiness of their counterparts during **nontask sounding and entertainment activities**. Generally, they consider people with strong work ethics who understand Japanese culture as worthy associates. One of the most important aspects of their business culture is trust between buyers and sellers, and they do not feel that everyone in the world shares these beliefs. For example, the Japanese do not feel that all business cultures offer buyers what they, as sellers, offer humbly and consistently. One of the reasons why the Japanese market is not very open to foreign products is the fact that many foreign sellers have not attained a high level of trust, and thus cannot negotiate seriously with the Japanese. To earn Japanese trust, sellers need to demonstrate similar traits of humility and dedication. Likewise, buyers must not take advantage of that same trust and humility, and must treat sellers with equal respect and care.

Persuasion

Since negotiations are primarily for working out the details of a predetermined agreement, the Japanese prefer a harmonious atmosphere with both parties respecting each other's needs. Trying to persuade or sway the opinion of the chief Japanese negotiator is usually ineffective, and if it seems pushy, it may be considered crass. The Japanese **prefer an exchange of information among the whole staff to reach a mutually-agreeable solution**. Western-style logic, however, is not always sufficient to persuade the Japanese, since they value the emotional and personal aspect of the relationship. They will, therefore, take into account the status of the relationship, and the desire to have it grow and strengthen, even if this means taking some initial loss. This philosophy of sacrificing in the interest of long-term success has helped Japan in almost every market around the world.

Since relationships are important to the Japanese, it is possible to persuade them during dinner conversations and by using personal appeals. These types of persuasion efforts assume several forms. One form occurs when the two parties have reached the relationship status in which one is comfortable enough to expose one's "*honne*" or "true self." This point in the relationship is usually reached after numerous meetings and several dinner and drinking excursions. In addition, this type of exchange tends to take place between the mid-level management, which we would consider to be boundary-spanning personnel, not top-level management. Once "*honne*" is reached the problem-solving style of negotiating (i.e., frank conversations addressing the concerns of both parties) that the USA, Canada and numerous European countries prefer can take place in its Japanese form. The conversation must stay very pleasant and both parties should put the other's interest ahead of their own (as is common among boundary-spanning personnel). In addition, the conversation should move back and forth between business and pleasure as is common in polychronic cultures. To reach and maintain "*honne*" one must be well-versed in Japanese culture, arts, history, sports and customs.

Another form of persuasion that is effective in Japan is known as "corporate pleading." "Corporate pleading" is quite effective in Japan, especially if the relationship is at risk. The Japanese will often do whatever they can to accommodate a trading partner's appeals. These pleas may take the form of explaining how much the company needs these products and services, and how important it is to secure them. Since the Japanese are highly team-oriented and coordinated, these pleas can take place at any level, especially among middle managers that socialize together. By mixing detailed information and facts with corporate pleas, negotiators can greatly influence Japanese negotiators. It takes a lot of patience to influence the Japanese, however, and foreign negotiators should always be patient.

The specific persuasion tactics that are likely to be effective in Japan are:

1) **+Visual Aids**. Although the Japanese avoid long periods of eye contact, they love to look at inanimate objects. Colorful pictures, charts, graphs and posters will greatly enhance one's presentation and correspondingly one's ability to persuade. Product samples are also a good idea.

2) The Japanese love to **"high-ball" or "low-ball."** Be prepared and respond in kind. However, after this initial exchange of outrageous prices, both sides should move very quickly to a more reasonable price.

3) The exchange of technical requirements, preferences, needs, etc. is appropriate at the negotiations table if it is done in a non-combative manner. The Japanese pay a great deal of attention to technical specification. However, it should be noted that most of this technical interaction should take place between mid-level management before the negotiations take place.

4) **Metaphors, stories and analogies** are a good idea in Japan if delivered in a friendly story-telling manner. Be sure to avoid anything that implies a threat or fear tactic.

5) **Distraction tactics** are useful in times of conflict and will definitely be used by your Japanese counterparts.

6) Certain requests that we might deem corruption may be normal business practices in Japan. Decide how you plan to initiate or respond to such requests.

7) **Stalling** is considered to be a very acceptable negotiation tactic in Japan. Your Japanese counterparts will stall.

8) **Start small and build.** Your Japanese counterparts are likely to prefer a small initial transaction. It is advisable to accept the smaller transaction. Thus, business may start slower than you prefer. However, this lays the foundation for future business and is a standard operating procedure for the Japanese.

9) Expect the Japanese to use the **"big-picture"** negotiation style. That is, nothing is decided until everything is decided. You should probably plan on a similar strategy.

10) As previously mentioned, **use "corporate pleading"** in informal settings.

11) Japan is a hierarchical as well as collectivist society. Referring to the **approval of others** and especially the approval of **respected higher authorities** in regards to your company, product, etc. should prove to be an effective method of persuasion.

12) Japanese businesspeople tend to be fairly analytical. **Summarizing previously-agreed-upon technical benefits** should be well received.

13) Discussion of harmonious future beneficial business relationships is an integral part of Japanese business culture. It is the basis for most introductory business toasts. Although this style of influence is very indirect, it can serve to alleviate tensions, provide minor support for argumentation, etc. Your **presentation of possible futuristic**

cooperative endeavors, the use of positive imagery, etc. should be beneficial during business presentations and negotiations.

14) Based upon the collectivist nature and desire for harmony in Japan, the **"Feel-Felt-Found"** objection-handling tactic should prove to be effective. Unfortunately, objections are cloaked and rarely stated in Japan. However, if an objection is revealed, then rephrase that you understand how they "Feel" and that another customer you had "Felt" the same way, but what they "Found" was that this was not a problem/issue once they engaged in your service/product's use. This can be effective if delivered in a harmonious and non-confrontational manner.

Tactics to avoid include:

1) **Do not discuss your BATNA.** In Japan, discussing alternative business arrangements is a polite way of indicating the negotiation is now finished with no agreement.

2) **Avoid surprises at the table.** Up-front surprises promote conflict and reduce harmony. However, surprises behind the scenes are to be expected.

3) **Do not self-promote.** Humility is considered a virtue.

4) **Do not engage in extensive information sharing.** Profuse information sharing is seen as foolish.

5) **Avoid Two-Sided Appeals.** In Japan, the presentation of the opposing side is not harmonious nor is it expected. Thus, a two-sided appeal, which provides both pros and cons of an argument/product, may cause doubt or destroy the harmony that has been fostered.

6) **Avoid direct conflict.**

7) Avoid direct eye contact, elaborate demonstratives, profuse smiling, and touching. For example, do not expect to gain favor by smiling, slapping them on the back, or looking directly into their eyes.

8) Do not use fear tactics, ultimatums, threats, loud voices, etc.

Resolving disputes

While mediators are common in many countries, in Japan the role of the *chukai-sha*, or "mediator," is almost institutionalized. The person who acts as the *shokai-sha* (introducer) usually acts as a *chukai-sha* if needed. These important individuals **usually mediate any problems that both staffs cannot solve on their own.** Inter-Japanese negotiations, and negotiations between Japanese and foreign companies are full of examples of important *shokai-sha/chukai-sha* who contributed greatly to making the deal.

One must keep in mind that the Japanese system is built upon problem avoidance, so disputes that arise in serious negotiations are usually solved through cooperation. After all, negotiations only take place when the two parties have established some measure of trust and good relations.

Group and individual dynamics

The Japanese have a **strong collectivist nature**, and they value teamwork and cooperation. These traits are apparent in the number of negotiators on a Japanese team, as well as by their meticulous teamwork and cooperation. Japanese society teaches cooperation and rewards individuals with long-term security and a strong sense of group identity. Japanese companies are known for taking care of their employees, and likewise, workers exhibit strong loyalty and dedication to their companies. The negotiating staff will work in concert to achieve the desired results, although each individual usually has unique tasks and knowledge. Foreigners should compliment the group, not just individuals, because without the rest of the group, individuals may not achieve the desired result. Companies and individuals that adopt the "John Wayne" style of sending one or two negotiators to Japan will probably not do as well as ones that send organized negotiating teams.

Risk

With their strong group loyalty and concern for long-term security, it is no wonder that the Japanese are **risk averse**, even more than the South Koreans and Taiwanese. A factor that prevents the Japanese from taking too many risks is saving face. If the risk fails, those who took it will probably feel ashamed and responsible for failing the group. One can argue that

Typical Japanese Style Contract

Tokyo Manufacturers and Osaka Retailers

Article 1:   This agreement between Tokyo Manufacturers located in Tokyo and Osaka Retailers located in Osaka, on this 1st day of January, 1999, is made in order to foster a mutually prosperous relationship.

Article 2:   Tokyo Manufacturers shall continue to provide products based upon Osaka Retailers' designs and specifications.

Article 3:   Osaka Retailers may register their designs in order to protect Osaka Retailers rights against third parties.

Article 4:   Tokyo Manufacturers shall not, without Osaka Retailers consent, produce products for third party purchase.

Article 5:   If either Tokyo Manufacturers or Osaka Retailers should suffer losses due to a violation of this agreement, the injured party may claim damages.

Article 6:   Two identical agreements are to be prepared and signed to evidence this agreement, whereupon each party shall retain one copy.

Tokyo Manufacturers: _____

Osaka Retailers: _____

the Japanese propensity not to take risks is the reason why it is sometimes hard to penetrate the Japanese market. A foreign unknown company or individual may be seen as a potential risk, so there is no strong incentive for the Japanese to become business partners. After all, in Japan, the idea is not only to "make the deal," but also to build for the future. The Japanese prefer strong business relationships that are guaranteed to bear fruit.

Decision making

Another reason for Japan's tremendous success in domestic and global business is its rational **bottom- up decision-making system.** With all their power and status, Japanese top executives are excellent listeners who expect their company experts to give them good council and recommendations. Foreign negotiators need to be patient as the chain of advice moves up from one level to the next. This is necessary since a consensus decision may take longer than an authoritative one. By involving all levels in making decisions, the Japanese can implement them very quickly.

Type of agreement

Like the Chinese, the Japanese **do not rely upon elaborately-written, highly-legalized contracts**. Unlike contracts between American firms, Japanese agreements reflect the positive relationship and good faith between the parties, and rarely include contingencies addressing breaches of contract or other negative issues. In other words, after the long and arduous work of establishing a relationship, the Japanese prefer a loosely-written gentleman's agreement that states the facts of the relationship, and very little detail. This does not mean, however, that both parties cannot put the true objectives of the venture in writing, stating who is responsible for what. Japanese contracts are more of a guide on how the two parties will do business, rather than legally binding and rigid documents. In case of future conflict, they prefer to renegotiate a mutual agreement, rather than hold each other responsible or go to court to remedy the dispute.

Japanese law began its modern foundation with the Meiji restoration in 1868. This event brought about a western-oriented government that began borrowing codes and laws from European legal systems. The Japanese civil and commercial codes of 1898 and 1899 were closely based upon German and French legal systems and remain in force today, although considerably amended and modernized. Post World War II events brought further changes in commercial and corporate law. In Japanese law there is no binding precedent, but there is a concept of a jurisprudence constant, which is similar to that found in France where a series of court decisions are used to support a favorable, consistent argument. Fundamentally, Japanese contract law is based upon the doctrine of good faith in performance and is similar to German, French and Anglo-American law.

Chapter 17

Korea (South)

- *Country Background*
- *The Korean Culture*
- *Business Protocol*
- *Communication Style*
- *The Korean Concept of Negotiations*

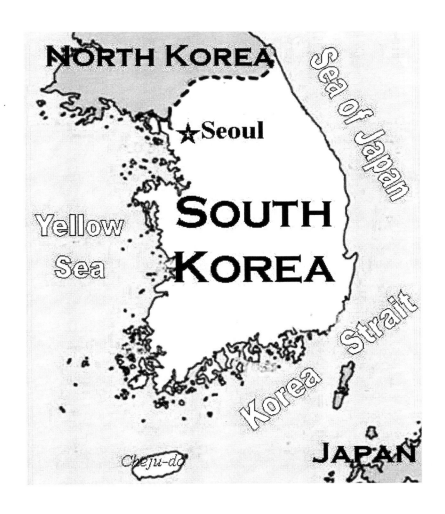

The Republic of Korea's economic recovery from a war-torn wasteland after World War II is perhaps unequalled in recent history. Unlike Japan and Germany, which had post-war support protection, larger populations, and a strong industrial and technological base, South Korea accomplished its economic miracle despite large defense expenditures. What the country had in its favor, however, was a resourceful and hard-working population with a strong desire to transform Korea from a Third World country into an economic powerhouse. Today South Korea boasts the world's 16th largest GDP with a fast-growing export-oriented economy. Korean products have penetrated worldwide markets, and have crossed the barriers that separate Japanese and Western technologies from those of developing nations.

Country Background

History

The human history of the Korean peninsula goes back tens of thousands of years. Large tribes controlled most of the peninsula during the Bronze Age, and these evolved into competing kingdoms that ruled the country. The best known of these is the kingdom of Silla, which existed from 75 BC to AD 935. The Silla dynasty ended with the rise of the Koryo dynasty, which gave Korea its present name. The Koryo dynasty ended in 1392 when the Yi dynasty seized power and held it until 1910, when the Japanese annexed Korea.

One of the constants in Korean history was Chinese influence on the peninsula and its inhabitants. Chinese culture, art, religion and government strongly shaped Korean culture and government.

The Mongols, who occupied Korea for most of the 14th Century, unsuccessfully attempted to invade Japan from Korea, and forced Koreans to participate in these attempts. The Japanese returned the favor by attempting their own unsuccessful invasions of Korea during the following centuries. Ironically, Japan, which had been forced to open itself to the world by the West, later forced Korea to open its doors to foreigners in 1876. Japan maintained a strong influence on Korea throughout the remainder of the 19th Century, annexed the country in 1910, and declared it a part of the Japanese Empire. Japan tried to change the Korean culture by

outlawing its language and "Japanizing" everything in the country. This difficult period ended in 1945 after the final Japanese defeat in World War II.

Unfortunately for Korea, Japan's defeat did not end its internal miseries. The victorious allies agreed to have two Koreas: communist North Korea, backed by the Chinese and Russians, and South Korea supported by the USA. War broke out between North and South Korea in 1950. South Korea, backed by the USA, went up against the Chinese-backed North Koreans. The war laid waste to much of the country and caused immense hardship on the population. When the war ended in 1953, there were two Koreas that are still divided by the 38th parallel, and a weary and impoverished population in both. Through a series of government and legal reforms, as well as USA support, South Korea started its strong march into the 21st Century. Despite occasional internal flare-ups, Korea continued to show strong economic growth. The recent Asian economic crisis, however, has led to layoffs and a $58 billion bailout by the IMF.

Government

South Korea is a republic with executive, legislative and judicial branches of government. The president or chief of state heads the executive branch, which includes the cabinet, a Prime Minister and a deputy prime minister. The National Assembly, or Kukhoe, represents the legislative branch. The public elects most of its members, with the remaining seats apportioned to winning political parties. The *Kukhoe* has the power to remove cabinet ministers and to approve Supreme Justice appointments. It also has the power to approve or oppose any emergency decision by the president. South Korea's judicial branch includes a Supreme Court and a constitutional court that has broad powers, including presidential impeachment and the dismissal of cabinet ministers.

The incorporation of foreign law into the legal system came in stages. Initially the Chinese dominated and brought the all-embracing concepts of Confucianism, which still influences the Korean approach to legal matters. Next the Japanese dominated and introduced their own version of the German code. During the brief USA military occupation, common law concepts were introduced. Korea's current legal system is a composite brought about by its adaptation to these influences.

During the first forty years of the Korean Republic there were nine amendments to the constitution. All of them permitted extensions to the presidential term of office, which ran counter to the intent of the constitution and were occasioned by political turmoil. These events promoted an autocratic presidency and weakened the legislative branch of the government.

The government has traditionally played a large role in business affairs and in setting the country's economic pace. Recent presidents and governments have eliminated much of the prevailing corruption, and have attempted to reduce the power of conglomerates by instituting fair-trade reforms.

Demographics

South Korea's population grew from 20 million in 1959 to over 40 million in 1985, and has now leveled off at approximately 50 million inhabitants. Korea is one of the world's most ethnically homogenous countries. About 20,000 people are of Chinese descent and the rest of the population is purely Korean. The population growth rate is now less than 1%. Life expectancy is 71 years for males and 79 for females. South Koreans are a very educated people; 98% of the population can read and write.

Economy

The driving forces behind South Korea's economic growth have been the well-planned development of an export-oriented economy, and a very successful shift to an industrial production base. This resulted in 10% annual economic growth in the late Eighties, which caused a tight labor market and strong inflationary pressures. The growth rate slowed down for a couple of years in the early Nineties, but bounced right back to more than 8% in 1994, which was much higher than the world average. This growth was attributed to booming exports, especially in the industrial sector. South Korea's economy is usually ranked around 12th in the world and around 30th place for per capita income. However, South Korea was one of the hardest hit countries in the 1997 Asian financial crisis, and the impact of the crisis will probably affect South Korean for many years to come. Major industries include automobiles, ships, steel, textiles and footwear. Agriculture accounts for 5% of the GDP, employing around 10% of the work force. Agricultural

products make the country self-sufficient in food, except for wheat. These include rice, barley, vegetables, fruit, livestock, chickens, milk, eggs, and the world's seventh largest catch of fish.

Korea enjoys a very healthy trade surplus. Export products include electronics, machinery, steel, vehicles, ships, textiles, clothing and fish. Major trade partners include the USA, Japan, and the European Union. Imports include machinery, electronics, oil, steel, textiles, chemicals and grains. The industrial sector accounts for more than 40% of the Korean economy.

The South Korean currency is the won.

The Korean Culture

Language

Heavily influenced by China for thousands of years, the Korean language in its written from is a mixture of Chinese ideograms and a native Korean alphabet known as *han'gal*. More than 50% of modern Korean consists of Chinese "loan" words. Because the Korean language was outlawed during Japanese occupation from 1910 to 1945, modern Japanese and Korean have similar grammatical rules, as well as similar levels of speech for "honorific" and "polite" terms.

Although the original *han'gal* was written from top to bottom and right to left like Japanese, almost all modern Korean today is written from left to right as in Western languages. The majority of South Koreans today learn English in school, which makes it easy for English-speaking business people to negotiate with their Korean counterparts.

Religion

Freedom of religion is an important element of South Korean society. Almost half (47%) of the population practices Buddhism. In contrast to China and Japan, which have very small Christian minorities, almost half (49%) of South Koreans are Christians. Very small sections of the population practice Confucianism and shamanism, or spirit worship, which is one of the oldest beliefs in South Korean society. Although religion is not prominent in South Korean business circles, religious beliefs play a role in shaping South Korea's values and beliefs.

Value system

South Korean values are strongly based on the Confucian principles that regulated the country for hundreds of years. These include hierarchical loyalty and duty to one's parents, family and society. Koreans tend to be far more outspoken, personable, more emotional, rougher, more aggressive in business/social affairs, and more hot tempered when compared to the Chinese or the Japanese. However, they are not as ethnocentric or anti-foreign. All of these differences may in part be due to South Korea's violent history as a small country torn between many stronger powers and a more marked influence from the West (i.e., Christianity, colonization, etc.).

Other Confucian values that dominate Korean society are the desire not to shame one's family, saving face, and dignity. These beliefs, which are shared by many Asian cultures, prompt individuals to be outer-directed versus inner-directed (i.e., more concerned with how other see them versus how they see themselves).

Other important Korean values include trust, reciprocity, and hard work. One must establish a relationship to do business based on reciprocal acts of hospitality and goodwill. Then the hard work begins. The Korean concept of hard work is almost unequalled in the world. Considering that many Koreans work 12-hour days and six-day workweeks, it is no wonder that this country transformed itself into a world economic power in such a short time.

Class structure / Stratification

Although South Korean society was traditionally divided into well-defined rigid strata, this has diminished considerably in today's society. The effects of this stratification, however, still manifest themselves in individual and business interactions among Koreans. It is not uncommon for two Koreans to "feel out" each other's status and background when they first meet, and to establish a hierarchical "pecking order." Connections, including family, school or friends, remain the primary means for obtaining good jobs and business opportunities. Korean social stratification criteria include schooling, ancestry, birthplace, family ties, and wealth.

Korean society traditionally treated men and women differently. Women did not receive the same education or opportunities. Most Korean women today have the same educational opportunities as men, but have not received complete equality. They are markedly excluded from higher management positions.

Safety

Personal safety is not a big concern for foreign business people visiting South Korea. The Korean population is generally very hospitable and honest. Crimes rates are very low. However, tourists are always theft-targets all over the world.

Safety of the society as a whole is a concern. Tensions have always existed between North Korea and South Korea and still continue today. Another concern may be a resurgence of student and labor demonstrations, which paralyzed the country in the mid-Eighties. One must keep in mind the turbulent nature of these demonstrations and the violent police response.

Business Protocol

Greetings and etiquette

Korean business etiquette is **highly formal**. A business-card exchange usually precedes any other greeting or business activity. These should be printed in English and Korean, and the presenter should use the right hand while handing them to the Korean counterpart. Most business introductions between foreigners and Koreans involve **a weak handshake and a slight nod between men**. Men and women can exchange nods, but rarely shake hands, although it is appropriate for Western women to initiate handshakes. Since there are very few surnames in Korea, it is common to address people by their title alone. Another form of address is adding the suffix *ssi* to Korean surnames, much like adding *san* to Japanese ones. Therefore, Mr., Mrs. or Miss Park may be addressed as Park*ssi*. It is inappropriate to address Koreans by their given names unless given permission to do so.

Time

South Koreans are **polychronic** and fairly punctual. South **Koreans definitely expect punctuality** from foreign counterparts, but they may keep them waiting in case of more important business. This is primarily due to the fact that top Korean managers are normally very busy and task-oriented, and may not always be able to finish tasks on time and prepare for the next meeting. South Korean business hours are normally 9 AM to 5 PM Monday through Friday, and 9 AM to 1 PM on Saturday. Most South Korean managers put in a lot of overtime and can be seen at their desks as late as 8 or 9 PM.

Since a great number of South Koreans are Christians, Christmas is not a good time to arrange business, nor is the period between July and August when many take their summer vacations.

Gifts

Exchanging gifts is common in South Korea, and a small exchange of inexpensive gifts may take place as soon as the first meeting. The best gifts are ones that originate from the presenter's country of origin, rather than Korean-made products. These may include chocolate, liquor, crafts or expensive pens. When giving gifts it is best to present them with both hands in the Korean tradition. It is customary for Koreans not to accept a gift immediately, so the presenter should persist. When receiving gifts, one should not open them immediately, but should give thanks, and reciprocate later with a gift of equal value. Since reciprocity is an important Korean value, one should bear in mind the value of gifts, and not give extravagant ones to associates who may not be able to reciprocate with gifts of the same value.

Business entertainment

Koreans prefer social conversation during lunch and only minor business issues are discussed. However, the ceremony of sharing food and drink together is important throughout Asia.

As in Japan, **the Korean business culture places a great deal of importance on after-hours entertainment**. It is customary to invite visiting business people to a *kisaeng* house, or to dinner with plenty of alcohol. A lot of non-task-oriented activity usually takes place at these events, as well as alcohol-induced discussions that may include business and social subject matter. Koreans, unlike Westerners, usually consider all these discussions to be meaningful despite the circumstances in which they take place. Therefore, it is

important for foreign negotiators not to promise anything that they cannot offer or deliver. The best subjects to discuss during these dinners are work, sports, and Korean culture. Although it is acceptable to discuss family, it is best to keep these discussions to a cordial exchange. Do not discuss private concerns, especially wives and daughters. Other sensitive topics include politics, communism and Japanese-Korean history. Whoever issued the dinner invitation usually pays, and the other party should reciprocate at a later date. Singing is a very important after-hours activity in South Korea. Foreign business people who can partake by singing a couple of melodies from their homeland may score big points with their Korean counterparts.

After a few such gatherings, it is possible to be invited to a Korean associate's home, which is an honor. Visitors should show up on time and remove their shoes before entering the house. When sitting on the floor around a table, men are expected to either cross their legs, or sit with the legs to the side. Women, on the other hand, always have their legs to the side. When using chopsticks, one shouldn't stick them in the rice or place them on top of the bowl, but should set them on the table or the chopstick rest when finished. It is also customary for guests not to eat all the food offered to them unless they want more, and not to fill their own glasses, which is done by the host. Finally, although an invitation to a Korean house honors a guest, the latter should respect the host's privacy and not venture uninvited into various rooms and quarters.

Foreigners should treat their Korean counterparts to equally lavish lunches and dinners in their respective homelands. Reciprocity is an important Korean value.

Dress

In agreement with the rest of their business protocol, Korean **business dress is conservative and formal**. Men are expected to wear suits, white shirts and ties when doing business. Women should also wear conservative and professional suits that are not revealing or provocative. High-quality and polished shoes are also the norm for men and women. Tall Western women should take care not to wear high heels so they do not tower over their Korean counterparts.

Communication Style

Business language

Koreans use **a high-context language**, much like their Chinese and Japanese neighbors. Following their tendency to save face and please others, Koreans place as much emphasis on what is not said as on what is said. Negotiators should be aware that Korean phrases that denote acceptance or confirmation have a different meaning or context from similar Western phrases. Although most South Koreans speak English today, it is essential to find out beforehand what language will be primarily used during the negotiations. Depending on the personnel and the previous relationship between the parties, it may also be a good idea to have Korean-speaking personnel or interpreters on board.

Non-verbal communication

Non-verbal Korean communication and gestures are based on formality and respect, and are rarely informal. Touching is rare in Korean society, especially among people of the opposite sex and/or those who are not good friends. As in many Asian cultures, however, **Koreans of the same sex may hold hands as a sign of friendship**, but Koreans do not like others to infringe on their personal space. Foreigners should pay particular attention to their foot positioning while sitting down. It is inappropriate to show the soles of the shoes to others. So is touching anyone with the feet, which is a taboo in Korean society.

Just as in Japan and China, pointing with one finger is considered rude, and the beckoning gesture consists of extending the palm face down and moving the fingers up and down. One of the most taboo gestures in Korea is blowing the nose in public, so it is important to try and do this as privately as possible. Korean women may cover their mouths when laughing, but men and foreign women do not have to do the same. Generally, Koreans seem more animated than the Japanese or Chinese, and they use more eye contact than Japanese negotiators.

The Korean Concept of Negotiations

Selecting personnel

According to Korean values, elders are revered and respected in all walks of life, including business. Although South Korean business has evolved dramatically during the last two decades, it is still dominated by older executives who have founded their companies or have served them for a long time. Today one can meet younger executives (many of whom are related to the founding fathers), and a great number of well-educated and sophisticated managers.

A negotiating team in Korea should include a Korean language expert or interpreter in case the negotiations take place in Korean. This is becoming less likely, however, since younger Korean managers are capable of speaking English. It helps to have at least one person who has good knowledge of the Korean language and culture. Try to match the Korean team on negotiators' status and numbers. Just as Japanese negotiators may gain an edge by bringing more people and experts to the table, so can Koreans.

Mature men with impressive status and credentials should lead the negotiating team in Korea. They should have a good understanding of the culture, be able to socialize with their Korean hosts (frequently without their spouses), and gain their trust and respect in every phase of the negotiations. The team should also include some technical experts, as well as support personnel, depending on the size and type of negotiations. It is much easier to have personal relationships with Korean associates than it is with the Chinese or Japanese. Many have observed that South Koreans are much more open to foreigners.

Negotiating style

Kibun, which roughly means "inner feeling" is one of the most important elements of Korean psychology and business culture. South Koreans will go to great length to protect a person's *kibun*, and they expect the same. While this "inner feeling" is hard to define, one can say that it takes a lot of politeness, tact and dignity to preserve one's *kibun*. An injury to one's *kibun* or face is probably an insurmountable mistake that should be avoided at all costs.

Compared to the Japanese, Koreans are much more animated and emotional, and they do not always exhibit the same spirit of mutual dependency that has characterized Japanese business for so long. The Western concept of fairness does not exist in the same form in Korea, where loyalty, especially to one's family and company, may supersede fair play. **Korean negotiators will try to find weaknesses in their adversaries**, so foreign negotiators should never appear rushed or lose patience. Koreans, like the Chinese and Japanese, will also use stall tactics to force the other side to make concessions before certain deadlines. Based on this, the foreign team should never inform Korean negotiators of their travel plans or other deadlines so they can negotiate on a level field.

Another important aspect of Korean negotiating style is their use of **distributive bargaining**. Koreans are hagglers when it comes to price, and they will raise the initial price to leave room for negotiations. Foreign negotiators should consider this tendency and make room for bargaining.

Issues discussed

Just like their close neighbors, Koreans discuss **relationship-based issues**, especially with new companies or negotiators. This is perhaps why business entertainment is just as important in South Korea as it is in Japan. Korean negotiators want to know about their counterparts' character, habits and intentions before they do any business with them. After establishing a relationship, they will eventually discuss substantive issues, such as pricing and other terms.

Establishing trust

Establishing personal trust between negotiators is very important to Koreans. While the Japanese have great group and company loyalties, Koreans have more personal loyalties to each other, and especially to their employers. This makes gaining trust and establishing relationships very important. The key to establishing trust with Korean counterparts **is past experience**. If the experience was a good one, then Koreans will remember it and treat the other party accordingly; if not, they will be cautious and methodical. Other trust-gaining methods include **non-task sounding and after-hours entertainment** and camaraderie.

Persuasion

Keeping face and harmony are the most important aspects of Korean persuasion. After establishing that both parties need each other to do business, it is vital to guard against anything that may be construed by Koreans as crude or improper behavior. This may include disturbing the harmony of the group through outbursts or accusations. It could also include embarrassing members of the Korean team and causing them to lose face in front of others. This is totally unacceptable, especially if it affects a senior Korean negotiator. Koreans are tough bargainers who will not mind equally tough adversaries who use strong bargaining techniques, but they will not tolerate acts that cause loss of face and disharmony.

Western negotiators, in particular, should take care not to lose their patience and tempers when dealing with Koreans. An important Korean persuasion tactic is delaying the deal as long as possible and stretching the patience of the other party. Perhaps the reasons why the Japanese are so successful in Korea is that they are masters of masking their emotions, and they can play the waiting game just as well, if not better, than the Koreans.

The specific persuasion tactics that are likely to be effective in Korea are:

1) **Visual Aids**. Colorful pictures, charts, graphs and posters will greatly enhance one's presentation, and correspondingly, one's ability to persuade. Product samples are also a good idea.
2) The Koreans like to **"high-ball" or "low-ball."** Be prepared and respond in kind. Koreans like to **haggle**.
3) **Metaphors, stories and analogies** are a good idea in Korea if delivered in a friendly story-telling manner. Be sure to avoid anything that implies a threat or fear tactic.
4) Certain requests that we might consider to be corruption may be normal business practices in Korea. Decide how you plan to initiate or respond to such requests.
5) **Stalling** is considered to be a very acceptable negotiation tactic in Korea. Your Korean counterparts will stall.

6) **Write everything down.** Take notes in an unobtrusive manner and later review them with your Korean counterparts.

7) Receiving the **technical specifications up-front** or in the beginning of the negotiation is a good idea in Korea.

8) Like most of Asia, Koreans will imply that they have influence with government officials or with important individuals. You may wish to **imply that you have influence** with certain people that are relevant to the transaction.

9) Considering the possible volatility of Korean negotiators, **diffusion questions** and **distractions tactics** can be very useful during periods of conflict.

10) Expect the Koreans to use the **"big-picture"** negotiation style. Nothing is decided until everything is decided. You should probably plan on a similar strategy.

11) Korea is a hierarchical as well as collectivist society. Referring to the **approval of others** and especially the approval of **respected higher authorities** in regards to your company, product, etc. should prove to be an effective method of persuasion.

12) Discussion of harmonious future beneficial business relationships is an integral part of Korean as well as other Asian business cultures. Your **presentation of possible futuristic cooperative endeavors, the use of positive imagery,** etc. should be beneficial during business presentations and negotiations.

13) Only use fear tactics, ultimatums, threats, loud voices, etc. when an agreement does not seem possible or in retaliation for a similar behavior. Otherwise remain very polite and civil at all times. This is an all-or-nothing strategy, is always kept in reserve, and is a response to latent conflict.

Tactics to avoid include:

1) **Do not self-promote.** Humility is considered a virtue.

2) **Do not engage in Two-Sided Appeals.** An appeal providing the other side with some negative information will appear amateurish.

3) Avoid extensive information sharing.
4) **Avoid direct personal conflict**.
5) Avoid extensive direct eye contact, elaborate demonstratives (although reserved non-verbal behavior is okay), and touching.

Resolving disputes

If problems arise during the negotiations, it is best to handle them on a personal level, and to get the head negotiators involved in reestablishing trust through personal interaction and after-hours entertainment.

Group and individual dynamics

Everything in Korean society points to its collectivist nature, and business is no different. Koreans are taught from childhood to respect family and society at large. They learn cooperation and teamwork in school and apply these principles for the rest of their lives. It is not surprising that Korean negotiators **are group-oriented**, and they will work together every step of the way to attain their goals. While the Chinese identify their sense of collectivism with work groups (*danweis*), and the Japanese with their corporations, Koreans tend to change their groups more readily, and their loyalty is more with individual managers than lifetime loyalties to companies. Therefore, they tend to have **more individual aspirations than their Japanese or Chinese counterparts**, and it is possible to have individual meetings/negotiations with Korean businessmen, which is very rare in either China or Japan. Any decisions and/or suggestions out of these meetings, however, have to be reviewed and approved by the group before final agreement.

Risk

Following a trend in collectivist and Confucian societies, **South Koreans do not like risk in business**. This ensures group harmony and eliminates any potential loss of face or group security. Rather than taking risks, many South Korean companies have opted for long-term commitments, even if this means low initial profit. This need for long-term security greatly outweighs the tendency to try for risky, but profitable ventures. By presenting any business to South Koreans as risky, foreign companies have much less success than those that promise long-term relationships and commitments.

Decision making

Unlike Japan, which has a well-established bottom-up decision-making system, South Korea has a variety of practices in that regard. Although Korean society at large is taught *pummi*, which means "deliberating," there are many forms of decision-making in practice today. **The founders or chief officers of some smaller companies make decisions on their own, while large corporations may practice a consensus approach**. South Korean managers will consult company experts and heads of departments before arriving at a decision. Korean decisions may take a long time by Western standards, especially if they involve government agencies. These usually start at the lowest level of government, and work their way upwards in a vertical system. South Korean companies can usually implement their decisions quickly upon reaching an agreement. Government agencies, on the other hand, may require more time due to the complex red tape in Korean government.

Type of agreement

Koreans in general prefer **written agreements that state the principles of the relationship**. They will prefer the contract to have some degree of flexibility, with provisions for negotiated modifications. Because of long periods of foreign domination, Koreans have only recently had the privilege of developing their own legal apparatus. Since their culture seeks to promote harmony, the legality of a contractual agreement is of less importance than the collaborative atmosphere out of which the agreement emerges. If notes have been taken and a consensus reached on the salient points of an agreement, then those elements can become the basis of a legal contract.

Larger companies prefer to enter into substantial contracts that spell out the details of the agreement. Smaller businesses often prefer flexible terms that they can modify if the need arises.

NOTES:

Chapter 18

Mexico

- *Country Background*
- *The Mexican Culture*
- *Business Protocol*
- *Communication Style*
- *The Mexican Concept of Negotiations*

For many years, Mexicans have referred to the United States as "el colossus del norte." Considering Mexico's vast human and natural resources, some North Americans now refer to Mexico as "the colossus to the south."

Sandwiched between two oceans to the east and west, Mexico is also strategically situated between the USA to the north and Central America to the south. It has an area roughly three times the size of Texas, and its enormous shoreline and other natural resources provide Mexico with a steady income from tourism, as well as mineral and oil sales.

The USA and Mexico share similar economic and political interests, but have different histories and cultural values. Despite these differences, Mexico's proximity to the USA has made the two countries major trading partners. From Mexico's perspective, no other country comes close to their trade levels with the USA.

Country Background

History

The human history of Mexico goes back thousands of years when Indian tribes cultivated the land and later vied for control of the best areas. The Mayan and Aztec cultures flourished in Mexico and produced well-structured societies that possessed advanced science and agriculture. Due to a combination of internal problems on the part of the Indians, and ruthlessness on the part of the Spanish conquistadors, the great Aztec empire came to a sudden end shortly after the Spanish conquest in 1517. Spain ruled until Mexico gained its independence in 1810.

Today one can observe the effects of Mexican history on the country's culture and beliefs. Although Spanish is the official language, there are almost 150 Indian languages currently spoken in Mexico. The Spanish brought with them a strict adherence to Catholicism. Moorish social patterns, still fresh in Spain, also influenced architecture, communications styles, and attitudes between men and women.

The USA and Mexico fought a war between 1845 and 1848 in which US troops marched all the way into Mexico City. The ensuing treaty forced Mexico to cede to the USA the lands that now constitute California, Nevada, Utah, Arizona, New Mexico, and parts of Colorado and Wyoming. Other historical events that took place in Mexican history include the revolution of 1910, and USA military incursions into northern Mexico at the beginning of the 20th century.

The tenuous historical relationship between the USA and Mexico is apparent in some negative attitudes the two peoples have had toward each other. This is more apparent on an individual level than a national or official one, as evident from the enormous economic and cultural exchanges between the two countries.

Government

Mexico is a federal republic with executive, legislative, and judicial branches. An elected president who serves a six-year term, and may not be reelected, heads the government. The bicameral National Congress is made up of a Senate with 128 members and the Chamber of Deputies with 500 members. The Partido Revoluciono Institucional (PRI) has dominated for many years, but other parties have made inroads in recent elections. Mexican citizens can vote when they reach the age of eighteen.

The highest court is the Supreme Court of Justice, whose judges are appointed by the president and approved by the Senate. The Napoleonic Code initially influenced Mexican Law. It was later revised to accommodate revolutionary demands for land reform. The Federal Constitution Article 27 indicates that original ownership within the territory of Mexico belongs to the nation. This article permits the Mexican government to impose restrictions or intervene even to the point of transferring the ownership of private property. This same right exists in regard to patents and the means of production associated with them. Patents may be subject to expropriation or their terms of duration reduced. This right, however, can only be invoked if it is deemed to be for the public good. Another facet of Mexican Law is that only native-born or naturalized Mexicans may acquire direct ownership of Mexican land.

Demographics

Mexico's population has reached 102 million, and is increasing by almost 2% per year. Following the United States and Brazil, Mexico has the third largest population in the western hemisphere. Mexico is a relatively youthful nation, for almost half the population is under the age of 20. It is also estimated that Mexico City will become one of the world's most populous cities with a projected 32 million inhabitants.

More than 60% of Mexico's citizens are mestizos who are a mixture of Spanish and Indian ancestry. Amerindians comprise the second largest ethnic group at 30%, and Caucasians constitute 9% of the population. A widespread educational system has contributed to a respectable literacy rate of 90%. The life expectancy for males is 69 years and 75 years for females.

Economy

Despite some economic and political setbacks and a large foreign debt, Mexico sustains a huge economy based on oil production, tourism, agriculture and manufacturing.

Mexico is presently the fifth-leading exporter of oil in the world. Other important mineral exports include natural gas, silver (top exporter in the world), salt, coal, iron ore, gold and copper. Service industries, such as tourism, banking and advertising, produce approximately 68% of the country's GDP. After oil, tourism brings in the second-largest influx of foreign funds.

Traditionally, Mexico has had an abundance of small farms and agricultural products. Agricultural production accounts for 5% of the GDP, but it employs 20% of the labor force.

Mexican industry today produces anything from textiles and tobacco to consumer products and motor vehicles and steel. The North American Free Trade Agreement (NAFTA) has increased trade between Mexico, the USA, and Canada, especially in the area of manufacturing. This is reflected in the growth of *maquiladora* factories all along the US-Mexican border. Taking advantage of NAFTA regulations, these firms import duty-free materials from the USA, and Mexican laborers assemble them for export back to the United States. The *maquiladoras* have created many jobs in Mexico, but some Mexicans complain that businesses are taking advantage of cheap Mexican labor while contributing to the pollution problem in the country. USA and

Mexican officials are trying to improve this situation through better enforcement of labor and pollution laws in Mexico.

The USA constitutes the dominant partner in Mexican exports, taking 88% of the total. In contrast, only 2% of Mexican exports go to Canada and 1% to Japan. Both export and import figures include in-bond industries, assembly plants in Mexico owned by US companies. Thus, almost 75% of Mexico's imports came from the USA, 11% from Europe, and 4% from Japan. These include metal working machines, agricultural machinery, electrical equipment, car parts for assembly, aircraft and aircraft parts.

The Mexican currency is the peso, which has suffered several instances of hyperinflation and fluctuating exchange rates for many years.

The Mexican Culture

Language

Spanish is the official language, although there are many Indian languages spoken by various Indian groups. The vast majority of Mexicans speak a Mestizo dialect of Spanish. Many in the upper class, however, speak a European dialect of the language, which is considered more prestigious. Most urbanites and business people also speak fluent English. Mexicans in general enjoy visitors who can speak Spanish and they truly love their native tongue. Visitors, especially those from North America, should not say that Spanish is an easy language to master. This may insult the hosts who might perceive this as a slight to their language. One should also remember that Mexicans consider themselves "Americans," and refer to USA citizens as *Norteamericanos*, which means North Americans, or *Estadounidense*, which means people from the US. Therefore, it is incorrect for USA. nationals in Mexico to refer to themselves as Americans, because all the people from Central and South American are also Americans.

Religion

Mexico does not have an official religion, although 90% of the population is Catholic, making Mexico the second largest Catholic nation of the world (after Brazil).

Protestants are growing in numbers and now account for 6% of the Mexican population. Religion plays a big role in Mexican daily life. Most Mexicans attend church and follow the church's teachings in family and social life. Mexican businesses close down during important religious holidays, including Easter.

Value system

Mexican values center around family, kinship and friendship. Although individuals are responsible for their actions, they take their families and close friends into account when making a group decision. Mexicans have intense relationships, and the family always exerts pressure and modifies the behavior of its members. Family members and friends frequently commit themselves to helping one another, especially in case of need.

Mexican society believes that each individual is spiritually unique, and that an individual doesn't necessarily distinguish himself through accomplishments, but through his dignity and inner spirit. This inner spirit must be protected at all costs, and a slight to a person's spirit is regarded as a grave provocation.

While some North Americans may define these qualities as vague or sentimental, they are very strong in Mexico. In contrast, Mexicans think that many North Americans are generally insensitive and only interested in material things. These feelings stem from differences in cultural and historical backgrounds, as well as a certain distrust of North American behavior due to the history of hostilities between the USA and Mexican nations.

In traditional Mexican society the behavior of men and women is quite different. Men are expected to be stronger and to be caretakers, while women are expected to be feminine and supportive of men. Both men and women generally shun North American or European women who break the mold and act aggressively. Likewise, men who enjoy nontraditional hobbies, such as cooking or needlepoint, should not advertise these traits to their Mexican hosts.

Machismo

One of the most talked-about and least-understood aspects of Latin and Mexican culture is machismo. This masculine trait probably has a foothold in all Latin cultures due to Arabic influences that go back to Moorish Spain. Many cultures that don't subscribe to machismo have a false impression of this strong cultural and individual trait. The myth about machismo is that it is blatantly disrespectful of women and the law, and manifested in sexual leers and pistol-carrying behavior. True machismo is less associated with sex and more broadly with authority.

A macho Mexican man is strong, courageous, and authoritative. Another interpretation, which comes as a surprise to many, is that macho men distinguish themselves intellectually in various fields including the sciences and philosophy. This is reminiscent of ancient Arab warriors/poets who were revered in society for their poetry and courage. The difference between the Arab and Latin cultures, however, seems to be in attitudes toward sexuality as part of machismo. Sexual behavior is less open and more discreet in the Arab world.

Mexican men revere their families and will traditionally take care of their mothers when they age. Many Mexican men show greater respect for their mothers than they show their wives. They often think that it is a weakness when North American men treat their wives better than their mothers.

Class structure / Stratification

Unlike its neighbors to the north, Mexican society is more class conscious. Mexicans in general do not believe that everyone is equal, and someone's accomplishments do not necessarily distinguish him if he doesn't have the right breeding and connections. There are great contrasts between the rich and the numerous poor. Mestizos dominate high political and armed forces positions, while those of Spanish ancestry tend to prevail in industry. Individuals with a lighter skin have traditionally had better economic and social status than individuals with Indian ancestry. Most Indian people are at the bottom of the stratification system.

Safety

Millions of tourists visit Mexico each year and enjoy themselves tremendously without encountering any crime or complications. As in any other country in the world, however, there is crime in Mexico. Business people visiting Mexico should use caution, avoid displaying money and valuables, and be cognizant of high-risk situations. Mexico is the main source for illicit drugs that enter the USA; avoid any contacts with drug traffickers, some of whom carry great amounts of cash for bribes and business deals, and are not averse to violence.

Drink only bottled water and avoid foods, especially salads, that are washed in tap water. Recommended immunizations should be obtained before your trip.

Business Protocol

Greetings and etiquette

Mexican men shake hands when greeting each other. Women often pat each other on the right forearm and shoulder in lieu of a handshake. If they are close friends or relatives, they may hug or kiss each other on the cheek. Men should wait for a woman to initiate a handshake before extending their hand. By the second or third meeting, Mexicans may consider a business counterpart close enough to kiss or hug. At parties or large meetings, it's customary to give a slight bow when entering the room. The host may introduce the guests to certain individuals, and one should greet them with a handshake and salutations. The same protocol applies for good-byes.

Titles are much more important in Mexico than in North America and most of Europe. One can address a person directly by using only the title, such as *Professor* or *Doctor*. People who are familiar with each other use first names, and it is best to wait for Mexican counterparts to initiate the change to a first-name basis. One should address persons without titles as Mr., Mrs. or Miss plus their last name, such as Señor Fernandez, Señora Fernandez, or Señorita Paz. Most Latinos have two surnames, one from their father, and the second from their mother. When addressing someone, it is customary to use only the father's surname. For example, Luis Fernandez Garcia is Señor Fernandez, and so on. One of the most common titles in Mexico is *"licensiado,"* which means the holder of a college degree. Using this or any other title in Mexico indicates respect and good manners.

Time

Mexico is a polychronic culture. To Mexicans, time is relative and fluid, and although they admire punctuality, not everyone practices it. Mexicans also prefer a slow pace of business, rather than rushing and setting deadlines. It is important to stress deadlines if they are important for business. Time in Mexico also means power, and executives may keep their business counterparts waiting in order to demonstrate their authority.

Business hours in Mexico are 9:30 AM to 6 PM and meetings may occur over breakfast, lunch or dinner. It's best to let the host decide when and where to meet. Lunch and the siesta may last from 1 to 3 PM.

Gifts

Gift giving in business is not required; however, small gifts or items with company logos are acceptable. One can also give a bottle of wine or nice cigarette lighters on subsequent visits. It is also customary to give gifts to secretaries, especially those in the private sector. To avoid any misunderstandings, it may be better if a female associate picks and presents the gift to a secretary, or the gift giver could say that his wife chose the gift. Dinner guests are not required to bring gifts, but the gesture is appreciated. Yellow and violet flowers represent death, and red flowers cast spells, so it is tactful to avoid these colors. Other gifts to avoid include silver, which is used to make trinkets for tourists, and knives, which denote the severing of friendship.

Bribery, or *mordida,* is not a crime in Mexico, but in most cases, a very acceptable form of doing business. Foreign executives and managers visiting Mexico should realize that to many Mexicans, *mordida* is simply an unofficial service charge, and therefore should not overreact or withdraw from negotiations if asked to pay *mordida*.

Business entertainment

Usually, one must know a person in Mexico before doing business, and that usually means knowing their family as well. **It is customary for Mexican business people to invite their guests to social events and dinners at home**. Visitors should graciously accept these invitations, which are meant to strengthen ties and allow both parties to know and trust each other better. Mexicans rarely discuss business at home and they genuinely make an effort to get to know their guests and their families. It's customary to arrive about 30 minutes late to these events, since the hosts may not expect the visitors to arrive on time and may not be ready.

The best topics to discuss outside the office include Mexican sights, history, culture and soccer. It's not a good idea to discuss controversial subjects such as illegal immigration to the USA or the Mexican-American war. Visitors should never offer to calculate or split a bill at a Mexican restaurant. Instead, they should symbolically haggle over the bill, and reciprocate by inviting the host to have dinner with them another time. Women should be careful not to initiate situations that may be misconstrued by Mexican businessmen. It is wise to have other associates present whenever meetings take place outside the office.

Dress

When many think of Mexico, they think of beautiful beach resorts, sandals and shorts. This describes the beach in Mexico, not the formal office environment that dominates most of the country, especially metropolitan Mexico City. **In most cases, men should wear a conservative dark suit and tie, and women should wear a dress or a skirt and a blouse.** Mexican negotiators care about what a person looks like and what he/she wears. If someone is badly dressed, he/she may be misjudged and mistrusted, so why take a chance on this issue?

For casual wear, men may wear a light shirt, and women a skirt or pants. Jeans are not usually appropriate except in very casual settings, and they should be pressed and new. Except for resort areas, shorts for both genders and revealing clothing for women are inappropriate and may raise some eyebrows. Men may wear the traditional Mexican *guayabera,* which is a light shirt that is not tucked in.

Communication Style

Business language

Mexicans use a high-context language when conversing and negotiating. The communicating style is indirect, and Mexicans may not immediately come to the point. They also dislike the North American style of getting down to business quickly, and would rather first converse at length to get to know someone. This may also include telling people what they want to hear, rather than telling them the "whole truth." Truth in Mexico is somewhat relative, and one can stretch it in the interest of preserving personal dignity and friendship. The overall tone of Mexican communication is warm and sincere, regardless of the discussion.

Non-verbal communication

Mexicans use non-verbal communication through gestures, body language and touching. They consider direct eye contact and gazing as confrontational, and they use intermittent eye contact when conversing. Mexicans also frequently exhibit passionate and emotional behavior even when discussing business. They smile and laugh frequently, and think that Anglo-Saxons are sometimes too serious and cold in comparison.

Mexicans converse at a much closer physical distance than North Americans and Europeans. Pulling away from someone may be considered unfriendly, and a Mexican may step nearer to reclose the gap. Mexican men make physical contact by touching the shoulders and holding one another's arm. To withdraw from such a gesture could be insulting.

Men should not put their hands in their pockets or put their hands on their hips, which may be construed as impolite and confrontational. Mexicans in public may catch someone's attention with a "psst-psst" sound, which is not considered rude.

The Mexican Concept of Negotiations

Selecting personnel

It is a good idea to have a local well-connected person make contacts and introductions for the negotiating team. This person could be an invaluable member of the team when it comes to giving advice on Mexican business and culture. If the person possesses the appropriate credentials, he/she can also help make appointments and possibly attend the negotiating sessions to add prestige to the team.

Negotiators in Mexico are chosen on the basis of status rather than experience. As a class-conscious society, Mexicans respect someone's station in life. A high-level negotiator in Mexico is also well-connected with influential political and economic entities. Most Mexican executives are men who possess strong personalities. They may resent having to negotiate with lower-management staff if they are upper-management executives. In other words, just as in most parts of the world, it may be best to send a negotiating team that mirrors the qualities and character of the host team. Women are accepted on the team, as long as they are not the decision-makers, and as long as they do not act in ways that offend the Mexican team.

The negotiating team should display their status level. If they have degrees and titles, they should mention them. Also, the team should stay at good hotels, eat at the best restaurants, and wear the best clothes and shoes while in Mexico.

Negotiating style

Negotiating in Mexico is a slow process that may require several stages. Following the cultural norm, it is essential to establish a strong and amiable relationship with the Mexican team to facilitate the negotiation process. The overall business atmosphere during negotiations is usually friendly and easy-going. Once the teams establish a good working relationship, it is possible to **bargain behind the scenes**, which is a preferred tactic of Mexican negotiators. Mexicans will also use **distributive bargaining** techniques when negotiating. They are sensitive to differences of opinion and loss of face.

Stalling and procrastinating may also be used in Mexican negotiations. Foreign negotiators should not assume they can get the deal quickly, and shouldn't try to offer one, which may instill distrust in the Mexican team. It is important not to rush Mexican negotiators by using North American or European standards of time. This may actually cause more harm than good.

Issues discussed

Personalismo, **which may be equated with long-term trust and friendship, is a big part of Mexican culture.** Mexicans like to build relationships before going into business. Therefore, the negotiating teams initially discuss issues that establish relationships and trust.

Establishing trust

Since they are a warm people, they like others who exhibit warmth and friendliness. Many **Mexicans like to start small with a minor transaction**. Once trust is established, they may expand the business dealings. The bases of trust in Mexico is established through personalized and warm interaction. The time it takes for "small talk" and personal interaction in Mexico is invaluable to gain trust and understanding. The two parties can talk about family, children, Mexican culture, soccer and other subjects that reveal their personalities and character.

The history of Mexico and the USA, especially dating back to the Mexican-American war, creates a lot of skepticism regarding USA intentions within much of the Mexican population. Yet, figures show clearly that the USA. is Mexico's largest trade partner. This demonstrates that Mexicans trust people in general, and can let go of their patriotic sentiments if it means doing good business with certain corporations or people.

Persuasion

Mexicans, unlike North Americans, value emotionalism and charisma in a person. A persuasive argument in Mexico includes dogma, emotion, and possibly a mixture of machismo and patriotism. Foreign negotiators in Mexico may have to persuade their Mexican counterparts that they are offering more than just products and services, such as a very beneficial relationship to the Mexican firm, family or society. Form may be as important as substance in this situation, and

Mexicans will be persuaded by friendly, emotional appeals from their counterparts. Who tries to persuade the Mexican team and how this is done is sometimes more important than the actual content of the persuasion.

Mexicans also appreciate presentations with tangibles and visual support, such as graphs, charts, samples and models. The negotiating team can use this support to prove the benefits of the deal. Another strong influence in Mexican society is Catholicism, which makes religion another factor in persuasive argument. Therefore, do not offend established religious or societal beliefs, but use these to advantage whenever possible. Mexicans also respect experience and historical knowledge, especially if applied properly to the business environment. Finally, forms of bribery may be very persuasive in Mexican business. One must keep in mind that this practice is not such a terrible thing in Mexico, but simply a method to "grease the wheels" and get people motivated. However, any such efforts should be done subtlety with finesse, not openly at the negotiating table.

The persuasion tactics that can be generally used with Mexicans or will be used by Mexicans are:

1) Mexicans love to **haggle** and are quite lively while doing so. **Distributive bargaining** is a favorite pastime. The Mexicans will almost always **"high-ball" or "low-ball"** a deal. Try to enjoy the process and you will be more successful.

2) **Diffusion questions** are often used.

3) **Distraction tactics** are useful in times of conflict and will definitely be used by your Mexican counterparts.

4) **Positive emotional tactics as well as personal appeals** should be useful in Mexico.

5) **Metaphors, stories and analogies** are a good idea in Mexico.

6) Certain requests that we might consider to be corruption may be normal business practices in Mexico. Decide how you plan to initiate or respond to such requests.

7) **Stalling** is considered to be a very acceptable negotiation tactic in Mexico.

8) Receiving the technical specifications up-front is almost always helpful.

9) **Write everything down.** Take notes in an unobtrusive manner and later review them with your Mexican counterparts. From the USA perspective, agreements have been known to mysteriously change in Mexico.

10) **Supported Facts.** The presentation of logical/factual information is always helpful. However, do not overdo it. The Mexicans will quickly tire of a highly technical and drab presentation.

11) Mexicans tend to use a little puffery, but less than one finds in Spain or Brazil. So, build up your firm, your products/services, and yourself with **slight exaggerations, enthusiasm, and non-verbal demonstratives**.

12) **Speak with conviction and confidence.** Mexicans tend to be great orators/story tellers and will expect the same from you and your firm.

13) **Visual proof sources** are helpful in almost any culture.

14) Mexico is hierarchical and individualistic at work and sport settings, but collectivist in the home. General associational appeals are likely to be ineffective in business. However, referring to the approval of respected **higher authorities** in regards to your company, product, etc. may prove to be an effective method of persuasion.

15) Because Mexicans are an emotional as well as a socially-engaging group, the **presentation of possible future cooperative endeavors** should be very persuasive.

16) Use a **"big-picture"** strategy. Nothing is decided until everything is decided.

17) Based upon the desire for harmony in Mexico, the **"Feel-Felt-Found"** objection-handling tactic should prove to be effective when delivered in a harmonious and emotionally expressive manner.

18) **Use silence as a persuasion mechanism**. Mexicans do not like silence. Thus, silence may make them feel uncomfortable and prompt concessions. However, only use this tactic late in the negotiations process after rapport has been firmly established. Using this strategy too early will destroy rapport-building efforts, cause boredom, and increase doubts.

Tactics to avoid include:

1) **Avoid conflict**. Do not be blunt and to the point. Mexicans are very concerned with loss of "face," especially with Americans. This is much more critical than in other Latin countries. Use your best "face" saving strategies in Mexico.

2) Do not use fear tactics, ultimatums, threats, yelling, etc. Mexicans are looking for an enjoyable, trusting, and harmonious exchange.

3) **Do not engage in extensive information sharing**. Disclosure of information is a bargaining chip in Mexico and should be used as an item of trade, not freely provided.

4) **Avoid long boring monotone lectures**. This type of lecture is not enjoyable anywhere. Variations in tonality, rate of speech, and pitch are even more critical in Mexico. Presentations must be accompanied by discussions, breaks, humor, etc.

Resolving disputes

The most effective way to resolve disputes in Mexico is **through personal appeal and dogma**. This may entail reverting back to the earlier stages of the negotiations when the two sides won each other's trust through *personalismo*. It is normal for Mexicans to argue and exhibit emotions in business, yet want to agree and eventually do so if they like and trust their counterpart. This is why establishing trust and a relationship is so important in Mexico.

Another way is to ask influential members of the team, or even outside well-connected people, to help resolve the disagreement. By keeping one's dignity and respect for others, rather than losing face and putting others on the spot during an argument, one has a much better chance of reaching an agreement. It's also important to not compromise too quickly in some situations, which may be perceived as weakness and cause a loss of respect.

Mexican Law provides for the arbitration of disputes. Articles 609 to 635 in the eighth chapter in the Code of Civil Procedure empower conflicting parties to subject their disagreements to arbitration. The National Chamber of Commerce in Mexico City has a standing arbitration committee that functions in accordance with official regulations.

Group and individual dynamics

There are two major influences that drive group and individual dynamics in Mexico. The first is a strong loyalty to one's family and the influence of family obligations. The second is deeply-rooted individuality and machismo. Mexican negotiators have **very high individual aspirations**, and depending on their status, may be very competitive with each other or with their foreign counterparts. On the other hand, **loyalty to the group, especially in a family-owned business, may precede any other rule** or principle. The negotiating team should try to understand the individual and group dynamics driving its Mexican counterpart.

Risk

Mexicans are risk averse. They will try to develop and pursue low-risk alternatives that are almost guaranteed not to hurt their business and their families. If a proposal carries risk with it, Mexicans are usually very skeptical and pessimistic. By presenting a risky proposal, or a proposal that Mexicans perceive as risky, a negotiator can lose ground and possibly the deal. Therefore, it is best to approach the negotiating process with appreciation for Mexican risk-adverse propensities.

Decision making

Mexican government agencies and traditional businesses **tend to concentrate power at the top**, and to delegate little authority. This top-down management style may be changing with younger Mexican managers, but for the most part it is still in existence. It is not unusual for Mexican top executives to make decisions with little or no consensus among the group. Their subordinates usually accept these decisions without much conflict since they accept and respect the powers of their superiors.

Senior Mexican managers, however, may rely on middle management for negotiations and reports. In a few situations, this may be frustrating for foreign negotiating teams, since in many cases Mexican middle managers are not as knowledgeable as their senior counterparts, and may not be able to make even small decisions or recommendations. It is important for the negotiating team to ascertain the roles and authority of their Mexican counterparts during the negotiation process so no mistaken assumptions regarding decision-making power are made.

Type of agreement

A written agreement is the most important part of an agreement between Mexican and foreign negotiating teams. Verbal agreements are not binding in Mexico, and should not be taken seriously, especially since Mexican negotiators sometimes say what their counterparts want to hear. However, under Mexican law **written memos or letters can be contractually binding**. Although not required, it may be wise to hire a lawyer or a legal expert to finalize the agreement between the two parties. Although verbal agreements are legally meaningless, it is important to enter agreements with Mexicans in good faith and trust on both sides. If Mexicans feel that they have been fairly treated by a partner who means well, they will support the agreement in any form.

The Federal Civil Code regulates a wide variety of contracts. Some contracts must follow administrative guidelines. The general law on commercial companies defines the contractual arrangement of a number of entities, including limited partnerships, limited liability companies, marketable share corporations, cooperatives, and joint ventures. Marketable share companies are currently popular because they are able to channel greater capital resources. A minimum investment and five shareholders are necessary to establish this type of entity as defined by Article 89 of the General Law on Commercial Companies. Foreign companies can operate in Mexico following authorization by the Secretary of Foreign Affairs.

Chapter 19

Philippines

- *Country Background*
- *The Filipino Culture*
- *Business Protocol*
- *Communication Style*
- *The Filipino Concept of Negotiations*

Most Westerners who come to the Philippines are pleasantly surprised to find the familiar conveniences of an American lifestyle and English spoken everywhere. Culturally, Filipinos are unique. The majority of Filipinos are of Malay descent, yet most have Hispanic surnames and are Roman Catholic. This is the only predominantly Christian nation in Asia. It has the third-largest English-speaking population in the world following the United States and the United Kingdom.

What gives complexity to the Filipino character is their colonial experience with imposed foreign values that the Filipinos either reacted to or adapted to in their own fashion. Almost 400 years of Spanish Catholic rule, followed by over 40 years of American free-enterprise colonization, reshaped Filipino society for better or for worse into what it is today.

Filipinos are a gregarious, happy, generous people. It is not difficult to win their friendship and goodwill. But to really know the Filipino culture one must probe past the Western veneer and an entirely different perspective emerges.

Country Background

History

The oldest human remains found in the Philippine Archipelago is a 22,000 year-old fossil skull cap found in the Tabon Caves in Quezon Palawan, but stone tools suggest primitive humans may have lived in the Philippines up to 500,000 years ago. The majority of the ancestors of present-day Filipinos came from Malaysia. From the 10th to the 16th century, foreign traders made their way to the archipelago. The Chinese brought porcelain and silk and profoundly influenced the entire Philippine culture. Around the 14th century, Arabs arrived. Islam was introduced, and remains a dominant influence in the southern Philippines. Because of this Muslim influence, that region of the Philippines put up a strong resistance to both Spanish and American colonization.

In 1521, Filipinos met Magellan's fleet, halfway through the first circumnavigation of the world. He named the islands after King Phillip II of Spain. Next came the Portuguese, the Dutch, and the British. However, the region fell under the colonial influence of Spain until 1899 when the territory was ceded to the USA at the end of the Spanish-American War. Filipinos had fought for independence against Spain and had proclaimed their independence on June 12. 1898. (In 1998 they celebrated the centennial of this event.) The Philippines then fought for independence against the United States in a conflict that lasted for 12 years and cost many thousands of Filipino lives. In order to use the resources of the colony more fully, the United States brought considerable infrastructural development to the country. Transportation, communication systems, and education were improved. In 1935 the nation became the Commonwealth of the Philippines, but was still under USA control. In 1941, the Japanese conquered the Philippines, but allied troops (both USA and Filipino) repulsed the Japanese in 1945. The Philippines finally gained independence from the United States on July 4, 1946.

The Philippines now face a future relatively free of foreign political influences, but without the millions of dollars the USA military poured into their economy. Currently, the Philippines is struggling with high unemployment, a stagnant economy, and a huge debt.

Government

Naturally, Filipino's tend to see their history as a long struggle for independence from foreign domination: first from Spain for almost 400 years; then from the United States for around 40 years; and from Japan for five years. The country's official name is the Republic of the Philippines and it is a unitary republic patterned after the United States. The first Philippine constitution dates back to 1935 when the Commonwealth of the Philippines came into existence under the guidance of the United States. The president is both the head of state and head of the government. Presidents are elected to six-year terms. There are two legislative houses: a 24-seat Senate and a 250-seat House of Representatives. Thirty of the house seats are nonelective, being allocated to various sectoral interests. Citizens are eligible to vote when they reach the age of eighteen.

Their legal system is based on Spanish and Anglo-American law. Supreme Court Justices are appointed for four-year terms by the president on the recommendation of the Judicial Bar Council.

Demographics

The Philippines is a nation of contrasts struggling to find its identity. It is a collectivist society, but its institutions are primarily Western. Its population of approximately 85 million is well-educated with a high degree of literacy (95%), yet there is considerable poverty. It is a working democracy, but real political and economic power is vested in a few.

Approximately 43% of the population live in the cities and 57% live in the country. The city of Manila is the most densely populated area. The population is expanding, with a growth rate of 2%. Life expectancy rates are 65 years for males and 71 years for females.

Ethnically, Filipinos are 92% Christian Malay, 4% Muslim Malay, 2% Chinese and a small smattering of other ancestry such as Spanish. A large percentage of Filipinos have mixed ancestry, such as 7/8 Malay and 1/8 Chinese.

Economy

The Philippine economy has been struggling for a number of years. It was beginning to recover from political turmoil and the fall of Marcos in the 1980's, when it was further damaged by natural disasters and the closing of USA military bases. With all these factors already impacting the country, it was not as deeply affected by the 1997-98 Asian recession as other Asian rim countries.

One of the primary limits on the Philippine economy has been inadequate electricity. It is estimated that the shortages in electrical power alone have cost the economy over a billion dollars in lost output every year. Brownouts also produce a secondary effect on employment and consumer spending, since firms are sometimes forced to reduce work hours or in some cases, lay people off. However, newly-built power plants are now producing electricity and others are being constructed. Coal and hydroelectricity have reduced the Philippines' dependence on imported oil from 95% of the energy supply in 1973 to 50% in 2000.

The Philippines is the world's leading exporter of coconut products, but their relative importance has declined and they now make up about 10% of exports. Increasingly important now are electronics (25%) and

textiles (20% of exports). Bananas and handicrafts have become growth industries. Overall, agriculture provides about a third of export revenue and employs about 40% of the labor force. Fishing, which accounts for about 5% of exports, has boomed with sales of shrimp to Japan.

Extensive cutting has depleted the forests, but mining remains important with gold, silver, copper, nickel, iron, lead, and chromium in rich deposits. The Philippines is the world's eighth-largest gold producer. Despite the international recession, the number of Filipinos working abroad, especially in Asia and the Middle East, has remained constant. Without the estimated 2 billion USD in annual remittances from these workers, the country's GNP would not have grown.

By GDP standards, the Philippine economy is usually placed around 40th in the world and slightly lower on the per capita scale. The Philippines enjoys a trade surplus but it is only marginal. Its major trading partners include the USA, Japan, Singapore, Hong Kong, and the UK. Major Philippine imports are raw materials, intermediate goods, capital goods, and petroleum products.

An English-speaking labor force, extensive natural resources, and a large domestic market put the Philippines in a strong position as it faces competition from China, Vietnam, and Indonesia. A top priority now is to address structural defects that have held the nation back, such as insufficient revenue, large corporate monopolies, and the extreme and explosive unequal distribution of wealth. These factors impede economic reform and discourage foreign investment.

The currency of the Philippines is the peso.

The Filipino Culture

Language

There are more than 11 languages and 87 dialects in the Philippine Archipelago. Nine of the major languages are spoken by 89% of the people. There are common roots and similarities in sound and grammar among these languages, but words introduced from Chinese, Spanish, and English have been added, all making for a complicated mix.

The national language, called Pilipino or Taglish, is primarily Tagalog-based. The US introduced English, along with the public school system, in the early 1900's. English is widely utilized in business and government. However, Americans do not always easily understand it, since Filipinos have added some of their own complex phonetic variations.

Spanish is another language spoken fluently by many Filipinos. Some also speak Arabic, Chinese or Nippongo.

Religion

Christianity is the dominant faith in the Philippines, with 83% Roman Catholic and 9% Protestant. During the centuries of Spanish colonialism, Catholicism was the only acceptable faith, and its teachings, vocabulary, and practices left an indelible mark upon the Filipino culture. Political channels for advancement were blocked to the Filipinos but membership in the clergy offered an opportunity to gain influence and prestige.

Islam is a significant minority religion composing about 5% of the populace, mostly in Southern Mindanao. A final 3% of the population is a mixture of Buddhist and some indigenous sects.

The historical tension between Christians and Muslims occasionally spills over into direct confrontation and violence.

Value system

Filipinos value group goals and long-term relationships more than personal goals and short-term results. Hierarchical positions within their culture are closely observed and older people are accorded special deference. They appreciate harmony, politeness, and modesty. They tend to avoid direct confrontation whenever possible and public conflict is generally regarded as a taboo because someone is bound to lose face.

A Filipino's first loyalty is to his/her family. Their identity is deeply rooted in a web of kinship that helps create their social environment. One value that is tied to family and society is called *hiya* (shame). If one fails to live up to the standards of one's family and/or one's society, one is then in a socially-unacceptable situation, which creates a moral dilemma for that individual. *Hiya* is a controlling element in Philippine society. Thus, social acceptance is a basic Filipino cultural value. A smooth interpersonal relation with a minimum of conflict is a sought-after goal. Another value that permeates the Philippine culture is the notion of reciprocity or the idea of a debt of gratitude (*utang na loob*).

Filipinos also place considerable emphasis on (*amor propio*) self-esteem. Anything that might hurt another should be avoided. Another ingredient in Filipino social acceptance is trust (*tiwala*). Trust is one of the attributes one expects from close kin and friends but not necessarily from all acquaintances. Conflict situations are usually avoided because "hiya" and "amor-propio" may come into play. Therefore, intermediaries are often utilized as a means of resolving differences. These intermediaries play an important role not only in family and friendship matters but also in business affairs, government transactions, and in dealing with any facet of the Philippine bureaucracy.

Women in the Philippine society have had a changing position. The pre-Spanish society was comparatively free of sexism; children traced their lineage bilaterally, and women held power on all levels. The Spanish influence added an element of courtly respect, but also largely removed women from positions of power. The wife has traditionally been a decision-maker for the family and participates in all key questions on economic and social issues affecting the family, but has limited status outside the domestic sphere. However, more women have moved into the business arena in recent times.

Class structure / Stratification

The real social unit in Philippine society is the *barangay* (the family — mother, father, children, and bilateral members, which includes maternal and paternal relatives). Family influence permeates all facets of Philippine society, for it is the primary unit of corporate action around which social, economic and religious activities revolve. Economic activities, such as agriculture, fishing, and cottage industries commonly involve all the kin group's adult members, and often the older children as well, in cooperative labor. Corporations are also family-owned. Nepotism in government and business is widespread and a reflection of family cohesiveness.

In Philippine society there is an upper class, which stresses the importance of holding office and being an aristocrat. There is also a middle class, those who have an education and important technical and/or manual skills. A large number of poor workers or unemployed, plus rural peasants, make up the most common class. There are also a large number of misfits, beggars, outcasts, and criminals, who steal or beg on the streets.

Safety

Personal safety and security is an important consideration. Homicides, kidnapping, con games, pick pocketing, and credit card theft all occur. Foreign visitors are often victimized, and travel by public as well as private vehicles can be risky. Travel off the national highways and paved roads, particularly at night, can be very dangerous. Any lost or stolen passports should be reported immediately to the local police and the nearest consulate or embassy.

Another safety issue worth mentioning is health. Filipinos make a distinction between private space and public space and do not think of public space as a shared community asset. Filipinos are personally clean and may live in well-groomed and attractive homes, while on the outside garbage is strewn all over the sidewalk and streets. Public sanitation is appalling and it is advisable to have all one's vaccinations and immunizations up-to-date before visiting there.

Business Protocol

Greetings and etiquette

It is customary for Filipino **men** to **shake hands** when being introduced. Traditionally there is almost no physical contact between men and women. They tend to keep themselves respectfully apart. Some **women will shake hands but only if the male initiates the gesture.** Physical contact is common between people of the same gender. Males will hold hands or place their arms around one another without any homosexual overtones. **Females will usually greet each other with a hug or a kiss on the cheek.**

Titles along with one's surname are commonly utilized when introducing people. One would make an introduction by saying Mr. Villegas, or Mayor Villegas,

or Attorney Villegas, or Assistant Secretary Villegas and so forth. Titles reflect status and are often utilized in lieu of compensation or higher pay. The wife of a man with a title might also be addressed as Mrs. Secretary or Mrs. Mayor.

Time

The Philippines is a **polychronic** culture. They like to do many things at once for the stimulation this provides. Appointments should be scheduled one month in advance of arriving in the Philippines. Midmornings or late afternoons are usually the best times to schedule appointments. For meetings, one generally finds that those with higher posts arrive later than those in lower positions. However, Filipinos are usually **punctual for business** appointments, so one should be on time for any business meeting.

Social events are another matter. If one were to arrive on time for a party, one would appear to be too eager and greedy for food. It is **customary to be** at least 15 minutes to a half-hour **late**. The more important the guest, the later the appearance.

The Philippines are eight hours ahead of Greenwich Mean Time (GMT + 8) or thirteen hours ahead of USA Eastern Standard Time (EST + 13).

Gifts

Gift giving is a **critical** part of Filipino hospitality. Unlike the custom in some western societies (e.g. Australia), it is not customary to bring food or a bottle of wine when one is invited to dinner. If one were to bring these items, it would imply that the hosts are not able to provide enough for their guests.

Giving **flowers or a dessert delicacy**, however, would not offend the hosts and would be well received. A thank-you note is appropriate afterwards and would undoubtedly be appreciated. At the conclusion of a dinner party, Filipinos give their guests extra food to take home — an ancient tradition called *pabaon*. It is customary to give gifts to employees at Christmas. This is also a good time to show appreciation to others you've had regular dealings with, such as customers, clients, etc.

Business entertainment

Business entertainment is a long established custom in the Philippines. There are numerous entertainment options, but most of them revolve around **eating and drinking**. There are business breakfasts, lunches, dinners and banquets. In fact, every social occasion will have food. The Filipino greeting "*Kumain ka na ba*?" literally translated means, "Have you eaten?" The eating festivities help establish rapport, build friendships, and create an atmosphere conducive to harmonious business negotiations, which are very important from the Philippine perspective.

It impresses the Filipinos if you are willing to eat everything, especially the dishes that make most foreigners squeamish. Be sure and smile while you eat to show your appreciation. It is appropriate to share a dinner with your Filipino partners upon the conclusion of a deal. Whoever issued the invitation pays. Remember Filipinos like to exchange greetings upon entering and when leaving.

Dress

Dress at the **executive level** should be a **conservative business suit for males**, and **women should wear white blouses and dark suits or skirts**. However, the heat and humidity often allow business attire to be more casual. For many **business occasions, dark trousers, a white short-sleeved shirt and a tie are sufficient for males, while a white long-sleeved blouse and skirts** would be appropriate for women. Filipinos are style conscious and appreciate clothing that is fashionable.

Often Filipino men will wear an embroidered shirt called a *barong*. The *barong* is the national dress for men, the equivalent of our shirt and tie. It is worn outside over one's belt and trousers and without a tie. There is also a long-sleeved variety made from pineapple fibers with beautiful embroidery, which can be worn to even the most formal of occasions.

Communication Style

Business language

Filipinos are a friendly people and they will converse about almost anything. They tend to process their information subjectively and associatively. They would rather attempt to solve problems personally instead of going by the book. As one listens to Filipinos talk, one hears mostly gentle and quiet sounds. The only time they are loud or boisterous is when they are telling a joke or having a good time.

The Philippines is basically a **high-context** culture. When a Filipino says yes to an agreement, it could have a variety of meanings. It could mean yes, or it could mean maybe, or it could mean I don't know, or it could mean if you say so, or it could mean I hope you realize I really mean no. The Filipino tries to live harmoniously. He tries to please his guest or his business acquaintance by trying not to say no. He very much prefers to avoid conflict. By not saying no, he hopes to stall until he can find a good excuse or a way out of the dilemma. He will look for a third party, an intermediary to help extricate him from this situation.

The only way to confirm if a yes really means yes is to get it in writing. A negotiated written settlement would make a Filipino feel honor-bound to live up to that commitment.

Non-verbal communication

As previously noted, Filipinos cloud all social intercourse with a pleasant, polite, harmonious façade, which includes an **extensive use of and observance of non-verbal behavior**. Not only is it important to listen to the words a Filipino is saying, but also to the sound of his voice and the nonverbal context of the exchange. Filipinos **greet each other with their eyebrows**. When eye contact is established, instantly the eyebrows are raised and lowered. This is a recognition signal. A **smile** along with it makes a friendly hello without words.

An abrupt backward toss of the head with hard eye contact is a challenge, and is often accompanied by asking what it is you want. Staring has various nuances, most of them negative. Staring is generally considered rude, aggressive, and provocative. Intense eye contact is usually a danger signal. To stand with one's hands on one's hips is considered arrogant and challenging, an aggressive posture.

Often when a Filipino makes a faux pas, he will scratch the back of his lowered head. When crossing a room and cutting through people conversing, one clasps one's hands together in front and advances with lowered head. Another variation used to advance through a crowd is to extend just one hand, fingers together, elbow bent, and head bowed.

An abrupt brush of the fingers on your elbow may seek your attention. It is considered insulting to beckon someone by crooking your finger; the proper form is to use your hand, palm downward. A palm-upward motion is considered rude. Snapping one's fingers or clapping to call attention to a waiter is also rude. One is expected to try to catch his eye and make a slight motion with one's hand upraised. In desperation you may get away with a soft pssst, but polite Filipino society frowns on any loud sounds to call anyone. Filipinos will point out a direction by pouting their mouths or shifting their eyes towards the direction they are indicating.

The Filipino Concept of Negotiations

Selecting personnel

Negotiators should be well informed about the Philippines. They should be **mature, experienced, patient, and reflect social status**. Understanding Filipino is unnecessary because English is primarily used in business. It is probably preferable to have the negotiators be **male**. Even though women are participating more and more in the business world today, most Filipinos feel the proper role for a woman is as homemaker and mother.

Negotiating style

Businessmen who come to the Philippines will find a climate conducive to multinational commerce. Negotiators should be aware of the **familial networking** that will effect all phases of the negotiations. The style of doing business in the Philippines is **moderately formal** and **non-directive**. Filipinos place **personal relationships** in very high regard. More important to them than the merits of a proposal are the people behind the proposal. Reputation and status are very important to them, so they will want to build a relationship with the company they are considering doing business with. It would be prudent to respect and facilitate this need on their part.

You can assume that your Filipino counterparts have already discussed the topics on the agenda but that doesn't mean they'll be ready to settle anything. Whatever the case, Philippine negotiations will take time and it is advisable not to push in order to get right to the point. At the top level, negotiations may move smoothly, but at the level of actual implementation, many individuals will have to have input. This is where subordinates and go-betweens are important to help move the process along. In addition, it is unusual to work out an agreement in one trip to the Philippines. Businesses who regularly negotiate Philippine contracts expect to take several trips over a period of months to complete a complicated business deal.

Like other Asian countries, Filipinos are also concerned about saving face. They never want to be embarrassed in front of family, friends, or close associates. They are always conscious of the impression they are making, how they are sitting, standing, or talking, and what others might be thinking of them.

No matter what the final results, the discussion should always end cheerfully. One may feel they are wasting time, but to a Filipino, cultivating a friendship, establishing a valuable contact, and developing personal rapport are what make business wheels turn.

Issues discussed

In a highly personal society, business is best done on a face-to-face basis in a warm, pleasant atmosphere. Since social contacts are more important in the Philippines than business issues, **one must establish rapport and be comfortable with the other person before proceeding**. Eventually, primary business issues will be dealt with, but only after all the relationship needs have been met.

This may mean one first goes out dining and, while you might want to get to the point immediately, the Filipino will talk about mutual friends and family. It is not uncommon for a Filipino to want to know all about a business associate's family, personal background and connections before discussing anything important. Thus, negotiations in the Philippines have **two phases, 1) relationship building, and 2) substantive issues**. However, non-task sounding will occur throughout the negotiation.

Establishing trust

Americans who work with Filipinos need to develop the ability to read the cultural cues and decipher the subtle messages behind them. They need to listen to their Filipino counterparts attentively if they are going to avoid misunderstandings. The nonverbal messages and the context in which the communication occurs are critical to establishing rapport and trust. The Filipino is also seeking trust and he will initially seek it **intuitively** and through the **establishment of a relationship**. They love to begin business relationships by wining and dining because it creates a relaxed and friendly atmosphere. They will ask personal questions in order to know the other person better. They are not necessarily seeking a friendship.

Friendship is another term that has a far different meaning for Filipinos than for Americans. Friendship for Filipinos takes considerable time to develop and involves real commitment. Filipinos expect their friends to lend them money when necessary, serve as a go-between in delicate matters, offer moral support in times of trial, and counsel them when making difficult decisions. They feel a considerable sense of loss when they are separated from a friend.

Persuasion

Filipinos like to haggle **(i.e., distributive bargaining)** in order to get a good price. One strategy is to start their negotiations at the lowest possible price and then work their way up to a more reasonable price. It is important to participate fully in this process, even though time consuming, because it is out of these interactions that a positive climate is established, rapport is achieved, and eventually a deal is agreed upon.

In some instances nothing happens without *lagay*, (a small bribe or what might be termed persuasive communication). There are those who claim it is not necessary to offer an 'unsolicited but expected' token of appreciation for services rendered, but others will point out that it is the only antidote for the agony of inaction. *Logay* is officially and publicly considered illegal and immoral; therefore, persuasive communication is unspoken and unwritten. Desk drawers of some petty clerks or bureaucrats are said to be left open in the expectation of something dropping in without anything being said.

In the Philippines, personal interaction, socializing, establishing contacts in the government, in the media, as well as in business, are all part of getting your viewpoint across, protecting your firm's interests, and finally closing a deal.

The persuasion tactics that can be generally used with Filipinos or will be used by Filipinos are:

1) Filipinos like to **haggle** and are quite lively while doing so. Distributive bargaining is a favorite pastime. The Filipinos will almost always **"high-ball"** or **"low-ball"** a deal.
2) **Diffusion questions** are often used.
3) Receiving the technical specifications upfront or in the beginning of the negotiations is a good idea.
4) **Metaphors, stories and analogies** are a good idea in the Philippines.
5) **Distraction tactics** are useful in times of conflict and will definitely be used by your Filipino counterparts.
6) Certain requests that we might consider to be corruption may be normal business practices in the Philippines. Decide how you plan to initiate or respond to such requests.
7) **Stalling** is considered to be a very acceptable negotiation tactic in the Philippines.
8) **Write everything down.** Take notes in an unobtrusive manner and later review them with your Filipino counterparts.
9) **Positive emotional tactics as well as personal appeals** should be useful.
10) **Supported Facts.** The presentation of logical/factual information is always helpful. However, do not overdo it. The Filipinos will quickly tire of a highly technical and drab presentation.
11) **Visual proof sources** are helpful in almost any culture.
12) The Philippines is a hierarchical as well as collectivist society. Referring to the **approval of others** and especially the approval of **respected higher authorities** in regards to your company, product, etc. should prove to be an effective method of persuasion.

13) Because Filipinos are an emotional as well as a socially-engaging group, the **presentation of possible future cooperative endeavors** should be very persuasive.

14) Based upon the desire for harmony in the Philippines, the **"Feel-Felt-Found"** objection-handling tactic should prove to be effective when delivered in a harmonious and emotionally expressive manner.

15) You may wish to **imply that you have influence** with certain people that are relevant to the transaction.

16) **Build trust through information sharing**. The Filipinos (perhaps due to USA influence) expect an exchange of information. However, do not disseminate volumes of information and never go as far as a two-sided appeal.

Tactics to avoid include:

1) **Avoid conflict**. Do not be blunt and to the point. Filipinos are very concerned with loss of "face."

2) Do not use fear tactics, ultimatums, threats, yelling, etc. Filipinos are looking for an enjoyable, trusting, and harmonious exchange.

3) Avoid overly analytical or dry presentations and do not speak in a monotone voice.

4) **Do not hurry to complete the transaction**. Allow for breaks, side conversations, etc.

5) **Avoid surprises at the table**. Up-front surprises promote conflict and reduce harmony.

Resolving disputes

In a culture where yes can mean no, I don't know, or maybe, and where there are eleven languages and about a hundred dialects, the possibilities for disputes would seem endless. However, Filipinos will go to great lengths to avoid a dispute. They abhor face-to-face confrontations and any scene that could lead to a loss of face. One has to keep in mind not only the individual psyche of the Filipino but also his or her public image and possibly the kinship and family ties of that particular individual.

Their primary methods of dispute resolution are **intuition and dogma,** (that is if it seems reasonable,

they will concede, or if someone in authority gives an opinion, they will defer). They prefer friendly diplomacy and the use of **intermediaries** whenever possible. Any approach used to resolve a dispute should be tempered by patience, sensitivity, and tact.

The Philippine judicial system is a third world amalgam of imposed or transplanted European and American laws, modified through local usage and at times via martial-law decrees. Bribery in the court system does exist and judges are sometimes paid off. However, resolving a dispute in a Philippine court is potentially a reasonable option.

Group and individual dynamics

From early childhood, Filipinos learn the importance of the **group** or context in which they live — family, neighbors, peers, associates at work, and other larger loyalties and identifications. Filipinos consider themselves individuals but always within the context of a group. They are defined by, and linked to the identity of the various groups, which offers them a field of action, support, and meaning. Thus, it is important to be sensitive to the quirks and moods of others and to develop skills in handling interpersonal situations. It is also important to be loyal to family, friends, and associates. Filipinos spend a lot of time and energy observing others and determining whether or not they are showing signs of stress or anger or friendliness. Maintaining good relations is more important to them than being right or completing a task.

Conversely, Filipinos are also acutely sensitive to how they are being seen by others. They feel implicated in any adverse commentary about one's family, friends, or associates. A considerable number of secondary values and behaviors emanate from these social frameworks. Filipino values do not imply a disregard for the individual, but merely an overriding concern for his/her group.

Filipinos profess a number of societal values embodied in concepts such as democracy and the Judeo-Christian ethic. At times personal and social values may be in conflict. For example, the ideals of the democratic process may run counter to the obligations one has toward one's family or peer group. These deep-seated values will tend to predominate over societal ones.

Risk

Like other Asians, Filipinos **do not like to take risks**. They have a need to carefully maintain correctness, and if one were to take a risk and fail, it would be embarrassing and a serious loss of face. By being low risk-takers, they protect their families, their friends, and their colleagues as well as themselves. Therefore, decisions are made slowly with a great deal of deliberation and every facet is thoroughly explored before a commitment is made.

Decision-making

Since Filipinos are group-oriented, but also hierarchical, they make decisions by **top-down consensus.** Filipinos invariably seek the consensus of the group because few individuals feel they have the final say on anything. Even the chief executives may not want to commit themselves and may say a proposal has to go to a board or a committee. However, this may be another way of saying no or maybe. In addition, access to the top executive is generally through intermediaries via numerous sessions. Thus, the decision-making process has a variety of group dynamics.

A final determining factor in this process may be the personal relationships between the Filipinos and the prospective business partner. If a strong relationship has developed and trust has been built, then an agreement has a better chance of being worked out.

Type of agreement

The Philippine legal system is quite complex. It is a voluminous composite of foreign and domestic legislation that is mixed with decrees issued under conditions of martial law. There is a large body of secondary legislation, involving administrative rules, regulations and orders.

In this legal environment it is advisable for all parties to choose a standard universally-accepted contractual document. **The contract language should be very specific, with all terms of the contract spelled out in detail**. All signatories should sign the document in the presence of a local authority or dignitary. It should be properly registered with the nearest appropriate governmental entity. **The presumption of legality will then be assumed, but may still be difficult to enforce.**

Chapter 20

Russia

- *Country Background*
- *The Russian Culture*
- *Business Protocol*
- *Communication Style*
- *The Russian Concept of Negotiations*

Russia is the world's largest nation with a territory about 1.8 times the area of the United States. Most of its land is in northern Asia, but the part west of the Urals is considered Europe. Russia shares a border with many countries, several as a result of the breakup of the Soviet Union into separate nations. These include Latvia, Lithuania, Estonia, Belarus, Ukraine, Azerbaijan, Kazakhstan, and Georgia, while older bordering countries are Poland, Finland, Norway, China, Mongolia, and North Korea. Even with the breakup of the Soviet Union, Russia alone still has the seventh-largest population of any nation in the world.

With its tremendous resources, vast lands, and educated people, Russia has much to offer the global business community, but convulsive upheavals and extensive corruption on both political and economic levels have led to unhappy circumstances for many of its people. As practiced in Russia, the worst characteristics of both remnant socialism and the new capitalism, and too few of the better features of either, have plunged most of the country into poverty and distress.

Nevertheless, many USA companies have investments in Russia, and despite the recent economic crisis, some have made good profits. Pepsi and Coca-Cola have long been successful there. In general, Russian consumers regard western products as superior.

Country Background

History

In the fifth century BC, Herodotus the Greek traveled to what is now Russia and noted that some of the people were agriculturalists; indeed the Greeks traded extensively for Russian wheat. However, most Russian inhabitants were nomadic hunters and/or pastoralists throughout the BC era. In the seventh century, Eastern Slavs migrated to what is now northern Russia and established the trading city of Novgorod on the Volkhov River. Fearing the nomadic tribes to the south, they asked the Varangians (Vikings) for protection. These Scandinavian Vikings moved south, ruled the Slavs, and established many trading settlements along the Neva River. They established Kiev as the capital city of the first Russian State and traded extensively with Byzantium. When Prince Vladimir took the throne in 988, he sought to unify his vast kingdom by making Byzantine Christianity the religion of all his subjects.

In the 1200s, the Tartar (Mongol) leader Batu Khan (grandson of Genghis Khan and cousin of Kublai Khan) captured and plundered Kiev. Consequently, Russian rulers moved their kingdoms to the north, and Moscow became the dominant Russian city, though still under Tartar rule. Czar Ivan the Great finally broke Tartar rule in 1480 when he refused to pay tribute and Ivan the Terrible defeated the last Tartar remnants in the 1550s. By then Russia was a large centralized state, but internal squabbles and foreign invasions continued to plague the country. In 1613 a national assembly elected Michael Romanov as czar and this family ruled for over 300 years. One of the most notable czars was Peter the Great, who modernized the government, encouraged trade with the West, introduced western culture, technology, and art, and built a new western-style capital at St. Petersburg.

During the 1800s, Russia experienced several wars, most notably an invasion in 1812 by Napoleon. His French troops were badly defeated as they retreated during the harsh Russian winter. The Crimean War of 1854-55 over control of lands of the Ottoman Empire led to Russia's defeat by the combined forces of Great Britain, France, and Turkey. Russian leaders saw their own "manifest destiny" in a drive to the Pacific. Russian expansion into Central Asia brought in areas such as Turkestan, Uzbekistan and Kazakhstan. As their frontier crossed Siberia and approached the Pacific, conflict over trading rights with China was successfully concluded, but the 1904-05 war with Japan forced Russia to give up Port Arthur.

Many factions united in dissatisfaction against the disastrous leadership of Czar Nicholas after Russia was attacked by Germany in WWI. Rule by the czars came to an end with the Russian Revolution of 1917. Vladimir Lenin led the establishment of the world's first communist state, the Soviet Union. After Lenin's death in 1924, Stalin seized leadership and dictatorially ruled until 1953. During this time Russia was industrialized and became a world power. For many Russian people, the most significant event was WWII, which they call The Great Patriotic War or sometimes just The Great War. After the Nazi invasion, twenty million Soviet people lost their lives and much of the country was destroyed. Every Soviet town and city built a memorial to their heroes and heroines who were eventually victorious.

After Stalin's death, leadership went to Khrushchev, who denounced Stalin's excesses, established less severe policies, and launched several new development plans. Khrushchev was retired in 1964, and Brezhnev became the primary leader. Russians sometimes call Brezhnev's era the "the years of stagnation" as much corruption and opportunism prevailed. The Central Committee of the CPSU (Communist Party) elected Mikhail Gorbachav as the General Secretary in 1985. Under Gorbachav's *perestroika*, efforts were made to establish more democracy and to introduce market principles to the centrally-planned economy. Though very popular abroad, he faced much opposition at home from entrenched bureaucrats and other opponents. Internal unrest (and rumored CIA involvement) led to Gorbachav's fall, the 1991 breakup of the Soviet Union into separate nations, and the quick establishment of a capitalist economy under the leadership of Boris Yeltsin. The economic transition was accomplished by encouraging foreign investment, auctioning off many state assets at fire-sale prices, and other quick methods of turning state property over to private ownership, all with very little regulation of the private financial and industrial enterprises that began to emerge. A robber-baron mentality, combined with vast corruption and mafia-type violence, still characterizes many sectors of the economic and political arenas.

Government

The Russian Federation includes 89 administrative units, including oblasts, autonomous republics, autonomous okrugs, krays, and the cities of Moscow and St. Petersburg. The executive branch has both a president who is head of state and a prime minister who is head of government. The president, who is elected by popular vote for a four-year term, appoints a council of ministers. The legislative branch is bicameral, with a Federal Assembly made up of officials from the 89 administrative units, and the State Duma with 450 seats, half elected from single-member districts and half from national party lists. Many new political parties have emerged; in 1999, about 150 parties and movements registered for the elections. Russia has universal suffrage for all those over eighteen years of age.

The judicial branch has a Constitutional Court, a Supreme Court, and a Superior Court of Arbitration, whose judges are appointed by the Federation Council after recommendation by the president. Russia has a civil law system and judicial review of legislative acts.

Demographics

Russia has 145 million people, a slight decline in recent years primarily due to out-migration. Life expectancy is 73 years for women, but only 63 for men. The vast majority of the population is of Russian background (81.5%); but other ethnic groups are present: 4% Tatar, 3% Ukrainian, and a smattering of Chuvash, Bashkir, Byelorussian, Moldavian and others. The educational system is quite good and has produced a literacy rate of 98% for this vast country.

Many of Russia's European cities are quite large. Moscow, the capital, has 8.7 million people while St. Petersburg has a population of 4.5 million. Russia's status as the largest nation in the world also means that much of her population is spread over vast territories from the Baltic area to the Pacific. Past efforts to develop Siberia have resulted in new industrial towns in isolated northern and eastern areas of the country.

Economy

With its abundant natural resources, Russia has mining and extractive industries producing gas, oil, coal, metals, and chemicals. However, great distances and the extreme northern climate of much of the country have hampered development. Forests and woodlands, particularly in Siberia with its vast coniferous forests and tundra, cover 46% of the land. Siberian permafrost also hampers development efforts.

Other industries produce all manner of goods from clothing to high performance aircraft and space rockets. However, Russia's industrial base has been declining. GDP fell every year since the start of reforms except for a slight increase in 1997. In twelve years, the capitalist miracle moved the second-most powerful nation in the world to the eighteenth position in economic production. Per capita income ranking is much worse at approximately 40th place. Inflation rates continue to soar. The labor force of 66 million has an official unemployment rate of 11%, but many more are underemployed. Thousands of people set up small sidewalk-table shops trying to sell whatever they can; some people call the country "a giant flea market."

Russia enjoys one of the highest trade surpluses in the world. Exports primarily consist of petroleum, natural gas, wood products, chemicals, and various manufactured products. Russia also exports gold, diamonds and strategic metals like palladium and uranium. The main trading partners are nations of Europe, North America, Japan, and some Third World countries. Imports are with the same countries and consist of machinery, various consumer goods, medicines, grain, sugar, and metal products. Foreign consumer goods are widely available.

Russian currency is the ruble. Over the past thirty-five years the value of the ruble on the world market has plummeted and is continuing to do so. For example, a 1970 Russian family who had saved the equivalent of one million US dollars worth of rubles would now be the owners of the equivalent of seventeen dollars.

The Russian Culture

Language

Russian is the official language and is spoken by 98 percent of the population. Russian is a Slavic language that is part of the Indo-European group. The Russian language is written in the Cyrillic alphabet and has 32 letters in its alphabet. It is helpful to learn these in order to read signs and to begin to understand common sayings. English and German are the most commonly taught second languages. In business circles, it is common to find people who speak English fairly well.

Within Russia there are also 140 other regional dialects and languages and five different alphabets. There were many more when the old Soviet Union existed; some people from the various republics still speak their native tongue.

Religion

The Russian Orthodox Church has a thousand-year history in Russia and is the main religion of the people. There are also some followers of the Islamic, Jewish, and other religions. Although the Russian Orthodox

Church has experienced a resurgence in recent times and more churches are opening, most people in Russia are not very religious since atheism was encouraged for many years.

Value system

The Russian Orthodox Church influenced values for many centuries. The tendency to philosophize, to discuss for hours, "to think, not do," may come from this background. Group loyalty and ideas of equality also derive from these roots. The importance of the group and the equality of its members have an ancient history in Russia. The peasants lived in the *mir* or village collective under the czars, so collective farms and factory work groups were indigenous developments. Russians like to do things in groups. This conflicts with the individualism that has also always existed and which has been greatly encouraged by the recent introduction of capitalism and the goal of individual achievement and wealth.

Russians love technology and admire western know-how in science and technology. Western consumer goods, especially from the USA, are greatly desired.

Class Structure / Stratification

Under communism, everyone was supposed to be equal, but party bosses and their families enjoyed power and privileges not accorded to the common folk, a system that demonstrated Max Weber's ideas of stratification based on the criteria of political party. Most people, however, did have free basic health care and education, and the government heavily subsidized such items as vacations, transportation, cultural events, and bread. The government no longer continues these programs, and many people have been plunged into poverty due to loss of jobs, nonpayment of wages, past extreme inflation, and the fall of the ruble which wiped out many a citizen's savings. Many older pensioners are especially in dire straits, as their pensions no longer cover the basic necessities.

Now a new wealthy class has emerged: the entrepreneurs and businessmen who have successfully taken over many enterprises or established new ones in banking, real estate, oil, and manufacturing.

Safety

Although most Russians are extremely hospitable and helpful, crime has increased. If possible, arrange transportation ahead of your arrival. There have been cases of muggings at railway stations and airports, of travelers taken to isolated areas, robbed, and abandoned. Even the "honest" taxi drivers generally think it fair to charge exorbitant prices to separate foreigners from their money. If traveling outside the big cities, it is wise to have a guide, especially if no one in your group speaks Russian. Hotels are expensive in the large cities, and are generally quite safe, though break-ins have occurred and one should take precautions with valuables.

Bottled water is readily available and should be used. Tea is a favorite drink and is safe. Public restrooms are often a disaster; better restrooms are found in most hotels and restaurants.

Business Protocol

Greetings and etiquette

The business environment is rather formal. Official requests for meetings are expected. Verbal communication by phone is not sufficient (and often difficult due to the inadequate phone system). The official communication should list the names and titles of all who are attending and the purpose of the meeting. Titles are important and should be used in the business arena. Do not use first names.

When the Russians arrive for a meeting, it is common practice to shake hands. The handshake should be firm. The Russians may appear solemn; smiling is not considered respectful on formal occasions. (Too broad a smile for no reason is a sign of idiocy, not friendliness.) An exchange of business cards is the usual practice. As phone books are a rarity, the business card provides needed information for business contacts. Be sure to include all needed information on yourself and your company on the card and have a Russian translation on the back. Some Russians may not yet have cards, but will appreciate yours. You can introduce yourself if your Russian contact does not.

The rituals of tea (or other drinks) with cookies or more substantial food, and small-talk about family and other personal topics will precede the substantive business discussion. Though the senior negotiator may sit at the head of the table, the more usual arrangement places the two negotiating teams on opposite sides of the table. Center seats are for the most senior officials, with interpreters and aides of descending rank on each side. Your team should each sit across from their peers. Also shake hands at the end of the meeting. Never shake hands over a threshold.

Time

Although you should be punctual, Russians generally are not. Some of the new businessmen, however, have adopted a more meticulous perspective on time and punctuality. The safest approach is to be on time, expect moderate punctuality from your Russian counterpart, and have some reading material in case you are kept waiting. In addition, the Russians are a **dualistic society** in-terms of their use of **time**. **St. Petersburg** residents tend to mirror Northern European neighbors with **monochronic** behavior and punctuality, while **Moscow** residents and **rural** Russians tend to be more **polychronic and less punctual.**

Don't schedule a visit near the end of July or during August when most people are on vacation, nor try to set up meetings on holidays such as the Orthodox Christmas on January 7, International Women's Day on March 8, Victory Day on May 9, Independence Day on June 12, or Constitution Day on October 7.

Gifts

Gift-giving is an old custom in Russia. The exchange of gifts is common at meetings or any get-together. The gift need not be expensive, though high officials appreciate new American electronics and technology. Large or small objects with company logos are good choices, as are pens, chocolates, videos, or lighters for the many who smoke. Marlboro cigarettes have long been a favorite gift for Russians. Although Marlboros may not be an appropriate gift for your business counterpart, Marlboros can keep your taxi driver happy. Russia is a nation of book lovers, so a good book about USA geography, history, natural beauty, or business is welcome. If invited to a home, which is an honor, bring flowers or another small gift to the hostess. You need not wrap your gifts, and can present them in a box or bag. Your host might not open the gift until after you leave; if so, you should do the same. Be at the house or apartment on time, for dinner will probably be served soon after you arrive. If your hosts are in slippers, remove your shoes and don the footwear offered. A gift for the children is not necessary, but is wise if you have developed a personal relationship. Some businessmen like to invite colleagues to their *dacha* or country home, perhaps for fishing or hunting. (The golf course is not yet a place for business deals.)

Blat is the Russian term for connection or influence and denotes an exchange of favors. Money and other gifts can be a part of this exchange, as well as help with official red tape or expedited agreement.

Business entertainment

Lavish entertainment is common. Banquets for foreigners are an old hospitality custom. Vodka toasts are interspersed with many food dishes. Though women may gracefully decline, especially after one glass, men will be pressured to drink—many. Expect to have your glass refilled many times by your dinner partner, and you should probably replenish their glasses if bottles are easily accessible. Be prepared to offer your own toasts. An agreement is often celebrated with champagne. It is hard to practice abstinence in Russia. (However, alcoholism is such a national problem, groups similar to Alcoholics Anonymous are officially being encouraged.)

Business lunches and dinners at restaurants have also become common in the larger cities. A night on the town, with floorshow or other theatrics, as well as a planned schedule of sightseeing, may be part of the entertainment. Russians feel the best way to get to know their foreign colleague is in a social setting. Do not discuss business on these occasions. They will probably ask questions about your personal life, family, and country. Other appropriate topics can include books, films, sports, and most current events. Reciprocal entertainment is appreciated. If you host a meeting, have tea, coffee, and bottled water available, along with something to eat—at the very least have cookies. If you entertain in a restaurant, you will need reservations, even for small groups, in most of the larger cities. Tipping is relatively new and large amounts are not expected. If your Russian colleagues come to the United States, they will certainly expect a banquet or other entertainment with lots of food and drink.

Dress

Rather conservative attire is worn for business meetings and banquets. A dark business suit with tie for men and an equally subdued suit, dress or skirt and blouse for women are expected. Do not overdress or unduly display wealth, for some Russians may see this as a putdown. Most Russians do not have a lot of clothes and may wear the same outfit several times in a week, though the new wealthy class can be more ostentatious.

Communication Style

Business language

Russians are generally known for being great orators, though a bit long-winded. The Russian language requires more time to express an idea than English does and when one adds to this their love of discussion, long meetings can result. Patience is a virtue. Although many Russian business people speak English, it is wise to have a competent interpreter present. Many Russian words have several meanings, and exact translation can be difficult. Some words used in English may have no counterpart, such as commerce.

Issues of business importance are not approached in a direct manner. Personal topics centering on family life, sports, or other neutral topics can help build a relationship and will eventually lead to substantive issues. A low-key approach is usual for initial meetings, but an emotional, direct manner may appear in subsequent meetings. Strength is respected and weaknesses searched for. Speaking loudly in public is not accepted behavior. In summation, stay calm, but strong, as you answer the issues raised and expect Russians to use a varying but usually **moderate-context** style of communication.

Non-verbal Communication

Russians use many hand gestures and facial expressions to help convey their ideas. Touching on the arms means progress is being made; hugs are an even better sign. Russian stand as close as 1-foot during conversation. Keep in mind that backing away may offend your Russian counterpart.

Staring is a common form of Russian non-verbal behavior; do not be alarmed or take offense if you are stared at. Clapping is a positive non-verbal signal and whistling is negative. When passing an individual (as in a theater row) you should face the individual. The "okay" sign and the "V" for victory sign are considered extremely rude in Russia.

The Russian Concept of Negotiations

Selecting personnel

The Russians will appreciate having someone who speaks Russian on your team. Other team members should have done some homework on Russian customs and current economic and political affairs. Although most Russian business people are men, women are accepted in business settings.

Russians generally select **higher officials for negotiations**. You should select personnel of equal status. Those of lower status who accompany the main official do not do much talking.

Negotiating style

Negotiations can be long and tedious. Drafts are often exchanged in advance to clarify objectives. Russians generally prefer to hear the other's position before presenting their own. Radical new ideas are best conveyed early, giving the Russians time to study them and formulate a response. Whereas Westerners prefer a detailed, one-issue-at-a-time style of negotiation, Russians like the "big picture" approach, at least initially. Details must be included later. Russians are great chess players and they plan several moves ahead. Expect delays and postponements. Be patient. More than one visit may be necessary. Negotiations in Russia generally take a long time. Compromise is generally not part of the Russian style, for they tend to think their initial offer is justified on moral, legal and ideological grounds. On the other hand, some of the new entrepreneurs are more used to wheeling and dealing and are quite amenable to haggling. Expect the unexpected.

Issues discussed

Russians will spend a great deal of time on non-task sounding. Conversation is a favorite pastime in Russia. Most Russians have had an excellent educational background in literature and music; they may wish to discuss these as well as sports, politics, etc. The time spent on non-business topics is based on enjoyment, building a foundation for the business relationship, and developing trust.

After socializing, business topics will be addressed. Russian experience in world commerce is limited, and many issues must be discussed in detail to ensure understanding. Do not take anything for granted. Expect stalling via changing the conversation to non-business topics. There is substantial bureaucratic red tape. Plan on spending a lot of time with numerous individuals.

Establishing trust

Russians tend to be distrustful and feel the need for self-protective measures. They tend to have a win-lose approach and hope to be the winners rather than the losers in a business negotiation. Win your Russian colleague's friendship first. Long discussions, drinking vodka with toasts, and exchanging family photos in an informal setting will help build a personal relationship. Building a personal relationship will increase trust, as well as successful business dealings.

Persuasion

Write down everything. In fact, Russians like to have a written and signed agreement on what has been discussed even if no agreement has been reached. This is good, for it helps clarify points of potential conflict as well as progress that has been made.

The specific persuasion tactics that are likely to be effective in Russia are:

1) **Supported Facts**. One needs to present logical/factual information that is accompanied by supportive documentation (proof sources).
2) Receiving the **technical specifications up-front** is an excellent strategy. You will need to be able to meet technical specifications as dictated.

3) **Get it in writing**. Write everything down throughout the negotiations. Take copious notes.

4) It is okay to **be blunt** and to the point in Russia. However, it is also permissible to **be vague and indirect**. Each strategy is considered acceptable. Use either/both to your advantage.

5) **Threats, enthusiastic demonstratives, and fear tactics** are effective in Russia. Expect them and use them in return.

6) **Use metaphors, diffusion questions and distraction tactics**. Russians are storytellers and will appreciate these tactics.

7) **Use the "big picture" method of negotiating**. Russians believe that nothing is decided until everything is decided. So, if you gave in too easily on a previous point, change your stance.

8) **Stall** for leverage and future opportunities. Your Russian counterparts are not concerned with time. They will be stalling and will not be insulted if you do.

9) **Act disappointed and/or insulted**. It is a favorite strategy of the Russians and is seen as an effective as well as acceptable negotiating strategy.

10) **Visual Aids**. Colorful pictures, charts, graphs and posters will greatly enhance one's presentation and ability to persuade. Product samples are also a good idea.

11) The Russians like **contingency bargaining**. However, they do not usually haggle a great deal. The "high-ball" or "low-ball" is not a big part of their negotiation style. Be prepared to trade extraneous items in order to move the negotiations along.

12) Certain requests that we might consider to be corruption may be normal business practices in Russia. Decide how you plan to initiate or respond to such requests.

13) The Russians are big on influence peddling (especially since it has historically been critical to prosperous business dealings). You may wish to **imply that you have influence** with certain people that are relevant to the transaction.

14) **Speak with conviction and confidence**. The Russians will do likewise.

15) **Surprise tactics** are acceptable strategies as long at they are artfully and tastefully executed.

16) **Summarizing previously-agreed-upon technical benefits** should be well received.

17) Like the French, the Chinese, and the Americans, the Russians view an effective tactic as an acceptable tactic, provided it is related to the business at hand and complies with their system of logic.

Tactics to avoid include:

1) **Do not engage in extensive information sharing**. Information should be traded, not used to build trust.

2) **Avoid Two-Sided Appeals.** It is best not to provide the Russians with additional information that they may try to use against you.

3) Avoid direct personal conflict. Business conflict is okay and is expected.

4) In general, avoid positive emotional tactics and personal pleas. This is not a steadfast rule in Russia, but will usually cost you more than you will gain.

Resolving disputes

Making sure your agreement is understood in detail and periodically verified is your best insurance. Although new laws regulating commerce have been enacted, the legal system still has difficulty enforcing contractual matters. This, added to increased Mafia–type activity, has made internal commercial relationships rather chaotic. Fortunately, foreigners have rarely experienced this type of violence. Disputes can be taken to the courts, the State Arbitrazh, or arbitration. Russian courts have jurisdiction over civil disputes where one or more of the parties involved is a private citizen. The State Arbitrazh handles disputes of a commercial nature when all parties are firms or registered entrepreneurs. Parties to a civil transaction can take a disagreement to arbitration and avoid both the courts and the Arbitrazh by stating in the contract that any disagreements will be resolved by arbitration.

Hopefully, disputes can be resolved in Russia without outside intervention. However, it may be difficult to do so. The Russians do not believe in compromise, since compromise is seen as a sign of weakness. Therefore, you must be able to **argue your case very effectively, present a great deal of information supporting your position, and be willing to concede on major issues** so that your Russian counterpart can feel that they have won.

Group and individual dynamics

Group work is customary in Russia. Under the communist regime group activity was planned, expected and carried out. This form of government was in place for 70 years. So, behaviors change slowly. However, the new entrepreneurs have little interest in group welfare. Numerous Russians have embraced capitalism and its individualistic ideals. Just like their Western counterparts, many Russians are becoming impatient capitalists who want quick profits and are not too concerned with a need for mutual prosperity. In conclusion, expect the masses to be **group-**oriented. However, if you are doing business with entrepreneurs, expect **individualism**. In a society as dynamic as Russia, generalizations can soon prove outmoded.

Risk

Russians generally avoid risk. The extreme climate forced peasants to face uncertain harvests and other natural ravages. Man-made disasters in the form of wars, revolutions, and jolting changes in political and economic policy have led to anxieties. Their life has been too harsh and they prefer some security and predictability.

Decision making

Russian's past history has led to an emphasis on group welfare, but also to some **top-down decision-making**. They are team-oriented, but the final decisions are made at the top. Power and control are sought after in Russia and are seldom relinquished.

Type of agreement

Agreements are customarily written and signed in both languages. Have a competent language expert present to make sure the two versions are the same, for translation can lose details and words can have different meanings. Have a lawyer look it over. Russian lawyers are becoming more familiar with commercial contracts.

A provision for periodic review of implementation is useful. In Russia, a contract is considered to be transacted when both parties reach an agreement on essential terms and both parties sign a written contract or each party signs a separate document. Russian courts will follow the literal meaning of a contract. If the wording is ambiguous the courts will follow the contract's general purpose.

NOTES:

Chapter 21

Saudi Arabia

- *Country Background*
- *The Saudi Arabian Culture*
- *Business Protocol*
- *Communication Style*
- *The Saudi Arabian Concept of Negotiations*

Saudi Arabia is one of the richest and largest countries in the Middle East. Its 865,000 square mile area comprises roughly 80% of the strategic Arabian Peninsula, abuts the Persian Gulf and the Red Sea, and shares borders with many other Middle Eastern nations. The Desert Kingdom and its royal family are also the custodians of the Islamic holy cities of Mecca and Medina. The discovery of oil in 1938, however, has provided Saudi Arabia with a steady income as well as added power and stability.

Today, the Saudi economy is one of the healthiest and most stable in the Middle East, and Saudi Arabia has consistently been a dependable trade partner with the USA, Western Europe and Japan. Saudi Arabia has also been a generous financial provider to other Islamic and Arab countries for many decades.

Country Background

History

In cultural and human terms, the history of Saudi Arabia can be traced to the beginning of Islam during the sixth century. Saudi society today is based heavily, if not wholly, on Islamic teachings and fundamentals.

The Kingdom's political history, however, dates back to the late 18th century when Mohammed Bin Saud, ruler of the Saudi clan, led a campaign to unite the area under his rule and captured Riyadh. Bin Saud was helped by Mohammed Bin al Wahab, the head of the Wahabi sect, which professed a return to the strict principles of Islam. The fruits of this alliance are evident today in the conservative posture of all aspects of Saudi society.

In 1902, Abdul Aziz Al Saud captured Riyadh and, after 30 years of a reunification struggle, declared himself as King of a united Saudi Arabia. The discovery of oil in 1936, however, changed the course of the nation's history. Over the years, oil revenues have been used to finance massive national development programs in education, roads and other transport, industrialization, urban development, and agriculture.

Government

Saudi Arabia is an absolute monarchy governed according to the Shari'a (Islamic law). There is no suffrage in Saudi Arabia, and the king appoints all cabinet members and the majority of important government officials.

The government is composed of 18 ministries, which are presided over by the Prime Minister or the first or second Deputy Prime Minister. The council of ministers is the legislative body, but no statute, code, treaty, international agreement, or concession is valid without the issuance of a royal decree. Draft legislation may be submitted to the king for royal approval.

There are four classes of courts in the Saudi judicial system: general courts, courts of appeal, the High Court of Justice, and a structure which accommodates a variety of complaint procedures. Its instrumentation varies from judicial to quasi-judicial boards, which adjudicate grievances, labor disputes, etc. The Shari-a has been supplemented by a growing body of statute law, which follows the dictates of the Shari-a while providing for the contingencies of a modern society.

Demographics

The Saudi population has now reached approximately 23 million. This number includes about 5 million residents who aren't citizens. According to Saudi law, these residents cannot become citizens.

A massive government-sponsored education campaign has raised the literacy level to 63%. The majority of young Saudis are well-educated, but a great number of older and rural Saudis are illiterate. Also, the education level and literacy rate for men (72%) is much higher than among women (50%) due to strict Wahabi teachings that do not encourage education for women. Life expectancy is 67 years for males and 70 years for females.

Economy

Saudi Arabia possesses a healthy oil-based economy with strong government support and control over major economic activities. The petroleum sector accounts for almost 75% of budget revenues and 35% of the GDP. Saudi Arabia has the largest petroleum reserves in the world, with 26% of the global total. Saudi Arabia's GDP rank is about 27th in the world, while their per capita income places them about 38th. Coupled with very low inflation and unemployment rates, the Saudi people have been accustomed to a comfortable economic existence and growth for several decades.

Petroleum and petroleum products make up 90% of the Saudi's billions in exports. The Kingdom exports 18% of its oil to the USA, 18% to Japan, and the remainder to various other countries. Saudi Arabia has one of the largest trade surpluses in the world. Imports include machinery, chemicals, foodstuffs, motor vehicles, electronics and textiles from the USA (25%), Japan (10%), Germany (7%), and several other European nations. As evident from these figures, the USA is Saudi Arabia's major trade partner for both exports and imports. Saudi citizens consider USA products and services to be of the highest quality and value.

The Saudi currency is the Riyal, which equals 100 halalah. The exchange rate is US$1 = 3.7450 SR (fixed rate since 1986).

Much of Saudi Arabia's labor force is composed of non-citizens. Manual and unskilled laborers come from Asia and Africa, while the majority of skilled workers come from North America, Europe and Japan. After the Gulf War, the Saudis replaced certain Arab workers, whose political views differ from those of the Saudi government, with workers from other countries.

The Saudi Culture

Saudi Arabia is a very conservative Arab nation and one of the most conservative countries in the entire world. This is reflected in the daily life of Saudi society, including religion, family, business, politics and entertainment.

Language

Saudis speak Arabic, which is a rich historical language and the language of Islam. Most educated Saudis also speak English, which is often used when conducting business with foreigners.

The Arabic language is a crucial part of Arab culture since it is the medium of the Koran, Arab history, poetry and identity. It is a very grammatically complex language that lends itself to rhythm and rhyme and is very pleasing to listen to when recited aloud. In addition to being an old language that hasn't changed much in almost 1400 years, Arabic is a rich language with a large vocabulary.

Saudis are proud of their Arabic language, so it's important to respect this heritage and to not show impatience when Arabic is spoken in social or business settings.

If the Saudi hosts don't speak English, one should bring translators to a business meeting. When living in Saudi Arabia, it's also helpful to learn some key Arabic words and greetings, such as *Assalaam Alaikum* (hello), *Shukran* (thank you), *Maa Assalama* (goodbye), *Aahlan* (welcome), etc.

Due to its complexity and distance from western languages, it's very hard for most westerners to learn Arabic. That's probably one reason why all Arabs appreciate foreigners who can speak Arabic.

Religion

Saudi Arabia is not only a Moslem kingdom, but also the country that houses Islam's two holiest cities and the site of the annual Hajj (pilgrimage) to Mecca. Over two million Muslims from Saudi Arabia and other parts of the world converge on Mecca each year in observance of the Hajj. In Saudi Arabia, Islam is not just a religion, but also a way of life. The faithful pray five times a day and practice the five pillars of faith all their lives (profession of faith, prayer, almsgiving, fasting and pilgrimage). Islam also teaches piety and living honestly and honorably. The orthodox doctrines inherited from the Wahabi teachings of the 18th Century have filtered down in the way Saudis conduct themselves in business and other aspects of life.

The vast majority of Saudis (approximately 90%) are Sunni Moslems, but there is a small Shia minority which is rather quiet and poor. Saudi citizens may not convert to another religion, and non-Moslems are denied entry into the holy cities of Mecca and Medina. Some western observers believe that Wahabi thinking is too rigid for the modern state of Saudi Arabia, but so far its puritanical practices have been firmly entrenched. It is both unwise and impolite for visitors to comment on Saudi Islamic practices and compare them to other religions and traditions.

Value system

The majority of Saudis believe that life has a predestined course prescribed by Allah. It's all right to have and endure hardships, since it's the will of Allah. Likewise, good fortune only comes through the blessing of Allah, so it's important to live honorably and patiently in all aspects of life.

Saudi culture is very male dominated. Men are perceived as strong, rational and self-controlled, while women are seen as weak, emotional and subject to temptation. Women in Saudi Arabia do not ride bicycles or drive automobiles (It's against the law!), and they must cover themselves to the ankles in public, as well as cover their hair.

While these traditions are restrictive by Western standards, the Saudis believe women are treated with great dignity and respect. For example, it is considered an honor for family members to drive a woman to do her errands, such as shopping or visiting friends. Men argue over the privilege of paying for a woman's expenses and shopping items, and it's not unusual for a woman to go shopping without money and expect a male relative to pay. Also, while they may be segregated from men in public, it is impolite to have women stand in line behind men, and they're usually escorted to the front.

The Saudi attitude on women dictates some important behavioral patterns for westerners. It's best never to ask about wives or daughters, unless the Saudi host mentions them first, or unless two families have established western-style friendships. Also, it's very important not to stare at Saudi women, even if they stare at western men. It's very wise to learn how to act and react around Saudi women, especially when among conservative hosts.

Class structure / Stratification

Family affiliations determine one's position in Saudi Arabia. The most elite class is that of the king and his family. After that, tribal affiliation, wealth, political power, and profession help determine class. Education is also important for gaining status and acquiring good jobs in the kingdom.

Family is the most important social entity in Saudi society. Families are extended and may live together in a large house. Marriage arrangements reflect both families' wishes and ambitions, but the couple has to accept one another. While family and political connections are of utmost importance, Saudi society also appreciates education and hard work.

Safety

Murder, drug trafficking and adultery are capital crimes in Saudi Arabia. The sentence for adultery is rarely carried out since the act has to be witnessed by four male adults. The severity of the sentence is indicative of a conservative society that protects and values personal honor and reputation.

Convicted murderers are publicly beheaded in Saudi Arabia, and repeat theft offenders can have their right hand amputated. Needless to say, the crime rate in Saudi Arabia is extremely low.

Westerners who are on business can expect to be safe in public as long as they respect the proper dress and public behavior traditions of the country. Overall, the Saudi population is pro-western and hospitable, but as evident from the 1996 bombing of the American barracks near Dhahran, and the participation of many Saudi citizens in the World Trade Center attack, there are anti-government elements that would rather see the American military out of the kingdom. The Saudi government remains wholly allied with the USA government and will do what it can to protect American citizens, provided they adhere to local laws.

Alcohol and drugs are strictly prohibited in Saudi Arabia, but smoking is allowed. Western visitors must adhere to the no drugs or alcohol policies of the country; otherwise they will be subjected to the wrath of the strict Saudi law. Visitors must not accept or should politely decline any prohibited substances, even if offered secretly or by a Saudi citizen.

It is equally important to adhere to and respect established traditions while in Saudi Arabia and thus not encounter the wrath of the Mutawain (religious police). This group enforces the modesty of dress in public, as well as enforcing other religious teachings. The Mutawain have full civil authority to arrest violators, sometimes superseding that of the civil police.

Surprisingly, some Mutawain are foreign-educated Saudis, but the majority are religious zealots who brandish — and use — camel whips when enforcing the law. Being a westerner or a woman in Saudi Arabia doesn't safeguard someone from running afoul of a Mutawah. The best guard is to learn and observe the established rules of public dress and behavior.

Business Protocol

Saudi business protocol is very formal, polite and conservative. Meetings start with lengthy greetings, introductions and polite inquiries about one's comfort and journey. Social occasions and meetings are an integral part of the negotiating process since this allows the hosts to know their counterparts in more depth. Although wives are invited to these functions, they rarely come, and a man may answer for his wife if she is invited. Introductions include the exchange of business cards, which should be printed in Arabic and English. It's wise to practice the proper pronunciation of Arabic names beforehand so no one will be offended at the start of the negotiations.

Greetings and etiquette

There are several greetings currently in use in Saudi Arabia, so it's best to follow their lead and use polite salutations whenever in doubt, such as extending the right arm and nodding the head slowly when exchanging greetings. Westernized Saudi men shake hands with other men and will ask about someone's health and family. Some will even shake hands with western women. It's a rare occurrence to meet a Saudi woman in a business setting, especially at a negotiation or in a management level. Again, it's best to follow the local lead whenever around women in a business situation.

The traditional greeting method among Saudi men involves each grasping the other's right hand and left shoulder and exchanging kisses on each cheek. Some may not actually kiss, but touch the cheeks or the heads while grasping each other.

Mispronouncement of Arabic names may signal a lack of respect in Saudi Arabia. Perhaps the best cure for this unfamiliarity is a bit of studying and homework before meetings. Visitors can ask their Saudi contacts to brief them on someone's title and the correct pronunciation of Arab names beforehand. Writing the names down in English helps. So does practicing before addressing someone directly. Most Saudis have a great command of western names, and they feel that they deserve the same treatment.

Arabic names are written in the same order as English names. The title is followed by the first name, the middle name, and then the surname. The middle name is often a patronymic, meaning it translates to "son of." For example, the king's name in Saudi Arabia is King Fahd Bin Abdul-Aziz Al-Saud. The title is king, Fahd is the first name, Bin Abdul-Aziz, which means son of Abdul-Aziz, is the middle name, and Al-Saud is the family name.

Westerners must not confuse the word "Bin," which means "son of" for the name Ben, and call Saudis by that name. They should also address individuals by their title, especially if they are members of the Royal Family or the military.

Saudis always use the right hand, unless necessity dictates using both hands or the left hand. Pointing at people in Saudi Arabia is considered impolite. When sitting down, it's best not to cross the legs. Keep the soles of the feet pointed downward. One should never use the thumbs up gesture, which is considered offensive to many in the Arab world. It's customary in the entire Arab world to offer a cigarette or coffee to anyone present before smoking or drinking coffee oneself.

Time

Traditional Arab patience makes for a polychronic culture that doesn't necessarily consider punctuality a virtue. Saudis may be late for meetings, and may be interrupted by family, telephone calls and coffee. Westerners shouldn't take offense at such behavior, but should anticipate it and make the best of it. In a society that values honor and personal values, one can win friends easily by showing patience and understanding for local customs and traditions. However, in accordance with western punctuality, they expect foreigners to show up on time.

There are, of course, a large number of western-educated Saudis in business today. These individuals vary in how they conduct business and treat time. Some may be just as prompt and focused as anyone in the west when it comes to meetings and setting objectives. Therefore, one can deal with such individuals just as dealing with business people in the United States, providing, of course that everyone stays within the prescribed parameters of Saudi society.

The business week in the Islamic kingdom is different than that in the Western Hemisphere. Friday is a holy day, and no business takes place on that day. Consequently, the Saudi business week is Saturday through Wednesday, since most businesses take Thursday off.

Government hours are from 7:30 AM to 2:30 PM, Saturday through Wednesday. Some banks open Thursday mornings. For the most part, Saudi tradition dictates six-hour working days, but due to the heat, working hours may vary. Some businesses close down in the early afternoon and reopen in the late afternoon or evening to avoid the sweltering heat. Due to the summer heat, many Saudi businessmen will set late appointments at their homes or offices. It's not unusual to have an appointment as late as midnight during the hot summer.

The Islamic calendar uses lunar months of 28 days, so paperwork usually carries two dates: Gregorian (Western) and Hijri (Islamic). No one conducts business during Eid Al-Fatr (the festival of breaking fast at the end of Ramadan), and Eid Al-Adha (the day of sacrifice). The dates for these holidays vary on the Western Calendar due to the difference between it and the Hijrah calendar.

Due to the short business day, try to set morning appointments, It's also common to keep people waiting for an appointment, so it's best not to plan more than one appointment per day.

Gifts

Although not required, gift giving is one of the oldest traditions in the Middle East. When giving or receiving gifts, one should present or accept them with both hands and thank the person giving them for his thoughtfulness or hospitality. It's customary not to open gifts in the presence of guests. Traditionally, Saudis who assist or broker a deal take a percentage, which may be determined beforehand.

Business entertainment

Much of what western people perceive as entertainment, such as local tourist attractions and nightlife, does not exist in Saudi Arabia. Instead the Saudi people entertain their guests by inviting them to their homes and other conservative social functions.

Saudi hospitality is legendary, and the Arab culture considers hospitality as one of the noblest characteristics one can possess. Visitors in Saudi Arabia can expect their business hosts to frequently invite them to their homes or to restaurants. When visiting Saudi homes, it is courteous, but not required, to bring a small gift, such as assorted sweets from a local market. If the hosts remove their shoes at the house, then the visitors should do the same.

When socializing, take the host's lead as far as asking about family members, especially women. The best subjects to talk about with Saudi men are soccer (football) and other sports, such as horse or camel racing. Visitors should firmly resist the temptation to discuss politics or societal issues. It is customary to stand up when others enter the room, unless they are servants. It's also considered rude to cross the legs casually, and especially to point the sole of the shoes in someone's direction while sitting down. When eating, one should never use the left hand to eat with or gesture toward people, even if left-handed. Some Saudi homes use western utensils, while others follow more traditional eating methods such as using hands and bread. It's customary for the host to inquire about the visitor's needs and appetite while eating and to encourage him to eat more. Visitors should not be annoyed by this tradition and should try to indulge, even in small quantities. Not eating a lot initially saves some space for additional nibbling.

Dress

Everyone in Saudi Arabia dresses conservatively. Western men shouldn't adopt the traditional Arab garb, but should rather dress in light suits that are well suited for the desert heat. Despite the heat, most of the body must remain covered and neckties are the norm in business environments.

Western women must be very cognizant of what's considered modest wear in Saudi Arabia. Generally, dresses must reach well below the knee if not to the ankle, with high necklines and sleeves that cover the elbows. Tight skirts or pants are not acceptable, and baggy clothes that don't reveal the contours of the body are the safest choices. Women should also consider carrying or wearing scarves to cover the neck in public, as well as hats to ward off the heat and cover the hair.

Communication Style

Business language

Negotiations will probably take part in English, or a translator may relay the information to an Arabic speaking decision-maker. As discussed earlier, Saudis are **high-context** people, and there is a lot of gesturing and body language.

Arab men may touch other men on the arm or hand, which is a sign of friendship. "Yes" from a Saudi delegation may not necessarily indicate an agreement, but it may also be a polite way of saying "continue," or "we're listening."

Arabs may speak gently or quietly, but they may also raise their voices and gesture emphatically while making a point. Loud discussions are not uncommon and aren't necessarily signs of anger or frustration, but may indicate interest and sincerity. This high-context society values trust and relationships. Therefore, it's normal to have more than one meeting to establish relationships and get to the heart of the negotiations. Visitors can expect coffee and personal conversations during these meetings.

Non-verbal communication

Arabs are sharp observers of others, especially of the eyes and body language. Personal space is less defined and Saudis may get very close to someone when conversing. It's natural for Arab men to observe the facial intonations and body language of their guests as they evaluate them and try to gauge their actions. They expect extensive eye contact as well as numerous gestures.

The Saudi Concept of Negotiations

Selecting personnel

Companies doing business for the first time in Saudi Arabia should secure a Saudi sponsor or contact before doing anything else. Banks doing business with Saudi Arabia may refer American business people to Saudi contacts. Another source for Saudi contacts is the USA International Trade Administration.

The Saudi contact/sponsor is a very important key to success in Saudi Arabia. Therefore, it's important to secure an individual with the right temperament and connections for that position. The Saudi contact can arrange introductions and meetings with influential people in the kingdom. Since the pace of business is slower in Saudi Arabia than in the West, it's important to be patient and anticipate delays and postponements before the deal is struck. Likewise, it's important not to pressure the Saudi contact and not to measure his performance by western standards.

One thing is constant when selecting your own negotiators; they should be men. Unfortunately, women in Saudi Arabia do not have a place in negotiations or high management. Conservative, well-groomed, sociable and patient men are best for the negotiating team, and they should take the lead over technically-adept but less-sociable members of the team. Saudis like to converse socially and maintain a conservative protocol most of the time.

Negotiating style

Saudi Arabians consider negotiations as the beginning of a long relationship. These are rarely viewed as win-lose situations or deal-makers, but rather as spirited meetings that lead to more business. While Americans place great emphasis on the written contract, Saudis prefer to base their business on trust and honor. Saudis also enjoy bargaining, so it's a good idea to leave some room for further negotiating.

Issues discussed

The issues discussed in Saudi negotiations are relationship-based. This includes getting to know the various team members, discussing long-term service agreements and other forms of commitment. The time spent on technical data and details is far less than relationship issues.

Bases of trust

Considering recent history in the Middle East, many Arabs do not trust the West or Westerners in general. Yet, Western countries constitute Saudi Arabia's major trade and business partners. The challenge for outsiders doing business in Saudi Arabia is transcending the barriers from being cold strangers to becoming warm friends.

One can establish this rapport and relationship through social activities, understanding the Arab culture, and a genuine honesty that convinces the hosts of good intentions. Arabs are much more judgmental of someone's character than North Americans or Europeans, and they do appreciate honorable people with good manners and education. From the other perspective, Westerners must respect Saudi thinking and try to honor personal pleas whenever possible. Even if a Saudi makes an error, it's wise not to put him on the spot and force him to admit it, which may cause him to lose face and to distrust his Western counterparts.

Persuasion

Saudis are generally more emotionally than logically driven. Their arguments tend to persuade emotionally and ethically rather than factually. Reasoning with Saudis using western logic may not always yield positive results. Using emotional arguments that appeal to the religious, personal and trusting nature of Saudis, on the other hand, may produce better results.

Another different aspect of Saudi culture, as compared to Western culture, is its view on evidence. Most Saudis have faith in their Islamic religion and use someone's faith and character as evidence, rather than emphasizing objective facts and figures.

The persuasion tactics that can be generally used with Saudi Arabians or will be used by Saudi Arabians are:

1) Saudi Arabians love to **bargain and haggle** and can be quite lively while doing so. Be prepared for a "high-ball" or "low-ball." It is likely they will ask for the moon with a very sincere face.

2) Always **get everything in writing**.

3) Saudi Arabians like to **imply that they have Royal Family influence** or influence with important individuals. You may wish to imply that you have influence with certain people that are relevant to the transaction.

4) **Stalling**. Take your time. Saudi Arabians are rarely in a hurry.

5) **Metaphors, stories and analogies** are often used in Saudi Arabia.

6) **Diffusion questions and distraction tactics** are useful in times of conflict.

7) Certain requests that we might consider to be **corruption** are normal business practices in Saudi Arabia. Decide how you plan to initiate or respond to such requests.

8) **Get it in writing**. Write everything down throughout the negotiations.

9) **Personal pleas** can be very useful in Saudi Arabia. Saudis never refuse a friend's personal request. However, it is acceptable to delay or avoid the request.

10) Receiving the **technical specifications up-front** is always a good idea.

11) Saudis tend to brag and use puffery. So, definitely build up your firm, your products/services, and yourself with **exaggerations, enthusiasm, and non-verbal demonstratives**.

12) **Speak with conviction and confidence.** Saudis tend to be great orators/story tellers and will expect the same from you and your firm.

13) Because Saudis are an emotional as well as a socially-engaging group, the **presentation of possible future cooperative endeavors** and/or multi-firm interactive simulations should be very persuasive. For example, if you are selling jets, then have them sit in the jet.

14) Use a **"big-picture"** strategy. Nothing is decided until everything is decided.

15) Loudness means sincerity so choose your moments to erupt.

16) Saudi Arabia is a hierarchical as well as collectivist society. Referring to the **approval of others** and especially the

approval of **respected higher authorities** (dogma) in regards to your company, product, etc. should prove to be an effective method of persuasion.

17) **Use silence as a persuasion mechanism**. Saudis do not like silence. Thus, silence will make them feel uncomfortable and prompt concessions. However, only use this tactic late in the negotiations process after rapport has been firmly established. Using this strategy too early will destroy the rapport, cause boredom, and increase doubts.

Tactics to avoid include:

1) **Avoid direct personal conflict**. It is acceptable to say what is on your mind. Some indirect conflict and/or a little banter are okay. However, direct personal conflict that causes someone to "lose face" will result in an emotional reprisal. Thus, avoid blunt and pointed statements regarding character or personal performance.

2) **Avoid long boring monotone lectures**. This type of lecture is not enjoyable anywhere. However, variations in tonality, rate of speech, and pitch are even more critical in Saudi Arabia. Presentations must be accompanied by discussions, breaks, humor, etc.

3) **Avoid non-professional behavior**. Saudis can be friendly, jovial, etc. but they remain professional at all times during work or leisure.

4) **Do not build rapport by asking about spouses or daughters**.

Resolving disputes

Due to the Saudi sense of evidence, it may be futile to argue certain points if they do not appeal to the Saudi sense of faith, family and honor. The best way to resolve arguments, therefore, is to understand the reasons for the objections and try to appeal to Saudi logic, while still trying to maintain trust.

Disputes may arise due to cultural and political differences that are much more important to Saudis than Westerners. It's best to be prepared and understand Saudi political views on issues of trade, politics and culture

before the start of negotiations. Finally, it may be very effective to appeal to the group leader, who has the authority to cool off the negotiating team and sway its opinion.

The rules of international law are recognized unless they conflict with the Shari-a. Legislation in the eighties provided a broad statutory basis for arbitration proceedings. Commercial disputes may be referred to the Chamber of Commerce and Industry, which is bound to adjudicate the matter if both parties agree to accept its jurisdiction.

Group and individual dynamics

Saudis are a group-oriented society, and it's safe to assume that the negotiating team and its individual members reflect the group's needs and desires. The group is primarily concerned with building a trusting relationship with the other team, and Saudi team members place an emphasis on saving face and not breaking ranks. This is why group consensus is important, though the consent of the group leader is crucial.

Risk

As evident from their conservative culture and social structure, Saudis avoid risk and have no gambling propensities. As a byproduct of this philosophy, Saudis want negotiations to succeed since they entered them knowing that the failure risk was minimal. Negotiators in Saudi Arabia must not urge their hosts to take risks or to think of the deal as a "good risk." This approach probably won't appeal to Saudis and may lead to negative results.

Decision Making

Decision making in Saudi Arabia is from the top down. Negotiators normally can make decisions, since the group probably agreed beforehand on the concessions and conclusions they are willing to make. If western negotiators know who the Saudi decision-maker is and what will make him happy, then it's good strategy to try and meet his demands. If he agrees, the group will follow. Saudis dislike conflicts and deviation from internal decisions.

Type of agreement

As a high-context society bound by honor and tradition, Saudis generally prefer brief, written agreements that discuss the principles of the deal. On a small scale, a gentleman's agreement normally has more power than a written one since it involves a man's honor and obligation. This, and other negotiating variables in Saudi Arabia, reflects the principles of Saudi society at large: conservatism, ritual, tradition and morality.

The most important statute in the commercial domain is the Commercial Code of 1931. This code provides for eight organizational business structures: partnerships, limited partnerships, partnerships limited by shares, limited liability partnerships, companies with variable capital, marketable share companies, joint ventures and cooperatives. Each of these structures is dealt with separately in the code. All companies with the exception of sole proprietorships must be registered with the Department of Companies in the Ministry of Commerce. Foreign firms seeking government contracts are required by law to have a Saudi partner or agent.

All commercial agreements between Saudi Arabian and USA businesses must be legalized by the following:

1) notarization by a Notary Public;
2) certification by the County Clerk where the Notary is commissioned;
3) certification under the seal of the Office of the Secretary of the state where the document originates;
4) authentication by the USA Dept. of State; and
5) legalization by a Saudi consulate.

Saudi associates can help with many of these steps. You may wish to obtain additional information about commercial transactions or other aspects of business from the USA- Saudi Arabian Business Council, www.us-saudi-business.org/rgcomm.htm.

Chapter 22

Singapore

- *Country Background*
- *The Singaporean Culture*
- *Business Protocol*
- *Communication Style*
- *The Singaporean Concept of Negotiations*

Singapore is favorably located at the southern end of the Strait of Malacca, the shortest sea route between China and India. Asian mariners knew of the island as early as the third century AD. By the seventh century, the maritime empire of Srivijaya, the first to arise in a succession of maritime states in the region of the Malay Archipelago, began establishing outposts. Singapore was probably one of its many outposts serving Chinese, Thai, Japanese, Malay, Indian, and Arab traders. An early chronicle refers to the island as Temasek, which means sea town. According to legend, a Palembang prince took shelter on the island from a storm in 1299. He saw an animal and mistook it for a lion. Temasek was then renamed Singapura, which means, "Lion City". Today, the island's inhabitants are energetic, intelligent, prosperous and self-confident, exactly the prerequisites needed for a society to have great cultural and economic achievements.

Originally the island was covered by a tropical rain forest and fringed with mangrove swamps. The landscape, altered by human hands, is now only 2.5% forest. Singapore is two degrees north of the equator and has a tropical climate. Its population resides in an area of 637.5 square kilometers (224 square miles). Today towering office buildings overshadow Victorian-era government buildings, symbolizing Singapore's transformation from a colonial port to an independent city-state with the highest standard of living in Southeast Asia.

Country Background

History

One of the earliest first-hand accounts of Singapore appears in a geographical handbook written in 1349 by Wang Dayun, a Chinese traveler. He noted that Singapore Island was a haven for pirates who preyed on passing ships and described a settlement of Malay and Chinese people who lived on a terraced hill that was purportedly the burial place of ancient kings.

What is fairly certain is that Singapore functioned for an extended period of time as a trading post under the influence of a number of different Southeast Asian powers. From ancient times, the Malay Archipelago

had served as a supply point and gathering place for sea traders of the kingdoms and empires of the Asian mainland and the Indian subcontinent.

By the early 1500s, Europeans appeared on the scene. When the Portuguese captured Malacca in 1511, the reigning Malaccan sultan fled to Johare in the southern part of the Malay peninsula, where he established a new sultanate. Singapura became part of that sultanate and the base for one of its senior officials. In 1613, however, the Portuguese burned down a trading outpost at the mouth of the Temasek (Singapore) River and Singapore was apparently unused as a port for almost two centuries.

In 1818 a Malay official of the Johare Sultanate and his followers resettled Singapore. They shared the island with several hundred indigenous tribespeople and some Chinese planters. The following year, Sir Thomas S. Raffles, an official of the British East India Company, arrived in Singapore and secured permission from the Malay officials to establish a trading post. Raffles named the port after its ancient predecessor and Singapore soon became a successful port. News of Singapore being a free trading port spread to passing ships, and traders from around the Orient began stopping at the excellent harbor to exchange their wares. The next half-century brought a widely diverse population and increased prosperity to the rapidly expanding seaport. In 1867, out of a need for a place other than fever-ridden Hong Kong to station British troops in Asia, London designated the straits settlement a crown colony.

As Singapore prospered and grew, the size and diversity of its population kept pace. By the 1870s, Singapore businessmen had become interested in the natural resources of the Malay Peninsula. The Chinese became the primary labor source for exploiting those resources. Although most of these Chinese immigrants merely passed through Singapore on the way to Malay mines and rubber plantations, the Chinese population on the island grew from 34,000 in 1878 to 103,000 in 1888. The affluent among this Chinese community gradually came to feel that their prosperity and welfare were tied to those of the crown colony and the British Empire.

British rule of Singapore lasted until the outbreak of the Second World War when the Japanese occupied the island from 1942 to 1945. At the conclusion of the war, Singapore again became a British Colony. The transition from a British Colony to the powerful city-state of today was marked by a surprising degree of civility and thoughtful planning. Under the British, Singapore had been permitted to manage its own internal affairs, but relied on Britain for military protection. The seeds of independence were sown with this arrangement, and the humiliating defeat of the British by the Japanese during World War II gave further impetus to the desire for self-governance.

The first representative legislature was elected in 1955. A Briton named David Marshall became the first Prime Minister. Marshall was committed to Singapore's independence and resigned when the British refused to go along with it. In 1958, a new constitution was ratified providing for limited self-government and Britain changed Singapore's status from a colony to a state. It was in the General Elections of 1959 that a new political party led by a Chinese lawyer named Lee Kuan Yew brought about separation from Britain, and union with the New Federation of Malaysia.

Singapore became an autonomous state within Malaysia, with its own constitution. It separated from Malaysia in 1965, when the legislative assembly passed the Singapore Independence Bill.

Government

Singapore's constitution provides for a parliamentary system of government patterned after the British system. The executive branch has a president whose duties are largely ceremonial. The president is be elected by parliament for a term of four years. A Prime Minister who has a cabinet selected from the ranks of parliament leads the government.

Legislative power is vested in a unicameral parliament with eighty-seven members who are elected for 5-year terms (or less if parliament is dissolved prematurely). The legislature consists of the president and the parliament. Members must be citizens of Singapore, twenty-one years of age or older, on the current register of electors, able to communicate in either English, Malay, Mandarin Chinese, or Tamil, and of sound mind. Members of parliament are elected by universal adult suffrage from forty-two single-member constituencies and thirteen group-representative constituencies. Voting is compulsory for all citizens above the age of twenty-

one. The group-representation constituencies elect a group of three members; at least one of whom has to be Malay, Indian, or one of Singapore's other minorities. Group representatives are intended to ensure multiracial parliamentary representation to reflect Singapore's multiracial society.

The judicial system is based on the British model. Power is vested in a Supreme Court, a Court of Appeals, district courts, magistrates, juvenile courts, and coroner's courts. British Law has been modified to a great extent by local legislation.

Demographics

Most of Singapore's first settlers were male immigrants seeking work. Today, its population of 4.3 million people are composed of 77% Chinese, 15% Malay, 6% Indian, and a sprinkling of other groups, including Europeans. It has four official languages: Chinese, Malay (official and national), Tamil, and English. Migration to Singapore declined in the 1930s, ceased during World War II and resumed on a minor scale after the war. In 1965, Singapore's government established strict controls on immigration, granting temporary residence only to those whose labor or skills were considered essential to the economy.

Singapore has a literacy rate of 97% for males and 90% for females. Life expectancy is 78 years for males and 84 years for females.

Economy

Singapore has excellent international trading links that evolved from its entrepot (a place where goods are stored and from which they are distributed) history as a free port with free markets. It is now a global city-state serving world markets and major multinational corporations. It has also become a service and manufacturing center. A slump in global demand for electronics slowed Singapore's export growth in 1996 and the Asian financial crisis in 1997 slowed growth even more. However, Singapore's economy today still ranks 36th and their per capita income ranks 24th.

Rising labor costs are currently a threat to Singapore's competitiveness, and the government's strategy of managing this problem includes increasing productivity, improving the infrastructure and encouraging higher value-added industries. In applied technology, per capita output, investment, and labor discipline, Singapore has the key attributes of a developed country.

While Singapore supports free international trade, the government is highly interventionist in its own economy. Since its independence, policies for industrial development were imposed at both the macro and micro levels. Singapore's government shunned the traditional system of import substitution, seeing it as more limiting than beneficial, and turned attention instead to exports. Singapore is one of the few countries where total trade (domestic exports, re-exports and imports) exceeds total GDP. It is the third largest oil-refining center in the world, despite being a 100% importer of crude oil. Its port is one of the largest in the world in terms of cargo tonnage.

Singapore has limited human and natural resources. As a result, they have focused on high value-added production. In addition to petroleum refining and electronics, Singapore's industries include oil drilling equipment, rubber processing and rubber products, processed food and beverages, ship repair, financial services and biotechnology. It has a labor force of 2.1 million. The unemployment rate is 3%. Singapore maintains an excellent trade surplus. Their major trading partners are Malaysia, USA, Hong Kong, Japan, and Thailand.

The currency is the Singapore dollar. The fiscal year is from the first of April to the 31st of March.

The formula that created Singapore's vibrant economy included investment in people, incentives for business and free trade policies. Considerable energy went into a free and effective educational system. They taught positive behavior and attitudes as well as knowledge and skills. Non-religious moral values were emphasized, resulting in a highly-educated citizenry that works hard, saves money and accepts civic responsibility.

Much of Singapore's economic development was financed through the private savings of its people. Their savings rate is among the highest in the world and is reinforced through required deposits to a central fund, which may be used for public housing or retirement at age 55.

A final factor in Singapore's economic success is the government's ability to convince the public of the realities of world economics: why wages must be limited; how resources must be conserved and prioritized; and why savings and foreign investment are essential. The government also has restructured the economy and placed more emphasis upon high-tech and high-skill industries such as automation and robotics.

The Singaporean Culture

Language

In colonial Singapore, the nearest approximation to a common language had been Bazaar Malay, which was a very simple language with a restricted vocabulary that many ethnic groups used to communicate with one another in the marketplace. The British Government, of course, used English, with translators employed when necessary, such as in the courts. Among the Chinese, a simplified form of communication known as Hakkien served as the language of the marketplace. The Chinese schools, of which there were many, taught Mandarin that became a language of prestige used at formal occasions. Sociolinguistically, Singapore's language system was both multilingual and diglossiac, which means there was more than one language with several dialects, both high and low, classical and vernacular, each used in different social contexts and carrying different levels of prestige. Bazaar Malay and Market Hakkien were the low languages and English and Mandarin were the high languages. In addition, other native tongues such as Teochiu, Tamil, Punjabi, and Pure Malay were used in the home and in other ethnic gathering places. In a 1972 survey of spoken languages among the citizenry, 73% could use Hakkien, 57% could use Malay, and 47% used and understood English. In a follow up survey in 1978, 67% claimed to understand Malay and 62% English. English is now replacing Malay as the common language, in both high and low language usages.

At various times in Singapore's history, campaigns have been initiated to replace the Chinese dialects with Mandarin. In 1979, there was a speak-Mandarin campaign sponsored by the government. By 1988, 87% of the Chinese population claimed to be able to understand Mandarin. People, however, did not agree on the appropriate contexts for using a language that they associated only with school. As a result, people were using English or their native tongue as an everyday language.

Religion

Early Indian and Chinese traders introduced Hindu and Buddhist beliefs, which supplemented the Malay animism that was already present. Later Malay immigrants were Muslims. As each of these immigrant groups came to Singapore, their religious congregations were also their social organizations. Colonial authorities refrained from interfering with the religious affairs of the ethnic communities and this fostered an atmosphere of religious tolerance.

Today, Singapore is a secular state where all religions are free to flourish. It strongly advocates religious tolerance and encourages religious communities to contribute to the harmony and welfare of the entire nation. In addition to the major religions of Buddhism, Hinduism, Islam, and Christianity, there are other religious faiths that include the Sikhs and Jains from India, the Parsis (who follow the ancient Zoroastrian faith) and some who adhere to the Jewish faith.

Value system

Singapore is a small society that was opened to the West through British colonialism and the early imposition of the English language. It has recently been considerably influenced by modernization and industrialization. Over time, ethnic affiliations have diminished as the forces of standardized education and the impartial application of laws and regulations have brought divergent groups into a shared national and cultural environment. Further exposure to international mass media along with the daily multicultural experience of employment in factories and offices has resulted in many shared attitudes among ethnic groups.

Government policies have also been a major factor, providing public services to all ethnic groups and reshaping society through a network of People's Associations, Resident's Committees and Parliament Constituent Advisory Groups. National holidays feature displays of the distinctive traditional cultures of the major ethnic groups, represented by costumes, songs and dances. Pupils in secondary schools take required courses in the ethics and religion of their designated culture.

The Singapore government holds nationwide campaigns periodically to heighten public awareness of a particular value goal. It also levies heavy fines and very strict penalties to discourage anti-social behavior. There are considerable differences between most Asian political systems, which are based upon group consciousness and conformity, and western systems derived from concepts of inalienable individual rights. Many Asians consider western versions of freedom to be immoral and selfish, preferring instead their own traditions because they prefer a settled and harmonious society.

Many Asian nations, including Singapore, have incorporated some western legal concepts into their political structures. In day-to-day living, however, they are ruled by oral traditions based upon centuries of village life. The "guided democracy" concept is an amalgam of values that treads a fine line between traditional Chinese authoritarianism and western representative democracy.

Class structure / Stratification

Singapore, with its multiplicity of ethnic groups, each with a different basis for social organization, social stratification and kinship structure, is a good example of a pluralistic culture. However, its economic success has enabled it to create a society without an underclass that is mired in poverty. There are no homeless and half the population lives in either low-rent or government-subsidized housing. The government also encourages home ownership. Health, sanitation and recreation standards approximate those in the West.

Due to the multi-ethnic nature of Singapore, the status of women varies considerably. Singapore law treats women's rights much the same as western nations. However, respect for religion translates into the supremacy of religious law in some instances. For example, having four wives is legal for Muslims as long as they comply with the provisions of Islamic law. In general, women in Singapore have higher status than their counterparts in many other parts of Asia. They have equal rights in court, can vote, own property and many earn their own incomes. Much of the alleviation of poverty and the decrease in income inequality that took place in the 70's and 80's was the result of the increased participation of women in the work force.

Among the Chinese, who constitute by far the largest ethnic group, the family is an integrated aspect of the economic structure. Chinese families with their numerous members and extended ethnic contacts provide the structure for both upward mobility and business initiatives. The Chinese believe that individuals should honor their lineage and clan with moral behavior, hard work, frugality and perseverance, and that one will then be rewarded with wealth and status.

The success of the Chinese in Singapore has influenced the Indian population to adopt similar approaches utilizing family connections to implement and expand their business options. The Malay population views the family from a different perspective. For them, relatives offer an emotional, rather than an economic advantage, and they are not likely to consider a business venture with their family members.

Singapore has become a meritocratic society and while the family may be the most important social unit, upward mobility in the form of political power, wealth and education are the new criteria for social status and measurements of success.

Increased family incomes made possible by full employment and the security of Singapore's government programs have to be distinguished from upward mobility, in which individuals move into more skilled and higher paying jobs and hence higher social classes. Residents from every ethnic community feel they can aspire to mid and high-level positions and that education is the key to potential success. Movement from menial to mental labor or from low-level blue-collar to white-collar positions is, however, difficult and rare. Nevertheless, surveys in the 1980's revealed that most Singaporeans considered themselves to be middle class. They justified this distinction by their savings accounts and their well-equipped homes and apartments and the opportunities they and their children have for education and advancement.

Safety

One of the major concerns people have when going to visit or work in a foreign country is personal security and safety. Singapore has a well-deserved reputation for being a safe place. It is one of the few places in Asia that has high health and sanitary standards and tap water that is fit to drink. It has very strict laws, excellent law enforcement and a very low crime rate.

While Singapore is clean and safe, there are definite health risks if you travel beyond its boundaries into the surrounding regions. Health authorities suggest the avoidance of milk products and uncooked vegetables. Eat only meat and seafood that has been thoroughly cooked and is still hot. Drink bottled water, avoiding ice. Protect yourself against mosquitoes. Singapore does require inoculations for yellow fever, typhoid, and cholera for people arriving from areas with outbreaks of these diseases. It is always sensible to have one's immunizations up to date for such diseases. It is also advisable to obtain vaccinations for hepatitis, which takes at least 6 months for full effect.

Business Protocol

Greetings and etiquette

Greetings and introduction rituals are usually **formal** and vary according to ethnic groupings. Among the Chinese, shaking hands is acceptable but there are cultural differences that need to be understood. The western-style handshake traditionally involves a firm grasp and three pumps and then a release. Chinese offer a **handshake**, which is soft, lingering, and sometimes two handed. Chinese men often greet one another with a **pat on the arm**. Shaking hands with a Chinese female is acceptable but not with Indian or Malay females. The woman takes the lead initiating contact in all greeting encounters.

Great respect is shown older people and introductions go according to rank with the **oldest person introduced first**. The western practice of saying the name of the most important person first is good etiquette. One should always use **Mr., Miss, or Madam** followed by the family name when introducing someone.

When giving one's business card, make sure you give one to each person present. Using both hands, present it with the print facing the recipient. The recipient will receive the card with both hands and look at it carefully. Do the same when a card is presented to you. Never write on a card or put it in your back pocket; business cards should be handled respectfully.

Time

The Singapore business culture is multi-focused and **polychronic**. They are generally **punctual** for all business meetings, but are usually tardy for social events. Appointments should be made at least two weeks in advance. Westerners are expected to be on time for business appointments.

Business hours are generally 9 AM to 5 PM, Monday through Friday. Some offices will be open for a half-day on Saturday mornings. The traditional lunchtime was from 12 noon to 2 PM, but efforts have been made to reduce this to a single hour from 1 to 2 PM.

Singapore is 13 hours ahead of Eastern Standard Time. If you fly to Singapore from the United States, you will lose a day on the flight over because you will cross the International Date Line. However, you will gain an hour for each time zone you cross. On the flight back the day will be gained back, but an hour will be lost with each time zone crossed.

Gifts

Singapore prides itself on being the most corruption-free state in Asia. Bribery is illegal and laws prohibiting it are strictly enforced. The government is scrupulously honest. **Do not give government officials any presents**. One can honor a business counterpart by presenting inexpensive gifts, such as flowers, candy, or pens with one's company logo. There may be legal and indirect ways to favor your counterpart by helping arrange for travel or educational opportunities in the United States.

If you are invited to the home of a business acquaintance, consider it an honor. Seek out the older members of the family first to pay your respects. A small gift of candies, cakes, or fruits can be sent as a thank-you gift after the event.

Business entertainment

In Singapore, business entertainment is cultivated as a means of impressing business counterparts, as a way of honoring them, as a way to determine the degree of their sincerity, and to work out business objectives. All of this helps cultivate a relationship out of which a harmonious business relationship might evolve. There are **business breakfasts, business lunches, business cocktails, business dinners and business banquets**. One should participate fully in this process. In Singapore, the establishment of a successful business venture may hinge on how well one does at these socializing events. In reciprocating, remember to choose a restaurant that can serve food that will be appropriate to the ethnic diversity of those you are inviting.

Dress

Because of the heat and humidity, Singaporeans usually dress more **informally** than western business people. In a more formal office environment, men might wear **light colored long-sleeved shirts, ties and dark trousers**. **Jackets are usually not worn for work.** In less formal offices, businessmen commonly wear short-sleeved shirts and no tie. Stripes and floral patterns are sometimes seen at these less formal businesses.

Businesswomen will wear lightweight business suits that tend to be more frilly and feminine than what western businesswomen usually wear. Hose are also worn in the more formal offices, but bare legs are common in less formal ones.

In restaurants, casual dress is appropriate although there are some that do not allow shorts, bermudas or slippers. Some first-rate restaurants and hotels require men to wear a jacket and tie or a long-sleeved batik shirt.

Communication Style

Business language

Asians respect and admire the courteous person. One must take the time to establish one's reliability, remembering that you are a representative and an extension of your business enterprise. One should speak in quiet gentle tones and always try to remain calm.

Leave plenty of time for people to respond to any statement you make. Asians communicate more contemplatively and like to reflect before responding. Westerners talk more rapidly, but oriental politeness generally requires one to pause before responding. Westerners often assume that they have understanding and agreement and continue talking without allowing the Asian the customary pause.

While each ethnic group in Singapore will communicate somewhat differently they all are **high-context** languages. They are not uncomfortable with periods of silence and in keeping with their cultural conditioning may frequently be indirect or vague when communicating. Among Asians one has to remember that it is considered impolite to disagree with someone, so they rarely say no. A foreign businessperson is expected to understand the difference between a polite and hesitant yes (which really means no) and an actual yes. If an Asian person qualifies their statement, such as "it might be difficult" that really means "no". Another way of saying "no" is for one to pretend the question was never asked. It is also considered polite among Singaporean Chinese to offer both positive and negative options for virtually all decisions. For example, instead of asking, "Would you like to have dinner?" they usually ask, "You want dinner or not?" The phrases involved (want or not want?, good or not?, can or cannot?) are direct translations of typical Chinese phraseology into English. To a foreign person, this can sound peculiar or aggressive if one is unfamiliar with this communication pattern.

In Singapore, women are now attaining high positions in business and technology. When conducting business with an individual of the opposite sex, be very careful to keep the level of the discussion professional. Any sign of flirting could destroy the woman's career and your business venture. It is appropriate to compliment her work, but say nothing about her appearance.

Non-verbal communication

Asians tend to be **very observant of all non-verbal behavior**. Saving face is very important in their lives. If an Asian expresses anger in public then he/she has shamefully lost face. Anyone who loses his or her temper is considered out of control and such a person will not be trusted or respected.

When to smile or laugh can vary cross-culturally. As in western societies, the Singaporean smile may hide embarrassment or shyness. The Asian half smile can mask bitterness, or discord, or loss of face.

There are nuances in body language that Asians consider inappropriate or even obscene, such as pounding one's fist into the palm of the hand or standing with one's hands on one's hips; both of these are interpreted as angry and aggressive gestures. Showing the soles of one's feet or shoes is considered impolite. One should never touch an Asian's head, including a child. Both Muslim and Hindu Singaporeans consider the left hand as unclean so one must use only the right hand to greet or to eat. It is also considered rude to point or beckon with one's finger. Instead, Asians beckon with the whole hand, palm down.

Colors have distinct meanings that must be considered when sending invitations or when wrapping a gift. For many Asians, particularly the Chinese, black, white, and blue signify death. Red, pink, and yellow are associated with joy. Five, eight and nine are good numbers. The number four is pronounced with a sound similar to the word for death and seven is considered unlucky.

When business negotiations involve members of the opposite sex, one should limit one's eye contact and be very circumspect with one's body language. Never touch, hug or kiss a person of the opposite sex in the casual-type gestures common in the West. They will be misread and can cause considerable animosity and embarrassment. Do not shake hands with a woman unless she initiates it. To show respect, one should smile, use quiet speech, and avoid any hints of familiarity.

The Singaporean Concept of Negotiations

Selecting personnel

Singapore's executives place considerable emphasis upon face-to-face contact. A personal visit to a potential business partner is much more effective than contact initiated by merely a letter or a fax. To be introduced by an intermediary who has some level of status can be of tremendous assistance. The intermediary can brief the Singaporean executives beforehand on the purpose of the approach, the size and scope of the foreign enterprise and the expertise and position of the person he is representing.

It may be a waste of time to send low-level company representatives to Singapore. To reach top-level decision-makers, companies must **send people of equal status and importance.** Singapore's executives tend to meet only with people of equal status. **Experience, rank, age and educational background** impress most Asians. The higher one's position in the company and the more experience one has, the greater the status one will have with one's Asian counterpart. In addition, any corporation that is doing business in Singapore or China should have someone on their staff who has some **knowledge of the Mandarin language.**

Most personnel, however, who fail in overseas assignments do not fail because of lack of professional skills, but because of an inability to adjust and adapt to an alien culture.

Traits that are important and should be considered in the personnel selection process include the following: a tolerant outlook, good communication skills, physical and emotional health, a positive and optimistic outlook, high self-esteem (but not egotistical), and a sense of mission. It is also helpful if the person is patient, friendly, kind, non-judgmental, courteous, diplomatic, and has integrity.

In terms of choosing someone who has high cultural adaptability, these factors would be important to look for: cultural empathy, love of exotic foods, willingness to learn a foreign language, political sensitivity, previous overseas experience, a tolerance for ambiguities, flexibility, an appreciation of different customs, and a willingness to learn from local people.

Negotiating style

As with most Asian cultures, relationship-based issues will come first. In Singapore, business negotiations are best approached in an atmosphere of friendship and harmony. For this reason **generalized topics are the entree of the negotiation menu.** These discussions may be only indirectly related to the organizational success the negotiation may eventually produce. Singaporeans are good bargainers and will use **distributive bargaining** techniques to reach an

agreement. Normally the negotiation time-line is greatly extended when dealing with the business representatives of a conflict-averse culture. As a rule, Asian negotiations tend to be subtle, prolonged and devious ordeals for westerners. This is not quite the case in Singapore. Singaporean business people are tough negotiators, but one of their top national objectives already partially realized is to become an "international total business center for manufacturing and services". Singaporeans are well aware of the negotiating style of westerners and they are masters of negotiation strategy; as a result negotiations in Singapore are quicker and more direct. These internationally-minded people have developed excellent skills that enhance the negotiation process. However, one should still pay attention to the basics: courtesy, patience, respect and the building of a relationship that leads to trust and long-term commitments. Singaporeans will drive hard bargains when it comes to price and production deadlines but one should determine one's walk-away point early and stick to it.

Issues discussed

Singaporean business people are team players. The business success they have enjoyed and developed has been built as much on group affiliations as on skill and talent. **They will not spend an inordinate amount of time on the relationship-based issues,** as most of their Asian counterparts are wont to do. Cooperativeness is high on their list of priorities and reasonableness is often used to describe them. They try hard to understand others and these virtues are what they admire, not personal drive, forcefulness, or individual self-assertion. They make decisions as quickly as possible and understand that **substantive** issues concerning prices, production schedules, and marketing deadlines are crucial to successful business ventures.

Establishing trust

For most Asians, establishing trust is a highly important issue. For this reason, they prefer to engage in a lot of **business entertaining.** They value long-term relationships that produce mutual understanding and good experiences. Singaporeans, however, have a shorter time perspective than most other Asians and they make decisions more quickly. **Immediate feelings, first impressions and observations** are given greater credence than in other Asian cultures. However, there is no substitute for factual information and objective data that is presented in a well-organized, easily-understood manner. Also, **past performance** can be the basis for trust.

Persuasion

"Keeping still" is an ancient Oriental virtue. The I Ching or Book of Changes stresses this virtue over and over again. Those who are influenced by it use guided imagery to visualize their minds as a still pond. They would like to negotiate in that kind of contemplative atmosphere where they can look at the whole picture in a holistic way.

Mirroring is a well-established persuasion technique. If one can cultivate a contemplative reflective demeanor, can speak in soft and muted tones, and can learn to speak slowly and allow periods of silence for others to give feedback, then one can be more persuasive in Asian negotiations.

The specific persuasion tactics that are likely to be effective in Singapore are:

1) **Supported Facts**. One needs to present logical/factual information that is accompanied by supportive documentation.
2) Receiving the **technical specifications up-front** is an excellent strategy.
3) Write everything down throughout the negotiations. Take copious notes. Having items agreed upon throughout the negotiations in writing will be a great deal of help. Once it is in writing it becomes a logical argument with a concrete basis.
4) **Build trust through information sharing**. The Singaporeans will expect a healthy exchange of information. Unlike most of Asia, the Singaporeans generally respect intellectual property rights and will not push for information that is proprietary. However, they will expect other information to be shared rather freely because they believe it is the best way to complete the negotiation.
5) Singaporeans like to **haggle**. Distributive bargaining is a normal part of life in Singapore. However, Singaporeans do not do as much haggling as their neighbors, so use some restraint. The Singaporeans will almost always **"high-ball" or "low-ball"** a deal.
6) **Stalling** is a way of life in Asia. Singaporeans stall a great deal less than their neighbors, but the negotiations will still move slowly from a western standpoint.
7) **Diffusion questions** are often used.
8) **Metaphors, stories and analogies** are a good idea.
9) **Distraction tactics** are useful in times of conflict.
10) Singapore is a hierarchical as well as collectivist society. Referring to the **approval of others** and especially the approval of **respected higher authorities** in regards to your company, product, etc. should prove to be an effective method of persuasion.
11) Discussion of harmonious future beneficial business relationships is an integral part of Asian business cultures. Your **presentation of possible futuristic cooperative endeavors, the use of positive imagery,** etc. should be beneficial during business presentations and negotiations.
12) **Visual proof sources** are helpful in almost any culture.
13) **Act somewhat disappointed and/or insulted at times**. It is a common and effective strategy in Asia.
14) **Summarizing previously-agreed-upon benefits** should be well received.

Tactics to avoid include:

1) **Do not self-promote**. Humility is considered a virtue.
2) **Avoid direct conflict**.
3) Do not use fear tactics, ultimatums, threats, loud voices, etc.
4) **Do not hurry to complete the transaction**. Allow for breaks, side conversations, etc.
5) **Avoid surprises at the table**. Up-front surprises promote conflict and reduce harmony.

Resolving disputes

As has already been noted, Asians love bargaining and the best advice is to maintain a posture of goodwill and patience. Try if you can to stay good-humored and avoid anger and paranoia. If an irresolvable dispute arises, one can take some satisfaction in the knowledge that Singapore's public service sector is highly regarded and considered to be almost entirely free of corruption. Their constitutional framework and the court system resemble that of its British model. **Logical arguments using empirical reasoning to resolve disputes** are a common occurrence in that framework. Singapore's business community has been influenced by and functions within that legal framework. Unlike many of the other Asian cultures that rely on past experience or intuition to resolve disputes, Singapore's society has developed a legal system that is efficient, uniform and based upon British Common Law which views only a final contract as binding. Disputes may be referred to an arbitration court, which has the same status as other courts.

Group and individual dynamics

Asian cultures tend to emphasize cooperation and **group** harmony. It is one of their core values. Asians have a saying, "The nail that sticks up gets hit on the head." It follows that individuals who stand out in the crowd, who differ with or question group values, will be placing themselves in an untenable posture leading to possible alienation or loss of respect. From their perspective, individualism is seen as egocentric and selfish.

Singaporeans are encouraged to be both competitive and cooperative. They want the best for themselves and their families, but at the same time they are reminded to strive for the good of the nation. Singaporeans are team players and their success in business depends as much on group affiliations as their individual skills and talent.

Risk

A culture that emphasizes strong group loyalty and long-term security is usually a **risk-averse** culture. Singapore's economic leaders have pursued conservative fiscal and economic policies designed to bear fruit over the long haul. They have stressed fundamental stability and a budgeted approach to economic development. While they are creative and imaginative in many of their business enterprises, they are very cautious about taking business risks. If they fail, they bring humiliation to their company and their society and they will personally lose face.

Decision-making

In Singapore, everyone on the team or everyone in the country shares the responsibility for a decision. Thus, Singapore's business executives utilize the **Singaporean version of the top-down consensus** decision-making model. They tend to be good listeners and will seek out the expertise and recommendations of their employees. Once the decision is made, they all share collectively in the consequences or good fortune of the outcome. This is the most common type of decision-making method employed in Singapore. However, like most Asian countries, Singapore is very hierarchical and thus is concerned with rank, age, etc. So, if top management makes a decision that does not conform to lower management's opinions, then lower-level management will pretend that they had reached the same decision and thus create an illusion of consensus and unity.

This is different from the western style of top-down consensus. The western style of top-down consensus occurs when top management consults with lower management, and then top management makes whatever decision they prefer. This is often followed by indifference from lower management, which results in the opposite of complete and unanimous support. The western executive's Singaporean counterpart is usually more interested in their lower management's input. However, the bigger difference is lower management's universal support of upper management in Singaporean enterprises.

The Singaporean decision-making system is very similar to that of mainland China. Both countries have extensive social welfare systems and very powerful governments. This has fostered a team viewpoint that is handed down from the top, but for the most part is still embraced by the populace. This attitude transcends government and also emerges in the business sector.

Type of agreement

While Asian cultures usually favor loosely-written relationship-oriented agreements, Singapore is a culture that has been heavily influenced by the British system from which it evolved. While Singaporeans may culturally favor a contractual agreement that is more of a guide than a legally-binding document, they have grown accustomed to the dictates of their adopted British legal system. **They now prefer contracts that clarify every aspect of the agreement and eliminate all ambiguities**.

Chapter 23

South Africa

- *Country Background*
- *The South African Culture*
- *Business Protocol*
- *Communication Style*
- *The South African Concept of Negotiations*

The Republic of South Africa has been called "a world within a country." It offers breathtaking scenery, a moderate climate, extended beaches, sophisticated cities, a diverse people, and incredible wild life.

The rest of the world now watches as South Africa struggles to leave behind the inequalities in wealth, education, social power, and human rights that typified the apartheid era, an era in which the potential of its people was denied and the nation internationally isolated. Nelson Mandela, once the world's most famous political prisoner, became the President of South Africa in 1994, and attempted to guide his country toward democracy and collective unity. Those efforts, with difficulty, are continuing today.

Country Background

History

Humans have inhabited the southern Africa plateau for over two million years; the remains of early predecessors of modern humans have been found at a number of sites. There is some evidence that hunters and gatherers of the late Pleistocene period (10-20,000 years ago) were the ancestors of the Khoi and the San. In the first century AD, the Khoi may have had domesticated goats and sheep; by the eleventh century, they had acquired herds of cattle. Many Bantu people also migrated to southern Africa and there is considerable evidence that the area was already socially-complex and economically-diverse with a rich agriculture by the time colonial settlers arrived.

The first European contacts resulted from efforts to find an ocean route to the Indies at the end of the 15th century. In 1488, a Portuguese expedition rounded the southern tip of Africa for the first time. Nine years later, a voyage under Vasco De Gama sailed from Europe to India. They landed to get water and traded for meat with the Khoi.

Dutch interest in South Africa was first awakened when a Dutch East India Company ship sank along the coast of southern Africa. The captain and crew were stranded there for several months. Upon their return to The Netherlands, they reported on the cape's potential as a midway station for supplying company ships on their long voyages to the East. The company's directors dispatched an expedition with a party of 100 men and four women. They landed at Table Bay in 1652, and it was from this nucleus that South Africa's Dutch settlement grew. The Europeans proved to be an insufficient labor force and attempts to recruit enough Khoi labor failed. Therefore, slaves were first imported from West African slave markets and later from Eastern Africa. Eventually, indigenous South Africans were also enslaved. (The British ended slavery in 1807, but near-slavery conditions continued for many.)

In 1679, German and Dutch settlers began to come from Europe, lured by offers of free land. In 1688, French Huguenots fleeing religious persecution accepted free passage to Cape Town. From the beginning, there was friction between the Europeans and the indigenous South Africans who saw the whites as intruders out to steal their livestock and their territory. Because of their superior armaments (and internal divisiveness among the Bantu), Europeans won these wars and confined the Bantu to the worst lands and/or used their labor in the mines and plantations. The discovery of diamonds and gold in the late 1800s brought British and other Europeans flocking to the region. Britain soon took control of much of the area and the Afrikaners (i.e., the original European settlers who were primarily of Dutch decent) moved inland. Several Anglo-Boer Wars finally resulted in British victory, but the Afrikaners set up their own independent regions called the Orange Free State and Transvaal.

In 1910, these two Boer states united with the two British colonies of the Cape of Good Hope and Natal to form the Union of South Africa. Their convention drafted a constitution that granted white people almost all political power. The first Prime Minister, JBM Hertzog, expanded the rights and powers of the Afrikaners. Later the National Party, which ran the country from 1948 to 1994, institutionalized and developed the policies of apartheid. Eventually, they took voting rights away from all non-whites and created an environment of total segregation. These political developments set the stage for violent clashes between the indigenous people and the armed forces responsible for enforcing apartheid policies. These brutal encounters motivated the various native groups to join forces; the African National Congress (ANC) was formed and Nelson Mandela emerged as one of its leaders.

After a number of years of demonstrations, bloodshed and pressure from around the world, the ANC was able to get the white leadership to enter into political negotiations. In 1990, Mandela was released from prison. From 1991-1993 the political parties gathered at the World Trade Center in Johannesburg and drafted a transitional constitution.

In April 1994, a turning point was reached for South Africa and its people. A new constitution was completed, a new flag and a new national anthem were chosen, and democratic elections were held.

Government

South Africa made a dramatic transition from an apartheid state to a promising democracy when it adopted its new constitution as the law of the land. South African citizenship became equated with equality for all people regardless of gender or race.

The first free elections in which all people could participate were held in 1994. The ANC won 62.6% of the vote, the National Party got 20.4%, and other political parties shared the remaining seats in parliament.

Elections are held every five years. The government has three separate branches: the legislative, the executive, and the judicial. The bicameral parliament is the legislative branch and consists of both the National Assembly, composed of 400 representatives who are elected by popular vote to serve five-year terms under a system of proportional representation, and the National Council of Provinces, which has 90 seats with 10 members elected by each of nine provincial legislatures for five-year terms. This branch has special powers to protect regional interests, including the safeguarding of cultural and linguistic traditions among ethnic minorities.

The judicial branch consists of the Constitutional Court; the Supreme Court of Appeals; the High Court; and the Magistrate Court. South Africa has a non-codified civilian system based initially upon Roman-Dutch Law. The main sources of law are legislation and case law, with custom and judicial precedence being of less importance. After South Africa was ceded to Great Britain, the British retained the Roman-Dutch Law but legislation thereafter was influenced by common law. This resulted in a mixed system with English legal doctrines superimposed on the earlier Dutch structure.

Geographics

South Africa is located at the southern tip of the continent of Africa, with a land area of 1,219,912 square kilometers, slightly less than twice the size of Texas. Its shares boundaries with Botswana, Lesotho, Mozambique, Namibia, Swaziland, and Zimbabwe.

Though subtropical along the east coast, the climate is mostly semiarid with sunny days and cool nights. The terrain consists of a vast interior plateau rimmed by rugged hills and a narrow coastal plain. South Africa's land is 10% arable with 1% in permanent crops, 67% in permanent pastures, and 7% in forests and woodlands. It has 12,700 square kilometers under irrigation, which is important due to the occasional long droughts. For this reason, there is a need for extensive water conservation and water usage threatens to outpace supply.

Demographics

South Africa's population totals 44 million. Its population growth rate is now almost zero. The ethnic composition is 75% Black, 14% White, 9% Colored, and 2% Indian (Asian), plus a small smattering of Chinese, Japanese and other nationalities. Life expectancy of the total population continues to drop and is now 48 years. Life expectancy is much higher for whites than nonwhites. Over 4 million South Africans currently have AIDS. The literacy rate is 82%, and again is much higher among white South Africans.

Economy

To understand the South African economy of today, one has to look at the yesterdays out of which the current economic structure emerged. South African economic policies are basically growth-oriented, free-enterprise capitalism. Capitalist motivations were the dominant force behind the freewheeling entrepreneurs who developed South Africa's mines in the late 1800's and continued to mold the actions of the businessmen who subsequently developed its manufacturing and commerce.

From the beginning, South Africa had an abundance of minerals, several of which are of worldwide strategic importance, and agricultural production was usually more than adequate to meet domestic requirements. Later, a highly diversified manufacturing sector was developed. By the 1980s, the World Bank classified South Africa as a middle-income country. However, a dualistic society existed with massive black rural poverty alongside white urban prosperity. This situation was largely the result of efforts by the government to enforce its concepts of separate development. The mobility of the country's largest labor force, the black workers, was severely restricted and they were forced to accept extremely low wages. These same factors also restricted the mobility of capital, the development of enterprises, and the ebb and flow of internal trade. The ideological imperatives of the system forced the establishment of two separate economies. All of this, along with international economic sanctions, gradually retarded economic growth and by 1980 brought some government recognition of the need for change.

Despite the efforts of South Africa's new majority-run government, income inequality remains extreme. A significant number of South Africa's white citizenry enjoy living standards comparable to those of Western Europe. In contrast, much of the remaining population suffers from third-world poverty patterns. The main strength of the economy still lies in its rich mineral resources, which furnish two-thirds of South Africa's exports. Government economic policy is currently focused on improving black living standards and providing jobs for the unemployed. The economy in recent years has absorbed less than 5% of the more than 300,000 workers annually entering the labor force (i.e., from population growth plus other individuals seeking employment in South Africa based on African immigration patterns). Local economists estimate that the economy must grow at least 5% annually in order to absorb the new entrants and begin to reduce the accumulated unemployed population.

The current labor force in South Africa is estimated at 17 million. Per capita purchasing power parity annual income averages $8,500. Occupational percentages are: 45% services, 30% agriculture, and 25% industry. Unemployment has held at 30% for years with an additional 11% underemployed. Some analysts say unemployment rates are even higher, for the economy has been in decline, and downsizing has been the prevalent policy of many corporations. The rate of inflation has recently improved to 5%.

South Africa's industries include mining (world's largest producer of platinum, gold, chromium), automobile assembly, metalworking, machinery, textiles, iron and steel, chemicals, and fertilizers. Agricultural products include corn, wheat, sugarcane, fruits, vegetables, beef, poultry, mutton, wool, and dairy products. South Africa enjoys a slight trade surplus every year. Commodities exported were gold and other minerals, metals, food, and chemicals. Important trading partners are Italy, Japan, USA, Germany, UK, other European countries, and Hong Kong. Import commodities are machinery, transport equipment, chemicals, petroleum products, textiles, and scientific instruments.

South Africa's currency is the rand (ZAR), 1R = 100 cents. The rand has been declining in exchange value in recent years. The fiscal year is April 1st to March 31st.

The South African Culture

Language

For many years, the official languages of South Africa were English and Afrikaans, the two major languages of the whites. The Afrikaans language is derived from Dutch. The Afrikaners and many of the Coloreds (i.e., those of mixed racial heritage) speak it, as well as those Blacks who have lived in predominately Afrikaner regions. Afrikaans is rarely used in Natal, a former British colony. English is common today, is used by a substantial number of Asians, and most urban blacks speak English in addition to their native language. Other regional languages include Northern Sotho, Ndebele, Pedi, Sotho, Swazi, Tsonga, Tswana, Vende, Xhosa, and Zulu.

Religion

Many aspects of indigenous belief systems, including religion, were fragmented as their social and structural supports were destroyed by white rule. Some rituals fell into disuse, but many vestiges of those systems remain, particularly in rural areas, and influence current values and thinking. The indigenous religious systems were specific to each tribe and were primarily concerned with health and prosperity in this world and the effects of ancestral spirits on the welfare of the living.

The Dutch Reformed Church has, in addition to the Afrikaners, a few blacks and people of mixed racial heritage as members. The Roman Catholic Church is found throughout English-speaking areas. The Methodist denomination has a large percentage of blacks in its membership, and there are many other Protestant denominations. However, the majority of the black population is affiliated with independent churches or with other localized indigenous religions. In addition to those of the Christian faith, there are Hindu and Muslim populations.

Value system

South African culture has a triple heritage of African, European, and Asian Indian values. For much of its history, these three have experienced conflict. Initially, African tribes warred against each other; later conflict centered along ethnic and racial lines as various immigrant populations sought to exploit the land and its human resources.

Today, South Africa is a republic of great diversity and a country in transition. In the second half of the 20th century, it suffered through the values associated with apartheid. Before 1994, the flag of South Africa was four flags in one, representing the flags of The Netherlands, The United Kingdom, The Orange Free State, and The Old Transvaal Republic. Today, the flag of South Africa is a five-colored flag representative of a new nation and a different value orientation.

The pronounced value orientation of South Africa today is called *Ubuntu*, which literally means "personhood - a collective morality". This value represents more than afrocentricity, because it is not a racial concept. While it is a uniquely African concept, it is also a universal one. *Ubuntu* in its most literal form is best understood by the African proverb "*Umuntu Ngumuntu Ngabantu*", which means "I am because we are; I am only a person through others." *Ubuntu* is expressed collectively in song, dance, work, story telling, and celebration rituals. *Ubuntu* is Africa's contribution to universal humanistic philosophy.

Class structure / Stratification

In South Africa under apartheid, class structure was based upon racial classification, which was guaranteed by the constitution. Within this system, the black citizenry were only slightly better off than slaves. The inequality of this system was so pervasive that four out of every five citizens had neither voice in how the country was governed nor any hope of a fair trial in its criminal justice system.

The British citizenry were the upper class and the wealthiest segment. The Afrikaners also had members among the elite and made up most of the middle-class farmers, merchants, and skilled workers. Racially-mixed people were generally unskilled workers. Although a few blacks achieved education and relatively low-paying professional jobs as teachers or nurses, most blacks were extremely poor even when they had jobs in the mines, factories, or as servants.

At present, these racial structures are slowly being dismantled. Some blacks are moving into the business sphere and even becoming entrepreneurs; some have found jobs with the new government. The black poor are still poor. Because the school system was so inadequate, half of the black population is essentially illiterate. It will take time to correct the damage that apartheid has done.

Safety

Safety in South Africa can depend upon what cities or areas one is traveling to. Crimes such as pick pocketing, con games, auto theft, breaking and entering, and street robbery are on the increase, and some cities are more unsafe than others. One is advised to take the same precautions one would take in any urban area: don't leave your luggage unattended; don't stroll the streets late at night; and always lock your doors. Whenever possible, travel with a group.

In the major cities and towns, the tap water is purified and fit to drink. If you're going north and into the interior, you should protect yourself against malaria-carrying mosquitoes by wearing protective clothing. There are also parasites in the lakes and streams of the northern and eastern regions of the country. Of course, one should be certain that all immunizations are up-to-date for travel in that part of the world.

Business Protocol

Greetings and etiquette

South African business protocol is generally **formal and conservative**. A firm **handshake** at the beginning and the end of the meeting is customary. Women may or may not shake hands, so it is best to wait for them to initiate a greeting before offering one's hand. South Africans introduce the most **senior people first** and use **Mr., Miss, or Mrs.**, along with the person's last name.

Business cards should include one's position in the company, one's education, and any titles or rank one has attained. South Africans are very conscious of status and rank, and respect well-educated and credentialed people.

Time

The whites of South Africa are **monochronic and punctual**. The blacks are generally **polychronic and less concerned with time**. Appointments should be scheduled well in advance (2 or 3 weeks) and one should always try to be on time. Businesses in South Africa are usually open from 8 or 9 AM to 5 PM, with a one-hour break for lunch.

Gifts

Gift giving is not a prerequisite for doing business in South Africa. However, polite and courteous behavior is much appreciated. **Thank-you notes** are always appropriate and the sending of **flowers, as an expression of gratitude,** might be worth considering, particularly if invited to a business acquaintance's home or shown an unusual kindness.

Business entertainment

South Africans enjoy **wining and dining** with business associates. These events are utilized as a means of getting acquainted. Lunch is the most common business meal and usually takes place at a local restaurant. Top executives may be treated to lunch at a really expensive and exclusive establishment. The habits for dining are fairly simple: wait until everyone is served before starting to eat, use your knife with your right hand and fork with your left, and wait until there is a break in the conversation before you speak. There are some topics to avoid in your conversations and naturally one of them is politics. Movies, sports, travel around the area, the beauty of the countryside and the wildlife are all safe topics, particularly if you've done some research and can speak knowledgeably about them in your conversations.

Dress

South Africa is a **conservative** country and its business attire reflects that orientation. **Men wear neatly pressed suits and ties, and women wear conservative dresses or suits**. The climate is subtropical with fairly warm days and the nights are fairly cool. During most of the year, light cotton clothing is appropriate during the day, while jackets, shawls, and sweaters are appropriate for the evenings.

Communication Style

Business language

The communication styles of South African business people vary with the racial and ethnic groups one is dealing with. **South Africans of British descent use low-context** forms of communication. They tend to be quite direct, non-emotional and will readily focus on substantive issues when negotiating. They place greater emphasis on verbal communication and utilize a minimal amount of body language.

The **Afrikaners are high-context communicators**. Relationships are important to them. After a relationship and some level of trust have been established, they will be ready to discuss substantive issues.

The **indigenous Africans** (i.e., blacks) are **high-context** communicators. They place a great deal of emphasis on relationships and the sharing of common experiences. Often demonstrating a dignified demeanor (such as Mandela), they can also be emotional when expressing their opinions. They will desire a high level of trust before dealing with any substantive issues. Any attempt to hurry this process along may be misinterpreted as manipulation or even dishonesty.

Non-verbal communication

The non-verbal communication patterns of the three ethnic and racial groups are quite distinct from each other. Body language among the South Africans of **British descent is quite subdued. They do very little gesturing and are quite unemotional.**

The **Afrikaners have a firmer handshake** than those of British descent; they make **good eye contact, are more emotional, and do more gesturing.** Their spatial needs are somewhat different and they will feel comfortable in somewhat closer proximity when communicating.

Indigenous **Black Africans** are generally more emotional than either the British or the Afrikaners and tend to **gesture more freely.** Prolonged eye contact, however, can be misinterpreted as confrontational or at least disrespectful.

The South African Concept of Negotiations

Selecting personnel

There are again distinct differences in the way personnel will be selected to represent the three basic ethnic and racial segments of the African business community.

The **British South Africans place considerable emphasis upon rank, social status and education.** When making their personnel selections, they will give greatest importance to these factors. The **Afrikaners and the Coloreds (those of mixed racial heritage)** place less emphasis on rank, social status and education. They will tend to emphasize **experience and maturity and will almost always want a male representing them. Indigenous Black South Africans** generally favor educated, experienced male personnel, but women are moving into business arenas.

Negotiating style

The South Africans of **British** descent have developed their own unique style of negotiating. They, **along with their Afrikaner neighbors,** utilize a pragmatic approach that focuses on the mutual benefit of all parties.

They refer to this negotiating posture as **"shopkeeper diplomacy".** This approach to negotiations views **compromise,** where all parties benefit, as the preferred outcome. There is much to be said for this style in that it fosters long-term amicable relationships and is similar to the win-win concept in American negotiations.

British and Afrikaner negotiators do not like to make quick decisions. They like to explore the facts and the technical data carefully before drawing any conclusions. They enjoy arguing, but prefer to do it as a polite back-and-forth exchange of ideas.

Many **Blacks of South Africa** have descended from tribal societies that were egalitarian democracies. Their cultures utilized **consensus and consultation strategies,** and stressed cooperation and harmony in the decision-making process. They have come from backgrounds that utilized **bartering, trading, and bargaining** tactics. These are the areas of their greatest strength.

With the new developments in South Africa, it is quite possible that negotiations with corporations from that country will now involve cross-cultural teams with representation from more than one ethnic group.

Issues discussed

The **British-descended South Africans will prefer to go into substantive issues** based on facts as quickly as possible. They may request the exchange of written agendas outlining an agreed-upon structure for the negotiations two or three weeks prior to the meetings. When the meetings actually start, they will prefer to bypass small talk and go straight into substantive and factual issues.

The **Afrikaners will be less formal, preferring to do some socializing before moving into a discussion of the substantive issues.**

Those South Africans of **mixed racial heritage will want to establish a relationship before proceeding into the factual phase of negotiations.**

The **Indian-Asian South Africans and Blacks will both favor spending time on relationship-based issues.** They will favor **non-directive discussions** that will establish rapport in the initial stages of the negotiations. They will resist moving too quickly into the substantive issues of the agenda.

With the changes that have taken place in South Africa, Blacks, Asians, and Coloreds are moving into managerial positions. As previously mentioned, it is possible that negotiating teams will be cross-cultural and ethnically-diverse units, and prior assumptions may not apply.

Establishing trust

The **British-descended South Africans, the Afrikaners, and the Coloreds** will look at past **performance and accomplishments as well as the size of the company**. These external factors are more important to them than relationship factors in the establishment of trust.

The **Blacks and Indian-Asians** will measure trust based upon the current status of the **personal relationship**. They will benefit from casual conversations and personal interactions that promote understanding and harmony.

Persuasion

The **British-descended South Africans favor empirical data** accompanied by charts and a presentation that features a factual analysis with supportive documentation.

The specific persuasion tactics that are likely to be effective with British South Africans are:

1) **Supported Facts**. One needs to present logical/factual information that is accompanied by supportive documentation.
2) Your initial presentation/offer is very important. The presentation/offer must include the benefits the South African firm will derive from the transaction along with the corresponding supportive documents. During the presentation, all options should be weighed, thus providing a logical path to your conclusions.
3) Receiving the **technical specifications up-front** is an excellent strategy.
4) **Get it in writing**. Write everything down throughout the negotiations. Take copious notes. Once it is in writing it becomes a logical argument with a concrete basis.
5) **Build trust through information sharing**.
6) It is okay to be blunt and to the point with British South Africans. Remember they view conflict as unavoidable. So, make your points and support it. The British South Africans will view this as an appropriate persuasion strategy.
7) This group is hierarchical. So, referring to the approval of respected **higher authorities** in regards to your company, product, etc. may prove to be an effective method of persuasion.
8) Use a **point-by-point** method of presentation, persuasion, and negotiation.
9) British South Africans tend to be fairly analytical. **Summarizing previously agreed upon benefits or listing the pros and cons** of the agreement can be an effective method of persuasion.

Tactics to avoid include:

1) Avoid the use of metaphors, emotional tactics, fear tactics, diffusion questions, distraction tactics, ultimatums, threats, loud voices, etc.
2) Haggling over price is okay but the price will probably not change more than 20%. So **do not "high-ball" or "low-ball."** In addition, it is probably best to wait to the end to discuss price. Both sides should start with reasonable prices, then attempt to meet each other's specifications and other requirements, and then the minor price issues can be resolved.
3) Do not use stalling, favoritism, or nepotism.
4) Avoid "small-talk"
5) Do not brag about personal achievements.
6) Avoid surprises at the table.

The **Afrikaners and Colored South Africans** favor a **factually-oriented presentation.** However, they **may also be swayed by personal appeals.**

The specific persuasion tactics that are likely to be effective with Afrikaners are:

1) **Supported Facts**. One needs to present logical/factual information that is accompanied by supportive documentation.

2) Your initial presentation/offer is very important. The presentation/offer must include the benefits the South African firm will derive from the transaction along with the corresponding supportive documents. During the presentation, all options should be weighed, thus providing a logical path to your conclusions.

3) Receiving the **technical specifications up-front** is an excellent strategy.

4) Get it **in writing**. Write everything down throughout the negotiations. Take copious notes. Once it is in writing it becomes a logical argument with a concrete basis.

5) Build trust through **information sharing**.

6) It is okay to be blunt and to the point with Afrikaners. Remember they view conflict as unavoidable. So, make your points and support it. The Afrikaners will view this as an appropriate persuasion strategy.

7) The use of metaphors, emotional tactics, fear tactics, distraction tactics and diffusion questions can be very useful.

8) Take your time. **Stalling** is acceptable.

9) **Speak with conviction and confidence.**

10) Use a **point-by-point** method of presentation, persuasion, and negotiation.

11) This group is hierarchical. Referring to the **approval of respected higher authorities** in regards to your company, product, etc. should prove to be an effective method of persuasion.

Tactics to avoid include:

1) Haggling over price is okay but the price will probably not change more than 25 to 30%. So **never "high-ball" or "low-ball."** In addition, it is probably best to wait to the end to discuss price. Both sides should start with reasonable prices, and then attempt to meet each other's specifications and other requirements and then the minor price issues can be resolved.

2) Avoid ultimatums, threats, loud voices, etc.

3) Avoid surprises at the table.

The **Blacks and Indian-Asians prefer appeals that are based on social and relationship-based issues**.

The specific persuasion tactics that are likely to be effective with Black South Africans are:

1) Get it **in writing**. Write everything down throughout the negotiations.

2) Build **trust through information sharing**.

3) The use of metaphors, emotional tactics, fear tactics, distraction tactics and diffusion questions can be very useful.

4) Take your time and **stall when it is useful.**

5) Black South Africans love to **haggle** and are quite lively while doing so. They will almost always **"high-ball" or "low-ball"** a deal.

6) Receiving the **technical specifications up-front** or in the beginning of the negotiation is a good idea.

7) Personal pleas often prove to be effective with Black South Africans.

8) This group is a hierarchical as well as collectivist society. Referring to the **approval of others** and especially the approval of **respected higher authorities** in regards to your company, product, etc. should prove to be an effective method of persuasion.

9) Discussion of harmonious future beneficial business relationships is an integral part of this group's cultures. Your **presentation of possible futuristic cooperative endeavors, the use of positive imagery,** etc. should be beneficial during business presentations and negotiations.

10) Based upon their collectivist nature and desire for harmony, the **"Feel-Felt-Found"** objection-handling tactic should prove to be effective when delivered in a harmonious and non-confrontational manner.

11) **Speak with conviction and confidence.**

12) Use a **big-picture** method of presentation, persuasion, and negotiation.

13) **Fatalistic reasoning** can be used effectively to build rapport and give minor support to one's arguments with this group. For example, "We were destined to do business."

Tactics to avoid include:

1) **Avoid personal conflict.**
2) Avoid surprises at the table. Up-front surprises promote conflict and reduce harmony. However, surprises behind the scenes are acceptable.

Resolving disputes

The **British South Africans** will try to **meet in the middle** and make compromises in order to resolve a dispute. They will favor an approach where all parties benefit. Failing to accomplish that, they will evaluate the evidence, explore all the facts, and then seek a legal solution.

The **Afrikaners and the Coloreds** will try to resolve disputes through **relationship-oriented appeals as well as an exploration of the facts**.

The **Blacks and Asian-Africans will favor relationship and emotionally-oriented approaches** to resolving disputes.

Under South African law, disputes can be taken to arbitration. The South African judicial system offers reciprocal enforcement and recognizes foreign judicial decisions, providing they had international jurisdiction and the capacity to adjudicate the issue. If the judgement of the foreign court was final and complete, then the decision will be accepted as conclusive. In South Africa, every court is bound by the decisions of the court superior to it.

Group and individual dynamics

The **British South Africans are individualistic**. They are very competitive and have high individual aspirations. They will often opt for their own personal success over a team approach.

The **Afrikaners and Coloreds are very resourceful and independent with mixed emotions about their commitments to a team approach**.

Blacks and Asian South Africans are team players. They are loyal to their families and it carries over to their group affiliations.

Risk

British, Afrikaners, Colored, and Asian South Africans are all risk averse. They will all favor pursuing low-risk objectives in their business transactions. However, **Black South Africans are more apt to accept risks in the pursuit of their business objectives.**

Decision-making

British South Africans favor a **top-down** centralized decision-making model.

Afrikaners favor a **top-down paternalistic** organizational decision-making structure.

Blacks and South African Asians use a **top-down consensus** style. They favor a centralized structure utilizing consultation and consensus, with **final authority held by an upper-management team.**

Type of agreement

Informal consent is sufficient for a contract in South Africa. Informal agreements through written correspondence are deemed to have been concluded at the date the letter of acceptance is posted. A contract for the benefit of a third party becomes irrevocable when accepted by the third party. There is no separation of civil and commercial contracts and formal conveyance of a contract involves registration.

British, Afrikaners, and Colored South Africans all favor explicit **written contractual agreements.**

Blacks and Asian South Africans favor oral, flexible, and implicit agreements. Indigenous cultures traditionally stress oral traditions and verbal agreements for which a man's word could be trusted.

Chapter 24

Spain

- *Country Background*
- *The Spanish Culture*
- *Business Protocol*
- *Communication Style*
- *The Spanish Concept of Negotiations*

The Kingdom of Spain, a nation of past glory and present prosperity, occupies the Iberian Peninsula and is situated in Southwestern Europe. The Atlantic Ocean, the Mediterranean Sea, and the Cantabrian Sea surround the peninsula. It shares a western border with Portugal and a northern border with France. Its territory also includes the Balearic Islands in the Mediterranean Sea, and the Canary Islands in the Atlantic Ocean. It has the distinction of being the closest European country to Africa; the 15-mile wide Straits of Gibraltar separate the two continents.

Spain has a total land area, including the Balearic and Canary Islands, of about 505,992 square kilometers, slightly over twice the size of Oregon. More than half the country is made up of vast, elevated tablelands—the *mesatas,* and five major mountain ranges that stretch across its topography. Spain has considerable natural resources, including coal, lignite, iron ore, uranium, mercury, pyrite, gypsum, zinc, lead, tungsten, copper, kaolin, potash, and hydropower.

Country Background

History

Over the course of its history, Spain was settled through a succession of prehistoric migrations and invasions emanating from Africa, Europe, and the Middle East. Little is known of the original inhabitants of the Iberian Peninsula beyond the fact that they were responsible for one of the world's most famous examples of cave paintings at Altamira.

By around 2000 BC, the Phoenicians and then the Greeks had established trading centers on Spain's Mediterranean shore. The Romans came during the first century BC. They heavily influenced Spain's language, literature, and architecture, and produced three Roman emperors. With the decline of the Roman Empire, The Suevi, Vandals, and Alans entered Spain. They were later subjugated by the Visigoths, who by the end of the 5th Century occupied virtually the entire peninsula.

At the beginning of the 8th Century, the Arabs entered from the south. They conquered the country quickly and their influence and dominance spread throughout the peninsula and lasted for almost 800 years.

Christian influences remained strong in the northern areas of Spain and eventually led to what became known as the re-conquest. It took the Christians 700 years to achieve an end to Muslim rule, a triumph that was completed in 1492 and is celebrated to this day during the fiesta known throughout Spain as the "Moors and Christians." Conquest of the Moors, along with the exploits of Columbus, became the springboard for the emergence of Spanish nationalism and the development of its colonial empire. Spain became a unified country in 1469 when King Ferdinand of Catalunya and Aragon married Queen Isabella of Castille. For several hundred years, this empire thrived and established Spain as one of the most powerful nations on earth.

Maintaining this colonial empire became increasingly difficult and disputes with the British, the French, and the Dutch strained Spain's resources. In 1808 Napoleon's troops entered and initially subdued Spain. However, a seven-year struggle ensued and finally culminated in Napoleon's defeat and the restoration of Ferdinand VII to the throne. Between 1810 and 1824, Spain's colonies in the Americas revolted and won their independence. In 1898 the Spanish American War brought an end to the Spanish Colonial Empire with the loss of Cuba, Puerto Rico, and the Philippines to the United States.

In the 20th century, Spain's deterioration continued and in 1923 the monarchy was ended by a seven-year military dictatorship. Demands for more democracy and less autocratic rule by both generals and kings finally led to elections in 1931, which were overwhelmingly won by those favoring a republic. The Spanish Republic broke up many of the great estates and curtailed the power of the Roman Catholic Church, which was perceived as closely tied to the monarchy. Thus, the Republic won the enmity of the wealthy landowners, the monarchists, the church hierarchy, and some of the generals. In 1936 Spain was torn by a civil war, which lasted 3 years and claimed the lives of over 450,000 Spaniards. Aided by Germany and Italy, General Francisco Franco defeated Republican forces and set up a fascist dictatorship; his rule lasted for 35 years.

Spain remained officially neutral during the World War II, but its close ties with Germany prevented its admittance to the United Nations until 1955. Spain's economy also suffered from UN trade sanctions in the late forties and early fifties. In 1969, Franco named

Prince Juan Carlos I as his successor, but remained in power until his death in 1975. When Juan Carlos assumed the throne he immediately implemented democratic reforms leading to civilian rule.

Government

The current constitution, finalized in 1978, made Spain a parliamentary monarchy. The Constitution provides for 17 regional governments with autonomous local control. The Chief of State is the King who heads the executive branch of the government. The head of the government is the Prime Minister, who is nominated by the king and voted into office by the National Assembly. Legislative powers are entrusted to the National Assembly, which is a two-chambered parliament consisting of the Congress of Deputies, which has 350 seats, and the Senate with 259 seats. Members are elected to four-year terms of office. All Spanish citizens are eligible to vote when they reach the age of eighteen.

The Supreme Court heads the judicial branch. Apart from the Constitution there is a Civil Code, which establishes the legal sources of Spanish law in the following order: laws, customs, and the general principles of law. A new subsequent law can only repeal current laws. The courts in Spain do not create laws; they only apply the legal norms. The present Civil Code of Spain was first set forth in 1889. Other special laws have been enacted to supplement and update the Code.

Spain joined the European Economic and Monetary Union (EMU) in 1998.

Demographics

Spain's population of 40 million makes it one of Europe's most sparsely populated countries, with about 78 people per square kilometer. It has a very low population growth rate. Life expectancy is 76 years for males and 83 for females. The literacy rate is 97%.

The Spanish people are a combination of Mediterranean and Nordic backgrounds. The earliest inhabitants mixed with later invaders including Celts, Carthaginians, Romans, Germanic peoples, and Moors. Several provinces emphasize their differences, such as Catalonia, Galacia, and the Basque Provinces in northern Spain. Since the Civil War, there has been a considerable migration of people from the rural areas to the cities, with more than 50% now residing in urban areas. Madrid, the capital, now has 5 million people in its metropolitan area.

One minority group in Spain is the Gypsies, who unofficially number almost 500,000 people. Spain also has 25,000 foreign permanent residents who are primarily from other E.U. countries.

Economy

When Spain's civil war ended in 1939, its economy was devastated. During the Second World War and its aftermath, there was little improvement, as Spain was hampered by UN sanctions and necessarily followed a path of self-sufficiency. Near the end of the 1950s, economic sanctions were lifted and the United States gave Spain much foreign aid in return for political support in the Cold War and the establishment of US naval and air bases in Spain. Along with the stabilization plan of 1959, this brought a positive trend to Spain's struggling economy.

A key factor in Spain's recovery in the 60s and 70s was tourism, which continues to be important to the Spanish economy. Approximately 70 million people visit Spain each year and contribute an estimated $30 billion per year to the economy.

Inflation and unemployment have at times reached crippling levels during the past 25 years. Over the past several years Spain has enjoyed a reasonable inflation rate, yet unemployment remains high at around 14% with many more underemployed.

Spain's economy ranks 10th in the world and their per capita ranking is 15th. Agriculture accounts for 4% of its GDP, which is still above the European average. Industry accounts for 31%.

Major industries in Spain include textiles and apparel (including footwear), foods and beverages, metals and metal manufacturing, chemicals, shipbuilding, automobiles, machine tools, and tourism. The agricultural sector produces grains, vegetables, olives, wine grapes, sugar beets, citrus fruits, beef, pork, poultry, and dairy products. Agriculture accounts for 8% of the country's labor force of 17 million. Spain's maintains a substantial trade deficit every year. Exports include autos and trucks, machinery, and foods. Its main imports are machinery, transport equipment, fuels, semi-finished goods, foodstuffs, consumer goods, and chemicals. Some of Spain's major trading partners are the Netherlands, followed by France, Italy, the USA, the UK, and Germany.

The currency is the Spanish peseta.

The Spanish Culture

Language

Spain has four major languages groups. The predominant language is Castilian Spanish, and it is spoken throughout Spain by approximately 74% of the population. It is the accepted language for business throughout every region of Spain. There are also three regional languages. Catalan, which is spoken in the extreme northeast by approximately 17% of the population, has close ties to the French language. Galician, which is spoken in the northwest by approximately 7% of the population, is closely related to the Portuguese language. Basque, which is spoken by 2% of the population in the north, is one of the oldest languages in the world. The Basques, who have fought for their independence in the past, claim to be a separate nation. These sentiments still persist, and their language is the predominant way in which they maintain their cultural identity.

Many Spaniards learn a second language. Traditionally that language was French, but more recently English has become popular. Most Spanish companies that are involved in international business ventures now have personnel on their staff who speak English.

Religion

Spain's constitution guarantees freedom of religion, which technically makes it a secular state with no declared official religion. In reality, the Roman Catholic faith has been an integral part of Spain and its history for over five hundred years. Today 99% of the population identify themselves with the Catholic Church, and the church still wields considerable influence even though a large portion of Spaniards are now non-practicing Catholics (especially the younger Spaniards). This influence can be seen in the numerous religious occasions and celebrations that occur throughout the year. Furthermore, the majority of Spain's most important buildings are churches and cathedrals. The influence of Catholicism has affected almost everything the Spaniards have done since 1492. There are other religions in Spain, but they are truly in the minority. There are a few Protestants and some Muslims, which together number less than one percent.

Value system

Family and individualism are the core aspects of the Spanish value system. In order of importance, family comes first, then individual aspirations, and last the needs of the collective group. Spaniards also tend to have intense relationships, and it is not uncommon for their bonds of friendship to last an entire lifetime. A commitment to family and friends is an intrinsic part of Spain's value system.

The Catholic Church has also nurtured Spanish values for over five centuries. Today these values are centered around loyalty to one's family, as well as a commitment to moral values and a code of honor that can be lost either by one's own actions or by those of one's relatives. While individualism is important, especially for men, family and friends are usually taken into account when individuals make a personal decision. Within the family framework there is usually one recognized head, and this is almost always the oldest member. This individual will receive considerable obeisance and respect. Spanish men also have strong bonds of loyalty to their mothers.

Today Spanish women are increasingly working outside the home and pursuing their own careers. They have also become more open and outspoken about their own needs and feelings. While divorce was previously unheard of in this Catholic country, it is now becoming a more common occurrence. The Spanish constitution of 1978 gave women equal rights with men.

There are substantial differences across the Spanish regions with regards to their value systems. Much like Italy, the Spanish north is industrialized and full of private enterprises. Thus, the northern Spaniards are career-oriented, possess a conservative business mentality, are more punctual, money conscious, etc. The Spanish south (also like Italy) is agricultural, more relaxed, passionate, etc. These differences are further exaggerated by differences in language, cultures, and economic disparity. The north is wealthier.

Class structure / Stratification

Spain still has a class-conscious culture; an individual's position in society is often determined by one's family of origin, as well as by one's occupation, professional accomplishments, and accumulation of wealth. Some of this class-consciousness can be traced back to Spain's aristocratic heritage, where one's family and one's connections were of primary importance. Today aristocratic heritage has little meaning, but the wealth that is associated with one's heritage still plays a critical role in the determination of one's status. Class structure is also somewhat determined by where one lives. Those who reside in rural areas tend to be poorer than those living in urban areas. The migration of people from the farms to the cities and improvements in the economy have brought about an expansion of the middle class.

As previously noted, women are now beginning to figure more prominently in education, politics and the work force. More equal opportunities under the rule of democratic law are beginning to soften the rigid lines of the old class structure.

Safety

With tourism being such an important part of the Spanish economy, it is not surprising that Spain is a relatively safe country to visit. The crime level in Spain is quite moderate when compared with that of other countries. Of course, there are precautions to take. Some apply primarily to driving a vehicle in Spain. It is advisable to have an international driver's license and proper automobile registration and insurance. The network of roads is excellent, but traffic tends to be quite heavy. Spaniards tend to be aggressive drivers, and if you are in an accident with a Spaniard, as is the case in most countries, the foreigner is usually found guilty no matter who caused it. If possible, keep all your valuables in the trunk of your car when leaving it unattended. The theft of valuables left in autos is a common occurrence. If traveling by coach or train, be careful of pick pockets and purse snatchers, who tend to prefer crowded locations.

Health standards in Spain have improved considerably. It is generally safe to drink the water and eat fresh salads. Food inspection standards have been upgraded. Now that Spain is a member of the EU, all food and drink has to be labeled in accordance with EU standards.

Business Protocol

Greetings and etiquette

Spanish business and social behavior is usually quite **informal**. Familiarity is a basic tenet of Spanish interaction in all but the most elevated circles. When meeting a Spaniard for the first time, a **handshake** is the normal greeting procedure. **Among close friends, Spaniards will add a pat on the back or a hug. Women will lightly embrace and kiss both cheeks.**

In the south of Spain, manners are slightly more informal than in the north. It is quite common at meetings or at restaurants for Spanish businessmen to take off their jackets or loosen their ties. **They also move very quickly to a first name basis.** If one is at a very formal occasion with a wide mix of rank, it is advisable to be circumspect and wait to see what others are doing.

If one has some fluency in Spanish, remember that Spain emphasizes the different forms of the pronouns "usted" and "tu" for "you." Generally, "usted" is used in more formal occasions and as a way of showing respect. It is probably advisable to use the more respectful term "usted" until one is asked to use the more informal term "tu"

Although Spaniards prefer to avoid formal titles, **the titles "Senor" and "Senora" should be used along with the person's surname when addressing or introducing a Spanish business person.** This is more complicated when written correspondence is involved. Most Spaniards have two surnames, one deriving from their father and the other from their mother. In written correspondence both names should be used with the surname of the father listed first.

For Spaniards any factor that impinges on their personal pride or honor will diminish a relationship. Relationships are important to the Spanish, for it is out of relationships that trust and respect are established. The Spanish also value modesty. Technical ability and professionalism are not as important to them as pride in one's self-reliance and personal worth. On the other hand, when addressing issues related to their ability to complete a task or their ability to fulfill your expectations or reaffirm the trust you have bestowed upon them, they may exaggerate their ability to complete the task.

Time

Spain is a **polychronic** culture; they like to do many things simultaneously. Southern Spaniards are not noted for their punctuality, but business meetings in Barcelona are fairly punctual. The pace of business tends to be slow in southern Spain and moderate in northern Spain. Social events rarely start on time in either area, but foreign business people are expected to be punctual. Business deadlines are taken seriously in most of Spain. A siesta in the middle of the day is now only practiced in rural Spain.

Urban office hours are usually 8 AM until 5 PM with one hour for lunch. The rural Spanish workday and store hours usually begin at 9 AM, lunch and the siesta may last from 1 to 4 PM, and work usually resumes from 4 PM to around 8 PM. It is not advisable to schedule meetings for Monday mornings because Spaniards celebrate very intensely on the weekends and are usually late for work on Mondays. Four-day work weeks are also not uncommon among higher-status Spanish business men.

One should remember that the Spanish write the day first, followed by the month and year, in their correspondence. Spain is also one hour ahead of Greenwich mean time (GMT + 1) or six hours ahead of US Eastern Standard Time (EST +6).

Gifts

Generally, Spaniards do not exchange gifts at initial meetings. After a relationship is established, gift giving commences. If one is invited to a Spanish business person's home, it is advisable to bring a gift; pastries, chocolates, or flowers are customary. Do not bring dahlias or chrysanthemums, which are associated with death.

Business gifts that are usually appreciated include: portable electrical products, local crafts, or illustrated books from your region of the world. Sport T-shirts and university caps are good gifts for children. Gifts should be chosen carefully, and should be of high quality and beautifully wrapped. If you are given a gift, it is customary to open it immediately. While giving and receiving gifts one should exercise grace and poise. In Spain, a gift is an extension of one's self. Thus, hastily discarding a gift, or not giving an appropriate gift, etc. are faux pas.

Business entertainment

Dining at a restaurant in Spain is a very popular form of business entertainment. These occasions are important because successful business ventures in Spain evolve out of **relationship building**. Spanish businessmen want to feel right about their foreign business partners, and they utilize dining opportunities in order to elicit and share information that will lead to bonds of mutual trust.

In most instances, a **Spanish businessman will make the first reservation and cover the check. Do not offer to pay for anything**, for this would be considered rude. **On the next occasion, you will be expected to reciprocate**. When inviting Spaniards to dinner keep in mind that they are accustomed to **excellent food and wine**. Make some inquiries and try to find a restaurant that serves gourmet food, fine wine, and offers the proper ambiance. One needs to be cognizant of the dining etiquette of Spain. In most instances only senior executives will be dining with foreign business representatives.

Business breakfasts are normally scheduled after 8:30 AM, since Spaniards tend not to be morning people. Business luncheons usually last one to two hours and are usually accompanied by a large meal. Spaniards rarely have their lunch brought in, so plan on meeting at a nearby restaurant. Keep the conversation light and do not delve into heavy business items during the luncheon. Most Spaniards prefer to relax a bit during lunch.

Dinners are usually scheduled around 9 or 10 PM, and they extend late into the night or early morning. At these dinner meetings you will note that **initially no attempt is made to discuss business matters**. Conversations will usually cover safe topics such as **travel, the weather, or sports**. Only **after coffee is served at the end of the meal will business matters be brought up**. It is acceptable in Spain to smoke and drink at these dinner events, but do not get drunk. Moderation in this context is imperative. The guest of honor will be seated to the right of the host. If you have been invited out, remember to compliment the host and headwaiter or proprietor of the restaurant before leaving.

Dress

The Spanish tend to be **stylish in their dress**, and are quite conscientious about their appearance. Well-made brand-named attire will be noticed and appreciated. Both men and women should adhere to current European trends. **Women should dress more stylishly than men.** Pantsuits are frowned upon, as are shorts for either gender. Spaniards tend to dress elegantly even for casual events. Clothing that is soiled, worn, or wrinkled lowers their impression of that person's social and business standing. When in an office or at meetings or a restaurant, it is commonplace for men to remove their jackets and loosen their ties.

Communication Style

Business language

The language patterns of Spain are **high-context**. Spain is a relatively homogenous culture. It is a country where the people share common experiences, common understandings, and a lengthy history. As a result there is **a lot of indirect and non-verbal communication**. Language alone does not convey the total context of all that is being communicated. When Spaniards communicate with one another, a great deal is implicit and understood between them that is beyond the understanding of someone from outside their culture. Therefore, when a foreign business person attempts to translate the words, he only gets part of what is being communicated. Communicating accurately in this kind of culture takes time. That is why building relationships and trust is important.

Non-verbal communication

Since Spain is a high-context language culture, the **non-verbal factors in their communication are highly developed**. Numerous gross and fine motor movements, as well as eye and facial expressions, convey a considerable amount of what is being communicated between them. Spanish conversation tends to be **lively and animated**, with **gesturing, grimacing, and eye movements an integral part of** the process. **However, non-verbal communication tends to be more subdued in northern Spain.** In negotiating sessions, Spaniards may exchange glances with meanings that are only evident to them.

When the Spanish converse, **spatial proximities are very close and eye contact is quite intense and direct.** Someone who stands back further than they are used to and doesn't make enough eye contact may be considered cold or disinterested. This is also true of silence; Spaniards tend to become uncomfortable during lengthy periods of silence.

The Spanish Concept of Negotiations

Selecting personnel

Spaniards attach considerable importance to **personal influence**. It is therefore desirable to have a local, well-connected person make contacts and introductions for the negotiating team. This person can also be valuable in briefing the team on Spanish customs and non-verbal idiosyncrasies. There may be instances where this local person can clarify subtle nuances in communications as the negotiation progresses. This person must be selected with great care, for once a representative is associated with your enterprise, it will be difficult to switch to another person.

Spanish companies tend to be family-owned, and until recently leadership was based more upon lineage than enlightenment. As the economy has gotten stronger, opportunities for upward mobility and promotions on the basis of ability and achievement have begun to occur. A new generation of negotiators chosen because of their training and accomplishments is emerging. Therefore, present-day Spanish negotiating teams **may have a mix of people in rank and status, along with some who have negotiation and/or other skills.** If you are negotiating with a multinational firm in Spain you can expect all members of the negotiation team to have been selected for skills, knowledge, and relevance.

Spaniards will tend to be responsive to a **foreign negotiating team that includes well-educated, high-ranking, and mature members. Female members of the team can expect to be the only woman at the table. However,** machismo and chauvinist biases are diminishing rapidly in Spain.

Negotiating style

The Spanish tend to view negotiations as an **enjoyable procedure**, and the process itself as a game or an art form. They approach the negotiating encounter with a **competitive attitude**; it is wise to allow some room for concessions and **bargaining**. Much of the historical negotiation training in Spain comes out of the French paradigm of Cartesian logic and debate. Thus, rationale arguing with a string of connected thoughts is viewed as effective and is expected.

Spanish negotiators also tend to be oriented toward the person, the relationship, and trust. Thus, they are not inclined to separate the task from the person. As previously mentioned, the Spaniards have different time perspectives than Westerners, and they will resist any attempts to hurry the negotiating process. Doing so will limit the **relationship-building** phase, which to them is a vital part of the process.

Initially, the Spaniards will be evaluating the individual members of the other team. This will involve asking personal questions about background, education, and interests, thus fulfilling their need to get to know their counterparts on a personal level. When they are satisfied and feel a degree of rapport has been established, they will be ready to move into the **substantive issues** of the negotiating process.

Spaniards appreciate people who approach the negotiating process quite **formally**; any presentation should be made in a very direct and clear manner. Eye contact is important because a lack of it is considered a sign of dishonesty. Spaniards admire modesty and are turned off by assertiveness. Presentations that are low key, understated (in terms of technical and financial details), and focused on the tangible aspects of an agreement will usually impress them the most.

Recently, Spanish negotiation training has been mirroring British and American paradigms. Thus, point-by-point presentations supported by empirical data have become more common place.

In conclusion, the Spanish negotiation systems are complex as well as in transition. As a rule of thumb, expect a trust-building component, followed by debate and argumentation, then a period of retraction and cooling off, after which empirical evidence will be presented in a point-by-point method, and last the negotiation will be concluded via oration, summation, and bargaining. Admittedly, these styles will ebb and flow with each negotiation and personality type.

Issues discussed

Relationship-based issues will be the first order of business. Friendships and long-term commitments are critical to Spanish executives. Once they feel comfortable, they will be ready for the more **substantive issues**. These can be anything from production schedules, warehousing facilities, and transportation costs to advertising time lines and other typical issues that are salient to an international business contract.

The issues discussed in Spanish negotiations **may vary considerably**. The Spanish are somewhat anarchistic and seem to resent agendas. Remember that they are also a polychronic culture, so they have a predisposition toward **simultaneous task activities**. This will often manifest itself in the form of **spontaneous debate**, where the meeting may become a forum for what may seem extraneous to the monochronically-oriented person. This does not mean that the Spanish do not value the importance of the agenda or the issues being discussed; it reflects instead their cultural conditioning.

To the Spaniards, **voicing one's opinion is the way to work toward agreement and harmony**. When meetings stray too far in the Spanish culture, the most senior person present is expected to act as arbiter and restore order. Whoever chairs the meeting will have to repeatedly pull the meeting back to the agreed-upon agenda.

Establishing trust

Establishing trust is a high priority in Spanish business negotiations. Trust is developed out of **relationship-based** activities. Dinners, conversations, and social events help the Spaniard to get to know the foreign business person. Spaniards will remember someone's past comments or behavior, and out of these experiences they will trust or not trust that person. If they do not trust someone, they will maintain a cautious posture that may impede business negotiations. If they do not have enough relationship-based information to form a bases of trust, they will try to intuitively determine a person's trustworthiness. Spaniards also attach a lot of significance to **perceived status**; they tend to more readily trust someone they perceive as a high- status person based on one's family background, occupation, education, wealth, etc.

Persuasion

If one has engaged fully in the earlier relationship-building activities, one's persuasion tactics will be more readily received. The Spanish will certainly use issues related to friendship to try to win concessions whenever they can. A persuasive argument in Spain includes logic and empirical evidence as well as dogma, emotion, and machismo. Form can be as important as substance in Spain. Style and conviction are critical.

Proposals that are practical and modest, rather than grandiose, will likely impress them. Yet one's individual ability or the firm's ability to complete the task should never be understated. The use of visual aids and samples can add credence to statements and presentations. Spaniards like to negotiate; therefore leave room for concessions, but counter by creating the impression you are willing to negotiate forever.

The persuasion tactics that can be generally used with Spaniards or will be used by Spaniards are:

1) Spaniards love to **haggle** and are quite lively while doing so. **Distributive bargaining** is a favorite pastime. The Spaniards will almost always **"high-ball" or "low-ball"** a deal. Try to enjoy the process and you will be more successful.

2) Receiving the technical specifications up-front or in the beginning of the negotiation is a good idea in Spain.

3) **Metaphors, stories, and analogies** are usually effective in Spanish business negotiations when presented in a Cartesian manner.

4) **Act disappointed**; the Spanish are highly competitive and by giving them the impression that they have won, one may be able to get additional concessions.

5) **Get it in writing**; if you have taken copious notes throughout the negotiations, they will probably prove to be of considerable value when it comes to the persuasion phase of finalizing the contract.

6) **Diffusion questions** and **distraction tactics** are useful when trying to re-focus and avoid conflict-producing issues.

7) **Acting as if you might leave** and implying that no deal is better than a bad deal can sometimes be a necessary concluding maneuver.

8) **Exaggeration is common and effective in southern Spain.** It is best to stay moderately humble and realistic with northern Spaniards.

9) As in France, your initial presentation/offer is critical to a successful negotiation. The presentation/offer must include the benefits the Spanish firm will derive from the transaction along with corresponding **supportive documents.** During the presentation, all options should be weighed, thus providing a logical path to your conclusions. In addition, an **historical overview is advisable. This is part of the Cartesian system of logic**. The historical overview provides supporting documentation, a track record of success and displays thoroughness. **Active participation** from others or questioning during presentations should be encouraged.

10) **Speak with conviction and confidence.** The Spanish are a very proud people and tend to speak with eloquence as well as bravado. You will need to do the same.

11) **Embrace indirect conflict**. The Spanish view it as positive, productive, and fun. However, avoid direct or personal conflict.

12) Take your time. The Spanish do not stall but they are definitely not in a hurry.

13) **Summarizing previously agreed upon benefits or listing the pros and cons** of the agreement is often an effective method of persuasion during the later portions of a negotiation in Spain.

14) **Build trust through information sharing.**

15) **Use silence as a persuasion mechanism**. Spaniards do not like silence and its use may prompt concessions.

Tactics to avoid include:

1) Do not brag about personal achievements. Most Europeans praise modesty. However, as in most of Europe, the presentation of documentation supporting corporate or individual achievement is very acceptable and expected.
2) Do not use fear tactics, ultimatums, threats, yelling, or other highly dramatic emotional tactics.
3) **Do not hurry to complete the transaction**. Allow for breaks, side conversations, etc.

Resolving disputes

The standard procedure in resolving any disputes that may arise would be to attempt to **answer their objection as factually and objectively as possible**. If you perceive that they are not accepting an objective answer, then perhaps you might change to a personal appeal or attempt to rephrase using Cartesian logic. Spaniards like to play devil's advocate. So, a rejection of your argument and/or presentation may merely be the Spanish version of a request for an encore in order to reinforce, remove doubts, and a check for puffery.

You might try to **diffuse the situation** by asking them what they would suggest. If that doesn't work, explore alternative options with them. Remember to try to remain friendly and affable. If you cannot do that, ask to **take a short break**. When the negotiations resume, if you feel your opponents' position makes sense and they are able to support it with documentation, you might yield. Then confirm that their concern has been dealt with to their satisfaction and move on to the next agenda item.

Group and individual dynamics

Spain is a country of contrast. They are a highly individualistic people, but are also deeply committed to their families. They are a relatively homogenous culture in terms of ethnicity and language, but their country has a long history of factionalism. Out of this milieu has emerged a people who are very **loyal to their friends and family, yet highly motivated toward individual achievement**. As individuals, they tend to be very competitive and even somewhat anarchistic. In this they are very much like Australians. They view one who always agrees with the majority as having neither

personality nor the ability for independent thought. As a result, they vacillate between their individual need for success or recognition, and their group, institutional, corporate, and societal commitments. Perhaps this in part explains why most successful Spanish businesses tend to be family-owned. Family loyalties offer the most permanent of Spanish group affiliations.

Risk

The Spain of the past is rapidly being pushed aside. An active and growing stock exchange, a thriving real-estate market, significant industrial development, and rampant consumerism have created a climate favorable to a new breed of entrepreneurship.

Traditionally, Spain was a risk-averse culture, steeped in fiscal conservatism and self-sufficiency and ruled by old-line families. In the old Spain, a Spaniard would never risk involvement in any venture that could possibly be detrimental to his family's status.

Today, Spanish executives are **moderate risk-takers** due to the transition to a pluralistic democracy, membership in the E.U., economic deregulation, and a wave of foreign investment that has opened new investment opportunities to the present generation. This generation is more flexible and astute in their investment strategies. While Spaniards still favor investments offering profits over market share, they are becoming more open to various investment strategies or business arrangements.

Decision making

The ideal business leader in Spain is a benevolent and courageous autocrat. Sharing the decision-making process with subordinates is thought to be a sign of weakness. When subordinates have a problem, they tend to expect the boss to solve it. Attempts to involve subordinates in the decision-making process tends to produce insecurity and anxiety.

However, in Spain's **top-down** management system, authority does not automatically go with status. Authority is also determined by the quality of a management person's relationships with subordinates. Therefore, some leaders who insist on rigid adherence to protocol and the following of proper chains of command may alienate subordinates. Loyalties in Spanish business enterprises tend to be toward personalities rather than the corporation. Spaniards do expect to be reprimanded, because it is the way a boss asserts his authority. Criticism is seen as an exercise of rank and an assertion of authority, rather than as feedback designed to improve job performance. Thus, the use of constructive criticism is an ineffective and sometimes a destructive management tool in Spain.

Appraisal systems in Spain are a rarity. When an employee's performance is reviewed and an evaluation is backed up by objective facts, it is usually resented. Spanish employees even resent positive feedback, because it implies a form of accountability they would rather avoid. Spain's management style is highly compartmentalized, bureaucratic, and run along top-down authoritarian lines.

Type of agreement

In Spain, the final contractual arrangements can take many forms. Traditionally, Spaniards considered one's word of honor, sealed with a handshake, as a sufficient gesture. The contract was seen more as a guide or an agreement in principle rather than a legally binding agreement.

Today, many Spaniards see the value of having every aspect of the agreement clarified, so that the **final written contract eliminates all ambiguities and is legally binding for all participants**. These contracts tend to be complex and extensive. The Spanish prefer, expect, and will argue for contracts written in Spanish.

Contract law

Spanish law has its roots in the Roman legal system. While Spanish law has evolved throughout the centuries, with major influences from the Napoleonic and British systems, it is largely unchanged. A major difference in comparison to the American legal system concerns the concept of jurisprudence. Like legal systems based on Roman law, Spanish law does not recognize precedents as binding. Precedents may influence the judge's decision, but do not automatically become law.

It should be noted that the Spanish law on contracts is very flexible. In fact, the parties to a contract may agree to whatever pacts, clauses, terms and conditions they deem convenient, as long as these are not contrary to the 'law, the moral or public policy'. As a result, under Spanish law the parties have considerable

discretion for establishing the rights and obligations corresponding to a supplier, an agent, a distributor, a franchisee, etc.

The elements of a contract in Spain are: 1) consent of parties; 2) true object that is the focus of the contract; 3) cause of obligation is established by the contract; and 4) in certain industries, the form of the contract is an element.

Like bilateral contracts in the United States, a contract in Spanish law is that figure of juridical business formed by the concurrence of two or more correlative wheels and that are reciprocally coordinated with the goal of satisfying the interest of the parties involved. There are three major principles that apply to contracts: 1) Principle of Autonomous Will, 2) Principle of Consensus, and 3) Principle of Compulsory Efficacy.

Principle of Autonomous Will. Article 1091 of the civil code established that obligations derived from contracts can be enforced by law and must be fulfilled according to the terms of the contract. Contractual conditions that must be satisfied are that the participants are free to accept or reject the contract and also to assign who will be the other party they enter negotiations with (according to articles 1254 and 1255 of the civil code).

Principle of Consensus. Contracts that are bilateral or multilateral juridical business in nature require the presence of several declarations of will. There must be converging declarations of will in order to form a contract (i.e., both parties must want to be in the contract of their free will). According to articles 1258 and 1272: "Contracts will be compulsory whatever the form in which they are accepted" as long as all elements are present. In some predetermined cases, you must have a specific form in which the contract is valid. For example, in public writing, there must be a lawyer that is registered with the court present. This applies to banking, transportation, insurance, and warehousing industries. Contracts developed within these industries must also be filed with, and are controlled by, the commerce department.

Principle of Compulsory Efficacy. Compulsory efficacy occurs when there is no exchange of tangible goods or real possessions, but of services. The parties that have entered the contract are forced to fulfill the contract.

NOTES:

Chapter 25

Sweden

- *Country Background*
- *The Swedish Culture*
- *Business Protocol*
- *Communication Style*
- *The Swedish Concept of Negotiations*

Sweden is one of the Scandinavian countries of Northern Europe. The Baltic Sea and the Gulf of Bothnia form its eastern coastline. To the south and west is Denmark and an arm of the North Sea about 80 miles wide and 150 miles long. Most of the west side of the country is composed of the border with Norway. The upper northern part of the country shares a border with Finland. The total land area is 410, 928 sq. km, slightly larger than California. The terrain is mostly flat or gently rolling lowlands with some mountains in the West. Its natural resources include zinc, iron ore, lead, copper, silver, timber, uranium and hydropower. Only 7% of its land is arable, 2% are in meadows and pastures, and 68% of the land is forest and woodland.

Country Background

History

Fourteen thousand years ago what is now Sweden was covered by a thick ice cap. After the ice age retreated, humans came to Sweden. The earliest evidence of human habitation dates to around 10,000 BC in Southern Sweden. This evidence consists of graves, dwelling sites, and tools from the Stone Age. The Iron Age, from 500 BC to AD 400, was a period in which agriculture began to play a prominent role as the population became less nomadic and more settled.

The Viking Age (AD 800 - 1060) is perhaps the most dramatic phase of Scandinavian history. Sweden was ruled at that time by a variety of territorial chieftains. Although their reputations are of violent war-like men, their main aim was often trade. There is evidence they traveled as far as India, China and North America.

The Vikings of Sweden directed most of their explorations and conquests eastward across the Baltic Sea and the rivers that flowed into it. They had two main advantages over those whose lands they ravaged. First of all, they had developed ships that could be sailed or rowed, and featured flat bottoms, which could come in close to shore and navigate up rivers. They were fierce in battle, believing that those who died gained eternal life in Valhalla, their concept of heaven. Their written Runic alphabet was inscribed on stones to document battles and deaths and also on arrowheads and axes. Many runestones are still found around Sweden with the oldest from around AD 200.

The biggest change for Sweden in the middle ages came with the emergence of the state as an entity to raise taxes, build fortresses and equip the military. The nobility gained in power during the middle ages and eventual divisions between the church, the nobility, the peasants, and the merchants grew into 4 distinct classes.

It was not until 1523 that Sweden established itself as an independent power under the rule of Gustav Vasa (1521-1611). Since that time the Swedish monarchy has been an inherited position.

Sweden had a long and complex history of expansion and conquest as they sought power and influence in Northern Europe. From 1521 to 1718 there was a succession of kings who first established Sweden as an independent power and then a dominating force in Scandinavia and nearby regions.

After 1721, the Swedish people tired of the burdens of taxation and conscription, and with a series of military defeats, the power of the kings waned. The ensuing shift from the power of the monarchy to that of parliament ushered in a period of freedom and enlightenment which eventually led to Sweden's evolution from an aggressive and war- like nation to a nation devoted to neutrality and pacifism.

Government

Sweden is a constitutional monarchy, although the head of state has no political power. In 1975 the constitution was revised for the first time in over 150 years. It is a parliamentary representative democracy. Elections to the unicameral parliament are held every 4 years and places are won through a proportional system. Each political party must win at least 4% of the national vote and 12% of a regional vote to be represented in parliament. Every Swedish citizen over the age of 18 is eligible to vote and around 90% do.

There are currently seven major political parties represented in the Swedish parliament. The leading party is the Social Democrats. Their primary support comes from the industrial unions and blue-collar workers. Their predominant ideology is focused on economic issues involving a more equal distribution of wealth and power. The next most popular party is the Conservatives, whose_constituency comes primarily from high-paid white-collar workers. The Centrists' main voter base is among farmers. The Liberal Party advocates a guided market economy with political democracy. The Leftist Party is the successor to the communist party. The Ecology Party, also called the Green Party, was founded in 1982 and attracts many young voters. Their primary focus is the protection of the environment.

Modern Swedish Law evolved primarily from Nordic sources. There were slight influences from the Roman Canonical and Germanic Law, which were evolving concurrently in greater Europe. Sweden has a strong legal tradition and their laws reflect a high degree of continuity.

One unusual feature of Swedish politics is the role of the ombudsman. These are officials appointed by the government to investigate complaints against public authorities and abuses of power. Another facet of Swedish government is the principle of openness. All documents must be accessible to the public unless they involve national security. These two features reflect the Swedish commitment to fairness and justice in their government.

Demographics

Sweden has one of the world's most homogenous populations. Of the current population of 9 million, only about 12% are foreign-born or first-generation immigrants. Most of the population is concentrated in the cities, for Sweden is one of the most urbanized nations in the world. The population is located primarily in the southern portions of the country where the climate is milder.

The capital, Stockholm, is home to approximately 1.5 million people. The second and third largest cities are Gothenburg and Malmo. Over 16% of the population of Sweden lives in these three cities and most of the rest live in smaller cities such as Snealand and Lund. For these reasons there are large areas of Sweden, particularly in the north, that are forested and are relatively uninhabited, providing some of the last true wilderness areas of Europe.

The population growth rate is almost zero. Life expectancy is high: 77 years for males and 83 years for females. The literacy rate is 99%.

Housing standards in Sweden are very high. Most homes and apartments are well equipped with modern appliances, central heating, good insulation, sound construction, and have efficient designs.

Economy

Sweden's evolution to a modern welfare state and highly successful economy is rooted in its unique history. Throughout the 19th century the population increased dramatically from 2.4 million in 1810 to 4.6 million in 1880. Swedes say this was due to peace, potatoes, and vaccine, all of which had been unknown previously. It was also due in part to land reform, which began in 1827 and parceled the land into more efficient agricultural units. Reforms continued throughout the 19th century with universal education for boys (1842) and a revamping of parliament into a bicameral system with voting rights to all property owners.

The Industrial age began for Sweden in 1870 with timber, iron, steel, textiles, and glass playing major developing roles. Swedish companies A.S.E.A., Ericsson S.K.F. and A.G.A. were founded, and inventors Ericsson (the rotary propeller), and Nobel (dynamite) thrived. Soon a new social class based on industrial workers began to grow and by the end of the 19th century, only 50% of the population still earned their living in agriculture.

As industry developed, so did the organization of labor unions. The year 1879 saw the first strike in Sundsvall. Sweden's current political parties have their roots in this time period. The Social Democratic Party came to power in 1920, and began to assemble the current Swedish social welfare system. In 1934 unemployment benefits were established. In 1946 pensions for all were begun. In 1947 a universal health care system was started, and in 1974 the parental leave act was added.

After the extreme poverty and insecurity of the previous century, Swedes were willing to pay higher taxes so that all segments of their society were well fed, well housed, well clothed, and well cared for. A complete welfare state is costly to maintain and Sweden was aided in this regard by a long period of peace and neutrality during World War I and World War II.

Over the years Sweden has established an enviable standard of living utilizing a mixed system of high-tech capitalism and extensive welfare benefits. It has a modern distribution system, an excellent internal and external communications network, and a highly skilled labor force. Timber, hydropower, and iron ore constitute the resource base of an economy that is heavily oriented toward foreign trade.

Despite the considerable influence of the government, Sweden's economy is a free enterprise system and a very successful one. It has the seventh largest economy in Europe, despite having a population smaller than that of Portugal or Greece. Part of Sweden's success can be attributed to the fact that they lead the world in the percentage of their population (over 50%) in the work force. Much of Sweden's industry is concentrated in a small number of highly efficient engineering firms, notably Ericsson, Electrolux, Saab and Volvo. Twenty of Sweden's largest companies account for about 90% of Sweden's industrial output; 50% of this is from the engineering sector. Agriculture accounts for only 2% of GDP and 2% of the employment in the country. Sweden enjoys a healthy trade surplus every year.

In recent years, growing unemployment and a gradual loss of competitiveness in international markets diminished this highly favorable picture. The unemployment rate is 6%. Sweden is ranked 20th in the world on GDP economic measures as well as on per capita income.

The Swedish krona is their currency.

The Swedish Culture

Language

The Swedish language, one of the Indo-European languages, is Germanic in origin. Swedish speakers can usually understand Norwegian and Danish and vice versa. There are about 18 million speakers worldwide, with pockets in Finland and Estonia. If one can speak German, Dutch, or Afrikaans in addition to English, learning Swedish becomes much easier. One may find they are able to read some basic Swedish with little effort.

English language instruction has been compulsory in the Swedish schools for over 40 years. Many Swedes can speak English, but as the language is seldom used, their abilities will vary considerably. However, one can certainly get by in Sweden without learning the language. If you go to Sweden and have a residence permit, you are entitled to 240 hours of free Swedish language instruction. Those who immigrate to Sweden are allowed paid time off from work for this language instruction.

Religion

During the Viking Age, the religion of Sweden was polytheistic. Odin was the principle deity, Thor the god of weather, Frej the fertility god, and Baldu the god of goodness and wisdom.

As the Vikings traveled through Christian lands and brought back slaves, some of them converted to the new religion. In 1008 King Olof Skotbonung was baptized and this marked the beginning of the end of the Viking Age and the old religious belief system. The country became Christian by the end of the 12th century. The Christian church gradually gained strength and influence and introduced the Latin alphabet and the Bible to Sweden.

In 1523, Sweden broke with the Catholic Church and joined the Protestant Reformation. Sweden was primarily affected by the winds of change coming out of Germany and the belief system they adopted was that of Lutheranism.

While most Swedes are Lutheran today, it is because they automatically became members of the church at birth. Since 1996, this has changed and one is no longer automatically a member of the church, but can opt to become a member at the age of 18. While 88% of the population are church members, only about 5% attend church with any regularity. Modern Sweden tends to be a secular society.

Legislation granting Freedom of Religion was enacted in 1951. All citizens are free to practice or not practice religion as they see fit. Religious education, however, is taught as part of the public school curriculum, and the morality of the church of Sweden is very much a part of the Swedish psyche.

In addition to Lutherans, there are about 100,000 Pentecostals, 81,000 Roman Catholics, 50,000 Muslims, 15,000 Jews, and a small number from the Orthodox, Hindu, Buddhist, and other Protestant faiths.

Value system

Sweden is a humanitarian culture where the quality of life and environmental issues are given high priority. They are highly egalitarian; consensus and compromise are deeply ingrained into every aspect of their culture and business operations. They are obedient to most authority and diligent in their duties. Women enjoy high standing, and it is estimated they hold 20% of all managerial positions.

Although there is a strong self-orientation and an emphasis on individual initiative and achievement, they also stress teamwork. They are not a status-hungry culture; one's ability is considered more important than one's station in life. They are also protective of their private life and refrain from mixing it into their business dealings.

Class structure / Stratification

Sweden is basically a middle-class homogenous society that minimizes social and ethnic differences. They are highly androgynous, with husbands and wives sharing the responsibilities of childcare. Since most of their necessities are taken care of by the efficiency of the state, there is a need to find challenges in life and this may account for their drive toward success in their business pursuits. Sweden has worked hard to eliminate its class system. The original 4 divisions of nobility, clergy, merchants, and peasants began to fade at the end of the 18th century and were almost gone by the beginning of the 20th century. In addition to the middle class, there is still an upper class that has greater influence and power and may have inherited wealth, but there is no infrastructure that sets this class apart. There are few exclusive clubs or schools. Swedes have a value orientation of doing their own dirty work, and the idea of expecting servants to do this sort of work for them is abhorrent.

A progressive taxation system tends to equalize the population. There is also a small class of people composed primarily of those who do not fit in, such as criminals and drug addicts. In the past decade there has been a shift to the right in Sweden and the division between the wealthy and this third marginal class of people has grown.

One remnant of the old class system that still remains is the royal family. The goal of abolishing the monarchy and becoming a republic has been part of the Social Democrats' manifesto for years, but it is not considered an important issue and is more or less ignored. The cost of maintaining the monarchy in Sweden is nominal compared with other European countries.

Safety

The **crime rate in Sweden is very low**. The most common offense is drunk driving, and the laws on this are very strict. As in many countries, violent crime is on the increase. Gun control is very stringent, and one's personal security is seldom threatened. Swedes drive on the right and keep their car headlights on at all times. Seatbelts are required both front and back. The roads are generally not crowded, except in the cities.

Business Protocol

Greetings and etiquette

Swedes are relatively **formal** in their business practice. **Titles and the use of Mr. and Mrs.** are normally adhered to in the initial stages of a business relationship. As they become more comfortable in the negotiations, they will tend to drop formal titles and will move toward a first name basis. A **handshake is always appropriate**, but there should be no touching on the arm, shoulder, or back when greeting one's Swedish business counterpart. As the relationship progresses Swedes become more flexible about physical contact.

Swedes are quite direct and may appear somewhat abrupt during introductions and even later negotiations. They **seldom engage in small talk and** tend to want to **get down to business rather quickly**. If the conversation does stray from the business at hand, safe topics include sports (particularly soccer), the countryside, and vacations. It is important not to pry into any personal matters. They are not very emotional, and look for sincerity, directness, and formality in their business meetings.

Time

Sweden is a **monochronic** culture and is similar to the USA in that regard. The business day starts **promptly** at 9 AM and ends at 5 PM with a one-hour break for lunch. Business appointments are usually made two to three weeks in advance. Punctuality is very important to the Swedes for both business and social occasions. In **fact, non-punctuality is considered a serious character flaw**. Meetings begin and end on time whether all the items on the agenda have been dealt with or not. Any items unfinished will be re-scheduled. The Swedes take approximately five weeks of vacation each year; July is the most common month for vacations.

The format for establishing dates on all meetings and correspondence is day/month/year, not month/day/year as is common for Americans. Another factor to remember is that it is important to ask for wake-up calls since days and nights vary considerably due to the northern latitude of Sweden. Missing a meeting because one is disoriented by this factor would certainly be a serious problem in this efficiently run punctuality-oriented culture.

Gifts

Gifts are commonplace for initial meetings with the Swedish. A guest can make a good impression by bringing high-quality USA liquors, which are quite expensive in Sweden. Flowers, cakes, wines, or chocolates are also appropriate gifts. Opening gifts in front of one's host is acceptable, but **showing excessive emotion or gratitude is not.** Swedes frown on excessive displays of emotion.

Business entertainment

Business lunches and dinners usually take place at refined/high-class restaurants. Gourmet dinners, combined with drinking, formal toasts and good conversation, are an integral part of Swedish business culture. Whether or not business will be discussed should be left up to the host. The best topics to discuss are soccer, vacations, nature and the environment. Toasts at lunch and dinner tend to be very formal. The most common toast is "Skoal" which means "To your health." A clink of the glasses, a smile and a drink of your preferred liquor follow the toast. Do not clink your glass until the "Skoal" has been announced. Toasting

and drinking is a formal occasion and should be considered an honor. Swedes do not like to take time away from their families, so business dinners are generally kept to a minimum.

Business is usually not discussed at informal lunches. As soon as lunch is finished the Swedes will be ready to get back to the business agenda.

Visiting a Swedish home is very rare. If invited, formal manners should be followed. The host will usually seat the guests. A gift of flowers or candy is appropriate.

Dress

In general, **Swedes dress quite casually in utilitarian clothing to protect against the weather, which can be cold and wet**. A good coat and boots are essential in the fall, winter, and spring. In the northern part of the country one can expect a lot of snow and ice from fall to spring. In the southern coastal cities such as Malmo and Gothenburg, it rains more than it snows.

For business meetings, conservative suits with fancy ties for men and conservative suits or dresses for women are appropriate. The Swedes do tend to dress more fashionably than other Scandinavians, and tasteful but not excessively expensive apparel is appreciated.

Communication Style

Business language

In business, the Swedes are direct, formal, and very straightforward. They appreciate direct eye contact and getting straight to the point. Superficiality, excessive salesmanship, and "small talk" put off Swedish people. Swedes are **very low context** and do not show emotion when speaking. They rarely use their hands while speaking and do not reveal facial expressions when discussing a point. This may seem strange to the more emotional Westerner. However, it is simply their way of showing that they are indeed paying attention. Swedes also show little or no sense of humor when negotiating. Consequently, any attempt to be funny by making jokes or sarcastic remarks would not be wise. Avoid arguing about or bringing up sensitive topics, and do not be surprised or offended if a Swedish counterpart interrupts such a discussion.

One should keep one's voice modulated and unemotional, as this will put Swedes at ease. Arguments that are well documented with proof, logic, and common sense will be recognized more favorably than irrational pleas. Reticence is considered a positive characteristic in Swedish business culture and one who acts in this manner will be an asset to the foreign negotiating team. Precise, concrete visual aids and graphs will also add considerable weight to any business discussion.

The Swedish conversational style is serial in nature, which entails uninterrupted listening by one party until the other has finished his/her point. The listener not only does not interrupt, but also displays no signs of acquiescence or disagreement to what is being said. This style is an important aspect of the Swedish communication system and permeates both social and business communication exchanges. Maintaining a calm and patient composure during business negotiations is a key factor in effective negotiations with the Swedes.

Non-verbal communications

There are few similarities between the USA and Sweden in the use of non-verbal communication. **Swedes do not use their hands, raise their voices, or express much emotion via facial or head gestures**. It is essential to take their words literally. If they do not agree with their foreign counterparts or one of their arguments, they will say so directly. In many ways this simplifies negotiations because it allows for minimal miscommunication or misunderstanding.

A nod of the head backward means "come here" and is similar to the motion of the index finger for Americans. Swedes are comfortable with silence. Silence provides time for them to gather and organize their thoughts, since they are very particular about their words and like to convey honest answers. It is important to listen intently while they are speaking. In some ways their style of speaking can be compared to the USA debate system, where one speaks his or her mind with no interruptions and then the other can rebut. When a participant agrees or has something to add to the speaker's point, s/he must wait for the appropriate time to speak. This system allows for a fair and reciprocal hearing of all points of view.

The Swedish Concept of Negotiations

Selecting personnel

Since personal status is of little consequence in Swedish business life, they focus instead on personal responsibility. An executive is foremost a managerial specialist, which does not make him socially superior to a specialist in some other field.

In selecting negotiating personnel, prior **negotiating experience and personal knowledge** is more important to Swedes than status. Consequently seniority is not of great importance either, and young men and women are frequently found in leadership positions on their negotiating teams.

Negotiating style

Swedes are systematic and their organizational approach is highly structured so that uncertainty and improvising is kept to a minimum. They do not appreciate an informal attitude in a business meeting.

In negotiations the Swedes want to get right down to the business at hand. They tend to not show their emotions. Swedes value consensus and will avoid confrontation. They appreciate precise and concrete presentations, but frown on humor, personal questions or any superficiality. They appreciate a task-oriented climate in their business meetings and prefer a **compromise** approach to negotiating. They do not like to carry over business discussions into lunch breaks. Relaxation is important, so they keep their business and personal lives separate.

Issues discussed

Swedes are rather ethnocentric and seem unaware that their business culture differs greatly from the international norm. They carefully plan out their meeting agendas and expect the same from their foreign counterparts. They value punctuality and if a meeting is scheduled to end at a certain time, it will. A direct approach to the business at hand is seen as a sign of efficiency and a wish to not waste everyone's time. Thus, only **substantive issues** are discussed in a very organized manner.

Establishing trust

In some cultures, a business relationship precedes a personal relationship, or vice versa. In Sweden, however, they tend to be kept permanently separate. Foreign business people who travel to Sweden often complain that their Swedish colleagues are all business and seldom reveal anything about themselves personally. This is because personal privacy is very important to them, and this keeps business life strictly on a business level. They believe that personal issues should not interfere with or cloud business judgment. Therefore, trust is not built on friendships initially. Trust for them evolves more from **hard-working result-oriented rationality** (i.e., **productive past performances)**. However, because their culture is nonhierarchical, they move rapidly from a formal demeanor to a first name basis regardless of job title, gender, status, or age.

Persuasion

The best way to convince them of something is to both listen to and offer **sound pragmatic arguments backed up by facts and figures**. Emotional pleas, favoritism and threats are not effective means of influencing Swedish negotiators. Negotiators should use empirical data, charts, and well-prepared presentations that show the benefits of a plan or a proposal.

The specific persuasion tactics that are likely to be effective in Sweden are:

1) **Supported Facts**. One needs to present logical/factual information that is accompanied by supportive documentation.
2) Your initial presentation/offer is critical to a successful negotiation in Sweden. The presentation/offer must include the benefits the Swedish firm will derive from the transaction along with the corresponding supportive documents. During the presentation, all options should be weighed, thus providing a logical path to your conclusions. However, active participation from others or questioning during presentations should be avoided.
3) Receiving the **technical specifications up-front** is an excellent strategy.

4) **Get it in writing**. Write everything down throughout the negotiations. Take copious notes.
5) **Build trust through information sharing**. The Swedes will expect a healthy exchange of information.
6) **Two-Sided Appeals**. The Swedes will probably complete extensive research regarding the negotiations. Thus, they will know the pros and cons, and a two-sided appeal is likely to be an effective persuasion strategy. In addition, the Swedes expect this type of presentation and are likely to present their information in a similar manner.
7) It is okay to be blunt and to the point in Denmark. Remember the Danes view conflict as a necessary evil. So, make your points and support them. The Danes will view this as an appropriate persuasion strategy.
8) **Summarizing previously-agreed-upon benefits** just before asking for a major concession should be helpful.
9) Use a **point-by-point** presentation as well as negotiation style. They will use it and expect the same in return.

Tactics to avoid include:

1) Avoid "small-talk"
2) Do not brag about personal achievements.
3) Haggling over price is okay but the price will probably not change more than 15 to 20%. So **never "high-ball" or "low-ball."** In addition, it is probably best to wait to the end to discuss price. Both sides should start with reasonable prices, attempt to meet each other's specifications and other requirements, and then the minor price issues can be resolved.
4) Avoid the use of metaphors, emotional tactics, threats, fear tactics, distraction tactics, diffusion questions, ultimatums, loud voices, etc.
5) Avoid supplification and emotional demonstratives.
6) Surprise tactics are inappropriate.
7) **Avoid stalling.** The Danes want to get down to business.

Resolving disputes

In Sweden "compromise" does not carry with it the negative overtones that it does in the USA. Anything other than a consensus is seen as unsatisfactory in the Swedish business environment. The Swedish mentality seeks agreement. However, the Swedes do not mind disagreement as long as reconciliation is eventually reached. This can make decision-making a very slow and frustrating process for a more action-oriented individual from a different culture. Thus, disputes are usually solved with **sound arguments based upon facts and logic**. The process is **slow, methodical, pragmatic and informal.**

Group and individual dynamics

For a considerable period of time, the principle of equal opportunity has had a profound influence in Swedish society. As with the Brits and Australians, there is a dislike for those who see themselves as superior achievers. It is referred to as "the law of Jante," originally a Danish "law". Its message is that one should not think of oneself as special or superior to anyone else.

Perhaps because of this factor, Swedish **companies** generally **have** a flat and **team oriented structure**. Matrix organizations are common and Swedes **often report to more than one manager**. This same factor would explain the open exchange of information at all levels in Swedish companies, since they believe the more one knows about what is happening, the more one will feel involved and motivated. Once separated from their group, Swedes become **deeply private, competitive and individualistic**.

Risk

Swedish executives are **generally willing to take risks**. One recent international study found that Sweden had the lowest "Uncertainty Avoidance Index" among all the countries compared, while Japan had the highest. However, while Swedish executives are willing to take risks, their decisions are usually made with great consideration.

Decision making

Swedish companies are very decentralized. A good manager in a Swedish firm is considered to be one who takes advantage of the natural creativity and motivation of his/her staff. Consequently, employees on all levels of Swedish organizations have the freedom to make decisions and solve unexpected problems without necessarily consulting with their superiors. Thus, decision making is neither hierarchical nor consensus. Nevertheless, during negotiations one can expect a **top-down style of decision-making (i.e., the senior person present will make the decision)**. Remember, however, that Swedish organizations are decentralized and you may see deviations from the top-down style.

Type of agreements

As previously noted, Swedes are very formal and pragmatic in their business dealings and they prefer, of course, to have **written contracts** whenever possible. This is not to say that verbal agreements are never made. They can be given considerable weight, but are not legally binding.

The Swedes have a pragmatic legal system, which is not totally spelled out in written law. It is therefore often subject to judicial interpretation. An example is the issue of foreign judgments, which generally are not recognized in Sweden. However there are exceptions, and foreign judgments, while not recognized, can have effect as evidence in a Swedish court of law. These sorts of ambiguities are not uncommon. It is advisable to have very formal written contracts with clearly spelled-out terms. The Swedes prefer written contracts and will usually agree to a highly detailed instrument.

NOTES:

Chapter 26

Switzerland

- *Country Background*
- *The Swiss Culture*
- *Business Protocol*
- *Communication Style*
- *The Swiss Concept of Negotiations*

Switzerland is a small, largely mountainous central European country, bordered on the west by France, on the north by Germany, on the east by Austria and Liechtenstein, and on the south by Italy. The country is a federal republic and its history, culture, economy, and unique character have been greatly influenced by the Alpine ranges that cover three-fifths of its total area. Deeply-eroded, steep-sided glaciated valleys separate these high, rugged, snow-covered mountains. In these valleys the broad river bottoms are used for cultivation.

In spite of its small size (15,943 square miles), minimal supply of primary resources, and considerable ethnic diversity, Switzerland is politically and socially one of the more stable nations on our earth. It has a great standard of living with a per capita income among the highest in the world. It is known for its banking facilities, the conservative character of its people and institutions, and its neutrality in Europe's two major 20th century wars.

Country Background

History

In its early history the Helvetic Celtic people inhabited what is now Switzerland. Its strategic location and vital Alpine passes brought many invasions and conquerors. Julius Caesar's Roman legions came in 58 BC, then later the Germanic Alamannians, Burgundians, Ostrogoths, and Franks. The region came under the control of the Holy Roman Empire in the 9th and 10th centuries, and by the 1200s, the Hapsburg family ruled much of what is now Switzerland.

Fearing the growth of Hapsburg power, two small regions in central Switzerland called Uri and Schwyz sided with the Holy Roman Empire in a dispute with the Pope and the Hapsburgs, and in return were granted more rights to self-government. When Rudolph I of Hapsberg became the Holy Roman Emperor in 1273, he tried to reimpose his rule, but was unsuccessful. Uri and Schwyz joined with neighboring Unterwalden in a mutual defense alliance and swore to fight for independence. Their new freedom permitted them to begin trading with other towns in their region, some as far away as Germany and Italy. As they prospered, they were reminded of earlier commitments they and their forefathers had made. As more and more people

embraced these ideas of mutual aid and independence, the concept became more than a pledge; it finally became known as *Eidgenossenschaft*, or the Society of the Oath.

In this oath, they pledged aid to each other against any foreign ruler who tried to conquer them. Eventually the oath became a covenant that brought forth a confederation first known as Helvettia. This confederation withstood civil wars, religious wars, French invasion, and attempts by the Austrians and Burgundians to test the resolve of the confederation and stem its momentum.

By the early 16th century, the confederation had not only maintained its independence but was expanding its military power. With 13 cantons as members, it challenged the French for control over northern Italy, but suffered heavy losses and began to question the wisdom of expansionist policies. Not long after, they adopted a policy of defensive neutrality and stayed out of foreign wars thereafter.

The reformation posed a serious threat to the political stability of the confederation and they lapsed into civil war. They were divided by language as well as religion, but external threats and invasions again united them and led to the formal recognition in 1648 of the confederation's independence by the Holy Roman Empire. After a century and a half of peace, French Revolutionary armies swept into the country and established the Helvetic Republic (1798). At the Congress of Vienna (1815) following Napoleon's defeat, independence was restored and Swiss neutrality was guaranteed by the powers of Europe.

An attempt by several Catholic cantons to secede from the confederation was prevented by force in 1847. The 1848 Constitution established 22 cantons (later 23) into the Swiss confederation and provided for a bicameral legislature and a representative form of democracy.

World War I brought political unrest between the French and German segments of the population, but Swiss neutrality survived and in 1920 the League of Nations made its home in Geneva. During World War II Switzerland mobilized an army of around 500,000 to protect its frontiers. Today, a national militia of 625,000 supports its policy of armed neutrality; Switzerland has national conscription for all men between the ages of

20 and 50 years. Since 1945, Switzerland has devoted its energies to continuing this neutrality, to improving its educational and welfare programs, and to developing its economy into one of the most enviable in the world.

Government

Switzerland is a federated republic consisting of 23 cantons and three half cantons. The federal government is divided into three branches: the Federal Council (executive); the Federal Assembly or Parliament (legislative); and the Federal Tribunal (Judicial). Each year one member of the Federal Council is chosen as the president of Switzerland, but the office is an honorary one. The Federal Assembly consists of two houses: the Council of States, composed of two members from each canton and one from each half canton, and the National Council made up of 200 members apportioned by the population of the various cantons. Each assembly has a 4-year term. Switzerland's federal court, the Federal Tribunal, is located in Lausanne; the other governing bodies are in Bern.

The Swiss have a multi-party political system. There are, however, few differences between the larger ones, so cooperation is common. On the right are the Christian Democrats, on the left the Social Democrats and the Swiss Socialist Party. The Radical Democratic Party represents the center.

Since 1959, government posts have been divided between these four parties. The coalition of the four holds three-quarters of the seats in the Federal Assembly and an even larger majority in the Council of the States.

The constitution of 1848 with revisions in 1874 provides for a federalist and democratic government in which political power is divided between the central government and cantonal governments. The 26 cantons exercise all the powers of government except those delegated exclusively to the federal government. Both the federal and cantonal governments have the right to levy taxes. The federal government regulates communications, higher education, and labor. Swiss citizens enjoy close control over the laws that govern them through the rights of referendum and initiative. Universal suffrage is enjoyed by all citizens over 18 years of age, although women were not granted the right to vote in federal elections until 1971. Indeed, the half canons of Appenzell Ausserrhoden and Appenzell

Innerroden introduced female suffrage for local elections only in 1989 and 1990. In 1984 the national assembly elected Switzerland's first woman cabinet minister (Dr. Elizabeth Kopp, a leading member of the Radical Democratic Party), who became head of the Federal Department of Justice and Police.

Demographics

Switzerland's population of 7.3 million is divided into major language groupings: 65% German, 18% French, 10% Italian, and 1% Romansh. The population growth rate is near zero. The population is unevenly distributed, with the principal concentrations occurring in the Swiss plateau.

Switzerland has a higher percentage of foreign-born residents than any other country in Europe. About 1 million people (15% of the total population) are foreign born. Nearly a third are from Italy. Large numbers of people from France, West Germany, and Spain also reside in Switzerland.

Switzerland has five cities of more than 100,000 people. They are Zurich, Basil, Geneva, Bern, and Lausanne, which together contain more than one-third of the population. None of these cities have a population of more than 500,000. Almost 100 other cities have populations of more than 10,000. The population density is 424 people per square mile, and 60% of the people live in urban areas.

The Swiss constitution requires school attendance for all children. However, each canton has the freedom to legislate, finance, and regulate its own educational system. As a result, the school systems of each canton are different with variations in curriculum, examinations, grading, as well as the dates for the beginning and end of the school year. In most cantons, children are required to attend school from the ages of 6 to 14 years of age. Instruction is conducted in the local language of each canton, and each child has the opportunity to learn one other language. Of the total population, it is estimated that 99% can read and write.

Swiss health and living standards are among the highest in the world. A complex public and private insurance system is administered through federal and cantonal jurisdictions. The Swiss enjoy an excellent life expectancy rate: 77 years for males and 83 years for females.

Economy

With the exception of abundant waterpower, timber, granite, limestone, and other building stones, Switzerland has very limited natural resources. Yet the Swiss enjoy one of the highest standards of living in the world. Its success is a prime example of a nation with limited natural resources that has prospered through the inventiveness, frugality, and the perseverance of its people, along with the development of a wide variety of manufacturing facilities. They are world famous for making watches and precision instruments. Far Eastern manufacturers cut heavily into Switzerland's share of the global watch market in the 1970's, but the Swiss watchmaking industry recovered in the 1980's with the manufacture and marketing of inexpensive electronic timepieces.

The Swiss economy is divided into 3 sectors: agricultural 3% (most of the land is too high or too rugged to be good farmland), industry 31%, and services 66%. The chief agricultural products are dairy products, fruits, potatoes, sugar beets, and wheat. Manufacturing includes chemicals, drugs, electrical equipment, machine tools, precision instruments, processed foods, textiles, watches, and wine. Services, which include banking, insurance, and tourism are the most important part of the economy.

The Swiss labor force is technically trained and highly skilled. The economy generates more jobs than its own people can fill, and the unemployment rate of approximately 2% is one of the lowest in the world. A shortage of unskilled labor led to the influx of a large number of temporary immigrants, most of them Italian. Immigrants make up 20% of Switzerland's labor force of 4 million people. Demand for such workers fluctuates with domestic and global economic conditions. The Swiss economy ranks about 19th in the world and enjoys a comfortable per capita income ranking of 16th. Switzerland's manufacturing industries process imported raw materials into high-quality products for export. To keep the cost of materials and transportation low, Swiss industries specialize in skilled precision work on small, valuable items. Most Swiss factories are small or of medium size and stress quality goods rather than mass production. Industrial and technical products include precision instruments, electrical generators, machine tools, and transportation equipment. Other products are chemicals, paper, processed foods, including cheese and chocolate, and silk and other textiles.

About two-thirds of the area of Switzerland is covered with forest, lakes, and mountains. Neither the soil nor the climate favors agriculture and Switzerland subsidizes the farms that do exist. Swiss agriculture is characterized by highly intensive production on small owner-operated farms. This system produces only about 65% of their needs. The rest of the food supply must be imported. Livestock raising is the most important agricultural activity and provides 75% of Switzerland's farm income, largely through dairy farming. Dairy products such as butter, the famous Swiss cheese, and other milk products account for the bulk of farm exports.

Despite the rugged terrain, Switzerland has an excellent transportation infrastructure. The electrified railroad system, which is almost entirely owned and operated by the government, provides fast and efficient service. The Rhine River connects Basel, Switzerland's only port, with the North Sea. Large barges can reach Basel, which processes about 8 million short tons of cargo a year. Geneva and Zurich have important international air terminals, from which there are regular flights to most parts of the world. The privately-owned Swissair, the country's only international airline, flies to about 40 countries.

Switzerland's policy of neutrality has kept them from becoming a member of the European Economic Community (common market), but the Swiss have joined the European Free Trade Association (EFTA). Switzerland's trading partners are primarily Western European countries and the United States, but it trades with nations throughout the world. About half of Switzerland's trade is with countries of the European Economic Community. Its leading exports are capital equipment, watches, and optical instrument products. Switzerland has a slight trade deficit. Imports are distributed among agricultural products, industrial raw materials, machinery, and fuels. The slightly negative trade balance is compensated for by the net income produced by tourism, the insurance industry, and international financial transactions.

Switzerland's currency is one of the world's soundest and its inflation rate is one of the world's lowest (usually less than 1%). The basic monetary unit is the franc, also called the franken or franchi (SFR).

The Swiss Culture

Language

Linguistically, Switzerland is a multi-lingual country with four national languages: German, French, Italian, and Romansch. It is primarily these language considerations rather than ethnic consciousness that define the different segments of the Swiss population. The Swiss constitution provides for three official languages: German, French, and Italian. Romansch is spoken only in the mountain valleys of the canton of Grabunden and constitutes just 1% of the population.

In a majority of the cantons, the most commonly spoken language is Swiss German, an Allemanic dialect of German differing vastly from both written German and other German dialects. Newspapers and magazines are written in standard German. In addition, standard German is commonly used in motion pictures and television productions. Swiss German is almost a separate language and even people who speak German find it hard to understand.

In Western Switzerland, French is the spoken language of about one-fifth of the people. Italian is spoken in the south by around 10% of the people. Both of these languages as spoken by the Swiss are similar to their standard forms in France and Italy. In the urban areas, many Swiss also speak English.

Religion

At the present time about 50% of the population are Roman Catholic and about 48% are Protestant. The percentage of Protestants has declined since World War II because of the influx of foreign workers, most of whom are Catholic. There are small minorities of Jews and old Catholics, a group found mainly in Switzerland and Germany that split from the Roman Catholic Church in the 19th century. There is no established national church, but cantons may designate one or more denominations as established churches, which may then be supported at least in part by cantonal funds. No citizen, however, is required to pay taxes specifically designated for support of a denomination other than his/her own. The Swiss constitution, reflecting concern over possible outside religious influence, prohibits the establishment of new parishes without federal consent, forbids the establishment of new religious orders or convents, outlaws the Society of Jesus (Jesuits) within its borders, and forbids all active clergy from holding seats in the National Council.

In Switzerland's past, religious belief systems have been a source of considerable unrest. During the Reformation and for centuries after, Protestants and Catholics had a history of contentious and at times bloody confrontations. Given the history of disagreements between these groups, the Swiss government assumed a moderating posture and mediated acceptable conditions for all. The Swiss have been able to come to terms with the cleavages of four languages and two religions. Perhaps part of this success is brought about through service in the Swiss military where all these potentially divergent groups are brought together to form a well-integrated force.

Value system

The value system has acquired many facets in its evolution through Swiss history. This is evident from the Society of the Oath in 1291 to the 1989 Swiss vote on a peoples' initiative (referendum) to abolish their army. The result was 1,052,218 votes to abolish the army and 1,903,797 to keep it. The fact that they would hold such an election says a great deal about this nation's values.

Another political example of the Swiss people expressing their values at the ballot box was in the 1970's. At that time there were over a million foreigners working in Switzerland. This prompted a people's initiative to reduce their numbers. It passed, but later the initiative was overturned by a national referendum, which overruled the proposal to oust the alien workers. The Swiss are a very ethnically-diverse people and these two political events say a great deal about their collective values.

Switzerland's social welfare system reflects another facet of their cultural values. Switzerland has compulsory health insurance for all its citizens. The federal and cantonal governments subsidize low-income groups. Switzerland has old-age, widow's and widower's insurance and invalid's insurance for all its citizens. In addition, there are compulsory unemployment, accident, and pension insurance programs for all salaried employees. It also has several different social security systems with separate budgets. Another area where the

Swiss values are exemplary is in relationships between labor and management. Switzerland has the lowest reported incidence of strikes in the world.

Swiss values helped attract the League of Nations to Geneva. Swiss values were instrumental in the establishment and continuing worldwide services of the Red Cross and the World Health Organization. On a personal level, Swiss values reflect orderliness, discipline, formality, propriety, neatness, tolerance of neighbors, and acceptance of government. They are hard working, value common sense, and do not make public display of their emotions.

The Swiss culture has historically rewarded self-assertion and sound work ethics for men, while the women of Switzerland have generally been ascribed nurturing roles that enhanced the quality of life within the Swiss family. There are still some classic role differences between the sexes, and discrimination against women still exists in some cantons. Women in general earn 33% less than their male counterparts. The Swiss have traditionally offered low-paying jobs such as salesclerk or teaching to women. There is, however, a very recent trend toward more women becoming executives in Swiss businesses.

Class structure / Stratification

Switzerland's class divisions appear to be divided into four distinct segments. There are the very wealthy industrialists and bankers who form the economic elite. International corporations such as Nestle's and pharmaceutical companies such as Sandoz and Roche provide the basis for highly paid executives and stockholders who enjoy privileged life styles.

The next segment is composed of the technically-skilled and white-collar workers and the various owners of numerous small businesses. They constitute a middle class that enjoys a very comfortable standard of living.

The working class of Switzerland, employed in the textile, pharmaceutical, and service industries, as well as the farmers, mechanics, and other hourly-wage earners enjoy a good living, partly because Switzerland has so many societal amenities that prevent anyone from falling into economic despair. Unemployment is low and there is a sound unemployment and retraining system for those who lose their jobs. Even the lowest level of Swiss society (i.e., the lower class) is relatively well cared for because of the well-organized social welfare system that undergirds the entire population.

Safety

Switzerland is one of the world's safest environments with a low incidence of violent crime. With the recession of 91-93 in Switzerland, there was an increase in vandalism, alcoholism, drug abuse, and petty crimes. Normal precautions should be taken; pickpockets and purse-snatchers do frequent tourist areas such as bus and train stations. Swiss laws are stringent and effective, and their police are well trained.

Business Protocol

Greetings and etiquette

In Switzerland greeting someone is a polite tradition. Initial business greetings include a handshake. The Swiss traditionally greet each other by placing cheek to cheek. But they are sensitive people and if they sense discomfort, they will stick to the handshake when being introduced and when parting. One should stand when being introduced and wait to be introduced by a third person. In the German areas of Switzerland, women often embrace but men do not. In the French and Italian areas, both men and women may embrace. The French may also kiss each other on the cheek.

The Swiss are very conscious of rank and title. The use of titles is a way of showing respect. **Status is important to the Swiss, so use titles whenever appropriate.** Be sure to include your own academic and corporate title on your business card. If your firm is an old one, have the year it was established on your card, because the Swiss respect age. **Always address the Swiss by their title or Mr., Mrs., or Miss, plus their surname.**

When arriving for an appointment, **give your business card to the secretary**. When you meet **your client, give him a business card as well;** the secretary will have kept yours on file. In most instances, first names are not appropriate for business acquaintances; they are usually reserved for close friends. A verbal greeting in the French area would be *Bonjour, Monsieur,* or *Bonsoir* if a meeting takes place during the evening, and for a woman, *Bonjour, Madame*. In the German-speaking areas, use *Herr* and *Frau* followed by their surname. A more informal greeting often used irrespective of locality is *Salut*, and *Ciao* for goodbye.

Time

Swiss business people are **punctual for both business and social events**. They take their appointments and time commitments seriously. Setting up appointments well in advance is highly recommended. They also expect prompt replies to any written correspondence. The Swiss are a **monochronic** culture and expect closure of a task before moving on to new tasks. Remember the Swiss write the day first, then the month, then the year when indicating a date.

The workweek is generally Monday through Friday from 7:30 AM to 5:30 PM with a one or two-hour lunch break. Most stores are open from 8 AM to noon and from 1:30 to 6:30 PM, Monday through Saturday. The larger stores do not close for lunch. The average workweek is around 43 hours.

Switzerland is one hour ahead of Greenwich Mean Time (GMT + 1) or six hours ahead of USA Eastern Standard Time (EST + 6).

Gifts

Gift giving is not a regular part of the Swiss business culture, but there are exceptions. In the few instances where gifts may be appropriate, they should be limited to tokens of some special significance. Interpreters or guides might appreciate a gift rather than a tip. If one is invited to a Swiss home, one might bring chocolates or a bouquet of flowers.

Business entertainment

Business lunches and dinners are popular events in Switzerland. Lunches tend to be rather informal, at times taking place in the company cafeteria. Power lunches have also caught on in the larger cities.
Business dinners are more formal occasions and a good opportunity to experience some of the finer restaurants. Toasting is traditionally a part of this dining experience. If your host proposes a toast, one should look directly at him or her and respond with **"To your health,"** or

something similar, preferably in the native tongue of the host. Then clink glasses with everyone within reach before drinking.

Dress

Conservative dress is the traditional attire of Swiss business people but they are also very style conscious. The weather is typical for a Central European country with elevations from 633 feet to 15,203 feet in a temperate climate zone. There is a considerable amount of precipitation and, depending on the time of year, one's clothing should reflect the season. In the summer, one will find the temperatures to be quite pleasant and not extremely hot. Depending on where one is going, the elevation, etc., it can be quite cool. Another factor in determining one's choice of attire is the part of the country one is going to visit.

Switzerland has many beautiful areas, often in high rugged mountains, and one would undoubtedly enjoy wearing a really comfortable pair of walking shoes, even hiking boots. Similarly, one should include a good pair of jeans, a hooded sweatshirt, a hat, warm underwear, warm socks, gloves, sunglasses, and sun block. A full wardrobe might include ties, several business suits, and several different pairs of shoes, again depending on the free-time activities one might be contemplating.

Currently, European styles vary only slightly from those that are fashionable in the USA. The **Swiss tend to dress stylishly**, which for business means they may not always wear a white dress shirt. A variety of colors in dress shirts and colorful ties are currently in vogue. The Swiss are not ostentatious or flamboyant; they appreciate style with modesty.

Communication Style

Business language

The Swiss are a multilingual culture; **the primary language is Swiss-German, which is a low-context language.** They tend to communicate directly, unemotionally, and logically. In the western part of the country, about one-fifth of the population speaks **French, which is a low to medium-context language**. In the southern part of Switzerland, the population speaks **Italian, which is a high-context language**. A significant percentage of the Swiss population also speaks English. Business negotiations, depending on what part of Switzerland you are in, could be conducted in German, French, Italian, or even in English in some instances. If you use an interpreter, speak slowly and clearly, avoid idioms, and frequently confirm that you have been understood.

Non-verbal communication

Switzerland is a conservative country and it follows that they **engage in very little physical gesturing**. There are some exceptions in that they can get quite physical when greeting friends or saying goodbye. There are some definite no-nos. Do not talk with your hands in your pocket. Do not sit with your ankle on your knee. Do not chew gum in public. The Swiss show considerable appreciation for the privacy of others, both in terms of their property as well as their personal privacy needs.

The Swiss value dignified and reserved behavior and most of them are very polite when conducting themselves in public. In the German areas, men tip their hats when passing acquaintances. It is also not uncommon for the Swiss to admonish strangers who engage in improper behavior on the street.

The Swiss Concept of Negotiations

Selecting personnel

The Swiss are very conscious of rank, title, and the extent of one's education. Swiss negotiating personnel are chosen based on their **overall knowledge, their experience, and their seniority** with their company. Swiss businessmen usually have a positive attitude, a desire to learn, and strong intellectual and linguistic skills.

Any foreign negotiating team would do well to focus on selecting personnel who can **match up with their Swiss counterparts**. They respect **age** and **experience**. They respect highly **educated** people and people who have an **important position** in the corporation.

Members of the team should be team players who are capable of independent judgments and recommendations. They will **respect** business people who have **integrity, a sense of fairness, have stamina, are disciplined, and yet have a team spirit**.

Negotiating style

The Swiss style is to regard negotiations as a **joint problem-solving** venture. They are relatively devoid of humor when they are focusing on business matters. They like to have an **agenda** and they like to proceed on a **point-by-point** basis. They have extraordinary capacities for organization and detail, and intricate charts, graphs, and similar forms of data presentation will usually accompany their presentations. The Swiss are not inclined to haggle. They will usually begin at or near the terms they are willing to accept and they will expect their counterparts to do the same. They do not like to beat around the bush and normally negotiations with the Swiss move forward at a brisk pace.

Issues discussed

The issues discussed in Swiss negotiations tend to be **substantive** and directly related to the business agenda. The Swiss rarely discuss non-substantive issues when they are at the negotiating table. Being a monochronic culture, they prefer to stay focused on each item on the agenda until it is resolved. They prefer a sequential type of business meeting that concentrates on the agenda. They may exchange pleasantries at the beginning of the meeting. They may ask about your trip, hotel accommodations, etc., but they soon get uncomfortable if this type of conversation begins to delay the start of the meeting. They like meetings to start on time and move right along on the agenda from one topic to another in order to accomplish the tasks at hand. The issues to be negotiated are more important to them than developing a relationship.

Establishing trust

The Swiss are logical and objective and they like to trust in facts to determine the truth. A well-prepared presentation including supporting documentation (i.e., charts, graphs, data, etc.) will be appreciated by them and will inevitably gain their trust. They are proud of their craftsmanship and appreciate quality workmanship in others. The Swiss are somewhat aloof and normally reticent at developing personal relationships. If they admire your work ethic, you will have moved forward in establishing trust with them.

Persuasion

The Swiss will listen to logical presentations. They will not be moved by emotional pleas, any displays of favoritism, or threats. Empirical data with charts and well-prepared presentations that clearly point out the opportunities inherent in a proposed plan of action will influence them the most.

Clarity is important to the Swiss; they will often question a point at great length if an aspect of a presentation is obscure to them. They are not necessarily conformist in their thinking or negotiating, and they appreciate creativity that may offer new insights in solving a problem.

The Swiss are good listeners. They value the bottom line, and they will be moved by any presentation that contains all the technical and mathematical data, as well as the methods that will be used to implement the plan.

The specific persuasion tactics that are likely to be effective in Switzerland are:

1) **Supported Facts**. One needs to present logical/factual information that is accompanied by supportive documentation. **Visual proof sources** are always a good idea.

2) Your initial presentation/offer is critical to a successful negotiation in Switzerland. The presentation/offer must include the benefits the Swiss firm will derive from the transaction along with the corresponding supportive documents. During the presentation, all options should be weighed, thus providing a logical path to your conclusions.

3) Receiving the **technical specifications up-front** is an excellent strategy. The Swiss are very technically oriented. So, you will need to be able to meet the technical specifications as dictated.

4) Write everything down throughout the negotiations. Take copious notes. Having items agreed upon throughout the negotiations in writing will be a great deal of help. Once it is in writing it becomes a logical argument with a concrete basis.

5) **Build trust through information sharing**. The Swiss will expect a healthy exchange of information. The Swiss respect intellectual property rights and will not push for information that is proprietary. However, they will expect other information to be shared rather freely because they believe it is the best way to execute the problem-solving style of negotiation.

6) **Two-Sided Appeals**. The Swiss will likely have completed or will complete extensive research regarding the negotiations. Thus, a two-sided appeal is likely to be an effective persuasion strategy. Two-sided appeals provide both the pros and cons of an argument/product. Of course, when making a two-sided appeal make sure the pros outweigh the cons.

7) **Speak with conviction and confidence.**

8) Switzerland is hierarchical. So, referring to the approval of respected **higher authorities** in regards to your company, product, etc. may prove to be an effective method of persuasion.

9) Use a **point-by-point** method of presentation, persuasion, and negotiation.

Tactics to avoid include:

1) Avoid the use of metaphors, emotional tactics, fear tactics, diffusion questions, distraction tactics, ultimatums, threats, loud voices, etc.

2) Do not use stalling, favoritism, or nepotism.

3) Avoid "small-talk"

4) Do not brag about personal achievements.

5) Haggling over price is not a good idea. The price will probably not change more than 10 to 15% in Switzerland. So **never "high-ball" or "low-ball."** In addition, it is probably best to wait to the end to discuss price. Both sides should start with reasonable prices, and then attempt to meet each other's specifications and other requirements and then the minor price issues can be resolved.

Resolving disputes

The Swiss can be very obstinate if they feel they have been wronged. However, their culture is highly developed in the art of conflict resolution and problem solving. As previously noted, the Swiss have the world's most enviable labor relations record. When a dispute arises, the Swiss will want to follow a **logical path**. They will refrain from emotional fixes and opt instead for well-prepared solutions. This may necessitate follow-up presentations, more data, or formal letters of explanation.

Groups and individual dynamics

A favorite Swiss slogan is "Unity yes, uniformity no." The Swiss work well together to achieve common goals, yet at the same time they are **highly individualistic**. As a culture, they value privacy and individual freedom; however, they also respect the role of government and authority in resolving differences. Switzerland's history of language and ethnic diversity is itself testimony to their ability to work together while appreciating and respecting individual differences. Even though the country has strong regional language and ethnic diversity, they have proven in their military, in the functioning of their government, and in their very successful business community, that the Swiss know a great deal about teamwork.

Risk

The Swiss are quite innovative; they weigh risks with an open mind. They also have a tradition of frugality so they will evaluate a proposal carefully, exploring the risk factors with carefully attuned attention. They normally like to proceed slowly and are **somewhat averse to taking risks**. They prefer, when possible, to make their decisions on rational, well-analyzed empirical data rather than luck or blind faith.

Decision making

For the most part, Swiss decision making follows a **top-down** format. Swiss managers and executives usually have strong technical backgrounds. They analyze data extremely well and prefer to make decisions based on facts rather than intuitive processes. They will utilize

feedback from all levels of their corporate team, but the chief executive will take responsibility for the final decision.

Type of agreement

Both German and French law influenced the Swiss legal system. Its contract law has evolved into what is considered a liberal system in that there are few mandatory provisions. This allows for the drafting of contracts that are specific to the negotiating circumstances. The Swiss government welcomes foreign investment, and the only area where they exercise control is in the acquisition of real estate.

After reaching a verbal agreement, the Swiss like to draft a **carefully-prepared document** that spells out the overall aspects of the **agreement in great detail.** They also like to prepare for any **possible contingencies** and leave little room for future interpretations **in a written contract**. The Swiss pride themselves on being responsible and doing their jobs with utmost efficiency.

Chapter 27

Taiwan

- *Country Background*
- *The Taiwanese Culture*
- *Business Protocol*
- *Communication Style*
- *The Taiwanese Concept of Negotiations*

Taiwan has one of the most dynamic and prosperous economies in the world, yet is relatively unknown. The country was formed in 1949 when the communist revolutionaries led by Mao Tse Tung defeated the nationalist government of China led by Chiang Kai Shek. The nationalists fled to Taiwan, an island 280 miles wide and situated one hundred miles off the coast of China. There they formed the Republic of China and proclaimed themselves the true government of China. Both Taiwan and the mainland government want reunification but only under their own economic and political systems.

Country Background

History

Taiwan's history is intertwined with its geography because its geography created its history. It was Taiwan's geopolitical location and its accessibility that attracted settlers from Luzon and Malaysia, and then more notably from China. There are eight distinct language groups so it is obvious that settlement came in waves and from different places.

The first political power that took notice of Taiwan was China. For centuries China considered itself to be the center of nations and Chinese emperors expected tribute from the subservient nations around their borders. In the 7th and 14th centuries, imperial expeditions were sent from China to explore the island. A migration of farmers and traders started in the 15th century.

In the 16th and 17th centuries Europeans became interested in Taiwan. In 1517, a Portuguese admiral became so enchanted with the island he named it Ilha Formosa, meaning Beautiful Island. The Portuguese also established a small but important trading presence. The Dutch, having already established themselves in Indonesia, sailed north in 1622 and visited the Pescadores, a group of small islands between Taiwan and the Chinese mainland. Within a few years the Dutch had built 2 forts on Taiwan. Shortly after, the Spanish came to Taiwan and started an outpost. In 1642 the Dutch, assisted by aboriginal warriors, kicked the Spanish off the island.

However, events unfolding in China soon resulted in the expulsion of the Dutch by the Chinese. By 1683 the Chinese had complete control of Taiwan. With Taiwan as a Chinese province, migration increased to the point where the Chinese dominated the aboriginal population. In 1895, following the first Sino-Japanese war, Taiwan and the Pescadores Islands were ceded to Japan. Taiwan was returned to the Chinese government following the 1945 defeat of Japan in World War II.

Internal developments within China also were to affect Taiwan. In 1911 a revolution on mainland China took place and a new Republic of China was proclaimed. Soon after, a destructive 38-year civil war divided China between nationalist and communist forces. Though briefly halted when both sides fought the Japanese invasion of China during World War II, the civil war resumed after Japanese defeat. Finally, communist power became consolidated under the leadership of Mao Tse Tung and the nationalist forces withdrew to Taiwan in 1949. Chiang Kai Shek proclaimed his government of Taiwan the true Republic of China, a claim that is still maintained today.

A number of western countries supported Taiwan as the legitimate Chinese government until 1971 when the People's Republic of China was admitted to the United Nations in place of the Republic of China. The USA opened relations with mainland China in 1979. Currently the USA retains unofficial relations with Taiwan through a non-governmental agency, The American Institute in Taiwan (AIT). A peaceful solution to this situation is still being sought. One option being explored is for Taiwan to become a separate and independent country.

After Chiang Kai Shek's death in 1975, his son Chiang Ching-Kuo succeeded him. Under martial law, Taiwanese business was allowed to flourish, farmlands were redistributed to farmers and agricultural output increased. Government corporations were created to absorb the excess military personnel. These companies focused on the construction of a heavy industrial base. Public schools were built and the infrastructure modernized.

In 1987 martial law was lifted and two years later political opposition was legalized, opening the way for the first multiparty democratic elections held in 1990.

Government

Taiwan's official name is Republic of China; it is also known as Nationalist China. The Kuomintang (nationalist party) is the oldest political party, and has been the ruling party since the Republic of China was established. It has claimed until quite recently that it is the sole legitimate elected government for the whole of China. Also until recently, no one was allowed to publicly or privately question the reality of this position.

In 1972 the United States changed its policy and recognized Taiwan as a part of China and therefore an internal problem of China. This also implied that USA intervention was not to be expected if China attacked Taiwan in an effort to take back the island. Already diplomatically isolated, a second blow came in 1978 when the USA broke diplomatic relations with the Republic of China (Taiwan) and established relations with the People's Republic of China (mainland China). With these developments, Taiwan embarked on a path of 'dollar diplomacy'. Ten major infrastructure projects were nearing completion and more were planned. These projects improved Taiwan's appearance as an investment site and delivered large contracts to companies in friendly countries.

The central government of Taiwan combines the cabinet and presidential systems. The president is the supreme leader of the nation; the head of the government is the premier who is appointed by the president. Under the president there are five yuans (councils) including executive, legislative, judicial, examination and control. There is a national assembly of some 344 seats and the legislative council has about 164 seats. The examination council fulfills the role of a civil service commission, and the control council is an investigative agency. All levels of local government, provincial and municipal, are self-governing. A governor heads the provincial government. The provincial council consists of 23 members selected by the national executive council and appointed by the president. The president is elected by the national assembly, which is composed of delegates elected from each county. The presidents of the various councils are nominated by the national president or elected by the provincial and municipal councils.

Geographics

The total area of Taiwan is 35,980 square kilometers, about twice the size of New Jersey. The land area includes the Pescadores and the Matsu and Quemoy Islands. The climate is tropical marine with a rainy season during June to August. The terrain of the eastern two-thirds of the island is mostly rugged mountains, but there are flat to gently rolling plains in the west. The elevation extremes range from the lowest point at the South China Sea to the highest point, Yu Shan, at 3,997 meters. Of Taiwan's total land area, 24% is arable, with permanent crops in 1%, permanent pastures in 5%, while forest and woodlands make up 55%.

Demographics

The Han Chinese comprise approximately 98% of the people; the remainder are aborigines of Malay descent. The population of 22 million lives together fairly amicably, but some tensions exist between the groups. The population growth rate is slightly less than 1% per year. The life expectancy at birth of the total population is 77 years: 74 years for males and 80 years for females. The literacy rate is 94%: 97% for males and 89% for females.

The population is distributed primarily in the coastal plains and basins, which are also the agricultural regions. The rough terrain of the central and eastern mountains dictates a fairly low population density. There has been considerable population relocation from the rural areas to urban areas. The most rapidly growing urban areas include Taipei (the capital), Kao-hsiung, T'ai-nan, T'ai-chung, Taipei county, and T'oo-Yuan county. The average population density is 1,387 persons per square mile, and is one of the highest in the world. To offset the growing population, the government has encouraged late marriages, female employment and single-child families. Family planning policies were implemented during the late 1960's and remain in force today.

Economy

Taiwan has a dynamic capitalist economy with considerable guidance of investment and foreign trade by government officials, and partial government ownership of some large banks and industrial firms. Real growth in GDP averaged 8% a year during most of the past three decades, but slowed during the Asian Financial Crisis. Taiwan's total economy ranks 16th in the world and their per capita income ranks 14th.

Exports have shown an even more prosperous rate of growth and provide the impetus for increased industrialization. The economy is divided into the following sectors:: agriculture 3%, industry 32%, and services 65%. Agricultural products include rice, wheat, corn, poultry, milk products, soybeans, pigs, beef, sugar, tea, canned mushrooms, vegetables and fish. More than 50 kinds of minerals have been found on the island but industries involved in processing these elements are of little economic significance. There are also limited quantities of petroleum, natural gas and coal.

Traditional labor-intensive industries are being moved offshore and replaced with more capital and technology-intensive industries. Taiwan has become a major investor in China, Thailand, Indonesia, the Philippines, Malaysia, and Vietnam. The unemployment rate is only 3%. The tight labor market has lead to the influx of foreign workers, both legal and illegal. The Chinese Federation of Labor, founded in 1948, is the only union sanctioned by the government, although other unions do exist. Strikes are illegal.

Major industries are electronics, textiles, chemicals, clothing, food processing, plywood, sugar milling, cement, shipbuilding and petroleum refining. Taiwan enjoys an excellent trade surplus every year. Exported commodities included machinery and electrical equipment, textile products, basic metals and chemicals. Trading partners are the USA, Hong Kong, E.U. countries and Japan. Imported commodities are machinery and electrical equipment, chemicals, precision instruments, metals and minerals.

For a number of years one of the factors complicating Taiwan's economic picture has been the larger economic opportunities presented by the Chinese mainland. Foreign firms that tried to do business with both Taiwan and the mainland were usually pressured into choosing one or the other, and usually at the expense of Taiwan. Within recent years Taiwan has benefited by joining the General Agreement of Tariffs (GATT) and the World Trade Organization (WTO). Tariffs are now lower in Taiwan than in China.

Taiwan's currency is the New Taiwan Dollar (NT$). The fiscal year is from July 1st to June 30th.

The Taiwanese Culture

Language

Mandarin Chinese is the official language of Taiwan, although Taiwanese (a southern Fukien dialect) is spoken more and more frequently. Eighty-five percent of the population are descendants of the Chinese who came over with Chiang Kai Shek and their language preference is the Mandarin dialect. Several other Chinese dialects such as the Hakka, as well as the aboriginal language, are still spoken. The Taiwanese do not use the modernized script currently used in the People's Republic of China. Chinese words usually have one, two, or three syllables and an ideogram or character represents each syllable. The Chinese are very proud of their language and appreciate foreign business people who can speak their language. English is a popular second language to study in school in Taiwan and many business representatives can speak, understand and correspond in English.

Religion

While religion is a major influence in the lives of the people, particularly the rural people, organized religions have never played a major role. Two principal religions in modern Taiwan are Taoism and Buddhism. Christianity is followed by only 4.5% and was introduced by the Dutch in 1622 (Protestant religion) and by the Spanish in 1624 (Roman Catholicism). Other religions, primarily Shintoism, are adhered to by only 2.5% of the population. Despite the tendency of the Taiwanese to adopt western values, Christianity has made a very limited impression.

Confucianism stresses loyalty to the ruler and to the social and familial hierarchy as a supreme value. The duty of all is to obey and conform to one's superiors in the hierarchy. Confucianism, while not a religion in the western sense, nevertheless has had an immense influence on the Chinese in Taiwan. Their ethics, their morality, and their academic standards have been profoundly influenced by Confucian teachings.

Value system

Within the Taiwanese value system, perhaps the most important concept is gaining or losing "face." It is a concept that focuses on prestige and dignity. From a westerner's perspective, the concept of "face" exposes one to a great deal of vulnerability and a much lower self-esteem. Westerners can generally understand what might cause Taiwanese to lose face. However, it is much harder to understand the concept of giving someone face. It is not that flattery is foreign to western business cultures, but rather that westerners rarely view obvious compliments in a favorable light and/or feel uncomfortable or even guilty about blatantly building up someone's ego. Coupled with this concern for face is the concept of *guanxi*. *Guanxi* can best be described as a special relationship between individuals who share some common history, which enables them to make extraordinary demands upon one another.

A value that is held in equally high regard is the importance of family and friends. They represent a network of confidants and business associates. This network is an integral part of doing business in Taiwan. Other important values include a high regard for the elderly and for people of higher rank. Education is also highly valued and considerable emphasis is placed upon it. It is seen as a key to upward mobility as well as conveying status and prestige.

In Taiwan the values and beliefs that have traditionally sustained Chinese civilization are becoming increasingly diluted as they come in conflict with the new emerging values of independence, individualism and the pursuit of profits.

Class structure / Stratification

Traditionally, the family system in Taiwan was as strong or nearly as strong as that in China, although the large extended family was less common. The long history of the Chinese people is a major source of cultural pride. This same history, with its millennia of accumulated tradition, weighs heavily in the heart of all Chinese. It defines their social, familial, commercial and political relations, as well as their relations with the spirit world and the physical universe. To deviate from expected behavior is to be labeled, stigmatized, harangued, and ridiculed. The Taiwanese relate thoroughly to their Chinese heritage.

Traditionally Chinese society had five classes: the royalty, the scholars (who came from wealthy backgrounds) followed by the merchants, farmers, and laborers. In feudal China only the scholars could serve in government and they enjoyed a privileged role.

Initially Taiwanese society was divided into well-defined economic and social strata, but this has diminished considerably in today's society. The effect of this stratification, however, is still manifest in individual and business interactions. It is not uncommon, for example, for two Taiwanese businesspersons upon first meeting to feel each other out in terms of background and standing in order to determine a hierarchical pecking order. As with other Asian cultures, one's family, school, or friend connections often determine the pace of economic advancement.

In Taiwan today there is a business elite who head up the country's major corporations. There is also a middle class composed of the technocrats who have the basic skills necessary to help a modern enterprise succeed. A third group consists of factory workers, etc., followed by farm workers and the servant class. The aboriginal population and a number of illegal aliens comprise the lowest class.

Safety

Taiwan has considerable problems with organized crime and corruption. However, for the average visitor it is a relatively safe environment. There are areas with pick pockets and thieves and where the kind of crimes associated with poverty and homelessness can occur. However, the population's good manners and strict values impress most visitors.

Another safety concern, of course, is one's health; be sure you have acquired all the recommended immunizations prior to leaving your own country,

<u>Business Protocol</u>

Greetings

When you are introducing yourself or are being introduced, it is polite to **shake hands first, then give your name card, using both hands**. You should also say your name accompanied by "I am pleased to meet you." A slight bow or nod of the head can also be an acceptable Taiwanese greeting.

It is considered good manners to use both hands when taking a name card that is being presented to you and then immediately scan the card as a show of respect. In the exchange of business cards, hold out your card with the writing facing the recipient. As in other Asian countries, it is considered demeaning to write on someone's card in his or her presence.

If you sit down at a table after being introduced, it is a polite custom to place any name cards you have received on the table in front of you so you can refer to them. If several people are involved in the meeting, place the cards in an order similar to their hierarchical arrangement. Place the highest-ranking individual farther in front of you, thus arranging the cards as a mini-organizational chart. One's title and level of education should be included on a business card, and business cards should be in English on one side and in Chinese on the other side.

It is customary in **informal situations to introduce the oldest person first**. In **formal situations the highest-ranking** person should be introduced first regardless of age. When introducing someone, use Mr. or Miss or any titles the person might have, followed by family name. In Taiwan, it is assumed that the first person to enter a room is the head of the group.

If the meeting room has a large central table, the principal guests will usually be seated directly opposite the principal host. Important guests are often escorted to their seats.

Time

The Taiwanese are **polychronic. T**hey will usually be on time for business meetings but they are not as punctual as many of their Asian counterparts. **They consider extreme punctuality to be a rigid** habit that can adversely affect the friendship between associates.

They tend to rationalize when other business commitments cause tardiness or attendance problems during negotiations. These problems can occur because of their simultaneous involvement in more than one negotiation or project at the same time.

Westerners who are monochronic will be frustrated when negotiations drag on and the Taiwanese skip from one topic to another, attempting to process all of the factors simultaneously. The monochronic individual wants to take one item at a time and wants the negotiations to lead to an agreement and conclusion. The polychronic person is more likely to favor a continuing negotiation process that leads to greater clarity.

The Japanese have been very successful in their negotiations with the Taiwanese and the Chinese mainland. They are also polychronic, so they structure negotiations in the same way as the Taiwanese, and are prepared to skip from one topic to another or even leave one project and pick up another.

Gifts

Taiwan is a culture where **gift giving has certain rules** and any gift one gives should suit the individual as well as the particular occasion involved. Lower-ranking people will receive correspondingly less expensive items. Gifts are symbolic of one's desire to build a relationship and the gift is less important than the conveyance of this sentiment. The Chinese traditionally decline a gift three times before accepting; this practice prevents them from appearing greedy. One should continue to insist until the gift is accepted.

Some currently popular gift items include appointment books, pen sets, imported liquor, travel books, calendars, calculators and magazine subscriptions. Good gifts for a first trip include items that might have a small company logo on them. Be sure the product was not manufactured in Taiwan. Gifts of food are always appreciated, but do not bring food to a dinner party, for this would imply that the host couldn't provide enough. One can send a gift of food afterward as a thank you; good choices are candy or fruit.

At the Chinese New Year, it is customary to give a gift of money in a red envelope to children and to the service personnel one deals with on a regular basis. This gift is called a *hon hong boo*. Give only new bills in even numbers and even amounts. It is customary to reciprocate a gift with one of similar value. Therefore choose a gift that takes into account the receiver's economic station.

Gifts should always be wrapped in bright colors. White and black symbolize mourning. Some gifts are very inappropriate, so be careful in your choices. Do not give clocks, umbrellas, white flowers, knives or scissors. All of these have negative connotations.

Business entertainment

Business entertainment is a cultivated art in most Asian cultures. It is used to impress and to honor foreign guests. It is also used as a means of developing rapport with foreign business counterparts. In Taiwan these activities help cultivate a relationship out of which a business venture will hopefully evolve. **There are business breakfasts, business lunches, business dinners and business banquets**. Involvement in these events is an essential foundation for a successful negotiation. One should reciprocate by inviting one's hosts to restaurants that offer similar quality food and services.

Dress

Historically, the Chinese culture had strict traditions concerning attire. Different materials, colors and styles reflected a rank or status as prescribed by law. In Taiwan modest and **conservative apparel** is what is expected for both men and women. Business suits with a white shirt and tie is the most common form of dress for a Taiwanese businessman. Women wear a conservative skirt and blouse or suit. Jackets may be removed if one's counterpart does so first.

Communication Style

Business language

The Taiwanese use a **high context** language that can contain many hidden meanings. Because most Taiwanese have been raised speaking more than one language or dialect and because of the island's cosmopolitan nature, Taiwan's population may be considered bilingual or trilingual. In addition, English and other Western languages are taught extensively in the schools from the primary grades through university, and are used in international travel and business. English is the most widely studied foreign language in Taiwan and virtually all students learn it. This does not mean, however, that English will automatically be used in business negotiations. Taiwanese negotiators might

choose their own language so they do not put themselves at a disadvantage, and it may be necessary to bring in a competent translator.

Taiwanese business language is full of polite escapes. For instance, if someone says something may be impractical, the true meaning may very well be that it's a bad idea. The Taiwanese are accustomed to using tactful and self-controlled language. They will shun direct communication and instead utilize language that contains many subtleties.

The Taiwanese do not take criticism well. They are more likely to consider it insulting and a form of arrogance. As a result, instead of criticism producing a change for the better, it may result in the opposite response and may make an enemy. As in so many other instances, the best way to make a point is indirectly.

Non-verbal communication

Because Taiwanese manners and ethics are enmeshed in personal relationships, the Taiwanese can be easily offended. One's voice slightly off tone, or a disapproving facial expression, or the hint of a criticism, or a tinge of superiority or arrogance, may make an enemy who will never forget. There is probably no chance at all of forgiveness unless somehow you become aware of your transgression and then humble yourself and apologize.

The apology is an especially important part of the interpersonal relationships because the Taiwanese take offense so easily. If they believe they have been slighted and do not get a quick, acceptable apology, they might seek revenge. Unlike most Westerners who take revenge quickly and openly, the Taiwanese prefer to wait and to get it in a subtle way so their targets never know what hit them. The Taiwanese also have long memories when someone has done them a favor, and the more time passes, the more strongly they feel compelled to return the favor.

Since the Taiwanese do not wear their emotions on their faces like Westerners are inclined to do, it is more difficult to judge their state of mind. The demands of their etiquette require that they develop considerable skill in acting, and they are masters at using body language to achieve their goals.

Another Taiwanese cultural trait that seems to mislead and frustrate some Westerners is their habit of smiling or laughing when they do not understand or are embarrassed. The individual who smiles at your question or request may not be turning on a friendly face. He or she may not understand what you are talking about, so unless you get a clearly positive response, it may be advisable to slowly go over it again.

Taiwanese have somewhat different spatial needs and tend to stand somewhat farther apart when conversing than Americans do. They also do not want to be touched, particularly on the head or shoulders. One should also avoid touching anyone with one's feet, and when sitting, feet should be kept flat on the floor. To indicate "no", one should shake one's hand from side to side with the palm down, and never point or beckon to someone with the fingers.

When visited by Taiwanese business people or government officials toward whom you want to show appreciation or respect, you should at least accompany them to the elevator (if there is one) when they are ready to leave. One should go all the way to the front door of the building if their goodwill is important. This gesture may seem conspicuous but it is an institutionalized part of Taiwanese etiquette, and whether one follows the custom or not, it tells them a lot about you.

Thus, the Taiwanese are **very conservative** when it comes to non-verbal communication and gestures, but are **very observant** of each other's non-verbal messages. Do as your Taiwanese counterpart does, and attempt to maintain a "poker face" during the negotiations.

The Taiwanese Concept of Negotiations

Selecting personnel

The Taiwanese will respect a negotiating team that includes persons with **seniority** and a **thorough knowledge** of their company and its products. It follows also that it is very important to have an older person on the team. The Taiwanese revere **age** and attach great status to older people. Sending a senior executive would show that a company is serious about starting a business relationship.

It is still **rare to have women** participate in business activities in Taiwan. Foreign women have the additional challenge of overcoming this bias. If women are to be included on the negotiating team, be certain to discuss this in advance with your Taiwanese contact. This will allow them time to adjust to the presence of a woman in negotiations.

Generally speaking, **the CEO of a major foreign company should not attend the early stages of negotiations**. The Taiwanese will assign lower-ranking personnel to these early discussions. **Higher-ranking executives will attend the final session and be present for the signing of a contract. At this time, a foreign senior executive is expected to be present.**

Negotiation style

The Taiwanese have a well-deserved reputation for being skilled and hardheaded negotiators. They take great pleasure in outwitting and gaining an advantage through their use of tactics and finesse. American negotiators frequently misjudge how well the negotiations are progressing. The Taiwanese will stress **personal interaction and friendship** but when serious negotiations begin, the Taiwanese usually become highly bureaucratized and require coordination with senior officials. The Taiwanese are good bargainers and they will use **distributive bargaining** techniques to reach an agreement.

The Japanese have been quite successful in their negotiations with the Taiwanese and the tactic they use is flexibility. If negotiations stall in one area, they shift to another project; they also move people in and out of their negotiating teams while keeping a small cadre of familiar negotiators on the scene. The Japanese also tend to be more aggressive in their negotiations than the Americans and seem less fearful of offending the Taiwanese. This may in part explain why the Taiwanese have tended toward a buy-American or European posture, for the Japanese drive hard bargains with them. (There are also old hostilities to contend with.)

The purpose of negotiations to most Taiwanese is to establish a good long-term business relationship. For this reason they may deliberately slow the negotiations down out of concern for the long-term success of the endeavor. This need is part of their cultural conditioning and should be taken seriously by a visiting team.

Issues discussed

The primary issues for the Taiwanese are usually both **relationship based and substantive**. They are more interested in a lasting business relationship that has long-term advantages than quick profits. They will also want to focus on the type of products or services offered and will listen intently to any presentations that might showcase new technologies. They may want to also satisfy their professional curiosities and ask questions about one's work place at home, what kind of office one has, and how many people the company employs, etc.

Establishing trust

Politeness and formality are important factors in establishing trust with the Taiwanese. While informality may be common elsewhere, Asians usually view it as impolite behavior. Taiwan is a hierarchical society that maintains subtle balances in their interpersonal interactions. Being direct in their society is not considered a virtue, but rather a sign of poor manners.

The Taiwanese also have a cultural predisposition to believe that inevitably negotiations must produce a winner and a loser. In response to this, some **American businessmen have found it useful to spell out in elaborate detail all the possible benefits for the Taiwanese, as well as the risks, and then to explicitly define what their companies hope to get. This sort of presentation is necessary to not only establish trust** with those present, but to also provide the data that will build trust within the Taiwanese hierarchy. It helps to emphasize the compatibility of the negotiating firms, as well as one's personal amicability and desire to work with your counterpart. While profits are important, **harmonious human interaction** precedes them in importance and helps establish the trust necessary for a long-term business relationship.

Persuasion

The Taiwanese are considered to be excellent negotiators. They may use problem-solving tactics, friendship, emotions, multiple bidders, prior documents, or change the negotiation team in order to gain an advantage. However, their traditional style of negotiating is based on **personal relationships** and **bargaining** in a holistic style.

Business people who have dealt with the ambiguities of the Taiwanese, their tenacity, their tendencies to be both unyielding and yet at other times highly adaptable, suggest that Westerners approach negotiations with the Taiwanese as though it were a sporting event. The play can get quite rough, and each side will do its best to win, but the end result should be something both sides can live with.

In daily life, the Taiwanese prefer harmony and little conflict. However, they are not naive in business; they believe the marketplace is a battlefield. Concessions are acceptable to them as long as they bring future gain. One of their favorite negotiating strategies is to be easy going initially and tighten the reins later.

Politeness, formality, patience, calmness and thoughtful reflections impress the Taiwanese. Search for their needs and interests and know your bottom line. Thoroughly research the organization and beliefs of the people you'll be dealing with and remember to be flexible.

The Taiwanese prefer a formal orderly presentation. Visual aids or other helpful props will also be appreciated. It is also worth pointing out that the American practice of the hard sell is usually a turnoff. The Taiwanese are practical and deliberate in their business transactions, and their demeanor is one of "restrained steadfastness."

The persuasion tactics that can be generally used with the Taiwanese or will be used by the Taiwanese are:

1) Taiwanese love to **haggle** and are quite lively while doing so. Distributive bargaining is a favorite pastime. However, given the chance, they will also engage in contingency bargaining. The Taiwanese will almost always **"high-ball" or "low-ball"** a deal.
2) **Get everything in writing**. The Taiwanese will attempt to put all of your requirements in writing while omitting theirs. The agreement will still change after it is in writing, but at least it will be a little closer to the original agreement if it was previously written down and agreed upon by both parties.
3) **Stalling** is a favorite technique of Taiwanese businessmen.

4) **Diffusion questions** are often used.

5) **Metaphors, stories and analogies** are a good idea.

6) **Distraction tactics** are useful in times of conflict and will definitely be used by your counterparts.

7) Receiving the **technical specifications up-front** or in the beginning of the negotiation is a good idea.

8) Expect the Taiwanese to use the **"big-picture"** negotiation style. That is, nothing is decided until everything is decided. You should probably plan on a similar strategy.

9) Taiwan is a hierarchical society. Referring to the **approval of respected higher authorities** in regards to your company, product, etc. should prove to be an effective method of persuasion.

10) Discussion of harmonious future beneficial business relationships is an integral part of Taiwanese business cultures. Your **presentation of possible futuristic cooperative endeavors, the use of positive imagery,** etc. should be beneficial during business presentations and negotiations.

11) Like most of Asia, the Taiwanese will imply that they have influence with government officials or with important individuals. You may wish to **imply that you have influence** with certain people that are relevant to the transaction.

Tactics to avoid include:

1) **Do not self-promote**. Humility is considered a virtue.

2) **Do not engage in extensive information sharing**. Profuse information sharing is seen as foolish.

3) **Avoid Two-Sided Appeals.** This show of good faith will not be reciprocated.

4) **Avoid direct conflict**.

5) Avoid extensive direct eye contact, elaborate demonstratives (although reserved non-verbal behavior is okay), and touching.

Resolving disputes

While in Taiwan, try to understand and adapt to their culture. It will take ***guanxi*, creativity and patience** to solve problems with the Taiwanese.

Have a team member who speaks Mandarin or get a good interpreter. Many disputes can be avoided if communication differences are addressed. Do not insist on having all meetings conducted completely in English and do not rely on your counterparts from Taiwan to provide your interpreter. By allowing them to speak in their own language, they will be able to express themselves more freely. While many people in Taiwan speak enough English to describe technical issues, their English can sometimes lead them to be perceived as defensive or negative by Westerners when they don't intend to give this impression.

Planning and decision making take longer since failure is not acceptable. Therefore, be prepared to allow time for the people from Taiwan to make their decision.

If you must use an attorney, make sure your Taiwanese colleagues understand that you are in charge and not the attorney.

The court structure of Taiwan is unusual and differs from European and Anglo-American models. The emphasis is on arbitration and compromise rather than the injunctive relief of grievances.

Group and individual dynamics

The Taiwanese are **very group oriented**. The heavy emphasis on shame as a social control mechanism from early childhood tends to cause feelings of dependency and anxieties about self-esteem. This naturally leads into self-consciousness about most social relationships. As a result, a great deal can be gained by helping the Taiwanese to win face and a great deal can be lost by any affront no matter how unintended. It is worth remembering that for the Taiwanese, sincerity is reflected in their desire to be absolutely correct.

Coupled with their concern for face is their concept of *guanxi,* a concept that has group dynamic implications of the most committed variety by western standards. The extraordinary emphasis Taiwanese negotiators place on friendship can be understood only in the context of *guanxi*, which is somewhat similar to networking but with a much greater commitment.

Risk

The Taiwanese are **somewhat averse to taking risks**. They will, however, take more risks than mainland Chinese or the Japanese. They will do everything in their power to modify the risk and they will research a project thoroughly before committing their resources to it. Taiwanese companies are also hierarchical and a business person's position is based on seniority. The higher the seniority, the greater the role in the decision-making process. Therefore, it is the senior executives who make the final decisions after receiving input and data from lower-echelon colleagues. The senior executives are less likely to take risks than are the younger generation.

Decision-making

In Taiwan, the **top person has absolute rule** and there is little delegation of authority. However, the company is an integral part of its employee's lives. The Taiwanese are very hard working and employees feel a heavy responsibility to their employers. If they make a wrong decision, they and the company will lose face. Decision making, therefore, becomes a time-consuming process that follows certain guidelines. The first rule they follow is the rule of patience. The Taiwanese must have time to digest all the information they need. They also take a long-range view of their potential commitments, and they want to be certain they are not making any mistakes. After an issue has been thoroughly researched and after consulting with his colleagues, the senior executive will make a **top-down final decision**.

Type of agreement

The laws of present day Taiwan were developed in mainland China. They broadly represent a European legal system which has been modified by its Asian jurisdiction. The Swiss and German codes of the 19th century were the primary legal models utilized by the Chinese. However, Taiwan does not have as complex or highly institutionalized legal system as the United States.

The Taiwanese culture has traditionally held a less than enthusiastic view of legal considerations and instead stresses ethical and moral principles. Americans are thought to be highly legalistic. Therefore, joint ventures and other contractual arrangements open the possibility for misunderstandings when it comes to finalizing an agreement.

For most westerners an agreement is a binding process, but for the Taiwanese an **agreement may simply be an accord that will start a relationship that further negotiations will clarify.** Americans prefer a carefully-worded contract; the **Taiwanese prefer a loosely-worded commitment**. These considerations point to a major difference in Taiwanese and American negotiating styles. Americans from the outset see the negotiating process as leading to consummation when an agreement is reached that will be binding on all parties and provide a given period of fixed predictable behavior. The Taiwanese, on the other hand, seem to have less feeling for the drama of agreement, and little expectation that any formalized contract will end the process of negotiations.

This is not to say the Taiwanese will not hold to an agreement; it's just that they have no inhibitions about proposing changes or even terminating a contract before the completion date if the terms permit it. Thus the Taiwanese will hold to an agreement, but signing the contract does not imply finality.

NOTES:

Chapter 28

Thailand

- *Country Background*
- *The Thai Culture*
- *Business Protocol*
- *Communication Style*
- *The Thai Concept of Negotiations*

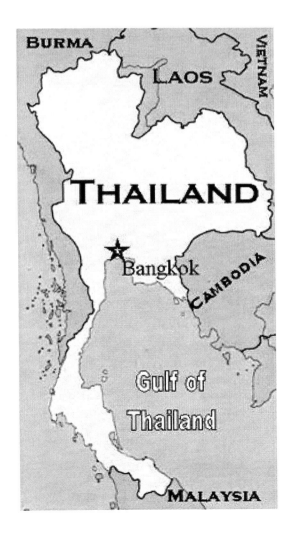

The name Thailand literally means land of the free. Thailand is the only country in Southeast Asia that has never been a European colony. However, most Thai have been affected by foreign contact and change for many decades, especially since the mid-19th century when the impact of European activity was first felt. Always able to harness the talents of its people and to make effective use of its natural environment, the Thai economy continues to function along open-market lines. The economy remains capitalist in orientation, largely operated by the private sector, with supportive infrastructure furnished by the government.

The land area is 511,770 square kilometers, about twice the size of Wyoming. Bordering countries are Burma, Cambodia, Laos, and Malaysia. The terrain includes a central plain, the Khorat plateau located in the east, and mountains elsewhere. The elevation extremes are sea level to the highest point, Doi Inthamon, at 2,576 meters.

Country Background

History

Thailand has an archaeological site in the northeastern part of the country that is believed to contain the oldest evidence of rice cultivation and bronze casting in Asia and possibly the world. Over time a number of migrations from southern China brought religious, social, political, and cultural innovations that influenced the later development of Thailand's culture and national identity. The dense forests of the region produced an abundance of food that supported first hunting and gathering economies and later agricultural communities. The development of rice cultivation enabled more complex communal, social, and political organizations to evolve.

The closely related Mon and Khmer peoples entered the territory along migration routes from southern China in the ninth century BC. The Khmer settled in the Mekong River Valley, while the Mon occupied the central plains and northern highlands that make up modern Thailand. In the sixth century the Mon established the Dvaravati Kingdom, while the Khmer were laying the foundations for their kingdom centered at Angkor. The Mon were receptive to the art and literature of India and introduced both Hinduism and Buddhism to the region. The Khmer eventually established dominance over the area but embraced the

religious and cultural concepts of the Mon. The Khmer built magnificent structures to glorify the monarchy but neglected their primary asset, which was an elaborate agricultural system.

The Thai regard the founding of the kingdom of Sukhothai in AD 1238 as their emergence as a distinct nation. Situated on the banks of the Mae Nam Yom, some 375 kilometers north of present-day Bangkok, Sukhothai was the cradle of Thai civilization. The Thai kingdom was not a single unified state, but rather a patchwork of self-governing principalities. Thai rulers were absolute monarchs whose office was partially religious in nature. They stood at the apex of a highly stratified social and political hierarchy that extended throughout the society.

The Thai always had a rich food supply. Peasants planted rice for their own consumption and to pay taxes; the surplus was sold and shipped abroad. In 1511 the Portuguese conquered Malocca and within five years had worked out a treaty to trade in the region. In 1592 a similar treaty gave the Dutch a privileged position in the rice trade. In the 17th century the Thai forged important commercial ties with the Japanese, the British, and the French and were successful at pitting one against the other so that they were not dominated by any one foreign power.

The country was called Siam from the 13th to the early 20th century. The name was officially changed to Thailand in the 1930s. Prior to World War II, Thailand looked to Japan as the only Asian government able to successfully challenge the European powers. Japan had used western methods and technology to achieve rapid modernization. When sporadic fighting broke out between Thai and French forces in 1940, Japan used its influence with the Vichy regime in France to obtain concessions for Thailand. During World War II, Thailand signed a mutual defense pact with Japan. In 1942, under pressure from Japan, Thailand declared war on Britain and the United States, but the Thai ambassador in Washington refused to deliver the declaration to the US government. As the war came to an end, Thailand repudiated its wartime agreements with Japan.

Government

In 1932, after centuries of absolute monarchy, a group of civil servants and army officers engineered a bloodless coup d'etat. The action was primarily directed against the ministers of the royal government and not the king. A provisional constitution was drawn up that stripped the king of his political power, but left the prestige of the monarchy unimpaired. The first parliamentary elections in the country's history were held in November, 1933.

From 1932 to the present, corruption and the political incompetence of its national leadership and the disruptive role of the military have plagued Thailand. Periodically, civil and political disorder has culminated in military usurpations of power, with constitutions abolished and martial law declared. Since 1932 there have been 18 coups that replaced one military government with another. Fourteen constitutions have been drafted, which tend to feature a British-style cabinet form of government. The power of the state is exercised through a centralized form of government, divided into the legislative, executive and judicial branches.

The latest constitution has been structured to accommodate both the military and the civilian bureaucratic elite. Up to 85% of senate membership in the late 1980s was drawn from the armed forces and the police. The intent of this arrangement was to induce the military to play its political role through the upper house rather than through coups and counter-coups.

The Thai legal system is based on a collection of major codes, with custom playing an important role in interpretation. The fact that numerous constitutions were regularly abrogated, suspended, and amended had little effect. Codification following civil code principles was carefully drafted and adopted piecemeal over a 30-year period of time. The two basic codes are the civil and commercial codes of 1935 and the criminal code of 1957.

The Thai judicial system has some overlapping and confusing spheres of authority. There is an extensive range of courts but at present there are no distinct administrative jurisdictions. Judicial decisions are based somewhat on precedent, but this varies depending on the judge. An earlier decision may not be binding on a similar case in the same court.

Demographics

Thailand's population of 62 million has a growth rate of 1%. Ethnically, the Thai make up 75% of the population, the Chinese are 14%, and a variety of other groups compose the remainder. Life expectancy at birth for the entire population is 69 years, but is 66 for males and 72 for females. In recent years, AIDS has slightly reduced the average life expectancy; over 2% of the population has AIDS.

The literacy rate is 94%: 96% for males and 92% for females.

Economy

Thailand is one of the more developed nations in Asia. The export of various manufactured goods, fueled by extensive foreign investment, has led to rapid economic growth. In the past decade, government policies that favor free-market trade and the investment of foreign capital have attracted billions, primarily from Japan and the United States. Manufacturing is concentrated in the capital city of Bangkok, where good transportation, communication systems, and support institutions in banking and marketing are readily available.

Thailand is the world's second-largest producer of tungsten and the third-largest of tin. A "frontier" atmosphere, with claim jumps, false registration certificates, so-called lost mines, and various types of violence, marks the tin industry. Other mineral resources are iron ore, manganese, lead, zinc, and various gemstones such as garnets, rubies and jade. Oil drilling and refining are developing industries; the Thai Shell subsidiary is one of the giants of the region.

Agriculture is still the main support for the majority of the population; 57% of the work force is agricultural. Farmers are generally small landowners who continually bring new lands into cultivation. Rice is the main crop, but tapioca, corn, sugar cane, cassava, tobacco, cotton, peanuts, cashews, and soybeans are also raised. The extensive Thai fishing industry ranks among the world's top ten.

Thailand's exports are 82% manufactured goods, 14% agricultural products and fish, and 5% raw materials. Their main trading partners include the USA, Japan, Singapore, Hong Kong, Germany, the UK, Netherlands and Malaysia. Thailand enjoys a healthy trade surplus. Imports are also primarily manufactured goods, followed by fuels, raw materials, and foods. Their real GDP places them at 30th place in the world's economies and their per capita income ranks approximately 45th.

Government support for economic growth is concrete. Several government agencies are in charge of developing and administering economic policy. Anyone doing business in Thailand will have to deal with some of them. The Ministry of Industry grants factory licenses and is in charge of industrial rules and zoning regulations. The Industrial Finance Corporation grants long-term financial credits to chosen companies, while the Bank of Thailand provides foreign exchange and helps finance special projects. The Board of Investment develops investment incentives. The Ministry of Commerce supports and controls international trade.

Thai currency is called the baht.

The Thai Culture

Language

A number of linguistic scholars trace the ascendancy of the central Thai dialect to the reign of King Narai in 1657-88. During his reign it became the standard dialect of Thailand for official business. There are four regional dialects in Thailand. Each region speaks the Thai language but with a distinct dialect that makes understanding one another difficult. As the educational system reaches larger numbers of the population, central Thai is spoken with greater fluency all over the country.

Before the advent of modern communication, regional differences also included costume, folklore, and other cultural traits retained in part because of the remoteness of many regions from the influence of Bangkok. Consequently Thailand has both a multi-lingual and multi-ethnic population.

English is an accepted language for business and is widely spoken in Bangkok commercial and government circles. Government offices and businesses will usually have at least one English-speaking employee. English is also spoken in most hotels and department stores. The Thai language is difficult to learn and in any dealings pertaining to consumer goods, a local agent or representative will be necessary to reach the non-English reading and speaking population.

Religion

Theravada Buddhism is the primary religion of over 90% of the Thai people. Other religions in Thailand include Hinduism, Christianity, Taoism, Animism, and Islam. Islam is the dominant religion in an area of southern Thailand where it is embraced by the Malay Thai.

Buddhism is part of Thai national identity. Religion, king, and national identity are inextricably intertwined. For many of the Thai people, however, their Buddhism is a combination of differing beliefs. They are quite tolerant of foreigners who adhere to other faiths and there are no religious taboos that affect their ability to engage in business or trade.

Value system

In the late 18th century and early 19th century Christian missionaries introduced formal western-style education to Thailand. Prior to that time scholarly pursuits had been confined to Buddhist temples where young men usually focused on the memorization of scriptures.

Emphasis on education grew after the 1932 coup as a result of the new constitutional requirement for a literate populace. By the mid 1980's nearly 80% of the population above the age of 11 years had some formal education. Today Thailand has one of the highest levels of functional literacy in Asia.

Also following the 1932 coup, a strong artistic movement began to flourish in Thailand. Drama, movies, and a variety of art forms moved out of the palaces and are now enjoyed by a wider audience. The Thai people have combined modern techniques in set and costume designs with traditional forms of drama to make regional art forms an integral part of Thai national identity.

Class structure / Stratification

In general, high status goes to those who wield power and control wealth. A rich villager wields political and economic power and has prestige. In the national system, the hierarchy of status began with the hereditary nobility: the royal family and the holders of royal titles. The royals still own considerable land and some of its members have political influence. The royal family, however, does not control the economy. The ruling class consists of several other levels: uppermost is the military and to a lesser extent the bureaucratic elite who have used their positions to further enrich themselves. Below the military elite are those who are highly trained in technical competence. These individuals enjoy considerable prestige but are not primary wielders of power. The Chinese Thai have considerable economic power but have served primarily as bankers, middlemen, and commercial entrepreneurs. Within the Chinese community there is a hierarchy of political influence.

Until the 1970s, the Chinese entered the bureaucracy only at the middle levels or if higher, as technical staff. This was in part a matter of Thai policy, but also a matter of Chinese orientation. The Chinese were not indifferent to political power or administrative skills as desirable qualities or as sources of prestige, but they adapted to the limits imposed by their minority status. By the 1970's, however, significant numbers of Chinese were being admitted to the higher bureaucracy. These were presumably the sons and daughters of wealthy entrepreneurs who had acquired the higher education necessary for admission to the bureaucracy's upper ranks. Below the hereditary nobility and the ruling class exists a socially and occupationally heterogeneous middle class that began emerging after World War II. Their middle class identity is based partially on income and partially on occupation.

There is also a large urban stratum of semi-skilled or unskilled wageworkers. Often from rural areas, they enjoy no steady employment and are to some extent indigent and homeless. Another group that enjoys a special status but is outside the traditional status hierarchy are the Buddhist monks and elders. Even the royal family and the ruling class show them a great deal of deference. A final group also outside the traditional status hierarchy, but at times with substantial incomes, are the many men and women engaged in illegal activities that are countenanced by the culture: narcotics dealers, prostitutes, and pimps.

Safety

By Asian standards, public health in Thailand is relatively good. Nevertheless one should either drink bottled water or boil all water for ten minutes. One should always wear shoes when walking outside to safeguard against parasites. Malaria, cholera, and tetanus do occur. It is advisable to plan one's trip well in advance so that one

has time to get all the recommended immunizations. Hepatitis immunizations require 3 injections over a 6-month period for full effect.

The crime rate rises and falls in proportion to the level of unemployment, population pressures, and where one is traveling in the country. Criminal activities in Thailand include all the usual forms of crime and are more common in Bangkok and the larger cities. There are high incidents of petty theft by youthful gangs who tend to prey on foreign visitors.

Very few policemen speak anything but Thai and they respond slowly to emergency calls. As in most foreign countries, one should be careful about traveling alone, particularly at night. Most crimes can be avoided if one is prudent. Two emergency phone numbers exist for English-speaking people: 2815051 or 2810372.

Business Protocol

Greetings and etiquette

Thai etiquette can be quite formal and complex. A cultural assimilation course would be time and money well spent for any potential Thai business visitors. If your time lines don't permit this, then get a competent *compradore* as soon as possible. A *compradore* is a Thai influence peddler, a financial broker. Even a poor *compradore* has status in Thailand. The really successful ones can open any door.

The *compradore* can be of assistance with letters of introduction and can help cut through reams of red tape. Every culture has their public trappings of respectability and protocol that must be respected if the venture is to succeed. **Introductions involving title, proper pronunciation of names, and proper order according to age and authority ranking must be done impeccably.** Intermediaries are established professionals who offer their services to foreign business entities. Every successful foreign business venture that has survived in Thailand will tell you how important they are.

Business cards printed in two or more languages create very favorable impressions. The Thai are more impressed by titles than degrees. The Thai are very friendly and open, but to them the handshake is an aggressive act. **Press your hands together with your elbows tucked in at your side, bow from your waist, and say "wai"** (pronounced like why in English). This is the traditional gesture used for greetings and departures. If one **speaks quietly** and engages appropriately in a customary greeting it will be greatly appreciated.

Initial meetings should include lunch or dinner. The first stage of negotiations is relationship building. The Thai eat an early dinner, usually no later than 6 PM. Thai cuisine is excellent and many restaurants in Bangkok have dishes that appeal to an international palate. Eating utensils include a fork and spoon. The atmosphere is quite informal. When you pay the check you can console yourself with the thought that you have just bought a lot of goodwill and respect.

Time

Thailand is a **polychronic** culture with customs evolving out of an agrarian lifestyle and a unique concept of time. They use three calendars: the Gregorian, which is the same as that used in the west, the Buddhist, and the lunar. They also divide the day into four six-hour segments. Each part of the day has a special name, so those who speak the language seldom make mistakes concerning time. The Thai are also familiar with the 24-hour clock, and visitors are expected to refer to it when setting appointments.

In their own way, the Thai are very punctual. They usually know the precise moment of a child's birth, for future use in fortune telling. The concept "a time and place for everything" has its own adaptation in Thailand. Each day has a color associated with it and it is considered lucky to wear the particular color of the day. There are numerous beliefs associated with the day, the date, and with numbers.

Although the Thai are **polychronic**, they are generally **punctual for business** appointments. **Socially, however, the Thai tend to be tardy.** So, for any event other than a business meeting, one can expect the Thai to be late.

Thailand is seven hours ahead of Greenwich Mean Time (GMT + 7) or twelve hours ahead of Eastern Standard Time (EST + 12).

Gifts

Giving and receiving gifts is an accepted and enjoyed activity in Thailand. Gifts should be carefully selected; they must not be too cheap or too expensive. If too expensive they will create a burdensome obligation on the recipient. If too cheap or common, they will have a less than desirable effect. Popular gifts include an **imported brandy or liquor, a doll in native dress, or an illustrated book from one's own country**. When invited to dinner one is expected to bring flowers or a cake or some fruit. Marigolds and carnations are flowers associated with bereavement, so avoid them. **Every gift should be beautifully wrapped and merely placed on a table in the proximity of the recipient.** If the gift is given almost anonymously and with a degree of humility, the Thai will feel most comfortable receiving it. **Gifts are not opened immediately and publicly.** The gift will be opened when the recipient can enjoy it privately.

Business entertainment

The path to business success in Thailand goes through the restaurants. Wining and dining is appreciated and thoroughly enjoyed. In **relationship-based** business cultures it is an absolute necessity to engage in this pleasurable activity. Bangkok's restaurants offer exceptional cuisine and excellent service. **The Thai love to eat in groups** and they prefer circular tables that permit optimal communication. Most Thai eat with a fork and spoon. They use the fork to push the food into the spoon, which is held in the right hand.

Buffet style dinners are very popular. This style also permits Westerners to select the foods that are more appealing to their pallet from the considerable culinary variety offered at these occasions. It is customary to invite wives to these events. If you are invited to a Thai home, find out as much as you can about the circumstances of the dining event. In that way you can bring an appropriate gift that will help enhance the occasion.

Dress

In Thailand clothes make the person. Success is reflected in the quantity and quality of one's attire. Some Thai will wear business suits with ties in stifling heat. Appropriate attire for the foreign businessperson is

lightweight and conservative: suits, sport jackets, slacks with short-sleeved white shirts and ties for men, and dresses or skirts and blouses for women.

Under less formal circumstances short-sleeved white shirts with or without ties are appropriate. For casual occasions, both sexes may wear jeans, but they can be too hot. Shorts are acceptable in the streets. Take at least one pair of old shoes with you. Wear them if you visit a temple. You will have to remove them to go into the temple, and new shoes will quite likely disappear.

Communication Style

Business language

Thai is a **moderate to high-context language**. They tend to speak softly. The raising of one's voice is associated with anger and potential loss of face. Unpleasant subjects and emotions are denied or avoided. Indirect forms of communication not associated with confrontation or conflict are used extensively. Social harmony is the goal and the Thai language is culturally oriented in that direction. Although most high-context cultures can be confusing and tend to project an element of secrecy or dishonesty to most Westerners, this is not the case in Thailand. The **Thai tend to exude (and admire in others) modesty, sincerity, honesty, an open and friendly posture and graciousness.** Unlike most of Asia, the Thai people are **only slightly indirect** and often tell you more precisely what they want. However, it is done in a gracious, harmonious manner.

If a translator is utilized, proper etiquette is to look directly at the person you are communicating with, using first person pronouns. When the other person is speaking, maintain eye contact, nod and pay full attention, letting the other person speak uninterrupted until finished.

Non-verbal communication

The **wai** is not just a Thai greeting gesture. It is an act symbolic of the Thai's respectful approach to human interactions, the singularly most significant nonverbal gesture in the culture. The *wai* is also an expression of inequality and subservervience. Those of higher rank do not customarily return the *wai* to those of lower status. Thank you *wais*, from a superior to one of inferior rank, are just not done, but those of lower rank express their

gratitude to their superiors with the *wai* gesture. Therefore, one never *wais* someone of lower social standing. If you receive a *wai* and wish to return it, make your *wai* slightly more casual. The safest people to *wai* are the elderly or a monk. The appropriate deference posture is to lower the head, bend the knees, and bend over slightly.

The next most common nonverbal communication in Thailand is the **smile**. The Thai smile constantly. In a culture that denies negative emotions, a smile is the perfect defense. Of course, smiles are not just defensive. They also express amusement, or they might express forgiveness or the pardoning of a wrongful break with etiquette. They might also express embarrassment, or the smile may be part of a good sales pitch. The head and the feet also have important nonverbal significance. Touching a Thai on the head is an insult, even among close friends. The feet are to be kept on the ground. Never use them to point or lift them high, particularly higher than another person's head. This can lead to awkward situations when one is a tall foreigner in a crowded location with people seated on the floor. In these circumstances, the Thai address the crowd with hand gestures, indicating the need for a pathway. Then they crouch or at least bend their back so their head is as low as possible. They pass through the ranks keeping their eyes toward the ground.

Status is defined through seating arrangements. If they seat you up front in a large gathering, you dare not move to another seat. Traditionally, Thai sat in large circular patterns. The seating was arranged according to rank, and those of **highest rank sat up front**. Rank was determined primarily by age. The Thai business community is breaking away from a lot of this ritualized behavior, but in the governmental sector it is still symbolically adhered to. When leaving, always let the **eldest person lead the way** unless they insist that you must go before them. **Rank is also expressed in the walking order.**

Whole books have been written on the significance of hand movements in the Thai culture. In the traditional ceremonial dances the hands primarily tell the story. It is a **taboo to point** at someone and no one slaps another person on the back or pushes him or her. The only touching allowed is a light touch on the elbow and that only between friends and colleagues of the same sex.

It is advisable for foreigners to refrain from all but utilitarian hand movements. **When you're not working with your hands, keep them down at your side, but not in your pockets.**

If you are at a restaurant you may **point your chin** to indicate a direction. You can call someone to you by extending the hand palm down and scooping with the fingers toward the floor. In passing plates or beverages at the table always use your right hand. **The left hand is used for hygienic toiletry purposes and should never touch food or another person.**

The Thai Concept of Negotiations

Selecting personnel

Thai businesses tend to be extended-family networks. Personnel are selected through lineage or patronage obligations. **Relatives will be hired first,** then others will be considered on the basis of friendship or favors owed. While this is nepotism to a Westerner, it is a completely proper way of doing business to the Thai.

Once a person becomes an employee in this family business structure, their position is viewed as secured for life. If performance is slipshod, if there is excessive tardiness or absenteeism, considerable finesse will be required. Only a fellow Thai is capable of motivating unruly, lazy, or incompetent Thai. Thai family patterns are patriarchal with great deference shown toward the elderly, who have more status and experience and make better team motivators. Only an older Thai has the status and experience required to effectively address Thai performance.

Thai personnel can be motivated, but they are not a naturally competitive or assertive people. They are a people who believe in cooperation and harmony. With competent indigenous leadership they become very industrious. Selecting the right personnel is crucial in Thailand.

Obviously, personnel considerations must be an early priority in the project flow chart. The ***compradore* is usually the first Thai a foreign business venture hires**. If you thoroughly brief him on your planned business venture, explaining the type of leadership required, he might not recommend his brother-in-law.

The Thai show considerable deference to a superior; experience, rank, age, and wealth impress them. The higher the position in one's company, the more experience the person has, and the greater status he/she will have with his/her Thai counterparts. The sex of the personnel is an important consideration. Like most Asian cultures, males are considered more proficient and superior to females, particularly when it comes to business matters. Therefore, the negotiating team that a Thai firm will select, and your firm should attempt to mirror, will tend to be **male, older, educated, have the ability to listen, have the ability to work harmoniously with colleagues and will always defer to superiors.**

Negotiating style

Initially, relationship-based issues will be the focus. Lunches, dinners, and drinking provide opportunities for the Thai to satisfy their need for rapport and friendship. They like to think of negotiations as the beginning of a long-term harmonious friendship. Maintaining this positive relationship as the negotiations move though the substantive issues takes considerable skill and time.

The Thai will nod and smile. They will **listen intently and pay close attention, but they will not ask questions or give any feedback.** The Japanese have been very effective in their Thai negotiations. They know the wisdom of being patient and the need for long-range goals, with modest short-term objectives.

Information is not quickly shared among the Thai. Open discussions are not a common event for them. Their methods are more reflective and subtle. Their orientation toward time enters into the negotiating process in that they are **not in a hurry**. While Westerners may find the Thai enigmatic acquiescence irritating, they must not show it in any way. The Thai will never say no; their style involves concession and compromise.

The Thai can be pragmatic and sometimes the key is to find the decision maker or someone who has the ear of the decision maker. The Japanese are very effective at securing trading and manufacturing advantages in this manner. Bribery usually involves intermediaries. Money does not always go to the top, so if you are planning on using this type of strategy, inside information is critical to finding the appropriate person.

Issues discussed

The Thai will favor **generalized topics indirectly related to organizational success**. Business issues in a highly personal society are best dealt with on a face-to-face basis. Social contacts and friendship are more important to the Thai than substantive business issues. **Once a climate of good will and camaraderie has been established and the relationship needs basically met, they will expect to enter into the substantive issues**.

Establishing trust

Initially third party introductions along with intuitive factors will provide an early basis for trust. Maintaining **proper etiquette** and showing **respect for the elderly** and those in authority is very important. Those who are courteous and considerate gain trust. Those who are abrupt and discourteous lose trust. By controlling one's emotions, **never showing anger** or causing someone to lose face, one will in time be considered trustworthy.

Persuasion

The "land of the free," the only Southeast Asian country never reduced to a colony, and the subject of that delightful musical, "The King and I," Thailand presents a number of challenges. The global free enterprise system offers amazing market opportunities in both directions. Selling the world on Thailand is the easy part. But how many Thai know that an American invented the ricksha? The Japanese know how to sell in Thailand and they've known how for a long time; the ricksha is a prime early example.

Thailand's elite are quite autocratic. The people, however, are mild mannered, friendly, and obedient. If superiors make autonomous decisions and inferiors unquestionably obey, would the inferiors automatically buy a product that superiors endorse? Not necessarily, because there are other values at work. Buddhism allows for selective conformity and there are a range of behavioral options open to the Thai. From a systems perspective it might seem they have narrowly confined roles, but the Thai think of themselves as a free people with numerous choices. The Thai are an individualistic and self-reliant people, always conscious of their position in their societal hierarchy. If a product can enhance their status and increase their self-reliance, it should be a saleable item. The proper introduction of a product can create a receptive climate. Advertisements on their radio and TV feature very subtle questioning techniques. Selective targeting of a segment of the Thai market could serve to establish product credibility. The Thai utilize circular reasoning patterns and have excellent memories. A product's track record determines its long-range success.

The persuasion tactics that can be generally used in Thailand or will be used by the Thai are:

1) The Thai love to **bargain and haggle** and can be quite lively while doing so. They will almost always **"high-ball" or "low-ball"** a deal.
2) As a negotiation progresses, the Thai may use the ploy "We are only a developing third world country" (i.e., **shaming**) and will seek compromises in their favor.
3) Always **get everything in writing**.
4) The Thai, like most Asians, like to imply that they have governmental influence or influence with important individuals. You may wish to **imply that you have influence** with certain people that are relevant to the transaction.
5) **Stalling.** It almost always happens. Plan on it and use it to your advantage.
6) **Metaphors, stories and analogies** are often used in Thailand.
7) **Diffusion questions and distraction tactics** are useful in times of conflict.
8) Certain requests that we consider to be **corruption** are normal business practices in Thailand. Decide how you plan to initiate or respond to such requests.
9) Because Thais are an emotional as well as a socially-engaging group, the **presentation of possible future cooperative endeavors** and/or multi-firm interactive simulations should be very persuasive.
10) Use a **"big-picture"** strategy. Nothing is decided until everything is decided.
11) **Positive emotional tactics as well as personal appeals** should be useful.
12) Thailand is a hierarchical as well as collectivist society. Referring to the **approval of others** and especially the approval of **respected higher authorities** in regards to your company, product, etc. should prove to be an effective method of persuasion.

13) Based upon the desire for harmony in Thailand, the **"Feel-Felt-Found"** objection-handling tactic should prove to be effective when delivered in a harmonious and emotionally expressive manner.

14) **Build trust through information sharing.** The Thais tend to be more upfront than most Asians and will expect reciprocation.

Tactics to avoid include:

1) **Avoid direct personal conflict.** Direct personal conflict will cause loss of "face."

2) **Thais view all conversations as enjoyable.** So avoid a serious/conservative business mentality. Keep the overall tone pleasurable.

3) **Avoid overuse of technical details** or dry presentations and do not speak in a monotone voice. Thais tend to like interesting, honest, and upfront presentations, and expect an unclouded bottom line.

4) Do not use fear tactics, ultimatums, threats, yelling, etc. Thais are looking for an enjoyable, trusting, and harmonious exchange.

5) **Do not hurry to complete the transaction.** Allow for breaks, side conversations, etc.

6) **Avoid surprises at the table.** Up-front surprises promote conflict and reduce harmony.

Resolving disputes

The Thai emphasize mutual trust in their negotiations. They prefer to **deny or avoid a problem** because it can effect harmony and jeopardize the relationship. Therefore, disputes can be difficult to resolve and one may have to take the position that no deal is better than a poor deal.

The most effective ways to resolve disputes in Thailand is **through personal appeals and dogma**. This may entail reverting back to the earlier stages of the negotiations when the two sides won each other's trust. Asking influential members of the team, or even outside well-connected people, to help resolve the disagreement can be very beneficial. By keeping one's dignity and respect for others, rather than losing face and putting others on the spot during an argument, one has a much better chance of reaching an agreement.

Contractual disputes must first be brought to the attention of the offending party before being brought to court. Disputing parties are expected to achieve a settlement outside of court. It is generally best to resolve disputes informally and mediation is commonly utilized. If a dispute is taken to court, the process tends to be lengthy.

The Thai legal system is based upon a collection of major codes. The constitution, regularly abrogated, suspended and amended, has had only slight effect on the development of the country's legal system, other than providing a somewhat inconsistent framework of government. Codification following civil law principles has been carefully drafted. The process has been going on piecemeal for many years.

Judicial decisions have limited precedence value in the Thai legal system. Depending on the judge, courts can be influenced by precedent as well as the practice of relying on a sequential line of strongly-stated decisions by authority on particular issues. However, even Supreme Court decisions only influence a current court decision if the judge decides it merits consideration.

The Sarn Rang Ngan Klan is the court for all labor matters. Above it are the appellate tribunals and then the Sarn Dika (Supreme Court), which is guaranteed as an independent entity under the constitution.

In 1938, Thailand passed legislation which provided guidelines to apply in the event of a conflict of laws. Where there is no provision in the act or in the laws of Thailand, the general principles of international law apply. However, if a foreign law is applicable but is not satisfactory to the Thai judge, then the internal law of Thailand must apply.

Group and individual dynamics

In most large-scale urban environments, people interact with others without common links of kinship. When Thailand was a monarchy and had an extended family agrarian organizational structure, it experienced centuries of stability. Modernization and urbanization have tended in a relatively short period of time to reverse this ancient and successful order.

The Thai are very group-oriented. Life spent in the company of strangers rather than together with trusted family members is an abnormal and insecure arrangement. Nepotism (favoring family members over strangers) is natural in any country with a strong agricultural tradition. Nepotism lends stability and continuity to the Thai work force, which is trying to adjust to an abnormal and insecure environment. In the earlier agrarian structures, family and social pressures kept people at their tasks. These earlier structures and their positive influences rarely exist in modern offices or factories.

In Thailand few workers are happy with purely economic incentives. The extended family and village structures of the past are relevant in the urban environment if they can increase the individual's chances of finding employment and of enjoying their work. When one has family members nearby in the work environment, it satisfies a deep-felt need.

Religious events are another source of social cohesion and organizational activity. They provide familiarity, inspiration, and linkages to the past. Successful offices and factories in Thailand are usually found when people enjoy their work and have opportunity to fulfill some of their emotional and spiritual needs. Nepotism is in many ways an attempt to recreate in the urban environment the conditions the Thai previously had in their agrarian past.

Risk

For centuries, land was the real source of wealth in Thailand. Agrarian cultures are **risk averse**. The fairly recent changes from an agrarian monarchy toward a modern industrial democracy have not gone smoothly and have created new insecurities. The king, although only a figurehead, has been the only politically consistent element.

Money is associated with status, but success on a day-to-day basis for the ordinary Thai involves more than money. The average Thai spends as much money on gambling as on religious activities. Gambling provides an inexpensive form of entertainment and is a diversion from the more urgent imperatives of day-to-day survival.

Fortune telling in all its forms is another major Thai industry. Intervention is sought in one's individual destiny. Knowing the future can minimize one's risk and improve one's chances of winning. Other than gambling, the Thai will only take **very moderate forms of risk.**

Decision Making

The fact that fortune telling is a major industry offers insight into the decision-making process for the ordinary Thai. Over centuries, habit patterns evolve and they become deeply ingrained cultural imperatives. When one is powerless then one must go outside oneself, individually and collectively, for guidance. Subjective decision-making networks are self-supporting and self-perpetuating entities that reinforce elitist top-down decision-making arrangements. The Thai are basically an obedient people. The **top-down decision making** model is firmly entrenched.

Type of agreement

Thailand's strong long-term economic prospects make it attractive to the international community. Officials throughout the Thai government have made it clear that they seek foreign investors. With the growing strength of the Thai private sector, potential partnerships beckon. A recent example is Nynex Telecom's entry into a strategic partnership with the Telecomasia Company. The first contract involved the upgrading of the Bangkok telephone system.

Within Thailand's constitutional framework are provisions relating to the laws of property. The legal framework is very similar to that of Germany and Japan. Thai contract law has also been influenced by Anglo-American common law. In the law of sales, ownership passes immediately at the time of sale to the purchaser. However, if the contract specifically states a condition or a term altering this event, then those specific terms apply. There is no law protecting industrial property rights in terms of patents, copyrights, designs, etc. Trademarks are protected under the Business Registration Act of 1956.

The laws regulating the formation of contracts are determined by the intent of the parties involved. All correspondence, memos, and written material can be used to determine intent. Intent clauses can provide additional legal options if problems arise.

Contracts can be made orally, but numerous provisions in the law protect the written contract, so oral agreements are not recommended.

NOTES:

Chapter 29

Turkey

- *Country Background*
- *The Turkish Culture*
- *Business Protocol*
- *Communication Style*
- *The Turkish Concept of Negotiations*

Turkey is an important country when viewed geographically, for it forms a land bridge linking Asia and Europe. Roughly rectangular in shape, most of its territory is in Asia, but a small portion is part of Europe. Within its borders lie the straits of Bosparus and the Dardenelles, a strategic waterway that has been fought over by many empires. Its surrounding waters, the Black, Aegean, Marmaran, and Mediterranean seas, were probably the earliest navigated trade routes.

The climate is temperate with hot dry summers and mild wet winters. The terrain is mostly mountainous, with a narrow coastal plain and high central plateau. Thirty-two percent of its land is arable with 4% in permanent crops, 16% in pasture, and 26% in forest and woodlands. Natural hazards include severe earthquakes, particularly in the northern part of the country.

Turkey has an industrious population, excellent seaports, and shares a border with eight neighboring countries: Greece and Bulgaria in Europe, and Georgia, Armenia, Azerbaijan, Iran, Iraq, and Syria in Asia. Turkey offers the international business community unique investment opportunities.

Country Background

History

A 6500 BC Neolithic community, which has been called the world's first town, existed at Catal Huyuk in what is now northwestern Turkey. Many civilizations followed, including the Hittites, the Phrygians, the Ionians, the Persians, the Macedonians, the Romans, and the Ottomans. Each civilization flourished, left ruins on the landscape, and a genetic imprint on the population.

The topography of Turkey consists of a high plateau rising gradually toward the east, with a number of inner valleys that undulate across the landscape. Rivers of immense historical and religious significance emerge from this plateau. On the eastern border with Armenia, Mount Ararat rises 5,166 meters. Many religious people believe that Noah's ark lies permanently ensconced somewhere in its upper regions.

The current Republic of Turkey emerged from the dissolution of the once splendid Ottoman Empire following World War I. In 1921 the Treaty of Sevres

divided up the remains of the old empire. Modern Turkish history begins with the war and revolution led by Mustapha Kemal against the European nations that had forced the concessions of Sevres. Turkey triumphed, and in 1923, the Treaty of Lausanne effectively established the modern boundaries of present-day Turkey. Mustapha Kemal was elected the first president, and was later re-named Ataturk (Father of the Turks) by his adoring countrymen. He abolished the harem and the veil, ended religious schools and courts, and adopted the Roman alphabet, the metric system, and a westernized law system. In succeeding years the internal pressures of conflicting ideologies and factions buffeted this young democracy. During several of these disruptive periods, the Turkish military was used to restore order. On several occasions the young republic teetered on the brink of civil war and political disintegration, but Turkey has repeatedly survived these disruptions and returned to stability.

Turkey was one of the few nations to remain neutral during World War II. During the Cold War it aligned itself with the West. In 1950 Turkey sent an infantry contingent to Korea, and in 1952 joined NATO. Turkey is a member of the United Nations and over fifty other world organizations.

Government

The Republic of Turkey is a parliamentary secular democracy. Its current constitution was ratified in 1982 and provides for an executive, legislative, and judicial branch. The executive branch has a president who is the chief of state, a prime minister who is the head of the government and a cabinet of ministers appointed by the president on the nomination of the prime minister. The legislative branch consists of a unicameral Grand National Assembly with 550 seats. Members are elected to serve five-year terms.

The Constitutional Court heads the judicial branch. The president appoints the judges. The judicial branch also provides for an appellate court, whose judges are elected by the Supreme Council of Judges and Prosecutors. The Turkish legal system evolved out of Islamic law, which was an all-encompassing system considered immutable and immune to intervention. The inadequacies of the Islamic legal system became obvious to the Turks, and gradually aspects of French, British, and Swiss legal codes were translated and utilized. This produced the development of two legal systems, one secular and the other religious, which were extant until the revolution. Within the first decade, 1922-1932, Turkey replaced almost the entirety of its legal system. In 1926 the Swiss Civil Code and Federal Code of Obligations were translated. Revisions are continuing: the commercial code was revised in 1956, bankruptcy laws were revised in 1965, and the civil code was revised in 1973. The reception of western law in Turkey is a continuing evolutionary process.

For the first 22 years of its existence as a democracy, Turkey had only one political party. This arrangement prevailed until 1946, when a second political party was formed. In 1950, this second party won a landslide victory. Each of these parties represented opposing economic philosophies and different segments of the electorate, again reflecting the factionalism in the society. At present, Turkey is a multiparty democracy, and its citizens enjoy universal suffrage at 18 years of age.

Demographics

Turkey's population of 67 million is growing. Life expectancy of the total population is 72 years, with males at 69 years and females at 74 years. Ethnicity is 80% Turkish and 20% Kurdish. Literacy rates for the entire population over 15 years of age are 85%, with 94% for males and 77% for females.

Economy

Turkey's location has made it a crossroads and a center for trade between East and West for centuries. It is the largest market in its region, and the business community has excellent entrepreneurial skills and experience. The economy is a complex mix of modern industry and commerce along with traditional village agriculture and crafts. The economy has a strong rapidly-growing private sector. However, the state plays a major role in some basic industries such as banking, transport, and communications.

Turkey's current economic situation is marked by strong growth coupled with a large public sector deficit. Real GDP has expanded by around 6% every year for the past ten years. However, inflation remains very high and the public sector fiscal deficit is usually more than 10% of the GDP. Turkey's real GNP ranks around 25th in the world and their per capita income ranks around 40th.

Turkey has a labor force of 23 million with 35% involved in agriculture. The service industry employs 40%, and 25% of its work force is in the industrial sector. Its industries include textiles, food processing, and the mining of coal, chromate, copper and boron. Other industries include steel, petroleum, construction, lumber, and paper. The unemployment rate is moderate at about 6%; however, many are underemployed.

Turkey's agricultural products include tobacco, cotton, grain, olives, sugar, beets, citrus, and livestock. Its exports are textiles and apparel, food, and steel products. Imports consist primarily of machinery and other equipment, fuels, raw materials, and foodstuffs. Turkey has a relatively large trade deficit that hampers their economic growth. Trading partners include Germany, the USA, Russia, Italy, France, and the UK.

Turkey's fiscal year is the calendar year. The Turkish currency, the Lira (TL) has had a lengthy history of depreciation.

The Turkish Culture

Language

The original speakers of the Turkish language came out of a region in central Asia that included western China, Siberia, and Kazakhstan. They came in large numbers as nomadic soldiers. Finding the Middle East more pleasant than the northern regions they had come from, they remained. Soon they expanded westward into Iran and Iraq, and then began raiding into the Byzantine Empire. They assimilated populations readily as they went along, having no concept of race to inhibit them. When they moved into Anatolia, the area that was known as Turkey, they became known as the people of that land, and were thus called Turks.

The Turkish language evolved out of the Altay branch of the Euro-Altay linguistic family. Over the centuries, the Turks occupied an extensive geographical area that included Mongolia, the Black Sea area, the Balkans, Eastern Europe, Anatolia, Iraq, and a considerable portion of northern Africa. A variety of dialects and accents emerged as the language spread over such vast distances. Historically, the language is divided into three main groups: Old Turkish (from the 7th to the 13th centuries), Mid Turkish (from the 13th to the 20th), and

New Turkish (from the 20th century to the present). During the Ottoman period, words from other languages, particularly Arabic and Persian, were assimilated.

In 1928, the Arabic alphabet was abandoned and replaced by a Latin one. A purist movement sought to reclaim the original Turkish language, and a language institute was established in 1932 to conduct linguistic research.

Turkish is an agglutinative language, which means it has a base to which other linguistic concepts are added. Each addition slightly alters the language's pattern and its meaning. This happens in the evolution of every language, but in the Turkish language you wind up with not just a larger word but also possibly a whole sentence in one word.

In the Turkish language the word order is different than English. Simultaneous translation is therefore more difficult than translating languages that have similar word orders, because you have to wait until the sentence is complete before beginning to translate. The language is also phonetic, and each letter represents a sound. However, dialect factors complicate the oral to written linkages. The modern Turkish language is a composite that includes many words of French, Italian, and English derivation. The Turkish language family has roughly 125 million adherents worldwide. The Ottoman Empire, out of which Turkey emerged, was the largest in the world during the 16th century. It stretched from central Asia to Vienna and all the way south to Saudi Arabia.

Religion

Turkey's constitution guarantees freedom of worship to all its citizens, and it also declares itself a secular state that does not interfere in the religious practices of its citizens. The Turkish population is 98% Muslim, 90% of whom are Sunni Muslim. The other 8% are divided between other Muslim sects. The remaining 2% are Christian or Jews.

The Pro-Islamic Welfare Party came out of the 1995 general elections as the dominant political party, which raised some fears that religious fundamentalism was taking over another country. However, others were quick to point out that they only represent 20% of the vote and that the other parties represent the true majority of the country.

Value system

Territorially, Turkey is a part of both Europe and Asia, and its value system is an amalgam of both east and west. This mixture has enriched Turkish life and culture. Turks are very patriotic with intense nationalistic passions. They are also a very friendly, generous people. Easily aroused to anger, they forgive and forget easily, too. They are individualistic and often find it difficult to work together in teams because they are very competitive. They want very much to be appreciated, and any hint of ridicule will offend them. In the company of two Turks you can expect them to speak Turkish, not because they want to be exclusive but because they don't want to give each other the chance to laugh at their idiosyncratic English language mistakes.

Education is a highly respected value in the Turkish culture. It offers an upwardly-mobile option that has the potential to transcend the chauvinism, nepotism, and factionalism that can cripple a modern industrialized secular state. Turkey continues to move in this progressive direction.

Class structure / Stratification

Many of Turkey's cultural traditions are rooted in values that are supportive of marriage and family support systems. However, one feature of Turkish society is the dominance of the male. While Turkish women have equal rights under the law, there is an inherited family structure that conditions them toward a submissive subservient position. They are defined as womanly in terms that are conceived and articulated by males. A womanly woman is quiet, shy, and fearful, yet a good cook and housekeeper. Suggestive clothing is out of the question—it is okay for males to be sexual but not females. Males are the decision-makers in this paternalistic and patriarchal society with attitudes inherited from Ottoman precursors. However, one Ottoman tradition has been shed; now no man can have more than one wife. Family systems are also structured to care for the elderly, up to the limit of each family's resources. The more senior a person is, the more respect they are traditionally given. This positive support is often sacrificed with urbanization, for extended families tend to be less common in the cities.

The Turkish language has within it the vestigial remains of linguistic class structuring. The Ottoman palace system was based upon rank, and was reflected in the language patterns of the elite and those who served them. This pattern linguistically implies servitude. Today, Turkey is a democratic society endeavoring to offer equal opportunities to all its citizens. However, traditional biases and practices have a way of prevailing over long periods of time. Turkey has a privileged elite who control the industrial, military, and legislative complex. These elitists, as would be expected, are protectors of their positions in the culture. Religious and regional prejudices also create situations that run counter to an egalitarian ideal. The Kurds are a prime example of a people who struggle with prejudices that devalue them as individual human beings simply because of their ethnic identity.

Safety

There is a complex array of factors to keep in mind when traveling in Turkey. Get all the required vaccinations, immunizations, and health briefings needed for your trip. Be careful of the water; drink only bottled or boiled water. Be aware of the typical minor crimes of pick pocketing and purse snatching, and also of some of the more sophisticated crimes that might involve team work like robbery, kidnapping and extortion. One worry in today's global environment is the threat of fundamentalist-inspired religious terrorism. Having an intermediary who can act as a guide and resource person is most helpful. The Turks are a very friendly and generous people; if you need help, ask anyone serving in an established position and you'll more than likely get the help you need. Turkish consulates are eager to help international business interests, for they feel global relationships will economically benefit their nation and help them learn better entrepreneurial skills.

In terms of hygiene, Turkey is a very clean country. Turks are very conscious of the need for cleanliness. There are foreign hospitals scattered throughout Turkey. The pharmacies are open from 9 AM to 7 PM and a 24-hour service exists in most urban areas.

Even if you have an international driver's license and consider yourself an expert, it is better not to drive. Turkey has one of the world's highest rates for road accidents. Traffic behavior is totally unpredictable. Take a cab or hire a Turkish driver.

For some nationalities, an entry visa is required for any visits that would exceed three months. For longer stays a residence visa is required. The Turkish embassy can enlighten you on the particulars applicable to your country of origin.

Business Protocol

Greetings and etiquette

Turkish **protocol and greetings are very formal.** They usually begin with a **handshake**, which should be firm but not a contest of strength. If you are astute enough to say and give the proper and respectful traditional word and introductory gesture, your efforts will certainly be appreciated. No matter how flawed your performance, they will not laugh at you, but will appreciate the fact that you tried. After you get to know them better, it may become a source of good-natured humor, which the Turks possess in abundance. Turkey's customs are numerous and complex and they vary considerably from region to region. With an intermediary as a guide, you may be able to make the right gesture and say the right word at the proper time. Initially that is all one can hope for.

In Turkey business is essentially a man's world, so it is unlikely that you will face an occasion where a woman represents Turkish business interests. There are religious prohibitions against opposite sex contact. If they are close, Turkish business acquaintances will greet each other with hugs and kisses, but only if they are of the same sex. Strangers do not greet each other so effusively. Turks also position themselves spatially about 1 to 2 feet apart when conversing after the greetings have been exchanged.

Business meetings tend to be very formal occasions in Turkey, with titles and surnames initially always used. Turkish people are not in the habit of exchanging business cards as soon as they meet. They are a frugal people and prefer to wait rather than possibly waste them on a business contact without a definite future. **If they do exchange cards, it is often a sign that they are ready to commit to a business relationship**. They may also send their business cards or leave their business cards as reminders of their business interests. It is not considered necessary to have your card translated into Turkish, but this should be done if you're going to be in the country for an extended period of time.

After you've been introduced, what do you talk about? The weather is not normally discussed. **Safe topics include economics, politics, football, and children.** Turks are concerned about inflation, and they will want to know about your country's rate of inflation. **They may ask how much you earn so they can compare their own life circumstances with yours.**

There are some topics best avoided: Cyprus, Bosnia, the European Union, and human rights. These are sensitive issues, and as a foreigner you may not have enough finesse to deal with these topics in a way that would not cause offense.

Time

Turkey is a **polychronic** culture, and consequently has a multi-tasked orientation. Punctuality is not a sacred cow to them. They will expect you to be on time because they know most foreign business people are punctual.

Business hours usually run from 8:30 or 9:00 AM to 12 PM. Lunch is usually from one and a half to two hours long, then its back to work for three more hours. The summer months of June, July, and August are popular family recreation times. There is absolutely no business conducted on Turkish holidays. They are based on international calendars and have fixed dates every year: January 1 is New Year's Day, April 21 is National Sovereignty and Children's Day, May 19 is Ataturk's Commemoration and Youth Sports Day, August 30 is Victory Day, and October 29 is National Republic Day. Religious holidays fall on different dates every year and are regulated by the Islamic calendar.

Dates in Turkey are written in sequential pattern with the day first, followed by the month, the day of the week, and then the year—for example, 4 October Sunday 1998. The comma and decimal point are also used differently. The dot denotes thousand instead of a comma (5.000.000,00 is five million). The representation of percentage is reversed (i.e. %75 instead of 75%). Turkey is two hours ahead of Greenwich Mean Time (GMT + 2), and from March to September clocks are moved one hour forward.

Gifts

Gift giving is a well-established custom in Turkey, and gifts are exchanged on numerous occasions. Gifts are viewed as a way of honoring the receiver of the gift. Gifts therefore have to be carefully selected so that they represent the appropriate status for the recipient. Too expensive a gift will put the recipient in an uncomfortable position of being overly indebted to you. In Turkey it is considered prudent to **buy modest gifts and present them with considerable deference.** Another strategy is to buy a modest gift and leave it on an entry table. It you present the gift directly to the person, it is customary to say something like, "This is not worthy of you but...." Wine does not enjoy the same popularity in Turkey that it does in Europe (remember it is an Islamic country); chocolates, fruit, or flowers are more appropriate. **It is not customary to unwrap the gift immediately** unless it is something that can obviously be shared, such as candy, or needs to be put in water and a vase, such as flowers.

Business entertainment

Business entertainment can take many forms in Turkey, and it is considered an integral part of the business process. **Dining at a restaurant is the most common form of business entertaining.** The Turks will generally take the lead as hosts. Whoever takes the initiative as host is expected to pick up the tab. A long business dinner is a favorable sign of business success. Restaurants in the major cities provide a wide variety of tasty cuisines.

Dress

Standards of dress are quite high. People put on their most respectable attire when going to work. **A suit and a tie are mandatory for males**, and they are worn even on the hottest days. Women are expected to wear respectable attire, but the rules are not quite as exact. The main expectation is that **women dress neatly and decently; a business suit is fine.**

Status and the desire for it are reflected in the clothing one wears, especially for males. The Turks subscribe to the dictum that the clothes make the man. An additional value believed to be reflected in a conservative well-groomed appearance is credibility. The businessman who dresses well is thought to be not only successful, but also an honest man. Of course, outward appearance does not always correlate with internal attributes of character, but being well-groomed will buy you the benefit of the doubt in Turkey.

Communication Style

Business language

Turkey's language communication is **high-context**. Homogeneity provides for many subtle nonverbal, almost subliminal, communication nuances. This often comes across as vagueness to those from a low-context culture. It is a business imperative that those with opposite communication styles build relationships. The relationship then becomes the basis for tackling business issues. A primary key to successful international business ventures in Turkey is therefore relationship-building activities.

The Turkish businessman distrusts anyone who is in too big of a hurry. Remember they are also polychronic, and what may seem to a monochronic person as a waste of time or stalling is their customary way of doing things. Their method for sizing you up involves dining, sharing personal histories, and comparing life styles, all the while watching you intently and noting every observable aspect of your demeanor. When this thorough evaluation has been completed, then the more substantive business issues can be approached. Remember also that Turks take business very seriously, so they prefer a more formal ambiance. **Only very close people call one another by their first names, and only then if they are of the approximate same age.**

Nonverbal communication

The Turks have a broad range and numerous forms of nonverbal communication. At the village of Kuskoy in the Black Sea region, people communicate with one another through whistles when they are out of voice range. Being a warm and friendly people, Turks generally **enjoy hugging, touching, and even kissing one another. Of course, there are Muslim religious restrictions regarding opposite gender contact that must be observed.** Turks engage in **very intense and direct eye contact, but there are also cultural guidelines that moderate this activity, especially between men and women.**

In Turkey official communication is carried out in a very serious manner and with utmost solemnity. Seriousness is associated with the truth. In any official context a **serious demeanor** is expected and creates confidence in the integrity of the transaction. The Turkish people have numerous folk mannerisms and beliefs that even the educated share. These subcultural beliefs are often expressed through nonverbal gestures. Pulling the earlobe and pursing the lips in a pressurized kiss is a way of sending a bullet to the devil's ears. Pouring water from a jug is a nonverbal way to wish friends a safe journey. Shoes are placed properly and with care lest they tangle the feet of their owners. A downward movement of the head means, "yes", and a no is expressed by a backward movement of the head while simultaneously raising the eyebrows and clicking the tongue. The shaking of the head from side to side means, "I don't know." If one were to join one's fingertips and collectively kiss them, the message sent would be "it's wonderful."

The Turkish Concept of Negotiations

Selecting personnel

Turkish negotiating teams tend to be selected on the basis of **status and filial considerations**. Many Turkish companies are family-owned, and family members are quite commonly chosen to be a part of the negotiation process. High-ranking senior members are considered essential and are invariably a part of the team. **When assembling a negotiating team, a Turkish intermediary should be considered a necessity.** It is probably wise to also mirror the Turkish team at least in having one high status and older male executive on the team. The Turks will assume that this older person will be making all the final decisions. A translator may be a necessary part of the team. If a woman is going to be on the team, it is probably advisable to clarify that up front with the Turks. Negotiators who are patient, mature, flexible, good at socializing, and willing to expand their knowledge of the Turkish culture are preferable.

Negotiating style

If you are going to negotiate effectively in Turkey, an ounce of preparation is worth a pound of reparations later on. The Turks have their own idiosyncrasies, most of which are charming ("whistling"), but some can be exasperating. Some of them form an integral part of their negotiating style, and are delightful in the proper context. When these negotiating postures are observed, precise culturally-specific counter moves must be made.

There are numerous examples. The one most often deployed is usually seen **in the opening stages of the negotiating process**. The Turk's posture when employing this negotiating scenario is to **act stubborn**; the foreign business representative is supposed to understand that they are only acting stubborn because an offer should never be immediately accepted. If misunderstood, this can set up a possible no-win situation or at least a stalemate where one party is making offers and the other is refusing. Play the game by their rules and if you don't personally know the rules make sure someone on your team does. Here is a brief outline of the Turkish negotiation style; mirroring it would be an appropriate negotiating approach: 1) do everything in slow motion with consummate solemnity; 2) every move should reflect the unity of your team. Numerous team meetings will therefore be essential. The team meetings will help slow the pace so you don't get ahead of yourselves; 3) know in advance that they are not going to accept your offer. This has some potential benefits. It opens up a number of options for you; and 4) continually brainstorm and map your strategy.

The next concept that relates to negotiations in Turkey is the concept of *Insallah,* which roughly translates as "God willing." The whole venture in the eyes of the Turks is only going to happen if it is the will of God. *Insallah*, "God willing," is an important concept in the Turkish negotiating style. When they make a suggestion that you appreciate but also have reservations about you can sit on the fence and buy time by saying "God willing." Then call a team meeting, particularly if your not sure of your next move.

The Turks like to get you off balance by using a placating ploy. The tactic involves building you up while lowering themselves. We see this in the western phrase, "Your wish is my command." It is an undemocratic holdover from more dictatorial times. This can upset the negotiating process if you do not play this game according to the rules. If a claim to inferiority is made to the senior member of your team, it should be accepted as though it was unquestionably true. However, if a claim to inferiority is made between persons of equal rank, a counter claim to equal inferiority must be made. This can start a seesaw game that can continue indefinitely unless someone invokes *Estagfurullah*. *Estagfurullah* is an Arabic term that means, "I beg the pardon of God." It is a culturally accepted way to end the inferiority game. It says, in effect, we are both inferior in the eyes of God, and we appeal to God for forgiveness.

The last pearl in this negotiating paradigm can be used when you are at your wit's end. The *allahaskina* is a prayer, which means "accept it for love of God." If you say *allahaskina* out loud and fervently, the Turks might gather together and agree that you are indeed at your wit's end, and therefore be willing to accept your generous offer.

Issues discussed

Initially, relationship-based issues will predominate. The Turks will feel uncomfortable dealing with substantive issues until they feel some degree of rapport has been established. Don't let your own cultural biases make you so inflexible that you overlook the relationship-based issues. Go fully into the generalized topics as though you are at a meeting among old friends. **Once a degree of relationship comfort has been established, then the substantive issues can be explored.**

Establishing trust

The Turks are basically a very trusting people. They know intrinsically the nature of honesty and integrity. If a Turk isn't honest in his own village, he will suffer extreme ostracism. They will also **assume you are trustworthy** unless you give them some reason to believe otherwise. During the **relationship-building** phase they will be watching and evaluating you. Their trust in you will be established through these **observations** and also their **intuitive readings** of you. In the long run, the record you establish in keeping your promises in the substantive areas will win or lose the opportunity for you and your company to continue to do business in Turkey.

Another strategy to maintain the Turks' interest and trust is to do some information sharing at the highest levels. Their hierarchical society is a carryover from their Ottoman period. Since they are hierarchical, the higher you go the better.

Persuasion

The Turks are a people with rich cultural traditions. They have strong emotional personalities. They are enterprising and have for centuries honed their skills in the art of distributive bargaining.

Persuasion techniques that are useful in negotiations with Turks or will be used by Turks are:

1) If you can reach agreement, put it in writing and ask them to initial it. Out of this process will come the final contractual agreement.
2) Ask for their list of **technical requirements up front**. This will enable you to integrate that into your later presentations.
3) Presentations should feature **visual aids** along with proofs that are consistent with Turkish business ideologies. **Personal appeals** can also be effective if they are **couched in patriotism**. This will be good for your country, etc.
4) The dictum, "the first person to quote a price loses," can be true with the Turks.
5) Decide in advance how you are going to handle any issues related to corruption.
6) If the Turks get upset, use **diffusion questions** such as, "What would you suggest," to ameliorate an issue.
7) Maintain a serious demeanor and a patient, deliberate disposition.
8) **Turks love to haggle**. For centuries they have honed their skills in bargaining at the marketplace. Be prepared to enjoy the process.
9) Turks like to **imply** that they have **influence** with important individuals. You may wish to also imply that you have influence with certain people that are relevant to the transaction.
10) **Stalling**. Take your time. Turks are rarely in a hurry.
11) **Story telling, using metaphors and analogies** are often used in Turkey.
12) **Speak with conviction and confidence.** Turks tend to be good orators/story tellers and will expect the same from you and your firm.
13) **Distraction tactics** are useful in times of conflict.

14) Turks tend to brag and use puffery. So, definitely build up your firm, your products/services, and yourself with **exaggerations, enthusiasm, and non-verbal demonstratives**.
15) Because Turks are an emotional as well as a socially-engaging group, the **presentation of possible future cooperative endeavors** and/or multi-firm interactive simulations should be very persuasive.
16) Use a **"big-picture"** strategy. Nothing is decided until everything is decided.

Tactics to avoid include:

1) **Avoid direct personal conflict**. It is acceptable to say what is on your mind. Some indirect conflict and/or a little banter are okay. However, direct personal conflict that causes someone to "lose face" will result in an emotional reprisal. Thus, avoid blunt and pointed statements regarding character or personal performance.
2) **Avoid long, boring, monotone lectures**. This type of lecture is not enjoyable for Turks (or most people).
3) **Turks view the negotiations process as fun and sporting**. So avoid a serious/conservative business mentality. Keep the overall tone light and sporting.
4) **Avoid overuse of technical details**. Turks tend to want to see an unclouded bottom line.

Resolving disputes

The Turks are a highly individualistic people and are very competitive. They are quick-tempered and hotheaded one minute and quite peaceful the next. Voices can be raised for no apparent reason. They are not an easy people to negotiate with, and they present interesting conflict resolution challenges for the business negotiator. Be sure to use the standard objection handling system: give them feedback on their objection (that is repeat the disagreement), and ask for clarification of their concerns. When you are ready to respond to their objection, you might then couch your responses in the Islamic format touched on previously in the section on negotiating style. Confirm with them whether or not you have answered or dealt with their concerns or objection before moving on. **Remember that saving** face is important and that truth seldom evolves out of the accumulation of objective facts in the Turkish viewpoint.

Group and Individual Dynamics

Turkish firms are hierarchical and tend to be family-owned. They do not have a high level of trust in one another, for they are a **highly individualistic people**. Their businesses are family affairs because loyalties are strong within families. They are also a patriarchal culture. Decision making is from the top-down. Those lower in the hierarchy mimic those above. Their group and individual interactions flow out of this matrix. Team members will tend to honor their filial commitments, but their high degree of individuality would suggest that they might place their own success and advancement above their concerns for the success of their group.

Risk

When Turkey emerged as a nation, the milieu out of which it arose was Islamic. Turkey was the first country in their part of the world to break from the organizational constraints which immutable Islamic law dictated. The eyes of the entire world were on the young Turks who broke from ranks and took considerable risks as a people. One could say that **the Turks are at least even with the Americans in their propensity for risk taking.** This is true despite their strong family ties. On a personal level, **risk taking appeals to their individualism.** In this context it can be seen as an exercise in self-reliance.

Decision Making

Historically, Turkey has evolved out of a patriarchal culture that cultivated **a healthy respect for authority**. This has produced a disciplined Islamic nation with fair laws, for Islamic principles play a subordinate role in the running of the government.

As mentioned, Turkish companies were traditionally family-owned. Family-structured corporations tend to have clearly defined chains of command. This system offers stability and tends toward a conservative business posture. Thus, Turkey's corporate organizational structures reflect discipline and a **top-down decision-making chain of command.** This model does not foster shared decision-making and it can foment

rivalries. This makes teamwork more difficult. Families do not necessarily work well as corporate teams, for their historical baggage tends to produce numerous complications, which erode economic efficiency.

Type of agreement

There was a time when a handshake and a verbal agreement could seal an agreement in this part of the world. Turkey is now ready to do business on a modern sophisticated level. **Legally-written contracts are commonplace in Turkey**.

One of the complicating factors in reaching a current legal contractual international agreement is that there is no uniformly accepted international legal system. The UN is probably the only forum out of which such a system could evolve. On a smaller scale, those countries seeking inclusion in the European Union are obliged to work out enormous changes in their codification systems. Within the European Union, the contract laws of each participating country must reflect compatibility across all of the borders of the participating nations.

From a strictly legal point of view, Turkey differs less today from other Muslim countries than it did fifty years ago. The Kemalist revolution introduced the Swiss Civil Code in 1926 and offered a model of uniformity in the judicial decision-making process. Recently, other Muslim countries have changed their old religious legal systems, for these absolutist beliefs have been obstacles to efficient business operations. These nations have also streamlined their legal codes. The transition to global economics is a reality for most of the Muslim world, and Turkey has shown the way in a number of areas. Because it wishes to become a full member of the EU, Turkey is currently involved in even more revisions of its codification system.

Chapter 30

The United Kingdom

- *Country Background*
- *The British Culture*
- *Business Protocol*
- *Communication Style*
- *The British Concept of Negotiations*

The United Kingdom of Great Britain and Northern Ireland encompasses England, Scotland, Wales, and Northern Ireland. During its height, the British Empire was arguably the largest in human history, as well as one of the most influential in terms of language, education, and culture. Former British colonies include English-speaking countries such as the USA, Canada, and Australia, which today are world leaders in their own right. Although it granted independence to most of its former colonies after World War II, the United Kingdom (UK) remains a world leader in trade and politics. In addition, it still has a number of smaller dependent areas worldwide, including many Caribbean islands, Gibraltar, and the Falklands.

Slightly smaller than Oregon in total area, the UK has 12,429 km. of coastline. The British Isles are only 35 kilometers from the coast of France, to which it is now linked by a tunnel under the English Channel. The climate is temperate with many rainy and overcast days.

Country Background

History

Celts settled the British Isles around the fifth century BC. Julius Caesar invaded England in 54 BC, but a more lasting Roman conquest took place in AD 46, bringing the isolated islands into contact with the rest of Europe. Pressured by the Barbarians raiding their homeland, the Romans gradually abandoned England. Left without Roman protection or a legacy of military knowledge, the Celts were no match for new settlers. The Angles, Saxons, and other Germanic people invaded and established many towns and kingdoms. The Vikings raided England for centuries. The Norman invasion in 1066 was the last successful foreign invasion of England.

The Normans brought with them a sophisticated governing system and feudalism on a par with France. The dynasties that ruled England for the following centuries were related to French royalty, and several conflicts took place on French soil over control of rights to the English or French thrones. This was manifested in the Hundred Years' War between the two countries, which lasted intermittently from 1337 to 1453 and ended with a French victory.

After the discovery of the new world in 1492, and the threat of a Spanish Armada invasion in 1588, England began to strengthen its navy. The resulting military and merchant navy made England the world's premier colonizing power and trading nation for many centuries. The Industrial Revolution, which started in Great Britain, brought the UK to the forefront of industrial nations. Ironically, it was after its World War II victory that the UK lost much of its world leadership and prestige, including the loss of the important colonies of India and Egypt. Even more surprising, Great Britain could not match the defeated nations of Japan and Germany in their economic recovery after World War II.

Government

The UK is a constitutional monarchy with an unwritten constitution that relies upon precedence and common law. Although the monarch is the nominal head of state, the true executive power lies with the prime minister and the cabinet. The prime minister is always the leader of the majority party in the House of Commons. Two parties, the Conservative Party and the Labor Party, have dominated British politics for decades. The legislative branch consists of the House of Lords, which has 1200 members, most of whom are hereditary peers, and the House of Commons, which has 651 elected members. The judicial branch is headed by the House of Lords, with several Lords of Appeal in Ordinary who are appointed by the monarch for life. The legal system is based on common law traditions with some Roman and other European influences.

Demographics

The UK's population has reached 60 million inhabitants. The population growth rate is one of the slowest in the world at 0.22%. Life expectancy is 78 year overall, 75 years for males and 81 years for women. Statistically, the population belongs to the following ethnic groups: English (81%), Scottish (10%), Irish (2.4%), Welsh (2%), Ulster (1.8%), Indian, Pakistani and others (2.8%).

The British literacy rate is an excellent 99%. High standards of education have a long history of development in the UK.

Economy

At its height, the UK led the world as the economic power with the most advanced industry and manufacturing. Other European nations caught up by the turn of the 20th century, and by World War II Germany and the USA had clearly passed Great Britain industrially and economically. With a leading tradition in science and research, which preceded the Industrial Revolution, the UK remains a world leader in technology and invention. Tough world competition, however, continues to diminish the industrial base.

Rather than compete with Japan, Germany and the emerging industrial nations after World War II, Britain's economy shifted from industry to services. This decision was influenced by the scarcity of raw industrial materials in Britain, and by the more cost-effective Japanese and American products. Unlike the Italian car industry, which withstood the Japanese onslaught by clinging to its artistic niche, the British automobile industry buckled and gave way in a market that it once pioneered.

However, the UK is still one of the world's great trading powers, as well as the 2nd ranked European economy. Great Britain is one of the most important banking, insurance, and business centers in the world. While industry continues to decline and now employs only 25% of the workforce, import and export trade has helped the economy grow. British agriculture, which only employs 1.2% of the population, is a model of efficiency for it produces 60% of the country's food needs.

The UK economy ranks 4th in the world. It recently surpassed France and Italy. Although quite respectable, per capita figures show a ranking of 23rd. The country has a major trade deficit. Exports include manufactured goods, fuels, chemicals and transport equipment. Major trade partners include the USA, Germany, France, and the Netherlands,

The currency is the British pound.

The British Culture

Language

English is a combination of Celtic, German (Anglo-Saxon), French (Norman), and some Latin (church influences). Although the UK is the birthplace of the English language, there are other languages spoken within the islands. For example, Welsh is spoken by roughly a fourth of the population of Wales and about 60,000 Scotsmen speak a Gaelic form of Scottish in the north. There are also various accents to the common English, such as Scottish, Irish, Welsh and some inner city accents.

Compared to many European languages, English is considered quite easy to learn, which may explain why so many Europeans can converse comfortably in English.

Religion

The UK has recognized the Anglican Church as the official religion since England's split from the Catholic Church during the reign of Henry VIII. Although the majority of Britons today are Anglicans (roughly 27 million), the Church of England no longer has political power. Other religions represented in British society are Roman Catholicism (9 million), Islam, Presbyterianism, Methodist, Sikh, Hindu and Jewish. Generally, however, religion is a very private subject and is rarely discussed, except in Northern Ireland.

Value system

The British are a very orderly and disciplined people. Their lives are highly structured, and individual achievement within the framework of society is highly cultivated. The emphasis on individualism and achievement in some British schools produces highly accomplished and knowledgeable students who possess strong leadership potential. The British are task and time-oriented. Recently, however, the UK has experienced a schism in its approach to work and duty, and many have questioned the implementation of the existing work ethic. Under Labor Party rule in the Seventies, the UK was transformed into a "welfare state" where the rights and income of all individuals were guaranteed for most of their lives. When the Conservative Party took over in 1979, it privatized many government services and reduced government spending on social welfare programs. The country has differing ideas as to what constitutes a fair government and fair working conditions. Today, one can argue that there are at least two kinds of Britons: traditionalists who wish to retain conservative British traits, and liberals who prefer "out with the old, in with the new."

The British are very proper and polite in general. Even the slightest physical contact is usually followed by an apology. They make only a few, select friends, and expect relationships to grow along defined guidelines. They have a very developed sense of humor, and are unashamed to make fun of even the most revered figures (as evident by the scathing nature of British tabloids). This is ironic considering that the British normally protect their privacy, and rarely discuss personal matters with anyone outside their immediate families. They also tend not to show outward emotion or public affection, even to close relatives.

Class structure / Stratification

The UK has traditionally been a class divided society. The old divisions of aristocracy and commoners, owners and workers, coupled with modern political differences, have contributed to a polarized society in some parts of the country. Indeed, the Labor Party was formed out of the dissatisfactions of the working class. Yet, although there have been many civil struggles throughout British history, few of these have been between the common people and the royalty-backed aristocracy. Instead, they usually involved backers of one sovereign over another.

The British people have always considered their monarchs symbols of a proud and independent nation. To revolt against the monarch would have been to revolt against the essence of Britain itself. There has also been extensive rivalry between the English, Scott, and Welsh populations. The nationalistic feelings of all three may have prevented them from disturbing the feudal system that existed after the Norman invasion, and thus opening themselves up to their neighboring foes.

Today Britain has many immigrants from its former colonies in India, Africa, and the West Indies. These newcomers face occasional discrimination and prejudice, but are fully protected under British law. Women in the UK have made great strides in business and politics. England has had many popular female sovereigns throughout its history, and Margaret Thatcher left her conservative legacy on British politics in the 1980s. Many female executives today make salaries comparable to their male counterparts.

Safety

Like most of Europe, the UK is generally a safe country, except for rare and isolated acts of political violence. Many of these are related to the ongoing struggle in Northern Ireland, and bombs have exploded on London streets. As a people, the British population is extremely law-abiding and proper. The majority of policemen do not carry guns, which is unheard of in other countries. Poor areas in London and other cities have a larger crime rate than the rest of the country, and visitors should use caution in such places.

Business Protocol

Greetings and etiquette

British **business protocol is conservative**, using a minimum of greetings, salutations, and gestures. Greetings usually involve a light handshake, and the ceremonial exchange of **"how do you do?"** This is a rhetorical, not an inquisitive question, and the proper response is "how do you do," not "fine," or the American statement of "pleased to meet you." The British are uncomfortable with effusive greetings and salutations. They prefer to keep all interactions at a professional business level. Women may or may not shake hands, so it is best to wait for them to extend their hand first.

A new trend in British business is to address associates by their first names. There are some exceptions, of course, so it is best to check with a secretary, or to ask politely. This new trend of informality follows the pragmatic atmosphere of British and international business.

Time

Great Britain is a **monochronic culture, with more emphasis on schedules than punctuality**. Business people should take London traffic into account when meeting for appointments, and should schedule these appointments well in advance. British business is usually open from 9 AM to 5 PM, but executives may leave around 5:30 PM. Generally, British office hours are less than Japanese, American, and German business hours. Although punctuality is important, the British may have "formalized" the habit of being 10 minutes late for everything, including work. Therefore, in modern Great Britain, almost everyone starts work 10 minutes late (but rarely more than 10 minutes), and arrives late for appointments and social occasions as well. They will, nevertheless, **strictly adhere to all schedules**.

Gifts

Gifts are not necessary when doing business in the UK. Rather than giving gifts, it is preferable to invite business associates to a nice dinner or to the theater. When invited to an English home, one may bring flowers, chocolate, or champagne. Local florists may assist in picking the right kind of flowers for the occasion.

Business entertainment

Business entertainment in the UK is much less important and lavish than in Asia or the USA. **Lunch is the most common business meal,** and it may take place at a local pub or restaurant. Only top executives are usually treated to lunch at expensive restaurants; otherwise, the location and food are usually reasonable, if not modest. It is possible to meet with British associates after work, but business is rarely discussed during these activities. The British do not switch the fork to the right hand, but keep it in the left hand, and the knife in the right. Also, one should keep the hands (not elbows) on the table at all times. Do not stare at or inquire about the food on other tables. Americans in particular should not become agitated when others smoke, or make "American" references about the health ramifications of some foods. This may be construed as obtrusive and rude.

There are many topics of conversation to explore when eating out, including the weather, football (soccer), or British sights and travel. Soccer is the most important sport in the UK, just as in the rest of Europe. One must pay special attention to the fact that English teams are not the only ones representing the UK. Scotland, Wales, and Northern Ireland have their own national teams, as well as their own professional leagues. (In fact, addressing Scots or Welshmen as Englishmen may be considered a grievous insult, so one must be careful not to do so). Furthermore, local club rivalries are so strong that it may be equally imprudent to choose one team

over another. Guests should listen, ask questions (the colors of the jerseys and the records of teams), and make only favorable comments on Britain's national sport.

Other conversational taboos include the situation in Northern Ireland, as well as comparisons with European and Asian nations that outperform the UK economically.

Dress

In accordance with their business culture, British dress is also conservative. Men should wear conservative suits, preferably in striped, dark gray or black colors. These should be of the highest quality, although they do not have to be new. A unique aspect of British dress concerns striped ties, which denote affiliation to certain groups or schools. Visitors must not wear such ties lest they offend or seem pretentious. One may sound naive by asking someone to explain the meaning of certain ties and emblems. Pens and other items in shirt pockets are considered to be in bad taste. British men prefer pocketless shirts.

Women should wear equally conservative business clothes, and should not wear pants. Very little makeup and perfume is used in business settings.

Communication Style

Business language

The British use **low-context** communication. British business people are not averse to saying "no," and will seldom go around a problem in communication. Their style is direct, calm, and cool, with very little nonsubstantive discussion. British English is different than "American" English in many ways, especially in some technical and cultural terms. For example, Americans may be called Yanks; an apartment is a flat; a bathroom is a loo; an eraser is a rubber and so forth. One can see how some of these differences in vocabulary can produce misunderstandings, and it is important to learn British terms, or ask for help in clarifying them.

The other differences lie in *how* the British and other English-speaking people use the language. The British sometimes complain that Americans do not finish their sentences and let them trail off without completing their thoughts. This demonstrates the British propensity for accuracy and preciseness, and the need to communicate with them in the same manner.

Non-verbal communication

The British use **very little non-verbal communication, touching or exaggerated gestures**. Apart from light handshakes in a business setting, touching in the form of backslapping or hugging makes them very uncomfortable. Getting really close to a British man or woman may be construed as intimate, romantic or unprofessional, not friendly. Consequently, they maintain a wider physical space than Americans or Asians. Likewise, excessive hand gestures and emotions may confuse or irritate the British, who prefer direct conversation with little eye contact.

There are, however, a few non-verbal clues in the British culture. One is tapping the nose to indicate confidentiality or secrecy concerning the verbal communication that proceeded or followed. The British victory sign made famous by Winston Churchill is a "V" sign with two fingers, with the palm facing outward. Giving the same gesture with the palm facing inward is a rude gesture. The British point with their heads, not with a finger, which is considered disrespectful.

The British Concept of Negotiations

Selecting personnel

Negotiations personnel are chosen based upon their **rank, status, and knowledge**. Social and business status is still important in much of British business, which has a tradition of ownership by eminent individuals and families. Many banking, insurance and service companies continue to be headed by people with high social ranking. While many of these do not have much to do with day-to-day operations, they wield enough influence to be present at important negotiations, or to appoint representatives with equal status. Knowledge is an essential ingredient in British management and is not hard to find, given their excellence in education and training.

Titles are different in the UK than in the USA. While a chairman is still a chairman, the British equivalent of a CEO is the managing director. Likewise, a VP is a deputy, and a general manager is a deputy director. A British manager is equivalent to an American assistant general manager.

Negotiating style

The British believe that the purpose of negotiations is for the **mutual benefit of all parties.** This pragmatic approach has given the British an excellent reputation as being fair and able negotiators. This style, which has sometimes been termed "shopkeeper diplomacy," believes that **compromise** between rivals is far more profitable than the defeat of one of the parties. In other words, the idea is to go for a win-win solution, rather than a winner who takes advantage of the loser. British negotiators will use honesty, frank discussions, and confidence to find the middle ground for both parties.

Unlike Asian business cultures, the British do not look for long-term solutions, but are rather interested in short-term profit. There are no accepted explanations for this, but it is not really different from many Western and Australian concepts of putting profit ahead of long-term relationships.

The British view time as a valuable commodity, so they will be organized and very time-conscious during meetings. They will attempt to follow a prescribed schedule, and will remind their counterparts of the necessity to do the same.

Issues discussed

The issues discussed by British negotiators are **substantive.** Since they believe in profit and success over relationships, the British spend very little time on nonsubstansive issues. They prefer to discuss the intricacies of each proposal, the terms, pricing, schedules, and solutions. Unlike Asian negotiators, the British are not interested in knowing their counterparts and establishing trust early on. To the British mind, there is a time and place for everything, and the time to get to know someone is not during business negotiations. This monochronic and perhaps impersonal attitude sometimes gives the British the image of being stuffy or cold. To them, however, this way of conducting business is acceptable, proper, and profitable.

Establishing trust

Although less common than in the past, the British system of **third party introductions** still exists in modern business circles. These introductions, or "letters of reference," help establish trust between parties that have had little prior interaction. Since it is hard to establish personal relationships with British business people, a letter verifying **past business performance** or **external recommendations** can be important in gaining their trust.

Persuasion

The British are persuaded by **logic, facts and unadulterated information.** One way to lose their interest is through irrational, emotional, and dogmatic appeals. They are very confident of their laws and procedures and will probably not deviate from them. Effective persuasion must take place within the realm of British law, and must not offend the highly logical approach of the British. Facts, figures, charts, and detailed information that convince them of the worthiness of the deal are more effective than dogma and emotion.

The British are particularly sensitive to "hard sell" approaches, which to them seem cheap and perhaps even unworthy of gentlemen. They consider some American salesmanship as too pushy or condescending, and are rarely persuaded by such tactics.

The specific persuasion tactics that are likely to be effective in the United Kingdom are:

1) **Supported Facts**. One needs to present logical/factual information that is accompanied by supportive documentation.
2) Your initial presentation/offer is critical to a successful negotiation. The presentation or offer must include the benefits the UK firm will derive from the transaction along with the corresponding supportive documents.
3) **Get it in writing**. Write everything down throughout the negotiations. Take copious notes.
4) **Build trust through information sharing**. The British will expect a healthy exchange of information. They respect intellectual property rights and will not push for proprietary information. However, they will expect other information to be shared rather freely.
5) Use **numerous small concessions** to build trust and a feeling of cooperation (i.e., shopkeeper diplomacy).
6) **Trade unimportant items for important items**. Concessions are always well received. However, one should attempt to preserve the most profitable aspects of the exchange.
7) Your **vocalics and non-verbal** behavior should convey **hospitality and friendliness,** but also **remain conservative and professional**. For example, say please often, sit formally, and smile pleasantly but not profusely.
8) Receiving the **technical specifications up-front** or in the beginning of the negotiation is a good idea in the UK.
9) **Two-Sided Appeals**. The two-sided appeal appeals to the UK's sense of fair play. Thus, it is likely to be an effective persuasion strategy.
10) **Summarizing previously-agreed-upon technical benefits** just before asking for a major concession should be helpful.
11) Use a **point-by-point** presentation as well as negotiation style. They will use it and expect the same in return.
12) The UK is a hierarchical society. Referring to the approval of **respected higher authorities** in regards to your company, product, etc. should prove to be an effective method of persuasion.

Tactics to avoid include:

1) Do not use favoritism or nepotism.
2) Avoid "small-talk" at the negotiations table. However, the use of dry humor will probably be useful during breaks and/or side-meetings.
3) Avoid the use of metaphors, emotional tactics, threats, fear tactics, diffusion questions, distraction tactics, supplification, and emotional demonstratives.
4) Do not brag about personal achievements.
5) Haggling over price is okay but the price will probably not change more than 25 to 30%. So **never "high-ball" or "low-ball"**. A civil personality is best when discussing price.

6) **Avoid misleading information**. It is likely to be detected and will result in the termination of the transaction.

7) **Avoid the "big picture" method of negotiating** unless you have a specific strategy for doing so. The "big picture" method of negotiating is viewed as a waste of time in the UK.

8) **Avoid Stalling.** The British want to get down to business. They usually proceed a little slower than Americans do, but they do not stall.

9) **Surprise tactics are inappropriate**. A surprise tactic would not be viewed as fair play and thus reduces levels of trust and/or cooperation.

Resolving disputes

Disputes may be addressed by returning to the original spirit of the agreement. If the dispute is regarding a perceived breach of schedule or conditions, then the other party must convince the British through **evidence** to the contrary. This may be as simple as showing evidence that the freight carrier did not deliver the goods on time, or that some other uncontrollable circumstances caused the problem. It may also be effective to appeal to "shopkeeper diplomacy" to resolve the dispute for the mutual benefit of everyone.

Group and individual dynamics

Mirroring their social values, the British are **individualistic**, but within the framework of a team. The educational and social systems produce highly motivated and educated individuals who are trained to think and analyze. Yet, Great Britain is a highly organized society where individuals are aware of their social standing at all times, and they respect authority. The British are fond of committees and special groups who work together to produce results, but their ultimate loyalty lies with family and country.

Risk

The British, like many European neighbors, are **low risk takers.** Business in the UK takes place methodically and is never rushed. This well-entrenched conservative approach continues to dictate the pace and type of business. Accordingly, one should not try to present risky proposals to British counterparts, no matter how attractive or lucrative they may seem.

Decision making

The British have **Top-down** decision making with senior management making most important and final decisions. They may appoint trusted staff to certain committees that analyze and make recommendations, but the highest executives are usually the final decision makers. In government-owned agencies, decisions may be even more complex. Government executives must consider many political and social factors before making decisions. This can be frustrating to a company that has little connection or impact upon these outside influences.

Type of agreement

An oral gentleman's agreement or a handshake constitutes a morally-binding contract. **Explicitly written agreements confirm the oral ones** and ensure accuracy and mutual understanding. Large contracts usually require legal experts and documents that are more complex. The British, who take their time in making decisions, rarely break their contracts and value their promises. They also prefer to resolve all disputes out of court.

Chapter 31

The United States

- *Country Background*
- *The USA Culture*
- *Business Protocol*
- *Communication Style*
- *The American Concept of Negotiations*

"Liberty enlightening the world,"—these words of Frederic Auguste Bartholdi, the Frenchman who created the Statue of Liberty, express the role America has hoped to play in the international business community. While many other nations set the stage and contributed to the social, political, and technical breakthroughs that have occurred in international trade, it was America which has generally led the way during the last fifty years of unprecedented growth in the world market economy.

Within the American fabric is woven all the threads of the human gene pool. Its citizens are bound together by a system of government that has offered a workable balance between individual freedom and collective conformity. From the beginning its citizens were steeped in values that disdained idleness and extolled the practical virtues of toil, self-reliance, and the seizing of opportunity.

Country Background

History

Evidence of man's earliest ancestors has never been found in the Western Hemisphere. Since modern types of Homo sapiens evolved in other parts of the world, a series of migrations were responsible for the presence of the first indigenous Americans.

The Vikings established settlements in Newfoundland around 1000 AD, but it was not until the fifteenth century that the nation-states of Europe were capable of sea travel over such a distance. By that time Europeans were increasingly involved in trade with the Orient, but the land routes that merchants had been using to bring the valued silks and spices from the East were blocked by hostile Turks.

Enterprising European mariners began to explore possible sea routes to the Orient. While some favored sailing south around Africa, others believed that the Indies could be reached by sailing directly west across the uncharted Atlantic. When Spain finally defeated the Moors in 1492, it was in a position to invest in a westward maritime venture led by Christopher Columbus. On October 12, 1492, after a six and one-half week voyage, land was sighted and the Europeans were convinced they had found India. At the time of this discovery,

independent tribes of indigenous peoples inhabited these areas and the Europeans erroneously named them Indians.

The news soon spread throughout Europe, where a number of countries were sufficiently developed to begin exploiting the new lands. Columbus's discovery gave Spain an initial edge. In 1565 Spain established Saint Augustine, the first permanent settlement in what was later to become the United States of America. Eventually, French, British, and Dutch, colonies were also successful, but the British proved more dominant then their European rivals. They defeated the French in war and established a dozen colonies along the Atlantic coast between 1607 and 1733.

The British colonies provided many raw materials for the mother country. While the colonies quarreled among themselves, they were essentially united by their loyalty to the king and their faith in a parliamentary form of government. The colonial system in North America worked quite smoothly until Britain unilaterally began to tighten its controls over the colonies, and ideas of independence began to gain advocates.

At the time of the 1775 American colonial rebellion the British were faced with a powerful combination of competitors and enemies, including France, which entered the conflict on the side of the colonists. Led by George Washington, the colonists won their revolution and created the new nation of the United States of America. The British officially granted independence at the Treaty of Paris in 1783.

The USA expanded its boundaries westward to the Pacific Ocean by purchasing the Louisiana Territory from the French and Alaska from the Russians, forcing Mexico to cede the Southwest and California, and winning a war with Spain to gain control of Hawaii, Cuba, and the Philippines. The last two areas were eventually granted independence.

In the 1860s the country experienced a great Civil War between the Southern slave states and the Northern free states, which ended in triumph for the North and the end of slavery.

Subsequent events included the development of industrialization, participation in two victorious world wars, and the expansion of global influence as the most economically powerful nation in the world.

Government

On July 4, 1776, representatives of the then 13 colonies met and drafted a Declaration of Independence. The colonial struggle had made the colonists wary of any form of centralized power. They came together from different backgrounds and regions, as Dutch, German, French, and English colonists. They declared their independence and became Americans united in an amorphous confederation, which eventually led to a new and still evolving governmental construct. The blueprint for this new government was a constitution adopted in 1787. It provided for three branches of government: the executive, the legislative, and the judicial.

The United States does not have a head of state, but only a head of the executive branch of the government. The president performs those functions associated with the duties of a head of state. He represents the United States in its relations with foreign governments, sends and receives ambassadors, and is the commander-in-chief of the armed forces. With the consent of two thirds of the Senate he concludes treaties, and with the consent of a simple majority appoints officers, judges, and department heads. He and the members of his cabinet are not responsible to the Congress, which differs from the parliamentary system.

Legislative powers are vested in a bicameral Congress, consisting of the House of Representatives and the Senate. Currently there are 435 representatives, who are elected every two years with proportional representation based upon population. The Senate has 100 members: two from each state who are elected for six years with staggered terms so that one third of the Senate are elected every two years.

The judicial branch consists of the Supreme Court with nine judges appointed for life by the president. There are eleven federal appeals courts, 90 district courts and a number of other courts with jurisdiction over taxes, customs, patents, etc.

The United States is generally regarded as one of the regions of Common Law, but it has features which are uniquely American. Legal development in the 13 colonies was never uniform, and they were organized at different times with different charters. Religious dissenters perceived the Common Law of England as a hostile force at odds with their religious practices. Their goals were to live by the word of God as expressed in the Bible. Lawyers were even forbidden to enter some colonies. As the population grew, commerce and industry flourished and eventually the need for lawyers became apparent.

The legal system that evolved was quite complex and heterogeneous. The rules of English Law were applied, but only insofar as they were not in contradiction to the constitution and customs of the new states.

The United States has a lengthy history of assimilating immigrants, and citizenship by naturalization is a comparatively easy process. America is regarded as a country that embraces free enterprise. Governmental regulations, however, are extensive and attempt to restrict monopolies and offer protection to small businesses, labor, agriculture, minorities, consumers, and the environment.

Demographics

The population of the United States is approximately 280 million, the third largest in the world. It is ethnically diverse: 83% are white, 12% are African-American, 3% are of Asian ancestry, and 1% are Amerindian. Included in these groups are individuals from almost every country in the world. The population growth rate is slightly less than 1%. Life expectancy for the total population is 78 years: 75 years for males and 80 years for females. The population is estimated to be 97% literate for both males and females. Immigration, both legal and illegal, remains strong.

Half of the population lives in urban areas of over one million people. The largest cities include New York City, Los Angeles, and Chicago, indicating a widespread pattern of population distribution.

Geographics

With a combined landmass and watermass of 9,629,091 sq. km., the United States is the world's third largest country. Bordering countries include Canada and Mexico. Its coastlines on the Atlantic and Pacific Oceans total 19,924 km. The climate is primarily temperate, but tropical areas include Hawaii and Florida, while arctic conditions exist in Alaska. The terrain includes a vast central plain with mountains in the west and lower mountains in the east. Alaska features rugged mountains and broad river valleys. Hawaii has rugged volcanic topography.

Economy

The United States economy has evolved into the most powerful, diverse, and technologically advanced in the world. The per capita GDP is among the world's highest. It is driven by a market-oriented economy, with governmental goods and services predominantly contracted through the private sector. United States corporations enjoy considerable flexibility in their freedom to expand their capital outlays, downsize their operations, or develop new products. In all economic sectors USA firms are at or near the forefront in technological advances, though USA advantages have slowly diminished since the early 1950s, the pinnacle of USA economic supremacy since other industrial nations had been devastated by World War II.

Technological advancement has created a "two-tier labor market", in which those lacking the education and technical skills to compete have lost ground to those with greater skills and education. As a result there is a large economically-stagnant segment of the population that is basically excluded from most economic opportunities. These economically-disenfranchised elements create social welfare and criminal justice problems. There is at present a need for greater infrastructure development, particularly in the older sections of the larger cities. Other problems include the rising costs of medical care due to new technology and large numbers in the aging population.

The USA labor force of approximately 140 million is divided by occupation into managerial and professional (30%), technical, sales, and administrative (30%), services (14%), manufacturing, mining, transportation and crafts (24%), and farming, forestry and fishing (2%). Unemployment is currently relatively low.

Major industries include petroleum, steel, motor vehicles, telecommunications, chemicals, aerospace, electronics, food processing, consumer goods, lumber and mining. Agricultural products include wheat, corn and other grains, fruits, vegetables, cotton, beef, pork, poultry, dairy products, forestry products and fish.

Even in the best of times, the USA has an economically unhealthy trade deficit. Major exports include automobiles, industrial supplies and raw materials, consumer goods and agricultural products. Major trading partners are Canada, Western Europe, Japan, China, and Mexico. Imported items include crude oil and refined petroleum products, machinery, automobiles, consumer goods, industrial raw materials, food and beverages.

The currency is the USA dollar (1 USD\$ =100 cents). The fiscal year is from October 1 to September 30.

The USA Culture

Language

George Bernard Shaw once said America and England are two countries separated by the same language. The American language differs from its mother tongue in phonetics and the use of some differing words. As a whole, English has the largest geographic spread and the largest vocabulary of any speech community in the world. English words have infiltrated most other major languages and American English has incorporated many words from other languages. The Native Americans whom the colonists dispossessed spoke several hundred different languages. Many of their words, especially place names, became a part of the American language. Further contributions came from the words and phrases of a wide variety of immigrants. With common usage they became an integrated part of the American vocabulary.

Spanish is the second most widely-used language and is prevalent in areas of Florida, the Southwest, and southern California. Spanish-speaking people have also contributed many words to the American vocabulary. Americans were never purists about their language. One word was as good as another, as long as it could be understood. Language was never a relic of the past but more an evolving entity of the present. In the twentieth century, radio and telecommunications have homogenized the American language, though regional accents still exist. The inability to speak English in the USA today is to live in relative linguistic isolation.

Religion

It would be difficult to understand America without an appreciation for its religious traditions. It has been called a nation with the soul of a church. Church and state have always been separate in the USA, yet over 75% of its citizenry belong to a religious group. Immigrants from all over the world have helped create a unique, experimental religious pluralism. While America is a secular state, its people are very religious without a single unifying religion. Of the total population, 56% are Protestant, 28% are Roman Catholic, 10% describe themselves as belonging to no religion, 2% are Jewish, and the other 4% are Muslims and other smaller religious groups.

Value system

America is a relatively young nation with a racially and ethnically diverse citizenry and an equally complex and contradictory value system. Its political values are rooted in its historical documents, the Mayflower Compact, the Declaration of Independence, the Constitution, and the Bill of Rights. These values are reiterated in numerous orations. They basically extol individual freedoms, the right to disagree and to be represented in government.

Current social values revolve around conflicts between earlier religious values of self-sacrifice and newer ones of self-fulfillment. Education, ambition and initiative remain strong, with affluence rather than other types of self-fulfillment as the desired reward. America's current wealth and the operative values of the market place are replacing its earlier religiously-influenced orientation.

Class Structure / Stratification

Ethnicity, color, and class determine stratification in the USA. Though most Americans enjoy a good standard of living, material affluence is uneven. One hundred and thirty-five years after slavery was abolished, race still remains largely synonymous with class. African-American (Black) progress toward equity with white society has been slow by every cultural/economic measurement. Hispanic Americans' (Latino) and American Indians' economic progress has been even slower. However, most Asian-American groups are not classified as disadvantaged minorities.

African-American infants are twice as likely to die as whites. They are three times more likely to live in poverty and will live six years less. They are one half as likely to go to college. Even if they graduate from college, they will earn only three fourths as much as whites. The death rate from homicide among black men is seven times higher than for whites. Unemployment among African-Americans is twice the rate of whites. African-Americans account for 10% of the work force, but are woefully underrepresented in prestigious occupations. They are readily hired as hospital orderlies, cab drivers, mail clerks, hotel maids and bus drivers, but only 3% of the nation's doctors and lawyers and 1% of its architects are African-American. However, some African-Americans have made great political and economic progress and there is a growing black middle class.

Hispanics Americans (Latinos) also have a small middle class, but as a group have an even lower economic status than blacks. One third of them do not have citizenship. The 1990 census revealed that 47% of eligible whites vote, 39% of blacks, and only 21% of Hispanics. About one half of those who did not vote said it was because they were not citizens.

American Indians, unable to continue traditional lifestyles after being forcibly placed on reservations in the 1800s, have historically lived in disastrous economic and social circumstances. The poverty on some reservations has been alleviated by the growth of the gaming industry, which has provided jobs and funds for social services, education and diversified economic development. About half of all Native Americans now live in urban areas. American Indian cultures are increasingly admired, both at home and abroad, and have added much to the richness of the American cultural mosaic.

If home ownership epitomizes the American dream, then homelessness is the most visible symbol of poverty. The number of homeless people has increased and causes major concerns in most large cities. However, the fastest growing category of housing for Americans in the last two decades of the twentieth century has been its prisons. The USA has the highest incarceration rate of any country in the world.

Traditional sex roles are also changing, but women have not achieved parity with men in pay or in power. Most women are in the workforce, even the mothers of young children. Adequate and affordable daycare is of concern to many of them, since the United States has no government-sponsored daycare programs. Due to the high divorce rate, single-parent households (90% of which are headed by women), have been increasing and are often economically disadvantaged.

Safety

There are legitimate concerns about personal safety when visiting America. Problems of substance abuse, crime, and violent behavior currently plague its cities. Drug abuse costs the USA about 1 billion dollars annually. Automatic weapons, urban gangs, particularly among the disenfranchised elements of the population, and homelessness (many of them mentally ill), are widespread.

Budget restraints have led to a lessening of expenditures on social services. The traditional inhibitors of violent and deviant behavior, such as churches, families, schools, and social taboos, have also been weakened. Most Americans, however, are law-abiding and helpful.

The wise traveler will avoid the more dangerous urban areas, will preferably travel in groups, and should rely on the counsel of locals and officials for guidance on safe procedures, particularly when arriving at airports and when carrying valuables. Most visitors do have an enjoyable and safe journey.

Business Protocol

Greetings and etiquette

American forms of greeting include smiles, nods, waves, handshakes, as well as a vast assortment of verbal greetings. The most common form of greeting in a business setting is the handshake. Male/male handshakes are very firm (sometimes slightly painful). Male/female and female/female handshakes are also firm but never to the point of pain inducement. A male should not shake a female's hand limply or with a partial grasp.

When meeting someone for the first time Americans usually maintain a respectful demeanor. They will usually use titles such as Dr., Ms., (pronounced Miz) or Mr., along with the person's last name. The order of names is first name, middle name, and last name. Americans like to move quickly into informality, with the use of

first names, or even nick names, which are usually abbreviations. Be sure your American acquaintances know the name by which you wish to be called.

Good friends and family members usually embrace and pat one another on the back. In casual situations a smile and a verbal greeting is adequate. When seeing someone at a distance, a wave is appropriate. Visitors can easily misinterpret Americans effusive greetings as an indication of deep and abiding reciprocal friendships, but greetings in America are basically superficial gestures. The greeting "How are you?" is not indicative of a concern for one's health. The appropriate response is "Fine, thank you", without elaboration.

Time

Visitors from other countries are either amazed or distressed by the rapid pace of American life and the emphasis placed upon punctuality and efficiency. America is a monochronic society and the dominant activity is "doing"; they have a preoccupation with time and getting things done. Appointment times are scheduled in advance and punctuality is expected. If one is going to be late, one is expected to call and let the other party know.

The contiguous 48 states have 4 time zones. New York is 5 hours behind Greenwich Mean Time (GMT -5). The state of Hawaii is 10 hours behind (G.M.T.-10), while most of Alaska is 9 hours behind (G.M.T.-9). In most states daylight saving time is in effect from mid-spring to mid-autumn. In written correspondence one must remember to write the month first, then the day, and then the year.

Gifts

Large business gifts are discouraged by law, which allows for only a $25 tax deduction. When visiting an American home it is not necessary to take a gift although gifts are always appreciated. One may take flowers, a plant, chocolates or a bottle of wine. Flowers are often sent before or after a visit and letters of thanks are good form.

At Christmas, gifts are exchanged. Business associates often give gifts that can be used in the office. The best gifts are items from one's own country. Personal gifts such as perfume or clothing are inappropriate for women. Gifts are usually unwrapped, shown immediately and shared. Taking someone out to dinner and or entertainment is a common gift.

Business entertainment

American business meetings are often held over lunch, which usually begins at 12 noon and ends at 2 PM. Lunch is usually a light meal, since work will be resumed directly afterward. Alcoholic beverages may be served, and one drink is customary. Dinner is the primary meal; it will start anywhere between 5:30 and 8 PM. A cocktail party may precede it. Business breakfasts are also common and they can start as early as 7 AM. On weekends brunches are common. They are a combination of lunch and breakfast and may begin anywhere from 10 AM to 2 PM A business agenda may be a part of the event.

When eating out, the cost can be shared. This is called splitting the bill or "going Dutch". If you are invited out for business, your host will usually pay. If you are invited out socially, you may be expected to pay for your own meal. When inviting a USA counterpart out socially, you should clarify whether you wish to pay. Before an unexpected visit to an American office or home, it is customary to call ahead. Most business parties are informal unless the host informs you otherwise. When food is served one is not obliged to accept; usually one can help oneself whenever one wants.

USA co-workers will enjoy learning about your country and toasts are a popular way of doing that. When dining, the fork is held in the right hand and is also used to cut food. When the knife is used, the fork is transferred to the left hand or laid down. Many foods are eaten with the hands; one can observe others or, if comfortable, do as one likes. Standards of etiquette are very forgiving and conversations are customary while eating. Americans will eat while walking or even driving their cars. There are numerous fast-food and drive-in restaurants. Tipping is expected when served by waitresses or waiters. Tipping is not necessary when one serves oneself and eats with disposable utensils and containers. Taxes are added to the cost of meals and they will vary from state to state.

Dress

Many visitors to America are shocked by the rather casual way many Americans dress. Business attire varies considerably, with a wide range of options. Some Americans wear conservative business suits while others dress much more informally. In rural areas and small towns, clothing standards are even less formal and less fashionable. If one wishes to wear conservative or traditional clothing from one's own country, feel free to do so. If invited out, one might ask the host to recommend appropriate attire.

Communication Style

Business language

America is a **low-context** culture; communication is direct and explicit. Little emphasis is placed upon personal relationships, and non-verbal communication has very little importance. Business is conducted at lightening speed compared to many other cultures. America's idealized imagery is rooted in its collective success and is reflected in its business language. Americans want to get to the bottom line (financial issues) quickly. Technology has reinforced this tendency to focus more on the immediate and the short term. American business language reflects that orientation in numerous ways. Phrases such as "Let's cut to the chase" and one-word encapsulations permeate the vocabulary.

Americans reward each other for achievement and tend to measure their self worth in proportion to their productivity and accomplishments. This practice evolved along with other aspects of industrialization over the last two centuries and has fostered materialism in conflict with their earlier spirituality. At the beginning of the 20th century, their business language reflected exuberance and optimism. They had recently taken over much of the continent and built the Panama Canal. As the century draws to a close their business language has begun to reflect more sensitivity for the environment and a greater appreciation for long-range planning.

Non-verbal communication

In the non-verbal domain Americans tend to stand near the center of a spectrum that extends to the lively Latin Americans on the one extreme and to the subtle Asians on the other. They are subdued in comparison to the Latinos but impulsive in comparison to the Asians. They also stand in the middle of the spatial comfort zone when conversing, which is about 2.8 feet apart for male/male interactions, 2.3 feet apart for male/female interactions and 2 feet apart for female/female interactions. .

Individuals of the same sex do not hold hands, because it is interpreted as a sign of sexual preference/desire. However, it is social acceptable for a female or male to touch a male in a business setting (for example, a pat on the arm or shoulder). However, it is taboo for a male to touch a female in a business setting (other than a handshake).

The index finger is used to point and one also can beckon by turning the palm up and using the index finger in a crooking motion. There are many different ways to call a waitress or waiter; one can make eye contact and raise one's eyebrows and one's head, one may wave with one's hand, or mouth words such as water, coffee, or check.

Americans like to use head movements. Especially, nodding yes (up and down) and no (side to side). Sometimes during moments of fabrication American negotiators will engage in **"double positive"** non-verbal behavior. "Double positive" non-verbal behavior occurs when someone dramatically shakes his or her head "yes" numerous times while making a very positive statement. This dramatic head movement is an attempt to hide one's self-doubt and increase believability.

Direct eye contact (30% - 60% of the time) is interpreted to mean sincerity, although it should not be too intense. Intense eye contact (more than 60%) indicates aggression or sexual desire. Infrequent eye contact (below 30% of the time) during a conversation indicates boredom and/or lack of interest. North Americans tend to **look-up and to the left during thought construction**. North Americans tend to look down when sad/disappointed or when examining their feelings. Of course, ethnic differences within the United States can mean much variance from these generalities.

In social settings postures can be very relaxed, with legs crossed, an ankle on the knee, or feet propped; all of these are considered socially acceptable. When an American crosses their arms or cliches their fists, this indicates that they are uncomfortable, uptight, mad or even feeling aggression/anger. In business meetings Americans usually maintain more erect postures and are less casual. When passing an item from one person to another, it can be handed or even tossed (as long as the distance is not too far and the item is light). There are numerous other hand-gestures and non-verbal forms of communication. The American "OK sign" and the "thumbs-up" are probably the most common (both mean good). Both of these can be interpreted as a vulgar gesture in some countries. One should always use non-verbal gestures cautiously, for their meaning can be quite divergent in various parts of the world.

The American Concept of Negotiations

Selecting personnel

Americans are result-oriented and personnel will be chosen primarily on the basis of their **past records**, particularly if they include successfully concluded previous negotiations. Valued qualities will include **technical expertise, strong educational credentials**, honesty, perseverance, trustworthiness and **linguistic capabilities**. Negotiating personnel will possess all or most of these qualities. Although not as important as in many other cultures, getting along with one's superiors in the USA should not be underestimated and will effect assignments, promotions, and income. Thus, personnel selection will also be somewhat based on favoritism, as it is (even more so) in most of the world.

Negotiating style

Americans favor a linear **joint problem-solving** approach. They will identify the problems and the opportunities, and then confront any issues that are in conflict. Points of disagreement will be thoroughly explored and all conceivable alternative objectives will be considered. When a decision is reached on an issue, a plan of action will be outlined, leading to timely implementation and appropriate follow-up procedures.

Americans value directness. They can be argumentative and they will question or challenge authority with little fear of losing face. Their style is to separate the people from the problem, and in this manner they separate their business from their personal life. Their negotiating style is to follow an agenda that will keep the process moving toward their objective.

At times this will create a combative negotiating style. **Both American men and women are prone to take this aggressive stance during negotiations**. In contrast, in other joint problem-solving counties such as Germany, men may take an aggressive stance but it is less likely that women from these cultures will use an aggressive style of negotiating.

Younger American negotiators avoid the gray areas during negotiating. Either they are completely up-front or they are more prone to mislead and fabricate. Misleading maneuvers can sometimes be detected in younger negotiators by loss of eye contact (up and to the left) and dramatic "double positive" non-verbal behavior.

Issues discussed

The issues favored by American negotiators are **primarily substantive**. The phrase "let's get down to business" is more than just a saying. Americans also **prefer agendas** and their agendas will normally not include time for relationship building. Ancillary topics are viewed as a waste of time. They are usually dedicated to getting the job done as expeditiously as possible. However, business meetings are usually started with a little "small-talk."

Americans from the Southern USA (Houston, Atlanta, and New Orleans) prefer about eight minutes of *small-talk*. Americans from the Northeast (New York and Boston) prefer two minutes of *small-talk*. The rest of the USA usually prefers around four minutes of *small-talk*. Compared to the rest of the world, this is rather inconsequential, for most other cultures (excluding Northern Europe) prefer anywhere from 20 minutes to two days of *small-talk*.

Establishing trust

Americans endeavor to establish trust through cooperative negotiating strategies that emphasize the free exchange of information. Their goal is to produce a legally binding, enforceable contract where all parties fulfill their commitments. Trust for them is best accomplished when all parties are willing to provide these legal guarantees.

However, on an individual basis, **Americans tend to trust by intuition.** Why is trust given so readily in the USA? First, Americans have generally had an excellent standard of living for over 60 years. This has minimized the needs and numbers of the "have-nots," who might be tempted or forced into a dishonest way of life. Second, religious, cultural, governmental, and legal forces have reinforced a belief that one is trustworthy until proven otherwise. However, it is common for an American to give you the opportunity to prove your dishonesty and you will be closely scrutinized during these tests. For example, an American may readily give you the opportunity to take advantage of them for a small amount (for example, $10 if an individual or $1,000 in a corporate setting). If you do not reciprocate, it will not be forgotten. This is seen as an inexpensive way of determining someone's trustworthiness.

One should note that the trust and gullibility of Americans (which is world renowned) is diminishing due to increases in intra/international economic disparities, extensive interactions/trade with other cultures, and the impact of previous outcomes based on this trust/gullibility. In an effort to avoid future harmful transactions, American firms/governments/individuals are attempting to strengthen international laws/jurisdiction, are starting to base their trust upon previous transactions, and are now studying the ethical systems/rules of other cultures.

Other factors that determine long-term trust and a deep level of trust in the USA are: 1) reliability (over a four-to-nine month time frame); 2) credibility (with other businesses in the same industry); 3) dependability (consistently meeting performance objectives); 4) continuous honest behavior; 5) information sharing; and 6) favors.

Persuasion

Americans appreciate well-prepared presentations that contain all the essential technical data. They will listen more readily to a logical argument than to an emotional appeal. One should remember they are extremely time conscious, so brevity is the watchword to keep in mind. Americans are team players, so naturally any approach that appeals to that value orientation will more than likely be effective. Presentations that mirror American imagery, however, might prove counter-productive, since this imagery permeates the planet. Americans appreciate originality, so be innovative. Like all human beings, they like to be entertained. Any presentation that effectively adds this element will have an attentive audience.

Americans have evolved into heavyweight international negotiators via a sophisticated educational network, based on access to an incredible amount of data. Presentations that are highly eclectic, fast-paced, imaginative, and contain precise empirical data would at least be entertaining to them. If you want a standing ovation, offer a bottom-line evaluation that honestly outlines profitability. An honest evaluation of the downside is also essential. For example, American corporations are legally obligated to follow environmental standards so any impacts should be presented in the proposed business plan. Americans are essentially optimists; a positive approach will appeal to their beliefs in the planet's future. Remember they also value honesty, not as a pious virtue, but because it is essential to credibility.

They are realists, however, and know that peace is best for business. They believe one way to achieve more harmony is through the crafting of legally enforceable international business contracts. The USA subscribes to the rule of law. It is a participant and a leader in numerous international organizations. A most persuasive element in their culture is the option of legal enforceability. If one can honestly offer some assurances in that regard, one may find they have persuaded the Americans to do business.

The specific persuasion tactics that are likely to be effective in the United States are:

1) **Supported Facts**. One needs to present logical/factual information that is accompanied by supportive documentation (proof sources). **Visual aids** should accompany a presentation or a proposal.
2) Your initial presentation is critical. A **logical, detailed and entertaining presentation** will gain the American's attention and interest.

3) Receiving the **technical specifications up-front** is an excellent strategy. You will need to be able to meet technical specifications as dictated.
4) **Get it in writing**. Write everything down throughout the negotiations. Take copious notes. In the USA, if it is in writing then it is more likely to be accepted as the truth.
5) **Expertise** goes a long way. Do not be afraid to self-promote yourself, your firm or your team
6) **Build trust through information sharing**. Americans expect a healthy exchange of information.
7) It is okay to **be blunt** and to the point in the United States. Americans view conflict as a necessary evil. So make your points and support them.
8) **Emotional tactics, threats, and fear tactics** can be effective in the United States under the right conditions. Scarcity tactics tend to be very effective. For example, "This is the last one left. You better buy today." However, these types of tactics must be used sparingly. Overuse will destroy one's credibility.
9) **Involvement questions** have proven to be very effective in the United States. Ask your counterpart how they would envision (involvement question) the outcome of the transaction.
10) **Problem questions, Implication questions and Need-Payoff** questions are also effective in the United States. These questions could expose a current problem your counterpart is having in their business, and how these problems are impacting your counterpart's productivity or profitability or image, etc., and can be rectified by interacting with your firm. Try to strategize and develop these types of questions before the negotiation begins. They will be invaluable.
11) **Always assume agreement** in the USA. Doubt and insecurity means death in American business. Confidence must be maintained at all times. **Speak with conviction and confidence.**
12) Use a **point-by-point** presentation as well as negotiation style. They will use it and expect the same in return.

13) **Summarizing previously agreed upon benefits or listing the pros and cons** of the agreement is often an effective method of persuasion in the USA. This type of tactic is usually effective with engineers, controllers, technical personnel, etc.

14) Referring to the **approval of others** and especially the approval of **respected higher authorities** in regards to your company, product, etc. should prove to be an effective method of persuasion. These tactics tend to be effective with personnel in management, H.R., and marketing.

15) The "**Feel-Felt-Found**" objection-handling tactic is usually effective in the USA.

16) Most Americans respond to the **good-guy bad-guy** team tactic in the desired manner.

17) Most Americans are very receptive to the get-rich-quick theory/concept. Do not underestimate its effectiveness. One third of all Americans plan on getting rich by suing someone, 1/3 by winning it via gambling, luck, taking risks, etc. and only 1/3 via their own earnings.

18) Americans tend to be very individualistic. So divide and conquer when possible.

19) Please refer to chapter one for more USA style tactics and expanded descriptions of some of the aforementioned tactics.

The specific persuasion tactics that should be avoided in the United States are:

1) **Avoid the use of metaphors, diffusion questions and distraction tactics**. Americans want to solve the problem as expeditiously as possible. These tactics only prolong the process, are boring, and are also ineffective and/or negative in the American's mind.

2) **Avoid misleading information**. It is likely to be detected and will result in the termination of the transaction.

3) **Avoid the "big picture" method of negotiating** unless you have a specific strategy for doing so. The "big picture" method of negotiating is viewed as ineffective and dishonest in the USA. The Americans' expect and may demand a point-by-point analysis.

4) Moderate haggling over price is okay but the price will probably not change more than 20 to 25% in the USA. So **never "high-ball" or "low-ball."** In addition, it is probably best to wait until the end to discuss price. Both sides should start with reasonable prices, attempt to meet each other's specifications and other requirements, and then the minor price issues can usually be resolved.

5) **Avoid Stalling.** Americans want to get down to business. Time is money.

6) **Surprise tactics are inappropriate**. Surprise tactics are viewed as unprofessional unless very artfully executed and undetected.

7) **Avoid personal pleas**. Most Americans view personal pleas as inappropriate, unprofessional, and unrelated to business.

8) Be careful about overuse of puffery. Big **exaggerations, too much enthusiasm, and/or excessive non-verbal demonstratives** are viewed as unprofessional, thought to be used by businessmen of lesser stature or by dishonest salespeople. Thus, it is safer to avoid these tactics.

Resolving disputes

In the USA as elsewhere there is a preference in favor of the **local law**. American courts are practical and not as strict as those in England. International businesses in the USA will be subject to the laws of the state they are registered in. Generally, when issues involve possible conflicts of laws, little distinction is made between cases involving states within the USA and cases involving a business entity of a foreign nation. In American legal parlance, state jurisdiction, in the context of international law, is equivalent to the German term, "International Zustandegleit," meaning the state as a whole. Therefore, to say a state has jurisdiction means the laws of that particular state apply first, and then the laws of the United States.

In 1945 the USA Supreme Court, in the case of the International Shoe Co. vs. the State of Washington, developed the "long arm of the law" concept. The length to which that concept may go in foreign judgments is not fully determined. American life flows across state and international boundaries with comparative ease and favorable foreign judgments frequently occur in USA courts. This is not to imply that all the issues related to international comparative law are in any sense settled. They are in fact in a state of flux. Foreign judgments, however, are readily expedited, if all the legal requirements for their recognition are satisfied.

The method of non-legal dispute resolution used within the United States is similar to their **joint-problem-solving** negotiating style. The issues will be addressed once again, analyzed and a mutually agreeable compromise will be sought. Supported facts are one's best method of persuasion in this situation. This may require counter or **follow-up presentations, more data, and a push to return to the objectives of the negotiations.**

Other remedies may include verbal apologies and writing formal letters of explanation or apology as a means of reducing the tensions. Dale Carnegie, in his book "Win Friends and Influence People," professed that the one who is correct should admit error, apologize and then deal with the more substantial matters. He felt it was always tougher for someone who truly made a mistake to admit it. This is sound negotiating advice, provided the dispute is not substantial.

Group and individual dynamics

America is a low-context culture in which social institutions, structures and systems, (the context), are given less emphasis than the **individual.** Individuality is a critical part of America's legal, political, and business system. Team players are prized, recognized, and valued but only because they are able to implement accomplishments for their superiors. At times and under many conditions, the media, government, educational systems, and businesses in the United States have attempted to encourage teamwork. However, the reward system in the USA is the opposite. Capitalism means individualism. Thus, individual achievement is paramount in the United States. Perhaps this is why entrepreneurship is pervasive in the USA, despite the rewards and comfortable lifestyle that is offered via the corporate career.

Risk

When law guarantees individual freedoms and when relative affluence is a fact of life, anxiety is reduced and risk taking becomes a more palpable option. When one adds the fact that most of the immigrants who came to the USA took enormous risks and were rewarded, one gets an appreciation for the American **propensity for risk taking**. Many comparisons can be drawn to the Australians' propensity towards risk taking.

American law encourages prudence, a quality that tempers risk taking and promotes a circumspect posture of informed investment. Americans will take risks but they will do their homework. They have access to enormous amounts of data, which helps to minimize their risks.

Decision making

Americans are products of their own sequence-oriented culture. Issues and alternatives are explored in a methodical manner. Decisions evolve in this framework incrementally, during stages of the deliberating process. Efficiency is a cultural imperative. Time management is the eleventh commandment, so decisions are arrived at quickly. The latest high-tech gadgets are utilized in this rapid decision-making process. Corporate decisions evolve out of "cost-benefit analysis," making the choices straightforward and impersonal, with little loss of face and conflict of interest factors considerably minimized. American businesses are structured so that any individual can be replaced without disrupting production. **Consensus in this framework is not an important consideration**. Top-level involvement is utilized in this organizational pyramid for the major decisions.

USA decision-making can best be described as **Top-down with imitation consensus. The senior personnel who are involved will always make the decision.** However, subordinates are almost always consulted due to their expertise and an effort to make them feel involved in the decision process. Sometimes the ability to delegate one's authority is seen as a managerial strength in the USA. Thus, decisions are often delegated. However, the senior member of those involved will make the decision. If a more senior member should become involved (for any reason), then the decision maker has now changed.

Type of agreement

The foundation for almost all commercial activity in America is the contract. The American Law Institute offers this definition of a contract: "a promise or set of promises for the breach of which the law gives a remedy, or the performance of which the law in some way recognizes as a duty". Not all promises or obligations are enforceable. In the environment of international business a legally enforceable contract may be as much myth as reality. A well-researched contract helps define the future; it results from the data available at a given point in time. Even the most carefully crafted instrument under these circumstances is fallible. The real strength of a contract is not necessarily its legality, though that is highly desirable. The real strength is in the mutual commitment of the people involved in carrying out the task. The rules of law are followed religiously in American business agreements, so that potential problems can be avoided. Globally there are void, voidable, or unenforceable contracts written every day. American businesses prefer to utilize attorneys with the expectation that legally enforceable international contracts can be crafted. Thus, American contracts tend to be **written, very detailed and very legalistic.**

NOTES:

Appendix A

Global Trade

- Terms and Conditions -

Letters of Credit

A "Letter of Credit" is an agreement between two banks (i.e., the importer's bank and the exporter's bank). The terms of sale are specified in the letter of credit. When documentation proving that the terms of sale have been met, the money is transferred between the banks. The buyer usually assumes the majority of the L/C costs. There are numerous types of L/Cs and various conditions that can be imposed. The eleven most common terms/types of L/Cs are as follows:

Commercial L/C: The general term for a letter of credit.

Revocable L/C: The terms of sale allow for changes to the L/C or the cancellation of the L/C.

Irrevocable L/C: Payment or terms cannot be changed/canceled without the consent of all parties.

Confirmed L/C: The buyer's bank has been reviewed and is acceptable to the seller's bank. In addition, the money's availability has been confirmed by both banks (i.e., in the importer's bank). Last, payment will be made immediately upon the receipt of the appropriate documents (e.g., Bill of Lading or Inspection Certificate).

Standby L/C: A stand-by L/C is used as a payment support mechanism. The stand-by L/C is used in conjunction with an open account. If the open account is not paid as its terms specify, then the stand-by L/C is executed and used to pay the importer's debt.

Revolving L/C: A revolving L/C is used in multiple shipments in conjunction with an open account. The L/C revolves from old shipments to new shipments. The prior shipments arrive and are paid via an open account system. The new shipments become subject to the terms of the L/C as the prior shipments are paid for.

Transferable L/C: Allows the L/C to be transferred to another party. (e.g., middleman to manufacturer/wholesaler). The transferable L/C permits changes in amounts and dates.

Assignment of: Allows the middlemen to transact the transaction without proceeds and without the supplier and the buyer having knowledge of each other. The supplier is paid when the middleman instructs the advising bank to pay the supplier after the required documents have been provided.

Back to Back L/C: Two letters of credit are used in conjunction (i.e., an L/C between the seller, the middleman and the buyer is used that is known as the "Master L/C," and an L/C between the supplier and the middleman is used that is known as the "Backing L/C"). The supplier must conform to both L/Cs in order to be paid. The middleman must conform to the master L/C in order to be paid.

Usance / Time L/C: Payment is due at a specific time (e.g., payment due 30 days after acceptance) as specified in the L/C.

Sight L/C: Payment is due upon sight of the documents (i.e., shipping documents, etc.).

Phase I: Contract Negotiations and Issuance of the Letter of Credit

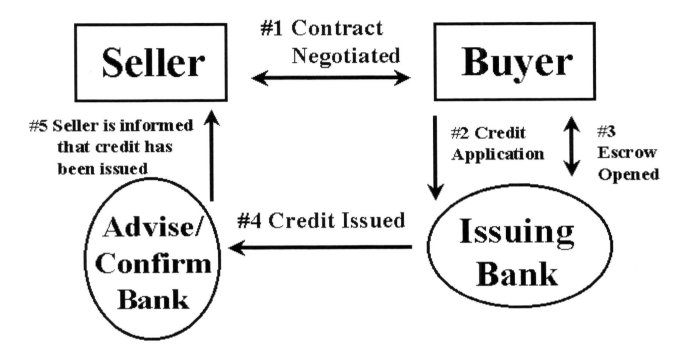

Phase II: Exportation of Goods and Exchange of Documents for Money

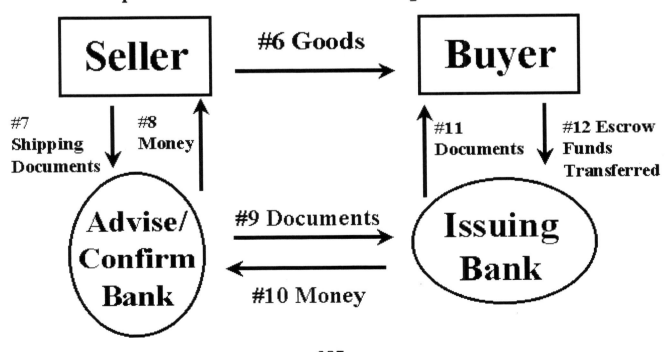

Letters of Credit

(Continued)

Strict versus Substantial Compliance

Generally L/Cs are subject to Strict Compliance not Substantial Compliance. However, a misspelling of words does not usually constitute non-compliance. If an invoice does not *exactly* describe the goods as specified in the L/C, then the obligation to pay is eliminated.

Documentation and Payment

L/Cs only deal with documents, goods have absolutely nothing to due with the financial obligation involved in an L/C transaction.

Advising versus Confirmation

Advising banks take reasonable care to verify L/C authenticity. Advising banks only pay after they have been paid. The advising bank does not assume financial risk. Confirmation of a L/C obligates the bank to pay immediately upon the receipt of the conforming (i.e., "clean" / "no discrepancies") documents from the supplier / exporter (i.e., the confirming bank must pay even before it has received funds from the issuing bank).

Using L/Cs as Loan Collateral

Although a L/C is not a guarantee of payment, it is an obligation to pay if all terms and conditions specified in the L/C are met. Thus, a L/C is viewed as excellent collateral. However, credit extension will be additionally based on the exporter's creditworthiness and prior exporting experience, the reputation and strength of the issuing bank, the terms and conditions of the L/C, and whether or not the goods exported are subject to price volatility.

Fees Charged on Export Letters of Credit

Fees are charged for advising, payment, discrepancies, communications, postage, and reimbursement. The fees are usually split between the buyer and the seller. The fees usually run between $150 and $250 for the exporter. The buyer's fees typically consist of a flat fee of .0025 (or more) of the total amount of the L/C plus some additional procedural fees.

Transferable Letter of Credit

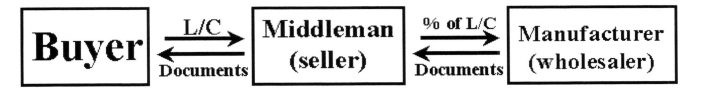

Assignment of Proceeds

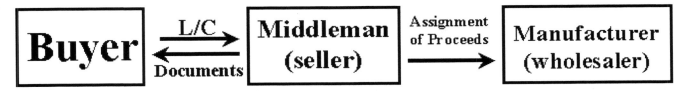

Back-to-Back Letter of Credit

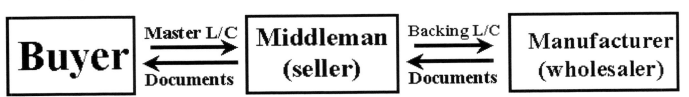

Documentary Collection

The exporter's bank collects payment due against delivery of documents. The exporter's bank, acting as an agent for the seller (exporter), presents documents to the buyer's (importer) bank. Neither bank is obligated to automatically pay under these transaction terms. The payment is made if the buyer is willing and able. However, documentary collection offers more security than an open account.

Types of Documentary Collection

Documents against Payment (D/P). AKA "Sight Draft" or "Cash Against Documents" (C.A.D.). The buyer must pay before the collecting bank will release the title documents.

Documents against Acceptance (D/A). An acceptance of a "time draft" by the buyer requires payment at a later date. The goods are released after acceptance of the time draft (i.e., not payment).

Advantages of Documentary Collection

Simple and inexpensive. Usually a faster receipt of payment than an open account. Seller retains title and the merchandise is not picked-up until payment/acceptance is made.

Disadvantages of Documentary Collection

The buyer can refuse to pay for any reason. If this happens the seller can 1) find another buyer, 2) pay for return transportation, or 3) abandon the merchandise.

INCOTERMS and the Corresponding Liabilities

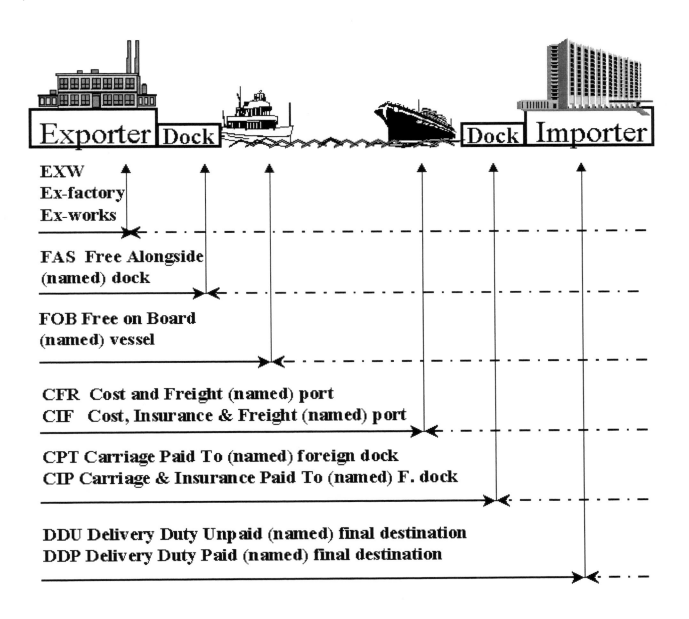

EXW
Ex-factory
Ex-works

FAS Free Alongside
(named) dock

FOB Free on Board
(named) vessel

CFR Cost and Freight (named) port
CIF Cost, Insurance & Freight (named) port

CPT Carriage Paid To (named) foreign dock
CIP Carriage & Insurance Paid To (named) F. dock

DDU Delivery Duty Unpaid (named) final destination
DDP Delivery Duty Paid (named) final destination

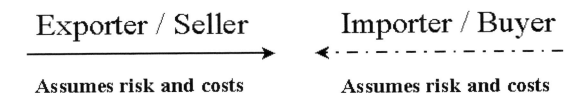

Exporter / Seller   Importer / Buyer

Assumes risk and costs   Assumes risk and costs

NOTES:

Bibliography

Acuff, F. (1992) *How to Negotiate Anything with Anyone Anywhere around the World*, Amacom, New York.

Adler, Nancy J. (1997) *International Dimensions of Organizational Behavior,* Southwestern College Publishing, Cincinnati.

ALM Consulting, Bischoff, F. C., and Marwick, K. P. (1994) *Doing Business in Russia*, NTC Business Books, Chicago.

Ames, Helen Wattley (1992) *Spain is Different*, Intercultural Press, Yarmount, Maine.

Ardagh, John (1987) *Germany and the Germans*, Penguin Books, London.

Ardagh, John (1993) *France Today*, Penguin Books, London.

ASM Group (1992) *Exporting to Canada*, Trade Media Ltd.

Axtel, Roger E. (1994) *The Do's and Taboos of International Trade*, John Wiley & Sons, New York.
—— (1993) *Do's and Taboos around the World.* John Wiley & Sons, New York.
—— (1991*) Gestures: The Do's and Taboos of Body Language around the World,* John Wiley and Sons, New York.

Balakrishnan, N. (1993) "Crack in the Cabinet," *Far Eastern Economic Review* 20: 18-23.

Bates, Chris and Ling Li (1995) *Culture Shock: Taiwan (a guide to customs and etiquette)*, Graphic Arts Center Publishing Co., Portland, Oregon.

Bender, David l. (1989) *American Values: Opposing Viewpoints*, Greenhaven Press, San Diego.

Bendure, G., & Friary, N. (1996*) Denmark: A Lonely Planet Travel Survival Kit*, Lonely Planet Publications, Hawthorne, Australia.

Bernhardson, Wayne (1996) *Argentina, Uruguay, and Paraguay*, Lonely Planet Publications, Hawthorne, Australia.

Boglioni, Guido and Church, Colin (1990) *European Industrial Relations*, Sage Publications Ltd., London.

Boye, Lafayette, and De Mente, C. (1993) *How to Do Business with the Japanese*, N.T.C. Business Books, N.T.C. Publishing Group, Chicago, IL.
—— (1994) *Chinese Etiquette and Ethics in Business*, N.T.C. Business Books, N.T.C. Publishing Group, Chicago, IL.
—— (1994) *Korean Etiquette and Ethics in Business*, N.T.C. Business Books, N.T.C. Publishing Group, Chicago, IL.

Boyraktarogher, Arin (1996*) Cultural Shock: Turkey (a guide to customs and etiquette)*, Graphic Arts Center Publishing Co., Portland, Oregon.

Braganti, N., and Devine, E. (1992) *European Customs and Manners*, Meadowbrook Press, New York.

Burgoon, Judee K., Buller, David B., and Woodall, W. Gill (1989) *Nonverbal Communication: The Unspoken Language,* Harper and Row, New York.

Caldwell, Malcolm (1968*) Indonesia - The Country and The People*, Oxford University Press, London.

Canadian Chamber of Commerce (1992) *Exporting to Canada*, Asian Sources Media Group, Hong Kong.

Castells, M. (1988) *The Developmental City-state in an Open World Economy: The Singapore Experience*, University of Southern California, Berkeley.

Central Intelligence Agency (2001) *CIA 2001 The World Fact Book*, www.odci.gov/cia., Central Intelligence Agency, Washington DC.

Chey, E.C.P., Lee, E. (1991) *A History of Singapore*. Oxford University, New York.

Claiborne, Robert (1983) *Our Marvelous Native Tongue: The Life and Times of the English Language*, Times Books Random House, New York.

Condon, John C. (1985) *Good Neighbors, Communicating with the Mexicans*, Intercultural Press Inc.

Cooper, Robert & Nanthapa (1996) *Culture Shock: Thailand*, Graphic Arts Center Publishing Co., Portland, OR.

Copper, John F. (1990) *Taiwan Nation - State or Province*, Westview Press, Boulder.

Craig, Joann Meriwether (1996) *Culture Shock: Singapore*, Graphic Arts Publishing Company, Portland, OR.

Crowley, William K. (1993) "Changes in the French Winescape," *The Geographical Review* 83: 252.

Culture Shock: Greece, (a guide to customs and etiquette), Graphic Arts Center Publishing Co., Portland, Oregon.
Culture Shock: Switzerland, (a guide to customs and etiquette), Graphic Arts Center Publishing Co., Portland, Oregon.

Curtis, Glenn E., ed. (1995) *Greece: a Country Study*, Federal Research Division: Library of Congress, Washington DC.

Danison, Lee, Hitchcock, Tim, Keirn, Tim, and Shoemaker, Robert (1992) *Stilling The Grumbling Hive*, St. Martins Press, New York.

Darnay, Arsen J., ed. (1996) *Manufacturing USA: Industry Analyses, Statistics and Leading Companies*, Gale Research, NY.

Deyo, F.C. (1981) *Dependent Development and Industrial Order: An Asian Case Study*, Praeger, NY.

Draine, Cathie and Hall, Barbara (1996) *Culture Shock: Indonesia, (a guide to customs and etiquette)*, Graphic Arts Center Publishing Co., Portland, Oregon.

Elegant, Robert. (1991) *Pacific Destiny*, Crown Publishers, NY.

Engholm, C. (1998) *When Business East Meets Business West: The guide to Practice and Protocol in the Pacific Rim*, John Wiley & Sons, NY.

Esterline, J. (1990) *How the Dominoes Fell: Southeast Asia in Perspective*. University Press of America, Lanham, MD.

Ferraro, Gary P. (1990) *The Cultural Dimension of International Business*, Prentice Hall, Englewood Cliffs, New Jersey.

Fishburn, D. (1996) *The World in 1997*, BPC Magazines Ltd., London.

Fisher, Glen (1980) *International Negotiation - A Cross Cultural Perspective*, Intercultural Press, Inc., Yarmouth, Maine.

Fisher, Roger and Ury, William (1991) *Getting to Yes*, Penguin Books USA Inc., New York.

Flower, Raymond and Falassi, Alessandro (1995) *Culture Shock: Italy*, Graphic Arts Center Publishing Company, Portland, Oregon.

Foster, Dean Allen (1992) *Bargaining Across Borders*, McGraw-Hill, Inc., New York.

Frazier, Gary and Rody, Raymond C. (1991) "The Use of Influence Strategies in Interfirm Relationships in Industrial Product Channels," *Journal of Marketing* 55: 52-69.

Frazier, Gary (1983) "On the Measurement of Interfirm Power in Channels of Distribution," *Journal of Marketing Research* 20: 158-166.

French Chamber of Commerce in Great Britain (1999) *Doing Business with France*, Kogan Page Ltd, London.

Fuller, B. (1993) *Discover Singapore*, D&N Publishing, Singapore.

Futrell, Charles M. (1996) *ABCs of Relationship Selling*, Irwin McGraw-Hill, Burr Ridge, Illinois.

Galey, Michael and Rollyson, Carl (1996) *Where American Stands*, John Wiley and Sons, New York.

Gochenour, Theodore (1990) *Considering Filipinos*, Intercultural Press, Yarmouth, ME.

Graff, M. (1997) *Culture Shock! A Guide to Customs and Etiquette*, Graphic Arts Center Publishing Company, Portland, OR.

Graham, John and Yoshihono (1984) *Smart Bargaining*, Ballinger, Cambridge, Mass.

Griffith, Samual B. (1963) *Suntzu: The Art of War*, Oxford University Press, London.

Hammons, Larry (1991) *Doing Business in Saudi Arabia*, Lawson Publishing, NY.

Harris, Philip and Moran, Robert (1991) *Managing Cultural Differences: High Performance Strategies for a New World of Business*, Gulf Publishing Co., Houston.

Harrison, Phyllis A. (1983) *Behaving Brazilian*, Newbury House Publishers, Chicago.

Hendon, Donald and Rebecca (1990) *World Class Negotiation:Dealmaking in the Global Marketplace*, John Wiley and Sons, New York.

Henley, Nancy M. (1977) *Body Politics: Power, Sex & Nonverbal Communication*, Simon & Schuster, New York.

Hoffman, A. and Finan, Gerard (1992) *Germany,* Societats-Verlag, Frankfurt.

Hofstede, Geert (1994) *Uncommon Sense About Organizations*, Sage Publications, Thousand Oaks.
—— (1984) *Culture's Consequences: Differences in Work Related Values*, Sage Publishing, Beverly Hills.

Hovde, B.J. (1948) *The Scandinavian Countries 1720-1865: The Rise of The Middle Class*, Cornell University Press, Itheca, New York.

International Business Practices in Argentina, (1997), www.smartbiz.coc/sbs/arts/bpr10.htm.

Jackson, Terence (1993) *Organizational Behavior in International Management*, Butterworth-Heinemann Ltd., London.

Jayapal, M. (1992) *Old Singapore*, Oxford University Press, NY.

Johnson, O., ed. (1997) *Information Please Almanac*. Houghton Mifflin Co., Boston.

Johnson, Thomas E. (1999) *Export/Import: Procedures and Documentation*, Amacon, New York.

Jolly, Adam (1997) *Doing Business in the Czech Republic*, Kogan Page Ltd., London.

Joshi, Manoj (1997*) Passport India*, World Trade Press, NY.

Juric, Jasna and Navarrete, Lilia (1996) "The Czech Republic," working paper.

Kenna, Peggy and Lacy, Sondra (1994) *Business Taiwan: A Practical Guide To Understanding Taiwan's Business Culture*, NTC Publishing Group, NY.
—— (1994) *Business Germany*, Passport Books, Lincolnwood, Illinois.

Kilanad, Gitanjali (1997) *Culture Shock: India*, Times Edition Ltd., London.

Kim, Shee Poon (1992) "Singapore in 1991: Endorsement of the new administration*, " Asian Survey* 17: 119-125.

Kjersgaard, E. (1990) *The History About Denmark*, Cultural Relations Department of Royal Danish Ministry of Cultural Affairs, Copenhagen.

Kydell, Margaret N. (1987) *Understanding Arabs, A Guide for Westerners*, Intercultural Press, Inc., Yarmouth, Maine.

Legg, Keith and Roberts, John (1997) *Modern Greece*, Westview Press, Boulder, Colorado.

Leifer, Michael (1992) "How they run?" *Far Eastern Economic Review* 46: 28-31.
—— (1993) "Goh steps out of the shadow," *The Economist*, 42: 98-101.

LePoer, B., ed. (1991*) Singapore: A Country Study*. Federal Research Division, US Library of Congress, Washington DC.

Leppert, Paul (1990*) Doing Business in Indonesia, (A Handbook For Executives*). Pallon Pacific Press, Inc., Chula Vista, CA.

Lewicki, Roy J., Hiam, Alexander, and Olander, Karen Wise (1996) *Think Before You Speak*, John Wiley and Sons, Inc., New York.

Lewicki, Roy J., Litterer, Joseph A., Minton, John A., and Saunders, David M. (1994) *Negotiation*, Richard D. Irwin, Inc., Burr Ridge, IL.

Longman, David Close (1995) *The Origins of the Greek Civil War*, John Wiley and Sons, New York.

Loo, V. (1983*) Insight Guides: Singapore*, APA Publications, Hong Kong.

Lovemore, Mbigi (1997*) Ubuntu, The African Dream in Management*, Knowledge Resources, PTY LTD.

Magnusson, Mangus (1980) *Vikings*, Elsevier-Dutton Publishing Co., New York.

Mbeki, Thabo (1996) "The Way Forward," *Southern African Decisions* 6: 14-17.

Mendoza, Plinio Apuleyo, et. al. (1996) *Manual Del Perfecto Idiota Latinoamericano*, Altantida, Buenos Aries.

Millar, Roderick and Reuvid, Johnathan, (1997) *Doing Business with Germany*, Kogan Page, Ltd. London.

Miller, Stuart (1987) *Painted In Blood, (understanding Europeans*), Atheneum, New York.

Milne, R.S., & Manzy, D.K. (1990) *Singapore: The Legacy of Lee Kwan Yew,* Westview Press, Boulder.

Mole, John (1995) *Mind Your Manners*, Nicholas Brealey Publishing, London.

Moran, Robert and Abbott, Jeffrey (1994) *NAFTA: Managing the Cultural Differences*, Gulf Publishing Company, Houston

Moran, Robert T. and Stripp, William G. (1991) *Successful International Business Negotiations*, Gulf Publishing Co., Houston.

Morrison, Terri, Conaway, Wayne A. and Borden, George A. (1994) *Kiss, Bow, Or Shake Hands*, Bob Adams, Inc., Holbrook, MA.

Motlen, Tim (1997) *Culture Shock: Czech Republic, (a guide to customs and etiquette)*, Graphic Arts Center Publishing Co., Portland.

National Trade Data Bank (1997) United States Department of Commerce, Washington, DC.

Nelson, Carl A. (1995) *Import/Export: How to Get Started in International Trade*, McGraw-Hill, Inc., New York.

Nierenberg, Gerard I. (1986) *The Complete Negotiator*, The Berkley Publishing Group, New York.

Nobel, J., Simonis, D., Armstrong, M., Forsyth, S., Simcock, C. (1997) *Lonely Planet—Spain*, Lonely Planet Publications, Hawthorne, Austrailia.

Nolan, James A., et. al. (1996) *Argentina Business: The Portable Encyclopedia for Doing Business with Argentina*, World Trade Press, San Rafael, CA.

Ohara-Oenereaux, Mary & Johnson, Robert (1994) *Global Work*, Jassey Bass Publishers, NY.

Otfinoski, Steven (1997) *The Czech Republic: Nations in Transition*, Facts on File Inc. New York.

Pervez Ghauri and Usunier, Jean-Claude (1996) *International Business Negotiations*, Pergamon, London.

Pope, Kyle and Paris, Jenny (1996) "Greek Premier resigns, sparking hope economic changes will continue," *Wall Street Journal*, Jan. 16, pA7.

Pounds, Norman J.G. (1994) *The Culture of the English People*, Cambridge University Press, NY.

Pye, Lucian W. (1992) *Chinese Negotiating Style*, Quorum Books, New York.

Rackham, Neil (1988) *SPIN Selling*, McGraw Hill, New York.

Richmond, Yale (1992) *From Nyet to Da: Understanding the Russians*, Intercultural Press, Yarmouth, Maine.

Roces, Alfredo and Grace (1995) *Culture Shock: Philippines (a guide to customs and etiquette)*, Graphic Arts Center Publishing Co., Portland, Oregon.

Rody, Raymond C., Winsor, Robert, and Kaufman, Gladis M. (1995) "Transaction Finalization Strategies: A Reclassification," *Proceedings for the 1995 Southern Marketing Association Annual Meeting*, Pp. 123-127.

Sabath, Ann Marie (1999) *International Business Etiquette: Asia & The Pacific Rim*, Career Press, Franklin Lakes, NJ.
—— (1999) *International Business Etiquette: Europe*, Career Press, Franklin Lakes, NJ.

Salacuse, Jeswald W. (1991) *Making Global Deals, What Every Executive Should Know About Negotiating Abroad*, Times Books Random House, Inc., New York.

Scher, Marion, (1996) *Business Manners in South Africa*, Franklin Publishers, Cape Town.

Schlosstein, S. (1991) *Asia's New Little Dragons*, Contemporary Books, Chicago.

Schuster, Camille and Copeland, Michael (1996) *Global Business: Planning for Sales and Negotiations*, The Dryden Press, New York.

Segall, Marshall H., Dasen, Pierre R., Berry, John W., and Poortinga, Ype H. (1990*) Human Behavior in Global Perspective: An Introduction to Cross-Cultural Psychology*, Allyn and Bacon, Needham Heights, MA.

Short, David (1996*) The Czech Republic: Customs and Etiquette*. Global Books Ltd, Kent, England.

Siegman, Aron W., and Feldstein, Stanley (1987) *Nonverbal Behavior and Communication*, Lawrence Erlbaum Associates, Publishers, Hillsdale, New Jersey.

Smith, M., Large, P., McLoughlin, J., and Chapman, R. (1985) *Asia's New Industrial World*, Methuen, NY.

Snensson, Charlotte Posen (1996) *Culture Shock: Sweden, (a guide to customs and etiquette*), Graphic Arts Center Publishing Co., Portland, Oregon.

Spanish Chamber of Commerce in Great Britain (1996) *Doing Business with Spain*, Kogan Page Ltd, London.

Strange, Morten (1996) *Culture Shoc:k Denmark (a guide to customs and etiquette)*, Graphic Arts Publishing Co., Portland, Oregon.

Tan, Terry (1994*) Culture Shock: Britain (A guide to customs and etiquette*), Graphic Arts Center Publishing Company, Portland, Oregon.

The Updated Guide to Foreign Investment in Argentina, (1997), www.mecon.ar/invest/www1.htm.

Turnbull, C.M. (1989*) A History of Singapore 1819-1988*, Oxford University Press, NY.

USDOC, Bureau of the Census, *Merchandise Trade - Exports by Country, Exports to France*.
USDOC, Bureau of the Census. *Merchandise Trade - Exports by Country. Exports to Switzerland*.
USDOC, International Trade Administration. *A Basic Guide to Exporting*.
USDOC, International Trade Administration. *International Business Practices. Region 2: Europe*.
USDOC, International Trade Administration. *Market Research Reports. Switzerland: Country Marketing Plan*.

Vatikiotis, M. (1992) "Double Blow," *Far Eastern Economic Review* 13: 38-48.

Vreeland, N., Dana, G.B., Hurwitz, G.B., Just, P., Shinn, R.S. (1997) *Area Handbook for Singapore*, US Government Printing Office, Washington DC.

Warshaw, S. (1988*) Southeast Asia Emerges*, Diablo Press, Berkeley.

Wenzhong, Hu and Grone, Cornelius L. (1991*) Encountering the Chinese*, Intercultural Press, Inc., Yarmouth, Maine.

Woodhouse, C.M. (1991) *Modern Greece: A Short History*, Faber and Faber, Boston.

World Competiveness Yearbook (2001) IMD International, Leusanne, Switzerland.

Yeo, A. (1992) "Towards Becoming an International Trading Centre," *Singapore* 1-3.